Human Services

Concepts and Intervention Strategies

Fifth Edition

JOSEPH MEHR
*Illinois Department of Mental Health
and Developmental Disabilities*

ALLYN AND BACON
Boston ▪ London ▪ Toronto ▪ Sydney ▪ Tokyo ▪ Singapore

Managing Editor: Susan Badger
Series Editor: Karen Hanson
Series Editorial Assistant: Deborah Reinke
Production Administrator: Annette Joseph
Production Coordinator: Susan Freese
Editorial-Production Service: Tage Publishing Service
Manufacturing Buyer: Louise Richardson
Cover Administrator: Linda K. Dickinson
Cover Designer: Suzanne Harbison

Copyright (c) 1992, 1988, 1986, 1983, 1980 by Allyn and Bacon
A Division of Simon & Schuster, Inc.
160 Gould Street
Needham Heights, Massachusetts 02194

This book is printed on
recycled, acid-free paper.

Library of Congress Cataloging-in-Publication Data

Mehr, Joseph
    Human services: concepts and intervention strategies / Joseph
Mehr.—5th ed.
        p.   cm.
    Includes bibliographical references and index.
    ISBN 0-205-13228-6
    1. Human services—United States.   2. Social service—United
States.   3. Public Welfare—United States.   I. Title.
HV9.M35   1992
361.973—dc20   91-26218
                                                                          CIP

Printed in the United States of America

10 9 8 7 6 5 4 3 2 1   96 95 94 93 92 91

PHOTO CREDITS—**Chapter 1:** David L. Ryan/*The Boston Globe.* **Chapter 2:** The Bettmann
Archive. **Chapter 3:** Ulrike Welsch. **Chapter 4:** Spencer Grant/Stock, Boston. **Chapter 5:**
Robert Maust. **Chapter 6:** Peter Menzel/Stock, Boston. **Chapter 7:** Alan Carey/The Image
Works. **Chapter 8:** (c) Frank Siteman/The Picture Cube. **Chapter 9:** Cleo Photography.
Chapter 10: (c) Meri Houtchens-Kitchens/The Picture Cube. **Chapter 11:** Mark Antman/
The Image Works. **Chapter 12:** (c) Jerry Howard/Positive Images. **Chapter 13:** (c) Sandra
Johnson/The Picture Cube. **Chapter 14:** Alan Carey/The Image Works. **Chapter 15:**
Andrew Sacks/Art Resource, NY.

In memory of Peter and Elizabeth

CONTENTS

Part III • The Contemporary Strategies

__PREFACE

As this fifth edition of *Human Services* goes to press, U.S. society continues to experience major transitions and profound uncertainties. We are witnessing unpredictable financial markets, major changes in tax legislation, an ongoing federal budget deficit with threats of social welfare funding cuts, and the continuation of a conservative Republican presidency. One constant in our society, however, is that many people need helping services, and many others are interested in providing those services.

Being interested in human services means being interested in and committed to finding solutions to the human problems that face people in modern times. These social and psychological problems are extremely complex and require a coordinated and integrated approach. This is what the human services are all about—helping ourselves and helping others to solve problems.

The term *human services* has become an all-encompassing phrase used to label services provided to individuals or groups who, for whatever reason, have failed to be included in the mainstream of the society and culture or who experience the pain and anguish of life in these troubled times. The clientele, depending on which expert one reads, includes 31 million poor, over 700,000 inmates of correctional institutions, 500,000 to 1 million children with school behavior problems, approximately 500,000 adults in mental hospitals and sheltered living facilities, close to 500,000 mentally retarded persons, and a large number of people with other severe problems who struggle daily with the problems of living.

In short, the field of human services is oriented toward dealing with all major social, psychological, and economic ills. Unfortunately, the dollar resources that exist at the federal, state, and local levels are limited, and it seems unlikely that they will increase greatly in the foreseeable future. In fact, in the 1990s, those dollars are shrinking. Our economy has been troubled by inflation, high interest rates, and deficit spending. Elected officials are cutting federal and state spending in an attempt to deal with these problems. These cuts will have major impacts on the human services. This fact has prompted the approach taken in the fifth edition of *Human Services*—that is, a focus on concepts and strategies that can have a significant impact on human problems in spite of limited fiscal and human resources.

People with major problems must receive the maximum application of resources if human services is to be a workable concept. Our primary concern must be with those who are at risk and with the conditions that have brought them to that low point of survival.

From this approach, dealing with the child-abusing parent is more critical than dealing with the parent of an underachiever, dealing with the dangerous adolescent gang member is more critical than dealing with the middle-class delinquent, and dealing with the psychotic housewife and mother is more critical than dealing with the dissatisfied homemaker. This is not to imply that the underachiever, the middle-class delinquent, and the dissatisfied homemaker do not have significant problems and do not deserve help but rather to emphasize that we must concentrate on the groups of individuals with the most severe problems and the fewest assets as the prime targets in the allocation of resources.

The content of *Human Services* reflects this view. The book does not ignore traditional systems for dealing with problem behavior but focuses primarily on newer approaches to human problems that hold promise for the future. These approaches are presented within the framework of human services concepts such as integrated services, recognition of the importance of environment and social institutions, rapid problem solution, and perhaps most important, a new consciousness about the directions in which we need to go in meeting the needs of both client and community.

Part I provides an orientation to and presents a perspective for viewing the field of human services. It examines the development of human services concepts. It distinguishes between integrative and generic concepts of human services, and places modern human services in an historical context. Part II focuses on the parameters of the field of human services. This part of the book discusses the roles of human service entry-level professionals and workers and explores human service problems and the boundaries of the field. Part III surveys the strategies that have been used traditionally to treat people in need. It concludes with examples of how human service workers can integrate these approaches into their work and emphasizes the importance of personal relationship factors in all human service delivery systems. Part IV explores the new strategies for helping people in need that are most closely identified with a human services approach. The section concludes with an examination of ethical and legal issues that impact on human service workers.

At the conclusion of the book, you will have a basic understanding of human services and the prevailing strategies for dealing with the major problems of people in need. You should also be able to understand the major approaches of professionals in correctional institutions, community mental health centers, mental hospitals, crisis centers, substance abuse service centers, mental retardation facilities, and multiservices centers. In addition, the role functions of human service workers should be clear: what they do, how they do it, and what effect they can have on people in need.

Acknowledgments

Many individuals have contributed to the development of the five editions of this text. The human service students and workers with whom I have had contact for the past twenty years have taught me as much as I have taught them. I owe a particular debt to Al Levitt, editor of the first and second editions of this text. Judy Shaw, editor of the third edition, also deserves thanks. The fourth and fifth editions owe much to the support of their editor, Karen Hanson, and to the human service professionals and educators whom she had critically review previous editions of the text. They are Carol A. Jenkins at Biola University, Tricia McClam at the University of Tennessee, Patrick McGrath at the National College of Education, and Cynthia Tower at Fitchburg State College.

1

Human Services:
A New Direction

- What is the meaning of *human services?*
- What recent circumstances have resulted in the growth of the field of human services?
- What are the differences between the concepts of *integration* and *generic human services?*
- What are the ten attributes of generic human services?
- What is a human service worker?

Human services is a phrase that is often used to group activities that focus on helping people live better lives. In the broadest sense, the human services include formal systems such as government welfare programs, education, mental retardation services, mental health organizations, child care programs, physical health care establishments, and the correctional services of the legal justice system. The phrase also has more specific meanings. Some authors have described its most important feature as a new consciousness among workers and clients in the formal helping systems. Others have focused on human services as a concept that embodies an integrated delivery of services to consumers. Still others have defined it as a sociopolitical movement that has aspects of a subtle revolution. Individual human service workers may focus on one or more of these factors as the most important aspect of human services, depending on their training, experience, and personal goals. The theme that all share is the improvement of quality of living for the most needy members of our society.

1

Antecedents of the Human Services Concept

Following the upheaval of global conflict in the 1940s, people in the United States began slowly to realize that all was not well with the traditional helping systems. Prisons were dramatically overcrowded, the crime rate was rising, mental hospital populations soared, and educational opportunities were unequally distributed. In spite of advances in social welfare policy, psychology, education, and social work, it seemed as if a losing battle was being waged. What was particularly striking about the battle was that the losers were usually members of the lower socioeconomic strata. It was most often members of this group who ended up on welfare; in the prisons, jails, and mental hospitals; and in the ranks of the educational dropouts. They had no money to purchase high-quality medical care, legal representation, or quality education. Several sociopsychological studies in the fifties and early sixties focused on some of these problems and drew them to the attention of professionals and the public (Goffman, 1961; Harrington, 1962; Myrdal, 1964; Redlich et al., 1953).

It was becoming obvious that, in most cases, those with the least need were receiving the most services, while those with the greatest need were receiving almost nothing at all. Although many helping professionals were being trained and were entering the world of work, by and large they offered their services to those who could pay—the white middle and upper classes.

The mental health delivery system is a particularly good example of the situation during that era. Beginning in the late 1940s, state and federal governments implemented massive training efforts to train psychiatrists, psychologists, social workers, and a host of other mental health professionals. (In fact, in a period of twenty-five years, over $2 billion was spent by the federal government alone on mental health training.) It has been reported that since 1948 the National Institute of Mental Health has funded the training of more than 50,000 mental health professionals: 12,000 psychiatrists, 11,000 psychologists at the Ph.D. level, 17,000 master's-level social workers, and 9,500 psychiatric nurses (*American Psychological Association Monitor*, 1976).

During this period, the great majority of these individuals were trained in public mental hospitals through the use of federal and state tax dollars. A small percentage of the patients in these institutions, those who were considered "good teaching cases," received excellent services. However, the rest were consigned to poorly staffed, overcrowded back wards in abysmal conditions. Once finished with training, many professionals quickly deserted the mental institutions for the more lucrative field of private practice, where they offered their skills to the better educated middle and upper classes who could afford to pay well for their services. In fact, only 9 percent of these trained professionals remained employed in the public mental health sector.

While the exodus of professionals continued, the hospital populations soared even higher during the late 1950s, until many institutions had two or three times as many patients as their rated bed capacity. It was during this period that some experts began to question the usefulness of the traditional medical-oriented approaches to dealing with people who had severe problems of life adjustment. However, the introduction of new drugs in the middle to late fifties both reinforced the medical approach to human service problems and paved the way for a conceptual change in mental health services. The masking of symptoms that resulted from the use of the new drugs for mental hospital patients was one of the major factors in the growth of the notion that many people who were in mental hospitals did not belong there and could exist in the community. Slowly but surely, the movement of patients from the hospitals to the community began.

The ability to control the more exaggerated behaviors of some patients (hallucinations, delusions) had a positive effect on the attitudes of mental hospital staff members. New ideas and treatments began to be introduced in the hospitals, such as patient government, group psychotherapy, and vocational rehabilitation. The movement of patients to the community gained momentum partly as a result of the success of the new modalities but probably more because of a new attitude on the part of many of the staff— something could be done. The change in attitude of staff members from a custodial approach to an active effort to help patients was a landmark change in the recent history of mental health services.

While changes were taking place in the mental health systems, similar events were occurring in the legal and correctional systems. There, too, recognition was growing that different standards were applied depending on race and socioeconomic class. White middle-class citizens tended not to be charged as frequently for crimes (even when they *had* committed the crime), tended to be found innocent more often, and tended to receive lighter sentences when found guilty. In the correctional system, prisoners were mostly black, Latino, or white members of the lower socioeconomic classes.

Recognition of the discrimination inherent in the differential treatment of low-income or minority group offenders and white middle-class and upper-class offenders has led to a gradual change in the judicial and correctional systems. Today there is much more sensitivity to the impact of social conditions on the likelihood of criminal behavior. In addition, there is much more concern with the rights of the accused and the convicted and a growth in programs that attempt to address the social causes of crime. Rehabilitation of offenders is more of a goal now, although the judicial and correctional systems are still haunted by the specter of retribution and punishment.

The changes occurring in the mental health and correctional systems, although based on problems within those systems, were reflective of changes in the culture at large. There has been, since the 1940s, a broad change in attitude from the conservative to the liberal in political and social life that has yet to run its course. Nicks (1985) should be consulted for a discussion of currently recognized inequalities in human services delivery systems. Fisher, Mehr, and Truckenbrod (1974) offer a more intensive examination of this process and its relationship to the human services.

A major expression of social liberalization can be seen in the civil rights movement beginning with the events around Selma, Alabama, in the 1950s. Although focused on the plight of black children and their problems in obtaining an education equal to that of their white counterparts, the civil rights movement has precipitated wide-reaching changes in the educational system. While still not entirely successful, desegregation progressed significantly during the 1960s, and we have witnessed the growth of a number of compensatory mechanisms, such as Head Start programs and busing. Among the broader effects of the movement has been the expansion of the concept that quality education is a right of all citizens, not a privilege, and that *all* disadvantaged persons must be served by the educational system.

For individuals with an investment in the notion that all members of our society have an equal right to needed services, the sixties were an exciting time. There was a massive growth in programs in all areas for the disadvantaged: the Economic Opportunity Act, the model cities programs, urban renewal, aid to education, and great strides in racial desegregation. As these programs continued, we seemed on the way to what President Johnson called the Great Society.

During the decade of the 1960s, one important approach for achieving the Great Society was the development of programs that created a new kind of worker. The Economic Opportunity Act of 1964, for example, resulted in the employment within one year of 25,000 paraprofessionals in community action programs and 46,000 paraprofessionals in the Head Start program for disadvantaged preschoolers. The Office of Economic Opportunity thus attacked the problems of the disadvantaged on two fronts: (1) it employed the disadvantaged, who would (2) help other disadvantaged people. This frontal attack on the problems of poverty was replicated in federal funding for similar programs in law enforcement and corrections, education, health, vocational rehabilitation, drug abuse programs, mental retardation services, and mental health. The programs have all been instrumental in the creation of a wide acceptance of new careerists in the helping services.

Even though developmental events in the areas of human services (mental health, mental retardation, corrections, public welfare, education, and so on) have not been completely parallel, the similarity is great enough to use mental health as an example. And the mental health system is particularly appropriate as an example since the concept that an individual's problems in living are internal in nature (caused by psychological problems of the person) has been widely adopted by the fields of correction, education, public welfare, and mental retardation.

In the field of mental health, the growing dissatisfaction with available services stimulated Congress in 1955 to pass a resolution that established a Joint Commission on Mental Illness and Health. The commission conducted a nationwide study on the extent of mental illness and its attendant problems, and the study and recommendations were published in 1961. Even more significantly, President John F. Kennedy appointed a cabinet-level committee to study the commission's report. In February 1963, Kennedy's message to Congress dealt with mental illness and mental retardation. In part, Kennedy said:

> I propose a national mental health program to assist in the inauguration of a wholly new emphasis and approach to care for the mentally ill. This approach relies primarily upon the new knowledge and the new drugs acquired and developed in recent years which make it possible for most of the mentally ill to be successfully and quickly treated in their communities and returned to a useful place in society.
>
> These breakthroughs have rendered obsolete the traditional methods of treatment which imposed upon the mentally ill a social quarantine, a prolonged or permanent confinement in huge, unhappy mental hospitals where they are out of sight and forgotten. . . . We need a new type of health facility, one which will return mental health care to the mainstream . . . and at the same time upgrade mental health services.

In effect, the problems of human services had obtained a national political priority. By the end of October 1963, a law (Public Law 88–164, the Community Mental Health Centers Act) was signed by the President; this law provided pressure on a national scale for the community mental health movement and indirectly gave impetus to the development of human services.

What is particularly striking about this period is that much of the pressure for change did not come from the established systems. Although there were a few groups in the traditional human services who were working in new directions, most of the pressure was coming from what has been called the *grass roots level*. It was during this period that much societal dissatisfaction found expression in events such as the radical student movement, the riots in Watts and Detroit, the Attica prison riot, the ecology movement, and the actions of people such as Cesar Chavez and the United Farm Workers Organizing Committee, Ralph Nader and the consumer movement, the gay liberation movement, and the Gray Panthers. While the broader society was embroiled in the turmoil of this period, a series of events in the mental health system was reflective of that turmoil and of a raised level of consciousness. It was also reflective of the dissatisfaction relating specifically to the mental health system itself. Events such as these were critical to the development of the human services concept.

Even though the concept that the community rather than institutional settings is the appropriate place for intervention predated the report of the Joint Commission, the enactment of Public Law 88–164 provided a major impetus for the changes of the sixties. It provided the sanction for moving patients from the institutional setting back to the community and for developing resources to support those patients once they had been moved. A major accomplishment of the federal legislation was the funding of about 600 comprehensive community mental health centers around the country. However, even in areas where these centers were not funded, local groups created county or city mental health centers that in many cases were supported by a local tax base.

The principal functions of the mental health centers as outlined in the Joint Commission's report were "(1) to provide treatment by a basic mental health team . . . for persons with acute mental illness, (2) to care for incompletely recovered mental patients either short of admission to a hospital or following discharge from the hospital, and (3) to provide a headquarters base for mental health consultants working with mental health counselors." In that early period, federally funded community mental health centers were required to have at least five essential services: (1) inpatient, (2) outpatient, (3) emergency services, (4) pre- and posthospital care, and (5) education and mental health consultation. The comprehensive mental health center was, in effect, proposed as a replacement for the large public mental hospital that had been the cornerstone of our mental health delivery system for 150 years.

Contrary to what might be expected, this concept was readily accepted by the administrators and staff members of most of the public mental hospitals even though it implied their demise as functional entities. Most of these staff members were proponents of the community mental health concept, at least in its early history, as a result of disenchantment with the existing system. It had been apparent for quite some time that the traditional public mental hospital was outdated, and workers in these facilities had already begun to turn to community programs as a possible alternative. Discharging patients into the community gained such momentum that during the 1960s many public mental hospitals reduced their inpatient populations by 50 to 75 percent. Figure 1-1 shows how one midwestern state hospital's population dropped from almost 7,000 patients in the mid-1950s to about 700 by the mid-1980s.

The patients, of course, did not change overnight. Many simply exchanged one type of institution for another, ending up in privately owned nursing homes or sheltered care facilities. Others, perhaps more fortunate, were able to maintain a minimal adjustment through funds from public welfare and supportive services provided by a local mental health center. Many ended up living isolated lives as homeless street people (Cordes, 1984). Some were lucky enough to be accepted into one of the growing number of community programs designed to assist them in dealing with their problems.

A particularly important aspect of the community mental health center movement for human services has been its emphasis on serving the most needy. As noted previously, not only were most of the public mental hospital patients who were being moved into the community originally from the ranks of the lower socioeconomic classes, but the priority for services in the new community mental health centers was being focused on those same socioeconomic groups. It had become clear from a number of studies that the greatest *need* for services existed in the urban ghetto and among the rural poor

Figure 1-1 *Population levels in a midwestern state hospital, 1915 to 1985.*

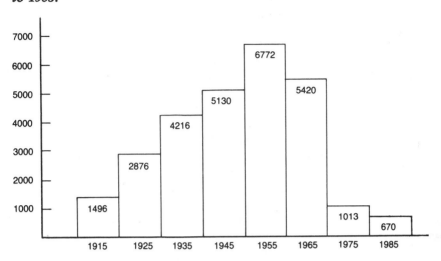

(Hollingshead and Redlich, 1965; Srole et al., 1962, 1978). However, once traditional services began to be offered to the poor, it became apparent that these services (the verbal "talking cure") were frequently not appropriate. The poor were not interested in *talking about* their problems; they wanted to *do* something about them, and frequently that meant dealing with problems of physical health, living accommodations, food, clothing, police, and money.

The traditional professionals, usually white and from the middle class, were ill-equipped to deal with such issues because of their critical insensitivity to the problems and life-styles of the client population. For these reasons and for the reasons of economy (lower salaries) and manpower needs, the community mental health centers and other public services agencies began to employ indigenous workers, paraprofessionals, case aides, or community mental health workers (Albee, 1961). By 1968, in community mental health centers alone, it was reported that 10,000 such people were employed (Sobey, 1970). These early paraprofessionals were the forerunners of today's entry-level professional human services workers.

The first steps toward recognition of this level of workers (individuals with less than a master's degree) occurred, of course, in the early programs where they demonstrated their effectiveness (Gordon, 1965; Rioch et al., 1963). Even though resistance to their use did (and does) exist (Rioch, 1966), a steady progression has occurred. In 1964, an associate-level degree program was begun at Purdue University to train mental health workers. By 1975, there were almost 1,000 training programs in the various subfields of human services (New Human Services Institute, 1975). Since the late 1960s, major steps have been made in the mental health field by a National Institute of Mental Health (NIMH) subdivision, the Paraprofessional Manpower Development Branch. This agency has funded numerous service-training programs whose goal is to develop service systems that use paraprofessional workers in innovative ways.

During the early 1970s, the agency began to focus on impacting large systems such as state mental health programs encouraging the development of large-scale career ladders for generalist mental health workers. To date, a number of states, including Illinois, Alabama, South Carolina, Massachusetts, Florida, Texas, Virginia, and Georgia, have developed or are developing such systems, either through the efforts of this NIMH branch or on their own.

Such strides were made that human services workers developed several national organizations that were similar to the organizations of the traditional human services professionals. Two such groups were the National Organization of Human Service Workers and the National Association of Human Service Technology. These two groups have now gone out of existence, but their role has been supplanted and expanded by two other healthy organizations. The current active human service organizations are the National Organization for Human Service Education (NOHSE) and the Council for Standards in Human Service Education (CSHSE). Founded in 1975, NOHSE is a membership association of human service educators, students, and human service workers made up of both national and regional groups. NOHSE sponsors regional meetings and a human service newsletter (*The Link*) and a journal (*Human Service Education*) focused on human services. Together NOHSE and CSHSE have for a number of years cosponsored an annual national conference on issues in human services.[1] CSHSE was established in 1979 to provide direction to education and training programs in human services by identifying criteria for curriculum, field instruction, faculty, student admission and advisement, and necessary resources. The Council Board's membership consists of regionally elected representatives of member educational programs. The council membership is open to any interested human service program. The council provides its members with a formal program approval process for human service education programs. The development of these two formal organizations is of major significance in the establishment of the human services approach as a viable field of study for the helping professions.

Although this brief description of the events of the last twenty years has primarily used the example of the mental health system, similar events have occurred in other subfields of human services. These events have been described by Pearl and Riessman (1965) and Riessman and Popper (1968) in the antipoverty programs, by Bowman and Klopf (1968) in the educational system, by Blum (1966) in the social services, and by Wicks (1974) in corrections.

To sum up, since the late 1950s and early 1960s a variety of circumstances—some planned, others unplanned—have come together to generate what is in effect a field called *human services*. Even though a list of the circumstances might differ depending on one's orientation, most of the following events probably would be included:

1. A dissatisfaction with the effectiveness of traditional service systems of the 1950s.
2. A growing sociopolitical awareness.
3. The stimulus of federal funding for "people programs" during the Kennedy and Johnson administrations.
4. A growing awareness of the relative inappropriateness of traditional helping technologies for the lower socioeconomic levels of society (and frequently for other levels as well).
5. The recognition of the degree of fragmentation of existing services.
6. The growing awareness of the need for new manpower resources.
7. The development of early sociopsychological intervention strategies.
8. Creation of formal human service organizations.

Some agreement exists about the events that have led to the development of the human services approach, but complete agreement does not yet exist in regard to just what the field is. Some professionals feel it is a totally new approach to providing innovative services to persons in need. Others describe it as a primarily organizational approach to the delivery of established services that have been developed by the traditional helping professionals. More and more think that it is a field with its own concrete identity, comparable to social work or psychology. In the material that follows, the primary current conceptions of human services will be explored.

Current Conceptions of Human Service Systems

The two major conceptions of human services that exist place primary emphasis on differing aspects of service delivery problems. The first conception deals mainly with the integration of existing services into a coordinated network at the local, state, or federal level. This has been termed the *human services integration concept*. The second conception, even though it includes the concept of system integration, focuses more on the issue of human services as a distinct new field, identifiable by the attitudes of its practitioners and the technologies it uses. This second concept, called the *generic human services concept*, forms the underlying fabric of this book.

Human services integration concept

The primary focus of this conceptualization of human services is its emphasis on integrating the various human service systems under one organizational or administrative system (Gage, 1976; Orlans, 1982). It has sometimes been called the *umbrella agency concept* (see Figure 1-2) It is the simpler of the two

Figure 1-2 *Umbrella agency concept.*

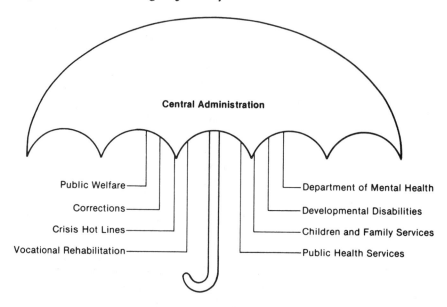

approaches and has fewer implications in terms of the types of services offered or the underlying conceptual frameworks. March (1968) describes programs under this framework as having the following features: (1) comprehensiveness of services, (2) decentralized facilities located in areas with a high population density, and (3) integrated administration that supports continuity of care from one service element to the next with a minimum of wasted time or duplication of activity. Four models of this type of organization, ranging from simple to complex, have been widely adopted: (1) the information and referral center, (2) the diagnostic center, (3) the one-step multiservice center, and (4) a linked comprehensive network (Demone and Harshbarger, 1974; Sauber, 1983).

A study reported by Parham (1974) gives a working definition for human services integration as follows: "The linking together by various means of the services of two or more service providers to allow treatment of an individual's or family's needs in a more coordinated and comprehensive manner."

Seven operational demands of human services integration are identified by Mikulecky (1974) in an analysis of reports from several regional conferences on service integration:

1. An integrated approach to planning. Within the planning process, certain specific things have to be done from an integrated systems approach. These include the following:

   a. Developing usage patterns of existing services, facilities, programs, and equipment, including behavioral patterns of use by the typical client in navigating his or her way through the service systems.
   b. Identifying gaps between services where problems or demands are likely to occur or may have occurred and the responsive service was not there to meet them.
   c. Developing an understanding and general awareness of where the services and programs of one or more agencies overlap with other agencies or duplicate each other's efforts in some inefficient way.
   d. Charting the potential utilization patterns by client-citizens of present and future services, using whatever possible alternative models and simulation of client and agency-management behavior to determine alternative policy choices.
   e. Ascertaining potential formal and informal linkages and relationships that might be developed among and between agencies that are most capable of complementing each other's activities.
   f. Exploration and investigation into new methods and techniques of service delivery.
2. *Community analysis* of the population, their needs and wants and how they are affected by the physical, social, and economic environment.
3. Acceptance of the responsibility of bringing the service to the client-citizen rather than expecting him or her to come to the location where it is offered (or even expecting that the client *know* it is offered).
4. Client-centered education in self-help and self-care.
5. Unification of administrative operations.
6. Integration of professional concepts of service (i.e., reducing interprofessional conflict).
7. Evaluation of the effectiveness of service integration over the various components acting alone and relatively exclusively, as has been the past practice.

A number of state governments appear to be using this conception of human services as an integrated system. To date, Georgia, Florida, Minnesota, and Wisconsin are well on their way toward such a model. The conception appears quite popular, and to some degree evaluation can demonstrate that it has improved the delivery of coordinated services to those in need (Frumkin et al., 1983). There does seem to be a major problem in the model's lack of careful attention to the very services it would integrate. This lack of focus is well illustrated in the seven operational demands listed previously. New methods and technologies in human services are given relatively little importance, for example. That this approach may be "old wine in new bottles" is a real concern. However, the basic concepts of service integration are unquestionably valid and desirable; in fact, they are an important part of the alternative generic concept of human services.

Human services involve activities of many kinds. As these youths wash graffiti off a city wall, they develop a sense of community while improving their neighborhood.

The generic human services concept

Even though the term *human services* is often used simply as a substitute for other terms (such as *social services*), it is becoming more and more apparent that human services is in reality a new field. The boundaries between the subspecialties of human services (mental health, corrections, child care, education, welfare, mental retardation, and so on) are becoming less well defined. The common attributes of generic human services become more obvious as those boundaries dissipate.

One well-known educator in human services, Dr. Harold McPheeters, has been involved in the field since at least 1965. In 1989, he was asked if there was something that could be called a human service delivery model and answered as follows:

> I don't know. I feel there needs to be a differentiation of the roles of human services and social work. I feel that human services has much more of an orientation to helping the client in any possible way—being with that client to get the job done to improve that person's functioning. Human service workers do whatever needs to be done—it might be psychological, or it might be assisting with medical needs or social needs. Human service workers are not constrained by any single philosophical orientation or technology. They're much more oriented to helping the client solve a problem whatever it takes, using a range of biological, social, psychological approaches. They ought to have the ability to deal confidently in all of those areas to help the clients. To me, this generic orientation to getting the job done is philosophically

the difference between human service workers and other professions. (McClam and Woodside, 1989)

We can look forward to a time when separate service subsystems no longer exist and individuals will be helped with all their problems through one comprehensive system, based on solutions to problems, rather than many different and unrelated service systems. Such a comprehensive service system would embody characteristics of the generic human services concept, such as the following:

1. Generic human services can be delivered only through an integrated service system.
2. Human services places increasing importance on environment (cultural expectations, here-and-now relationships) as a factor in problems of life adjustment but does not ignore psychological issues.
3. Human services focuses on problem solution rather than on treatment.
4. Human services has a major task of understanding the impact of social institutions, social systems, and the social problems of client-consumers.
5. A major task for human services is identifying and using *experiences* by which people grow or mature.
6. Human service workers are identified by their competencies rather than by level of formal education or type of educational degree.
7. The focus for training human service workers is an emphasis on learning skills, but knowledge is not ignored.
8. The human service system demands evidence that its technologies and approaches *work*.
9. Human services is pragmatic and eclectic. It uses all the things that work in dealing with client-consumer problems.
10. Human services is parsimonious.

It is obvious from this list that human services is not a new science or field of knowledge; it is, however, a new approach to using the understandings and discoveries of the current sciences and professions. Human services, while not antagonistic to the traditional professions, is a new mixture of attitudes, approaches, and behaviors. This will become clearer as we examine each attribute individually.

1. *Generic human services can be delivered only through an integrated service system.* This concept of the integration of service has been examined more fully earlier in this chapter. The client-consumer *must* be able to obtain all the needed services through the same system if the problem of fragmentation of services is to be avoided. To receive *only* psychological support when you have concrete problems such as lack of decent housing, no employment, or no social contacts does not deal with the total pattern of problems and is likely to be ineffective.

Put yourself in the client's place. How would you react if you were an unemployed single parent with two preschool children, living in an unheated three-room apartment, with no money for rent, barely enough food, and no funds to pay for child care so that you could hunt for a job? Would you be angry? Would you feel hopeless and depressed? A counselor at a mental health center could try to help you with your angry, hopeless, or depressed feelings, but the other problems would still be there. In an integrated service center you would get help for all or most of these problems at the same time: job training; advocacy with the gas company so that the heat could be turned on; help with temporary public aid money, food stamps, and arrangements for child care; and counseling for the emotional problems.

2. *Human services places increasing importance on environment as a factor in problems of life adjustment but does not ignore psychological issues.* Until recently, most of the human service subspecialties focused on the inner person, the psychological dynamics that caused the problem or illness, to the virtual exclusion of environmental factors. The true human service approach seeks an appropriate balance between psychological dynamics and here-and-now factors. Such an approach recognizes that it is inappropriate to deal with personality characteristics or maladaptation until real progress is made on the client-consumer's security needs, such as food, shelter, and safety. In effect, it is futile to deal with the psychological dynamics of a symptom pattern unless attempts are first made to deal with such precipitating factors as social isolation, loss of employment, or lack of monetary resources. However, once basic needs have been dealt with, the client's behavior, thinking, and feeling may require change.

3. *Human services focuses on problem solution rather than treatment.* The concept of *treatment* implies illness, and a great deal of evidence exists that once begun, many of the traditional treatment systems are virtually interminable. Human services focuses on the development of solutions to real-life problems and the development of problem-solving capacities in the client. This basic process must occur before treatment can be effective. It is conceivable that once the human service problems are dealt with, treatment will be unnecessary.

4. *Human services has a major task of understanding the impact of social institutions, social systems, and social problems.* The problems and processes of the *inner* person are dealt with as well as possible, considering the current knowledge and resources of the traditional professionals: the social worker, psychologist, psychiatrist, and so forth. But it is on a critical area that these professions have generally ignored that human services focuses: the social-institutional environment. This is not to say that the field of human services should ignore the issues of the inner person. These issues are important, and human services must incorporate them into its system; however, the prime focus must be on the problem areas that have not been dealt with. Human

services must look for new answers to human problems that can supplement and complement the already widely accepted strategies. These answers are most likely to be in the arena of effects of social institutions, new institutions such as peer groups and consumer groups, cross-cultural issues, community political attitudes, quality of life, social change, and many others.

5. *A major task for human services is identifying and using experiences by which people grow, mature, or change.* Even though the traditional helping services are considered to be growth experiences, it is imperative to identify additional experiences of this type, preferably ones that are natural or built into our existing systems (Wilson, 1983). The recent growth of self-sustaining communities of ex-mental patients who provide one another with social and emotional support and cooperate in business ventures for their livelihood is a good example of this process, as are the work-release programs in corrections. Other examples are Alcoholics Anonymous, Synanon, and peer therapy programs (see Rosel, 1983). This process is extremely important in terms of resource use and staffing since the communities are generally self-supporting and require little funding from the tax base.

6. *Human service workers are identified by their competencies (their ability to do things) rather than by levels of formal education or type of educational degree.* In current systems, the educational degree is the prime criterion for employment, size of salary, importance, power, and credibility in spite of the relatively well-established evidence that the degree one holds has relatively little to do with one's ability to work effectively with clients. The tremendous growth in the use of entry-level professionals and studies done on their effectiveness indicate that relatively uneducated staff members can competently perform a large percentage of the tasks currently done by traditional professionals (Hattie, Sharpley, and Rogers, 1984). Human service workers, then, are identified by what they can do, not by how far they went in school or what they studied.

7. *The focus for training human service workers is an emphasis on learning skills, but knowledge is not ignored.* Although a human service worker needs to *know* many things, knowing does not necessarily imply being able to *do*. The focus in the traditional fields has been on knowledge rather than on experience and behavior, with the significant exception of medical training. The current trend, even in the traditional professions, is now toward more use of skills-focused degree programs, such as the Doctorate in Psychology, which focuses on practical experience rather than on book learning. Since human services focuses on doing, it makes sense that human service training or degree programs must focus on competence-oriented education and training in addition to academically oriented education.

8. *The human service system demands evidence that its technologies and approaches work.* The helping services have often been based on unprovable as-

sumptions and have rarely been evaluated in terms of effectiveness. Does what we are doing really work? A major attribute of human services *must* be valid evaluation and a commitment to act on the results of that evaluation. The delivery of a particular service must be based on its effectiveness in problem solution rather than on the deliverer's *belief* that it is good for the client or on the fact that the deliverer enjoys doing it.

9. *Human services is pragmatic and eclectic; it uses all the things that work in dealing with client-consumer problems.*   All too frequently, valid solutions are not used by a system because they do not fit into a set of rigid assumptions about treatment. A case in point is the rejection of behavioral (learning theory) technologies by systems that are predominantly psychodynamic in orientation. Human service systems employ technologies on the basis of their effectiveness rather than on the basis of theoretical preconceptions.

10. *Human services is parsimonious.*   By and large, human service systems are tax-supported since their focus is on dealing with people who do not have the ability to pay. A major problem has always been that there never seems to be enough tax money to fund complex services for all those who have been identified as needing services (McQuaide, 1983). A compounding factor in most of the traditional systems has been the issue of overtreatment, that is, delivering long-term services to a small percentage of potential clients, which in effect ties up the system and prevents services from being delivered equally to all. A major attribute of human service systems, then, is parsimony—providing a minimum level of effective intervention for the client but avoiding creating an overdependency on services in the client. This approach ensures that the greatest number of client-consumers will receive services.

A good example of this concept is the problem of phobias, or irrational fears. In the traditional mental health services system, a phobic client usually is dealt with through psychotherapy. This type of intervention generally is involved and time-consuming, often taking years to effect a relief of symptoms. Recent techniques developed by behavior therapists can often effect symptom reduction within a few weeks to a few months. In the interest of parsimony, the behavioral techniques would be the service of choice in this case, since more clients could be effectively dealt with using the available staff resources. The concept of parsimony implies delivering effective services to the greatest number of clients possible, through the most efficient use of resources possible (Johnson, 1983).

The ten attributes of the generic human services approach in effect define the concept. In condensed form, the definition can be expressed as follows:

Human services is the field of endeavor that helps individuals cope with problems in living that are expressed in social welfare, psychological, behavioral, or legal concepts. Human services is characterized by an integrated, pragmatic approach focusing on problem solution within the client's life space, utilizing change strategies affecting both the internal person and his or her external environment.

What Is a Human Service Worker?

Just as there are two conceptions of the field of human services, the integration concept and the generic concept, there are several possible definitions of human service workers.

A human service worker is anyone who is trained or educated in helping activities. This definition fits in with the use of the term *human services* as a broad phrase that subsumes all of the established helping professions and helping activities. But if this definition were to be used, it would include all members of the traditional helping professions and virtually everyone else who provides helping service to the needy. For our purposes, it is much too broad.

A human service worker is a person who does not have traditional professional academic credentials but who, through experience, training, or education, provides helping services. If human service workers were defined this way, traditional helping professionals would be ruled out. And indeed, although some members of the established traditional professions approach their work from a framework that embodies some of the attributes of human services, many do not. The large majority of traditional professionals maintain a self-identity related to their specific academic training. They do not identify themselves as a *human service worker* but as a *social worker* or *psychologist*, for example. For that reason, this definition is closer to the mark.

The problem with this definition is that, like the previous one, it includes too broad a range of those who provide helping services. It would include volunteers, policemen, paramedics, helpful and concerned bartenders, and so on. While these people may provide helpful efforts as adjuncts to formal human services systems, there is little utility in a definition that includes this group as human service workers.

A human service worker is an individual who, through training and experience or formal education in a human services curriculum, develops a role-identity as an entry-level professional possessing the knowledge, skills, and attitudes that characterize the generic field of human services. The field of human services and entry-level human service professionals are characterized by a multidisciplinary or interdisciplinary viewpoint, a concern for the whole person, and a recognition that the field of human services can lay claim to a philosophical uniqueness that continues to evolve dynamically (Kronick, 1986; Macht, 1986; Mehr, 1986). This last definition attempts to communicate that there is something different about people who are human service workers. They contribute something new and different to the helping services, something beyond what the traditional professions offer. The human service professional is a new type of worker: a generalist change agent.

Summary

1. The perceived failure of the established helping systems and the major societal changes of the 1950s and 1960s have led to the development of a new field of endeavor: human services. The field has come to be characterized by new attitudes on the part of staff members and an increased emphasis on providing services to the most needy. It focuses on the poor and disenfranchised rather than on groups that have always been able to pay for services.

2. A major impetus to the growth of the field grew out of legislation in the 1960s, particularly that which resulted from a study commissioned by the Kennedy administration. Adequate and equal services became a national political issue after Kennedy's message to Congress in 1963. Since that time, there has been a major growth in the availability of human services to the needy.

3. The need for additional people to deliver relevant services to the needy led to the use of nonprofessionals in many fields. Between 1964 and 1975, almost one thousand college programs were developed to train human service workers.

4. One approach to human services focuses on integrating various service delivery systems under a single administrative organization. This approach has been criticized for not placing enough emphasis on new service methods and technologies.

5. The generic human services approach adds to the concept of integration a focus on the types of methods and technologies used to help people in need.

6. Generic human services share a number of characteristics:
   a. Integrated services
   b. Emphasis on environmental factors
   c. Problem solution
   d. Understanding of social institutions, systems, and problems
   e. Identification of growth experiences
   f. Competence of workers
   g. Development of skills in workers
   h. Evaluation of services
   i. Pragmatism and eclecticism
   j. Parsimony, or efficiency

7. *Human services* can be defined as a field that helps individuals cope with problems of a social welfare, psychological, behavioral, or legal nature. Human services is characterized by an integrated, pragmatic approach

focusing on problem solution within the client's life space, utilizing change strategies affecting both the internal person and his or her external environment.

8. A human service worker is an individual who, through training and experience or through formal education in a human services curriculum, develops a role-identity as an entry-level professional that embodies the knowledge, skills, and attitudes that characterize the generic field of human services.

Discussion Questions

1. In what ways is the human services approach reflective of broader-ranging changes in society?

2. Why could one consider human services a grass roots movement?

3. An important aspect of human services is serving disadvantaged populations. Why?

4. What major problem exists in the integration approach to human services?

5. What are the attributes of the generic approach to human services?

6. In what ways are the integration approach and the generic approach similar? How do they differ?

7. Why do we need a human services approach?

Learning Experiences

1. Ask two different community providers to define *human services*. Compare their definitions.

2. Check the racial mix of people receiving public financial aid in your community, county, or state. Is it reflective of the overall population? If not, try to find out why.

3. Determine whether your community, county, or state has the integrated approach or the generic approach to human services, or neither.

Endnote

1. National Organization for Human Service Education, National College of Education, Executive Office: Building Six, 2840 Sheridan Road, Evanston, IL 60201.

Recommended Readings

Frumkin, M.; Imershein, A.; Chackerian, R.; and Martin, P. "Evaluating State Level Integration of Human Services." *Administration in Social Work* 7 (1983) .

Mikulecky, T. (ed.). *Human Services Integration*. Washington, D.C.: American Society for Public Administration, 1974.

Sauber, S. R. *The Human Services Delivery System*. New York: Columbia University Press, 1983.

2

A History of Helping

- How long have people offered helping services?
- Why are demonic possession and exorcism mentioned in a text on human services?
- How did the view that disturbed people are sick affect helping services?
- What three viewpoints about human behavior have developed since the turn of the century?
- What is the social welfare movement?

The field of human services shares with the other helping professions a history that can be traced back into antiquity. The study of the history of helping services illustrates that the type and extent of assistance provided to needy people is dependent on the "self-evident truths" of particular historical periods. Those so-called truths include how a society or culture defines the concept of *needy* and what it considers an appropriate response to human problems.

Suppose, for example, that a person has no livelihood, cannot pay for shelter, food, or clothing, and has no other person to support and care for them. For a society to support such a person constitutes a burden on the self-supporting members of the society. The extent to which members of different societies or cultures have viewed that burden as acceptable or appropriate varies widely.

One culture at a particular point in history may hold the belief that poverty is due to laziness, lack of motivation, or poor character and either offer no assistance or grudgingly offer only minimal assistance. Another culture may view poverty as a god's punishment for sin. Assistance depends on the person repenting the sins, and aid may then be offered through a religious organization. A third culture may view poverty as caused by impersonal, uncontrollable external factors. Assistance may be offered willingly since poverty could strike any member of the group.

Throughout history many different beliefs have been held about why people behave the way they do, why they become disadvantaged, whether their problems ought to be of concern to the culture at large, and what ought to be done about them.

The history of human services concerns the changing ways in which societies and cultures have organized to deal with the problems of people. At different times the problems people have posed for society have been ignored, treated harshly, or dealt with in a more humane manner. The type of response has depended on the beliefs held about the causes for human behavior and about the "right" way to deal with those causes and the people who suffer from them. We like to think that the beliefs of today are truer than those held 100 years ago. One hundred years from now, some of today's self-evident truths may seem as much in error as those described in this chapter.

The Dawn of Time: Early "Human Services"

Before the development of written language, when humans were primitive wanderers who survived by hunting for meat and gathering fruits and nuts, life was extremely harsh. A tribe or clan could ill afford to have nonproductive members. The disabled elderly, the deformed, and crippled or infirm children often were killed or banished and left to die. Even then, however, there was at least some concern for the joint welfare of the group and some sharing of resources (Landon, 1986). From today's perspective, though, there was little in the way of human services.

In those early times, troubled human behavior and environmental catastrophe were attributed to the intervention of spirits, as were positive events, such as a good hunt or the birth of a strong infant. When an individual clan member behaved in a manner that was unusual, it was obvious to peers that he or she was being controlled by a spirit. If that behavior had a positive result (for example, predicting an avoidable catastrophe) the individual was usually honored and frequently became a tribal witch doctor with great power and prestige. If, however, the behavior was perceived as being negative (casting spells resulting in a poor hunt or a drought, harming another through magic), it was believed that the person was possessed by an evil spirit, and formal responses to the problem were made.

Scientists have found evidence tens of thousands of years old that a procedure now known as trephining was used as a treatment for primitive people believed to be controlled by an evil spirit. Since it was believed that the evil spirit entered the person's skull and controlled his or her behavior from that location, it made sense to make an opening to let the spirit out. The process was directed by a witch doctor or holy person and consisted of using a sharp rock or clam shell to chip a hole several inches in diameter in the subject's skull. Skulls have been found with bone growth around the trephined hole, indicating that some subjects lived several years after the procedure and, we can presume, manifested a more acceptable form of behavior. If the behavior did not improve, it is probable that the person was expelled or abandoned by the clan. In most instances, of course, the subject died as a result of the massive injury and subsequent infection. This concept of demonic or spiritual possession has had a long history of acceptance, but over time, other forms of social control also developed.

With the passage of time and the development of agriculture, more complex societies developed, particularly in the Near East around the Nile River basin and the Mesopotamian area. Complex societies required even more social control of human behavior. Around 2500 B.C. the Code of Hammurabi was developed. The Babylonian ruler Hammurabi's code covered the gamut from major laws to very detailed regulations for business, labor, wages, and behavior. This code illustrates a harsh approach to the control of human behavior: "If a man break a man's bone, they shall break *his* bone." Yet the code also showed compassion, such as providing for the adoption of orphaned infants.

This mixture of "eye for an eye" justice and some concern for social welfare is also present in the later writings of Hebraic law. The Hebraic (Jewish) tradition of law, as set down in the Talmud, recognized that people who were disabled or otherwise disadvantaged deserved some assistance (Scheerenberger, 1983). This principle is embodied, for example, in the Hebrew practice of leaving a generous amount of grain unharvested around their fields for the use of widows and fatherless children (Landon, 1986). The care and protection supported by Talmudic writings was mirrored by the charity of other eastern religious groups such as the Moslems. The giving and receiving of charity (alms) was becoming more widely accepted. Charity continues to be important in most religions.

The Enlightened Greeks: "Human Services" and the Golden Age

During the so-called Golden Age of Greece, much progress was made in the areas of politics, the natural sciences, and philosophy. It was a time of personal freedom and education, at least for the upper classes. The era is famous for the introduction of the basic concepts of democracy, but we usually forget that it was a period of great deprivation for most people and a time when slavery flourished. For most classes of people, life continued to be brutal. In some cultures, such as those of Athens and Sparta, infanticide was practiced on some occasions. Deformed or disabled children were often killed at birth, as were some unwanted female children even if they were robust and healthy. However, infanticide was not common to all cultures. For example, across the Mediterranean Sea in Egypt, infanticide was not practiced.

Judeo-Christian concepts of charity were not widely accepted in ancient Greece. It was at this time, though, that one change in viewpoint about problem behavior appeared. This change in the concept of helping is generally attributed to the efforts of the physician Hippocrates, who lived from the fifth century B.C. to the fourth century B.C. He has since become famous as the father of medicine and the originator of the physician's Hippocratic oath.

Hippocrates pronounced that much problem behavior was a function of natural illness and rejected the notion of demonic possession. Rather than religious treatment for the afflicted, he preferred medical treatment. Several of his theories were held for more than one thousand years before falling into disrepute.

During this same period a "modern" concept in corrections had its beginning. A common concept in law today is that if a person suffers from diminished responsibility and commits a crime out of impulse or inability to understand the difference between right and wrong (the justification varies from state to state), he or she should not be punished. The particular concept is laid out very well in Plato's *Laws:* "Someone may commit an act when mad or afflicted with disease. . . . Let him pay simply for the damage; and let him be exempt from other punishment."

In education, the Socratic method was the common approach in the schools, which were only for the wealthy: Young men would seek out well-known philosophers and would learn by being asked questions for which they had to seek out the answers. Otherwise, few people could read or write; the lower classes were totally uneducated. Children learned informally through practice and observation or apprenticeship to a craftsman. Few children received any formal training.

The general welfare of the population was not of official concern during this period. However, for individuals who were needy but conformed to general cultural expectations, some helping services were available. At times pensions were provided for the crippled, sometimes the needy were given free grain, and some residential institutions were set up for the orphaned children of men killed in battle (Trattner, 1979, 1986). But, although the Roman philosopher Cicero stated that "Justice commands us to have mercy on all," charity was the exception to the rule.

Though the concepts discussed here were at the forefront of intellectual thought in this period, the common person who violated cultural expectations was still frequently treated as if possessed, whether he or she was behaving in a manner we would today label as mentally ill, socially disadvantaged, retarded, or delinquent. Differentiations were not commonly made, and such persons usually ended up expelled from the community, imprisoned in dungeons, or enslaved in galleys. The more enlightened concepts of Hippocrates, Socrates, Plato, and their followers lasted for almost

700 years, but by A.D. 200 there began a rather overwhelming return to the concepts of demonology. By the fifth century, western civilization had entered a bleak period known as the Dark Ages.

The Dark Ages: "Human Services" in Medieval Europe

The Dark Ages was a period of upset, strife, and turmoil in western Europe. The fall of the Greco-Roman Empire to the "eastern barbarians" led to a turning away from much that had been discovered in the preceding 1,000 years and a return to demonology. Demonology was now related to Christianity rather than pagan beliefs. The "new" religion, Christianity, was strong and healthy and invested in spreading "the one true belief."

The period is called the Dark Ages to signify that the light of learning went out all across Western society. During this period, people were property, owned by feudal overlords. Society was harsh. A child found stealing a loaf of bread would be hanged as quickly as an adult. In essence, there was no childhood. Children were seen as small adults and treated as adults. They worked as soon as they were able. Except for the wealthy few, there was no education, no way to learn to read or write. Most of the population was illiterate.

The Dark Ages was a bleak period, but the Roman Catholic church, in spite of its belief in demonology, encouraged some humane institutions. The clergy set up monasteries, many of which became social service agencies of a sort. The income from church lands and donations was used to provide monetary assistance to the worthy poor. Monks and nuns reached out into the homes of some of the poor to provide food, clothing, and succor. By the eleventh and twelfth centuries, secular relief was provided by craft and merchant guilds (guilds were somewhat like today's unions) for destitute members and their families. Religious and lay groups opened hospices that offered shelter and care for weary travelers, orphans, and the aged, the sick, and the poor. It was an era of contrasts and inconsistency.

Russell (1960) describes the Dark Ages as an era of repression and constriction by the dominant religion. The "pressure cooker" aspect of the period may explain the outbreak of unusual forms of group hysteria, such as the *Saint Vitus's dance*, or *tarantella*. A quote from Sigerist (1943) describes the "affliction":

The disease occurred at the height of the summer heat. . . . People, asleep or awake, would suddenly jump up, feeling an acute pain like the sting of a bee. Some saw the spider, others did not, but they knew that it must be the tarantula. They ran out of the house into the street, to the market place, dancing in great excitement. Soon they were joined by others who like them had just been bitten, or by people who had been stung in previous years. . . . Thus groups of [people] would gather, dancing wildly in the queerest attire. . . . Others would tear their clothes and show their nakedness, losing all sense of modesty. . . . Some called for swords and acted like fencers, others for whips and beat each other. . . . Some of them had still stranger fancies, like to be tossed in the air, dug holes in the ground, and rolled themselves into the dirt like swine. They all drank wine plentifully and sang and talked like drunken people.

The prevalence of these strange behaviors and other individual problems were of great concern to the clerics of the period. The behaviors were unexplainable except through reference to concepts of good and bad, sanctity and sin, God and the devil. These notions led to one of the most disreputable systems for dealing with people who have problems in entering the mainstream of a culture. This was a time when witch-hunting became one solution to problems of human behavior.

One common belief was that people who behaved unacceptably were possessed by the devil, and only through God's intervention could the devil be cast out. Early in the Dark Ages, a technique known as *exorcism* began to be used by Roman Catholic clerics to help those considered to be possessed. Initially, the technique was rather kindly, consisting of praying to God to cast the devil from the subject's soul. It was believed that the subjects were usually possessed against their will.

As time passed, however, the theory changed to the belief that, in many cases, the subject *willingly* embraced the devil, or sold his or her soul in order to gain magical powers over others. Once this assumption was made, clerics added more severe techniques to the exorcism process. After several hundred years, exorcism came to include attempts to make the subjects' bodies unfit habitations for the devil. The process consisted of cursing the subjects; smearing them with feces; beating them with whips; placing red hot coals on their feet, hands, or stomachs; and a variety of other tortures.

By the 1400s, the quest for security led to spiritual explanations for deviant behavior. Persons behaving in violation of acceptable standards began to be labeled witches or warlocks and were considered heretics since they did not follow the teachings of the church. In 1484, the Pope issued a proclamation that was accepted as being divinely inspired. "Desiring with the most heartfelt anxiety . . . that all heretical depravity should be driven far from the frontiers and bournes of the faithful, we very gladly proclaim and even restate those particular means and methods whereby our pious desire may obtain its wished effect" (Szasz, 1970). In 1486 two monks, Jacob Sprenger and Heinrich Kramer, expanded on the "means and methods" in a book commissioned by the Pope titled *Malleus Malleficarum* (*The Hammer of Witches*). It was a document that "proved" the existence of witches and warlocks and told how to identify them and how to treat or help them. It became one system for dealing with the types of people to whom today we would apply the human services systems.

Even as some unfortunate individuals were viewed as possessed or in league with the devil and were "treated" accordingly, others were treated less viciously. Side by side with the torture and executions of witches and warlocks, other disturbed people were consigned to hospitals or poorhouses or assigned to the care of their relatives, neighbors, or communities through legal court proceedings (Allderidge, 1979). But still others were left alone to beg for alms if they could not support themselves. Vagabonds were simply expelled from community after community and left to survive as best they could. The era was a strange mixture of brutality and charity.

The Voice of "Reason"

Even while the superstitions of the 1400s continued, a few courageous individuals began to have doubts. By the 1600s, some people, such as Czech educator John Amos Comenius, advocated early childhood education, and some private schools for children were started. Still, only the wealthy could afford such luxuries. Punishment of children who broke laws was still harsh, but the punishment for adults was even more severe. Adults had to face being burned at the stake, whether witches or not, and cruel forms of slow death, such as being crushed by rocks or boiled in oil, were common. Lesser crimes merited penalties such as having one's tongue torn out.

Slowly, punitive attitudes began to wane. By the 1500s, the decline of the church as a ruling body and the erosion of feudal systems led to a growing involvement of civil law and government in human services. In 1536, the Henrican Poor Laws were passed in England. These laws provided for the punishment of beggars and vagabonds but offered civil relief for the "worthy poor." The state assumed responsibility for these whether they were young, old, disabled, or able-bodied. The laws were expanded in 1601 into what are now known as the Elizabethan Poor Laws. Henceforth, social welfare would be seen as having a dual role: provision of charitable relief and a means toward correcting behavior (Landon, 1986; Romanyshyn, 1971).

The correctional aspect of civil services is illustrated by the changing response to people who in prior centuries had been labeled as witches or warlocks. Toward the end of the era of witch-hunts, it was more difficult to label people who behaved oddly as witches. A number of individuals began to propose that people who behaved strangely, who did not fit into the mainstream, were not possessed by the devil but were instead "sick" (Neugebauer, 1979). Although the causes of the sickness were not clear, by 1547 an asylum had been created in London at St. Mary's of Bethlehem (known as *Bedlam* soon after) to give shelter to such persons (Bynum, Porter, and Shepherd, 1985). In the new world, in 1752 Pennsylvania Hospital was being used in such a manner, and in 1773 Williamsburg Hospital was founded as an asylum.

Although originally humanitarian, by the late 1700s such facilities had turned into little more than dungeons where the deviant could be locked up until they died. The inmates consisted of men, women, and children who had serious behavior problems or who were poor and could not pay their debts; vagrants; and those who had committed criminal acts. They were poorly fed, chained to walls, tormented by guards, and poorly clothed. Placement in such a facility meant almost certain death from typhoid, dysentery, or a host of other infectious diseases.

Outside the walls of the asylums, however, rational and scientific thought blossomed in the eighteenth-century Age of Reason. It was during this period that physicians began to become a major force in the development of approaches to personal and social maladaptation. In 1792, after the French Revolution, Philippe Pinel, a physician, became director of La Bicetre, the asylum in Paris. Following the footsteps of a layman, Jean-Baptiste Pussin, who was the first to institute reforms, Pinel continued to humanize the institution by removing the chains and providing reasonable shelter, food, and clothing for the inmates (Weiner, 1979). While Pinel succeeded in France, the same change occurred in England under William Tuke. In the United States, the concepts were advocated by Benjamin Rush, a physician and signer of the Declaration of Independence. Although considered humanitarians, both Pinel and Rush still advocated coercion, intimidation, and terror as useful tools in "moral treatment."

From the late 1700s to the 1850s, the first of the major medical theories of deviant behavior was developed: masturbatory insanity. The theory was strongly advocated as factual by Rush as well as by numerous eminent physicians of the nineteenth century. From 1850 to 1900, masturbatory insanity was advanced as the major causal explanation for all manner of deviances. It was believed to cause, for example, general insanity, weakness, impotence, consumption (tuberculosis), "dimmers of sight," vertigo, epilepsy, loss of mental powers, criminality, and death (Szasz, 1970).

In brief, the theory was that excessive masturbation caused such behaviors as a result of the loss of seminal fluid, which was considered a life force. Each person has only a certain amount of the life force at birth, and using it thus prematurely was said to cause a physical and mental deterioration. The obvious treatment was to prevent excess sexual activity, and the methods used varied from surveillance and physical restraints to surgical procedures such as severing of the dorsal nerves of the penis or removal of the clitoris. The theory prevailed until early in this century and was accepted as fact by most European, English, and American physicians, educators, and criminologists.

The late 1700s to the 1800s saw many changes in human services. In the United States, there was a clear separation of church and state. Although religious charity continued to be an important source of human services, social welfare increasingly became a major focus of civil government. In the nineteenth century civil solutions to human service problems included institutionalization in county poorhouses, prisons, mental hospitals, schools for the retarded, and orphanages.

The growing numbers of urban poor in a land where wealth was considered a virtue and dependency a vice led to great concern over the problems of social disability. In 1843 a private voluntary organization, the New York Association for Improving Conditions of the Poor, was formed. This group was concerned with the evil effect of poverty on community life but to a large extent saw poverty as the result of irresponsible behavior by those who *became* poor. The needy were seen either as "worthy poor" (widows, orphans, the sick, in dire straits through no fault of their own) or as "unworthy poor" (able-bodied persons who had no income because of "laziness" or "character faults"). As in previous eras, civil authorities attempted to discourage the "unworthy" from asking for help through the use of shame and humiliation (Landon, 1986). For example, in prerevolutionary times the poor were treated as morally deficient. They had to swear to the "pauper's oath" and their names were entered on the "poor roll" exhibited in the city hall or in the market-place. Local newspapers published the names of all paupers with the amounts of their relief allowances. In Pennsylvania at that time, all members of a pauper family had to wear the letter *P* on the shoulder of the right sleeve.

This attitude began to change partly as a result of social upheavals during and after the Civil War. It was obvious that increased numbers of poverty-stricken widows, orphans, disabled veterans, and civilians who had lost everything were not personally responsible for their condition but were victims of events beyond their control. There came a growing acceptance of the notion that the poor *deserve* services. By the late 1800s there was an organized charity movement funded by private contributions and public tax money.

Fragmenting Human Behavior

The late 1800s was a period characterized by an increased interest in discovering the reasons why people behave as they do: why they steal, act violently, do not learn, do not work, use drugs, or get depressed. A new approach to answering these questions involved the application of the scientific method. Human behavior was becoming the province of various scientific disciplines, and this led to a fragmentation of concepts about human behavior into various schools of thought.

Although that trend was becoming *apparent* in the eighteenth century (1700s), most disturbed individuals were still regarded as "sinners." In the middle and late nineteenth century, there occurred a greater differentiation of subclasses, such as "mentally ill," "criminal," and "mentally retarded." For a period, it was strongly felt that specific organic causes would be discovered that would support the differentiation of problem behavior into specific categories. There remains some validity to this approach, particularly in the areas of the few behavior disturbances related to specific organic causes (such as organic brain syndrome in the field of mental illness and mental retardation as a function of lead poisoning or inheritance). However, most behavioral dysfunctions today cannot be so easily pigeonholed.

In the late 1800s, three persons contributed greatly to the differentiation of subfields of mental illness, retardation, and corrections or criminology: Emil Kraeplin, Edward Seguin, and Cesare Lombroso. Kraeplin and Lombroso were particularly important for emphasizing organic factors in the development of deviance. Seguin, although not focusing specifically on organic causality, believed that the mentally retarded were suffering from "prolonged infancies." He became a major force in the development of special institutions for the training of the retarded and in the identification of techniques for the training process itself (Scheerenberger, 1983).

Seguin's method was to train perceptual processes before conceptual functions, a principle still utilized in early childhood education for both normal and retarded children. Seguin, a Frenchman, emigrated to the United States in 1848 and was the guiding spirit of the U.S. special education field in its early years. In Europe, the concern for the educationally handicapped led to the mental measurements movement in the late 1800s under the guidance of Alfred Binet, designer of the first intelligence test.

In criminology and corrections, the organic approach was supported by Cesare Lombroso, an Italian physician and anthropologist at the University of Turin. He proposed an early theory that criminals represent a biological phenomenon of physical degeneracy and that they can be identified by physical characteristics. In addition, he proposed a classification system with four specific subsets (Ferrero, 1911):

1. *The born criminal:* an individual who has inherited atavistic traits. The criminal behavior is instinctual; one-third of the criminal population was considered to be in this class.
2. *The "insane" criminal:* an individual who performs criminal acts as a result of being insane and who bears no responsibility for his or her behavior.
3. *The criminaloid:* an individual who has latent criminal "tendencies" [and who acts on the impulses] only under significant "stress."
4. *The noncriminal:* an individual who under *no* circumstances would commit a criminal act.

Current theories of criminal or delinquent behavior are an outgrowth of concepts that have a heavy sociocultural aspect; that is, the criminal or delinquent is either psychologically "sick," does not share the mainstream cultural values, or both.

Perhaps the most dominant criminologist of the twentieth century was Edwin Sutherland who died in 1950 (Gaylord and Galliher, 1988). He provided a distinctly social/environmental interpretation of crime and delinquency that contradicted both organic and psychological theories, which were common in the early 1900s. Sutherland proposed that criminal behavior is learned just like noncriminal behavior, often from associating with others who favor criminal pursuits.

While Lombroso worked on his theory of criminality, Emil Kraeplin, a German physician-researcher, studied individuals who manifested severe behavior disorders that were labeled *mental illness*. He followed the prevailing scientific approach in that his emphasis was on the *classification* of behavior. It was Kraeplin who introduced the term *manic-depressive psychosis* and promoted the terms *dementia praecox* (later called *schizophrenia*) and *paranoia*. Today's psychiatric diagnostic labels are based on his general system of classification. Kraeplin was a highly influential scientist. His advocacy of the position that behavior disorders are caused by physical problems of heredity and metabolism contributed greatly to the organic approach to human problems.

Most important in this period were two developing avenues of investigation and theorization: the focus on organic medical causes and the focus on psychological or functional causes. The organic approach led to the wide variety of physician-dominated strategies of the early and mid-1900s. The functional or psychological approach, after many modifications, spawned the human services concept.

The organic approach

The organic viewpoint was particularly common through the 1940s and has many adherents today. Its prevalence may be explained partly by its early successes. During the late nineteenth and early twentieth centuries, several discoveries were made. Foremost among these was the cause of an illness called *general paresis*. It has been estimated that around the turn of the century, up to one-third of institutionalized mental patients had this disorder, which appeared much like schizophrenia with an accompanying neurological impairment.

By 1913 it was proved that general paresis was caused by a syphilitic destruction of brain tissue (tertiary syphilis), and by 1917 fever treatments had been introduced to combat the disorder. Following the introduction of penicillin during the 1940s, the disease virtually disappeared. This, plus the discoveries of the causes of certain mental disorders associated with nutritional problems, aging, and toxic states and of genetic and toxic causes of mental retardation, strengthened the search for an organic answer to *all* behavioral disorders. Scientists even began searching for biological causes of such diverse problems as poverty, various criminal behaviors, depression, anger, and war. There was, in effect, a desperate rush to redefine and seek cures for all human problems as medical in nature (Valenstein, 1986).

The organic treatments were well received by staff members in institutional settings, especially mental hospitals. Various chemical and mechanical means were used to generate high fevers in paresis victims to kill the syphilitic spirochetes, including the injection of sulfur in oil and injection with malaria. By the 1920s the bromides were being used as sedatives, and in 1928 Ladislaus von Meduna introduced the first of the shock therapies.

Meduna began to experiment with the induction of convulsive seizures in schizophrenics in the hope that the process would alleviate schizophrenic symptoms. That is, in fact, what he found. Following the injection of metrazol, a camphor derivative that causes convulsions, the patient was "in better contact." By 1935, Dr. Meduna was reporting impressive cure rates. At about the same time (1933), Manfred Sakel reported his accidental discovery that insulin shock would produce very similar types of improvements in schizophrenics.

Finally, in 1938, an Italian physician, Ugo Cerletti, reported on the beneficial effects on schizophrenics of electrically induced convulsions (Szasz, 1970). In a very short time, these physical treatments became uncritically accepted by every mental hospital in the western world in spite of the disastrous side effects of the convulsions, which included broken bones, broken backs, and (although still disputed) significant memory loss. Physical injuries were controlled a few years later by the use of muscle relaxant drugs before the shock treatments. Little stood in the way of shock therapies' becoming the most common form of treatment in institutions through the early 1960s. Electroconvulsive therapy, in fact, is still used on a wide variety of people, from those with moderate depression to those with more severe disorders (Sackeim, 1985). It remains, however, a rather controversial treatment.

In the mid-1930s, one additional form of treatment was introduced. A Portuguese physician, Egas Moniz, in 1935 introduced a surgical procedure known as *lobotomy*. Moniz had noted a relationship between certain structures of the brain and aggressive behavior. He believed that certain repetitive responses, particularly aggressive actions, were a function of a "cycle of ideas." He felt that if the neural connectors between the location of the ideas could be cut, the acts would be interrupted (Valenstein, 1973). Moniz experimented with his procedure, generating evidence that it worked, and soon it became relatively common in "last resort" cases and, unfortunately, even in cases that one would have difficulty defining as "last resort." In fact, from 1935 to 1950, at least 40,000 known lobotomies were performed in the United States alone. The side effects were severe, including a loss of creativity and intellectual ability, the development of childlike behavior, and loss of social sensitivity. By the 1950s, such controversy had been generated that the operations decreased sharply and were performed in only a few centers.

The emphasis on the organic approach remains strong. One major advance in the treatment of human problems has been the discovery and development of a wide variety of tranquilizers and mood elevators since the early 1950s. They have contributed to a major turnaround in the treatment of seriously disturbed individuals in our society and have become widely used in prisons, jails, counseling centers, employment agencies, day care centers, and mental hospitals. Also, it would be difficult today to find a public school system in which some children are not regularly placed on drugs to help control their behavior. One article (Bruck, 1976) reported that from 500,000 to 1 million school-age children were taking stimulant medication on the recommendation of school physicians and officials.

Since the early 1950s, a major research effort has tried to find organic causes for virtually every conceivable problem from the major psychoses to minor problems of living. Investigations have been conducted and are being carried out in brain chemistry, nutrition, brain structure, genetics, and a host of other areas in the hope of finding medical answers to human disorders.

The functional or psychological approach

Even though the organic approach has a significant contribution to make to our efforts to understand human behavior and develop strategies for dealing with problems, this approach leaves much to be desired. The many questions it leaves unanswered stimulated the growth of a second major approach, the *functional* or *psychological approach*. Although the major advances and developments in this approach mainly date from the current century, its antecedents can be tracked back to the 1700s and the work of Anton Mesmer.

Mesmer was a physician who noted that some of his patients' complaints diminished after sessions in which he had given them no recognized medical treatment. He came to the conclusion that people had a life force

Mesmerism was a spectacular treatment in the 1700s; it later fell into disrepute.

called *animal magnetism* and that some individuals became sick because their animal magnetism was diminished in strength or because they were born without it. He also felt that he must be passing some of *his* animal magnetism to his patients when he talked to them and touched them. (Somewhat egotistically, Mesmer believed that he had more animal magnetism than most people.) The infusion of his magnetism into patients, he felt, caused their cure. Mesmer was heatedly attacked by other more traditional scientists of his day, and he was ultimately branded a charlatan or con man. His short-sighted contemporaries could not accept that Mesmer had discovered a legitimate phenomenon, even though his theory was in error.

By the late nineteenth century, mesmerism had been renamed *hypnotism* and had become more or less respectable. A number of respected physicians began using it to study problems in behavior. A major discovery was that the symptoms of a disorder called *hysteria* (paralysis, deafness, lack of physical sensitivity) could be produced in normal subjects through hypnosis and could be removed from hysteric subjects while they were in the hypnotic trance.

At this time in Vienna, a young neurologist, Sigmund Freud, became interested in the treatment of hysteria. In 1885, he went to France to study with a French physician, Jean Charcot, an expert in hypnotism. Upon returning to Vienna, Freud entered private practice with an older friend, Josef Breuer, a physician who was using the hypnotic method. Breuer found that if patients were encouraged to talk openly and emotionally about their problems under hypnosis, they would awaken feeling relieved. The technique was called the *cathartic method*. It was through this technique that the concept of unconscious processes was formulated. Freud later found that hypnosis was not necessary to the process. An uncontrolled, free monologue on the part of the patient, with no restraints, had the same effect. He called this process *free association*.

With the publication in 1900 of one of his early works, *The Interpretation of Dreams*, Freud began a long career of developing and refining a revolutionary approach to human maladaptation. At first reviled and rejected because of their emphasis on the sexual, his theories gradually gained wide acceptance. By the 1920s and 1930s, specialists in other fields were using Freudian concepts as an integral part of their thinking. Anthropologist Margaret Mead, for example, began an ongoing integration of these concepts into her study of primitive cultures.

Freud was unquestionably one of the geniuses of our time. He advanced our understanding of human behavior, society, and culture. Although there is perhaps not as much hard evidence regarding his theories as one might desire, they are broadly accepted and act as a fundamental cornerstone for many approaches to human adaptation problems. In regard to supportive evidence, recent work seems to provide some methodological support for a number of his critical concepts (Silverman, 1976). His major contributions are the concepts of unconscious motivation and of stages of development, the notion that deviance is the exaggeration of normal behavior, and the development of a psychological treatment methodology: psychoanalysis (Mehr, 1983).

Today, there are only approximately 2,500 fully accredited Freudian psychoanalysts in the country. However, many thousands of professionals in the fields of corrections, early education, mental health, public welfare, and the other areas of human problems are basically psychoanalytic in orientation. By the 1960s, Freudianism had become the dominant theoretical conception of human behavior as reflected in newspapers, weekly magazines, radio, television, and movies.

From the human services perspective, if one were to criticize psychoanalytic theory, the criticism would be that it focuses too exclusively on the inner person, relatively ignoring social, cultural, and economic factors in human behavior and deviance. In addition, to use psychoanalytic techniques effectively requires many years of intensive training. Also, the treatment is intensive, usually requiring many years for each client. For these reasons, the subfields of human services generally have not used psychoanalytic treatment technologies, or have tried to use them and have been ineffective.

In spite of the criticism of Freud's psychoanalytic technique, it was the first of the *functional* approaches. *Functional* is used here in the sense that all behavior is seen as having a psychological *function* of meeting the person's needs. As a result of Freud's breakthroughs in theory and practice, there has been a tremendous growth of theories that purport to explain human behavior in general and abnormalities or maladaptations in particular. One work (Harper, 1960) lists thirty-six major psychological therapies, including the various offshoots of traditional psychoanalysis. There are many more if one adds systems such as primal therapy, logotherapy, reality therapy, neurolinguistic programming, and gestalt therapy.

It was not until the early 1940s that a major competitor to the psychoanalytic frame of thought appeared. In 1942, Carl Rogers's *Counseling and Psychotherapy* was published. Rogers's background was in theology, education, and clinical psychology. He reacted negatively to the psychoanalytic view of the person as a base animal in need of socialization and to its authoritarian approach to treatment. Rather, Rogers viewed human beings as basically striving for "good" and felt that within each individual there was the potential for the development of a mature self. For Rogers, the purpose of the therapist was to provide the setting in which clients could comfortably examine their problems so as to change their perceptions about their world and their place in it. *Client-centered therapy* (Rogers, 1951), as it is called, has become an extremely popular theoretical and functional system.

Rogers's early work was done on a very select client population. He worked mainly with bright, young students in university counseling centers. His technique has been criticized as being effective with merely one type of person: white, middle-class or higher, verbal, and with neurotic problems. Although Rogers and his followers have tried to prove otherwise, the criticism is still expressed.

There is some disagreement as to whether it can be experimentally proved that verbal psychotherapy works at all (Eysenck, 1966), although much current research is very supportive of psychotherapy's usefulness and effectiveness (Smith, Glass, and Miller, 1980). Even among those who accept its validity, there is growing concern about its effectiveness with those who suffer disruptions in their ability to cope on a long-term basis with life in a complex society. Rickard (1971) lists the critical deficiencies of the verbal therapies (or as he calls them, the interview therapies) as the behaviorist sees them:

1. The strength of interview therapies lies to a large extent in the ill-defined patient-therapist relationship. Since relationships grow slowly, a severe restriction is placed on the number of clients who can be seen in the lifetime of a hardworking therapist.

2. Interview therapy demands that communication, primarily verbal, be established between client and therapist. Small children, severe retardates, recalcitrant juveniles, and seriously disturbed psychotics are examples of vast populations notorious for poor communication skills.

3. The interview therapist must undergo expensive professional training. Much of this skill is frankly artistic and difficult to teach, even in the master-apprentice relationship. The subtleties of psychotherapy cannot be easily encompassed in a curriculum and thus readily passed on to a psychological technician. The present extremely expensive, time-consuming approach to training interview psychotherapists is inadequate to meet existing and projected needs.

4. The interview therapies in general are difficult to evaluate. This criticism applies in various degrees to all psychotherapeutic techniques, but the interview therapies are especially vulnerable. Interview therapies fail to specify goals except at quite molar levels: improved self-concept, fewer inhibitions, less repression, etc. Most of the goals of interview therapy are intrapsychic ones occurring within the context of the psychotherapeutic relationship.

The behavioral approach

The third major approach to appear in the past century is based on learning theory. It has been called by a variety of terms including *behaviorism, behavior modification, behavioral theory,* and *behavioral therapy.* While in many ways behaviorism was a contemporary development with Freudian psychoanalysis and predated Rogers's client-centered therapy, it was not until relatively recently that the behavioral approach became popular. The reason for this is not clear, but its current popularity may well have something to do with the last two decades' growing concern for quick, effective treatment that can be delivered economically to large numbers of clients.

Behavior therapy in its most simplistic form can be defined as the application of learning theory to the problem of changing behavior. The basic concept is that most behavior, adaptive or deviant, is learned and that deviant behavior can be unlearned. Simply put, adaptive behavior is reinforced and maladaptive behavior either is not reinforced at all or is negatively reinforced.

Behavioral approaches had their roots in the work of the Russian physiologist Ivan Sechenov in the mid- to late 1800s. Sechenov claimed that psychic or mental activity depended entirely on external stimuli and their link with reflexes. A major step forward occurred at the end of the 1800s when Ivan Pavlov, another Russian physiologist, accidentally discovered *classical conditioning*. In his work with dogs, Pavlov found that if he repeatedly paired the ringing of a bell with the presentation of meat powder on a dog's tongue, eventually the sound of the bell alone would produce salivation. The flow of the dog's saliva had become *conditioned* to a new stimulus.

Pavlov's findings were expanded upon in the work of J. B. Watson, a U.S. psychologist. Watson held the view that all behavior is learned, including disturbed behavior, through association or conditioning of stimuli and responses. In a now classic experiment Watson and a student, Rosalie Rayner, conditioned an eleven-month-old child named Albert to be terrified of furry objects (Jones, 1974). In a later study they *deconditioned* the fears of a child named Peter. These two studies became very influential in supporting the view that emotional disturbances such as phobias (irrational fears) could be learned and also that disturbed behavior could be unlearned.

Many thousands of psychologists have contributed to the development of learning theory and its application to human behavior. One who is very well known is B. F. Skinner. Skinner followed in the footsteps of Edward Thorndike, who had formulated the "law of effect," which states that behaviors followed by positive consequences are likely to be learned, and those followed by negative consequences are less likely to be learned. Skinner formulated the concept of operant or instrumental learning. This is the concept that the occurrence of a behavior is instrumental in whether or not it is learned. The behavior "operates" on the environment, resulting in a consequence, and in turn the environmental consequence "operates" on the behavior in the form of reinforcement or punishment. B. F. Skinner has been a vocal advocate of the view that we must focus on observable or measurable events rather than on mental events if we wish to understand and modify (change) behavior. The instrumental or operant learning approach has made major contributions to the understanding of human behavior and remains a major viewpoint today.

A third important behavioral approach has grown out of an awareness of the limitations of the conditioned learning and operant learning approaches. Both neglect the importance of internal mental events. Since the 1960s a number of learning theorists have focused on the manner in which internal mental events such as thoughts, beliefs, and emotions influence behavior. For example, social learning theory emphasizes modeling or observational learning: how people learn by watching and imitating others (Bandura, 1977, 1982). Other theories developed in the 1970s and 1980s focus on cognitive mediating events. A mediating event such as a thought (cognition) may be activated by a stimulus, and then may initiate the behavior. The same stimulus may result in different behaviors, depending on the intervening internal events. This type of cognitive theory has gained significant popularity in recent years (Meichenbaum, 1977).

Behavior therapy has been cited in the National Institute of Mental Health's 1975 report, *Research in the Service of Mental Health*, along with the use of the major tranquilizers, as one of the two major developments in the field since the 1950s. It has become a common technique, particularly in public institutions, since the mid-1960s. Although there was a flurry of interest in it during the 1920s and 1930s under the leadership of J. B. Watson, during the 1940s and 1950s it lost impetus. However, during the 1960s, there was a surge of activity in the area, and the work of many researchers and therapists has stimulated a tremendous growth of interest in behavioral techniques in the fields of early childhood education, mental health, corrections, and retardation.

Social Welfare:
Toward a Community Approach

Although history seems to have been marked by inhumane approaches to disadvantaged and problem-ridden people, there have always been people who were charitable toward the less fortunate. Through most of history, charity was given for the benefit of both the needy and the *giver*. Charity was a moral virtue that raised the giver's status and moral standing while helping the needy.

As societies became more complex, simple charity no longer appears to have been adequate in dealing with the needy. A major change in perception occurred in the 1500s, when the view developed that civil governments should address the needs of persons through civil legislation. The Elizabethan Poor Laws established in England in 1601 founded a system that provided care and shelter (of a primitive sort) for the poor who could work, in state-run "workhouses."

Nearly 200 years later, the industrial revolution resulted in large concentrations of disadvantaged people in urban areas. To deal with this problem, many public and private institutions were opened. These included workhouses; debtors' prisons; penal institutions; houses for orphans, delinquents, and unwed mothers; and mental institutions. These institutions required workers and "helping" services to become more formalized. However, these institutions left much to be desired in terms of their conditions. The concern of some private citizens over these conditions led to a number of attempts at social reform.

In the middle nineteenth century, one of the great reformers appeared in the United States. Dorothea Dix, a retired schoolteacher, was requested to teach a Sunday school class at the East Cambridge jail. She was shocked at the general conditions of prisons and was particularly appalled at the manner in which those who were considered insane were handled. In midwinter, they were huddled in unheated cells, given slop to eat, and untreated for physical illnesses. She began a personal investigation of conditions in jails, debtors' prisons, and asylums across this country, exposing the ill treatment and brutality that had become common following the decline of the reform movement stimulated by Pinel and Tuke. Her exposés hit a responsive chord with the populace and with legislators, and by the time of her withdrawal from active lobbying for improved conditions she was directly responsible for the establishment of more than thirty mental hospitals in the United States and Europe. Her main efforts were focused on the plight of the insane, but her reform efforts were also significant in the areas of corrections, education, poverty, and the provision of physical health services to the indigent. In a sense, her efforts at reform foreshadowed the advocacy role of human service workers.

The social welfare movement made major strides in the 1800s and early 1900s. For example, in 1880 the Salvation Army, founded in 1878 by William Booth in England, was imported to the United States. Although a religious organization, the Salvation Army utilized military rank for its members and focused primarily on implementing social welfare programs. It currently works in seventy nations and operates more than 3,000 social welfare institutions. Another important development was that of the concept of settlement houses. In the United States, many new immigrants were arriving, and settlement houses were established to help them since they were often poor and had difficulty fitting into American culture. The role of a settlement house was twofold: (1) to be of help to the immediate neighborhood surrounding the house; (2) to change, as much as possible, the social condition that made living in a slum a wretched and demeaning existence. Many early settlement workers hoped to build a bridge between the wealthy and poor citizens of major cities. Early settlement workers were often upper-class women who donated their time; later, some of those who came as immigrants became workers.

The first recorded settlement house was begun by Stanton Coit in 1866. Settlement house workers saw themselves as friends and neighbors of the disadvantaged. They were advocates for the poor and often organized self-help clubs in disadvantaged neighborhoods. Their efforts can be characterized as early social action programs.

One settlement house is well known: Hull House in Chicago, which opened in 1889. Here social work was born. Today, the Jane Addams School of Social Work at the University of Chicago is named after the founder of Hull House. By the 1920s, the settlement houses had become institutions that employed people trained in the new career of social casework.

Unfortunately, the standardization of charity work into social casework had certain undesirable results. Social casework began to emphasize the individual's contribution to his or her problems rather than the contributions of a negative environment to social problems. This emphasis on individual culpability was given impetus in the 1920s by the publication of a major text called *Social Diagnosis* by a highly regarded social worker named Mary Richmond. The emphasis of social diagnosis was on individual problems and their individual remediation. This individual focus paralleled the fragmenting of the study of human behavior into the various schools of thought described in this chapter. Especially in the 1920s, social work in a sense "surrendered to Freud" and the psychoanalytic viewpoint (Trattner, 1979, 1986). An individual clinical model of social casework predominated through the 1960s and is still somewhat common.

The past eighty years have again seen accelerating change. In the period from 1910 to the present, the depression and World War II resulted in tremendous economic, social, and psychological upheaval. As after the Civil War, it became apparent that social as well as strictly personal factors were important in the existence of human service problems.

A period of major significance began during the Great Depression of the 1930s. Franklin D. Roosevelt was elected president in 1932 and took office in early 1933. President Roosevelt brought with him his experience of trying to deal with a depressed economy as governor of New York. During the depression, one-third of the U.S. labor force was unemployed. Roosevelt was committed to sweeping social change in an attempt to get the economy back on track and to deal with the human misery resulting from the depression. He promised a "New Deal" for U.S. citizens.

During Roosevelt's three terms in office, many of today's social welfare entitlement programs were begun. One of the most important was the Social Security Act of 1935. It established ten different programs: old-age retirement; unemployment compensation; state public aid for the elderly, blind, and dependent children; maternal and child health services; services to crippled children; child welfare services; vocational rehabilitation services; and public health services. It was a truly sweeping piece of legislation and resulted in dramatic changes in how we deal with the disadvantaged.

Social Security legislation was further broadened under President Eisenhower in the 1950s, to include coverage of the self-employed, clergy, farm workers, and members of the armed forces. In addition, Eisenhower established the federal Department of Health, Education and Welfare and signed the Civil Rights Act of 1957, which was the basis for the civil rights activities in the 1960s.

The major legislative and systems changes which occurred from President Roosevelt's time through the Eisenhower years helped to create a foundation for the human services programs to come. A new perspective was being developed about the rights of the disadvantaged and their entitlement to services. The more recent antecedents of the human services approach have already been described in Chapter 1. During the Roosevelt to Eisenhower eras, the previously fragmented conceptions of human behavior began to move in the direction of a new integration in service delivery. (See Table 2-1.) Social welfare began to emphasize community approaches and a growing concern with social action, advocacy, and social development reminiscent of the settlement workers' approach years before.

Table 2-1 *Historical highlights and their relationship to the development of human services*

Historical highlights	Relationship to human services
Trephining	First known attempts to change behavior of people who had difficulty belonging to the mainstream of their culture.
Hippocrates	First movement away from spiritualistic explanation of human behavior.
The Dark Ages	Return to religious explanation of human behavior. Development of exorcistic treatment.
The Age of Reason	Beginning of major medical model explanations of human behavior.
Humanitarian reform	Pinel and Tuke emphasize that humans should be treated as sick, not bad. Dorothea Dix crusades on behalf of the "insane," the poor, and the criminals.
Fragmenting human behavior	Kraeplin, Lombroso, and Seguin contribute to the development of three major subfields—insanity, corrections, and retardation—leading to the subsequent fragmentation of the study of human behavior. Three schools of thought develop—the organic, the functional, and the behavioral—that attempt to explain and change human behavior based on distinctly different theories and ultimately set the stage for the development of the human services approach.
Integrated social welfare	Social welfare approaches are embraced by organized private charity groups. Social action and advocacy approaches are begun in settlement house settings but are eclipsed by the development of an individually focused social diagnosis/social casework viewpoint. The mid-1900s see the return of a social action development focus and the beginning of an integration of various schools of thought into a generic human services approach.

Summary

1. The beliefs that a society or culture holds at any period of time have a major effect on how the society or culture perceives the needs of its members. Societal responses to disadvantaged people are determined by the same "truths."

2. Primitive people believed that human behavior is often controlled by spiritual entities. Although some needy people were treated charitably, most were viewed as an unacceptable burden and were dealt with harshly.

3. As social organizations became more complex, codes of behavior were established such as the Code of Hammurabi and the ethical writings in Hebraic law. The codes were mainly primitive but did establish charity or helping behavior as important social behavior.

4. The Golden Age of Greece was a period of heightened interest in the reasons for human behavior and a time when greater concern for the principles of human services was expressed, at least in regard to the wealthy classes of free men.

5. The Dark Ages saw a return to spiritualistic or demonic theories of maladaptive behavior. The responses to disadvantaged people were often brutal. However, some charitable institutions were established to provide services to the "worthy" poor or disabled.

6. The end of the Dark Ages was marked by great inconsistency. The persecution of disturbed people as witches and warlocks occurred even as institutions were created to feed, clothe, and shelter many types of disadvantaged people. Civil governments began to take on responsibility for dealing with the disadvantaged.

7. A century ago, the methods of scientific investigation began to be applied to the issue of human behavior. Three major schools of thought developed about why people behave as they do. The study of human behavior was fragmented into the organic, functional, and behavioral viewpoints.

8. The organic approach focused on finding physiological causes for behaviors such as criminality, mental illness, and inability to learn.

9. The functional approach searched for psychosocial reasons for behavior such as crime, mental illness, poverty, and life dissatisfaction.

10. The behavioral approach explored how behaviors could be learned. It attempted to develop a rationale for explaining behaviors such as crime, poverty, depression, anxiety, and fear as being due to inappropriate learning experiences.

11. Social welfare has become the province of civil government during the past 100 years. It began as an organized charity movement dealing primarily with the "worthy poor," moved into a social action phase with the settlement house, and switched to focusing on social diagnosis and individual treatment. Most recently, social welfare has moved again toward social advocacy and social development. To some extent it integrates the knowledge and techniques developed by the various behavioral science approaches.

Discussion Questions

1. Why was so little charity present in preliterate tribes and clans?

2. What was the significance of the Henrican and Elizabethan Poor Laws?

3. What were the positive and negative outcomes of the development of the scientific approach of the late-nineteenth-century work of Kraeplin, Lombroso, and Seguin?

4. What was the significance of the discovery of the cause of general paresis?

5. How might one criticize the Freudian approach?

6. How did the settlement house movement foreshadow today's human services approach?

7. In what way is the current spirit of the times influencing how we conceptualize human behavior?

Learning Experiences

1. Read Ken Kesey's *One Flew Over the Cuckoo's Nest.*

2. Attend a revivalist meeting. What does it remind you of?

3. Survey your friends.
   - How many of them believe in astrology? Why?
   - How many of them believe in demonic possession? Why?
   - How many of them have taken tranquilizers? Why?

4. Pretend you live in another period of history. Would you be a "helper"? If so, how would you behave?

5. Visit a local museum to get a feeling for the historical periods represented.

Recommended Readings

Alexander, V., and Selesnick, S. *The History of Psychiatry.* New York: Mentor Books, 1968.

Landon, J. W. *The Development of Social Welfare.* New York: Human Sciences Press, 1986.

Romanyshyn, J. M. *Social Welfare: Charity to Justice.* New York: Random House, 1971.

Scheerenberger, R. C. *A History of Mental Retardation.* Baltimore: Paul H. Brooks, 1983.

Trattner, W. I. *From Poor Law to Welfare State: A History of Social Welfare in America.* (3rd. Ed.) New York: The Free Press, 1986.

3

Human Service Workers:
Agents of Change

- Can human service workers be considered professionals?
- What are the thirteen basic role functions of human service workers?
- Why are human service workers described as generalists?
- What are some real-life examples of the functions of human service workers?
- Is there evidence to support the competence of human service workers?
- Do human service workers need to be credentialed?

In Chapter 1, human service workers were described as being characterized by a dynamically evolving generic human services viewpoint, by a multidisciplinary (or interdisciplinary) focus, by a concern for the whole person, and by an approach that involves being a generalist change agent. That description leaves many questions unanswered. Are human service workers professionals? What do they really do on a daily basis? Can human service workers be as effective as traditional professionals? Do human service workers need special credentials?

Human Services, A New Profession

With growing acceptance of the evidence that one does not have to be a highly credentialed member of a traditional professional discipline to provide competent helping services, there has been a great deal of concern given to developing expanded roles for human service workers. Before examining these roles, however, it is important to consider briefly the professional–nonprofessional issue. It has been the prevailing attitude that professionals are the most qualified service deliverers and that the higher the educational degree and the longer the educational process, the better. For example, the psychoanalyst (ten years of specialty training) is viewed from this perspective as being "better" than the psychologist (six to seven years of university training), and the psychologist is "better" than the social worker (six years of university training). Some professionals have adopted and encouraged this attitude to the extent that critics have described it as professional myopia (Morris, 1974). Psychologists, of course, would not agree that psychoanalysts are better than they, and social workers would not agree that psychologists are better than social workers! All would probably agree that each has a different focus and a contribution to make.

Sometimes the terms *nonprofessional* and *paraprofessional* are used to denote people without bachelor's or master's degrees, who are presumed to have less ability or expertise than the traditional professionals. However, although it is perhaps not extreme to require ten years of training to pursue the complex practice of psychoanalysis, to place the same expectations on all practitioners of helping services is absurd (Vidaver, 1973). In fact, relating professionalism to academic credentials alone (which is what happens in most instances) is a distortion of the true meaning of *professional*. Bay and Bay (1973) feel that the usual concept of professionalism is eroding rationality in health care. They quote sociologist Philip Slater (1970) as asserting that "the principle behind every professional organization is (a) to restrict membership, and (b) to provide minimum service at maximum cost." These two goals are, of course, totally unacceptable from a human service perspective.

The true professional ethic, however, should relate more to how people behave in their work and how well they do it as well as to their credentials or training. *Profession* is, in fact, defined as an occupation or vocation requiring training in the liberal arts or sciences and advanced study in a specialized field, *or* as the body of qualified persons of one specific occupation or field. Significantly, a widely accepted definition of *professionalism* is the condition of having great skill or experience in a particular field or activity. Thus, it is rational to consider the competent human service worker a true professional.

Human service workers by and large do consider themselves professionals. Instructors in human service education programs in colleges and universities view their graduates as entry-level professionals, the term *paraprofessional* having outrun its usefulness (Kronick, 1987). However, the issue is not one of self-perception, but of how others view us. Feringer and Jacobs (1987) point out two significant problems facing human services in the process of professionalization.

1. There is insufficient recognition by the public for human services as a profession. For example, our degrees are not sufficient and necessary conditions for employment. Furthermore, the public does not differentiate us from similar and other related classes of workers.

2. There continues to be a fragmentation in human services education. While providing a great deal of freedom for responding to local needs, we are limited in our ability to create coherent progressions of learning and articulation agreements between levels of curricula.

Will these problems be resolved, and will human service workers achieve recognized status as professionals? It seems very likely, since substantial progress has already been made. We can appreciate the progress that has been made by comparing the development of the field of human services with the development of social work as a recognized profession.

Social work, like human services, traces its roots to humanitarian or charitable activities throughout history. The formal beginning of the profession of social work, however, is often traced to the establishment in 1898 of a summer school of philanthropy by Mary Richards, the director of the New York Charity Organization Society (Landon, 1986). This school later became known as the New York School of Social Work. A comparable event in human services was the establishment of the Purdue University two-year program in mental health technology in 1966. In the ten years following 1898, many new schools of social work were established around the country. In the ten years following 1966, hundreds of human service worker programs were established in community colleges, four-year colleges, and universities.

The next major step in the professionalization of social work was the establishment of a professional organization in 1918, and several others in the years that followed, all of which finally joined together in 1955 in a national organization that had local and regional chapters. The existence of a national professional organization allowed social workers to establish criteria for professionalism in social work and provided advocacy for the profession itself. The development of a national membership organization was preceded by the establishment (in 1946) of a national Council on Social Work Education whose purposes were to set standards, review and accredit programs and procedures, and distribute materials related to social work education.

Do these developments in social work have a parallel in human services? They do to some extent. During the past twenty years a number of national organizations of human service workers have formed, but for a variety of reasons most did not survive. One, the National Organization for Human Service Education (NOHSE), is, however, strong and healthy, with a number of regional and local chapters. Unfortunately, it has a membership of only about 600 people, whose primary focus is on education of human service workers. A second organization, the Council for Standards in Human Service Education, could be compared to the Council on Social Work Education in 1946. What has not developed in the field of human services is a stable, viable, national organization of individual human service workers. It may be coming: The National Organization for Human Service Education does accept as members human service workers employed in field settings. Perhaps if that membership keeps growing, we will see a functional national organization of human service *workers* splitting off from NOHSE sometime in the years to come.

Human services is a young field, only about twenty-five years old. It took social work, psychology, and nursing each about fifty to sixty years to become full-fledged recognized professions. From that perspective, the future of professionalization in human services may be very bright. The human service worker may soon be recognized by all traditional professionals, the lay public, and every social systems agency as a professional who has accepted human service credentials.

Role Functions of the Human Service Worker

As the use of people we now call human service workers has expanded, there has been increased concern with determining realistic and legitimate role structures for them, and reasonable models for interaction between human service workers and the established professionals. Suggestions have ranged from proposals that human service workers be assistants to professionals, doing menial tasks, to proposals that they do everything the established professionals do.

Concern over this issue led a consortium of community colleges in fourteen southeastern states called the Southern Regional Education Board (SREB) to try to develop a rational model of appropriate roles and functions for such workers. The results have broad applicability to human services in general. Over a period of several years, the project identified thirteen functional roles and four levels of workers who could or would perform human services (SREB, 1969). The project attempted to identify the needs of the clients, their families, and communities and then proposed activities or functions to meet those needs. The proposal included the following categories:

1. *Outreach worker*—reaches out to detect people with problems, to refer them to appropriate services, and to follow them up to make sure they continue to their maximum rehabilitation. (For example, an outreach worker may work with senior citizen centers. The worker would become aware of the seniors' needs, identify persons who need assistance, and refer them to appropriate services.)

2. *Broker*—helps people get to existing services and helps the service relate more easily to clients. (This role involves making contacts with the relevant agencies that offer service and helping the client obtain the most appropriate services.)

3. *Advocate*—pleads and fights for services, policies, rules, regulations, and laws for the client's benefit. (Advocacy may involve individuals or

groups. The advocate generally can exert more influence on the powers that be than disadvantaged groups or individuals. The changes in services, policies, laws, and rules that advocacy can achieve may have a positive impact on large numbers of people in need [Sosin and Caulum, 1983].)

4. *Evaluator*—assesses client or community needs and problems, whether medical, psychiatric, social, or educational. Formulates plans. (This role is important in assessing the effectiveness of services delivered to individual clients but is also applied to the evaluation of whole programs and agencies.)

5. *Teacher-educator*—performs a range of instructional activities from simple coaching and forming to teaching highly technical content directed to individuals and groups.

6. *Behavior changer*—carrries out a range of activities planned primarily to change behavior, ranging from coaching and counseling to casework, psychotherapy, and behavior therapy.

7. *Mobilizer*—helps get new resources for clients or communities. (Mobilization means becoming an initiator of new resources. It often involves bringing agencies or groups of service providers or citizens together to form networks that can support one another, share information, and advocate for change [Grossinger, 1985; Sarason et al., 1977].)

8. *Consultant*—works with other professions and agencies regarding their handling of problems, needs, and programs.

9. *Community planner*—works with community boards, committees, and so on, to assure that community developments enhance self and social actualization or at least minimize emotional stress and strains on people.

10. *Caregiver*—provides services for people who need ongoing support of some kind (e.g., financial assistance, day care, social support, twenty-four-hour care).

11. *Data manager*—performs all aspects of data handling, gathering, tabulating, analyzing, synthesizing, program evaluation, and planning.

12. *Administrator*—carries out activities that are primarily agency or institution-oriented (budgeting, purchasing, personnel activities). (This role generally develops after a person has had substantial experience working with clients. The transition from direct care work often requires additional training [White, 1981].)

13. *Assistant to specialist*—acts as assistant to specialists (e.g., psychiatrist, psychologist, nurse), relieving them of burdensome tasks. The types of tasks include administering psychological tests, taking blood pressures, escorting clients to agencies, and other duties which are viewed as an ineffective utilization of a specialist's time.[1]

In addition to identifying specialist functions, SREB specified the following four levels of competence at which these functions could be carried out:

- *Level I: Entry Level*—persons with a few weeks to a few months of in-service instruction but with little experience.
- *Level II: Apprentice Level*—persons with substantial formal training or experience; equivalent to the associate of arts degree.
- *Level III: Journeymen*—substantial formal training or experience functioning at the baccalaureate degree level.
- *Level IV: Master or Professional Level*—highly competent, equivalent of a master's or doctorate.[2]

These broad guidelines have been well accepted by many in the human services, and further work has refined them. For example, in one major study 358 tasks of human service workers were identified (Austin, 1975, 1978). The study identified common tasks that cut across the various subspecialties of the Florida Department of Health and Rehabilitative Services, an umbrella agency, and provided empirical support for the rough categorizations of SREB.

The activities that human service workers engage in have been further detailed by the SREB (1979). Project staff members from that organization combined several task lists. The lists had been developed by projects around the country using job analysis of functioning human service workers. The projects included data from Texas, Illinois, Florida, North Carolina, and the United States Navy. Substantial work on these task lists resulted in the selection of 141 tasks that were organized into a survey administered to more than 200 human service workers across the country. The data indicated that human service tasks cluster around four main areas: (1) linkage/advocacy, (2) treatment/planning, (3) administration/management, and (4) therapeutic environment control.

The thirteen functional roles SREB had identified earlier (SREB, 1969) can be fitted into this more recent classification system.

Linkage/advocacy
1. Outreach worker
2. Broker
3. Advocate
7. Mobilizer

Treatment/planning
6. Behavior changer
10. Caregiver
13. Assistant to specialist

Administration/management
4. Evaluator
11. Data manager

12. Administrator
8. Consultant
9. Community planner

Therapeutic environment control
5. Teacher-educator

This clustering of tasks is self-explanatory. With the exception of therapeutic environment control, the earlier SREB descriptions define the new clusters accurately. Therapeutic environment control involves more than just teaching. It involves activities such as teaching self-help and living skills and also involves structuring new environments, maintenance of stable behavior in old environments, and provisions for disruptive behavior.

Why is there so much emphasis on identifying tasks in human services? Human services is a broad field, new on the helping scene, so practitioners are still struggling with its identity. We need to know what human service workers do specifically, if for no other reason than to determine how to train, educate, and retrain individuals to work in this area.

Although definitions of the human service worker may vary, all share one characteristic. In effect, what is being described by these projects is a *generalist worker*, a concept that was touched upon by the Southern Regional Education Board (1973, 1978). SREB describes five characteristics of the generalist that are applicable to human service workers.

1. The generalist works with a limited number of clients or families (in consultation with other professionals) to provide across-the-board services as needed by the clients and their families.
2. The generalist is able to work in a variety of agencies and organizations that provide human services.
3. The generalist is able to work cooperatively with all the existing professions in the field rather than affiliating with any one of the existing professions.
4. The generalist is familiar with a number of therapeutic services and techniques.
5. The generalist is a human services professional who is expected to continue to learn and grow.

These projects have made excellent beginnings in the identification and definition of human service worker roles and functions. There appears to be increasing agreement between such groups, at least on the broad outlines. It appears that the field is moving toward identifying a core group of functions that will be the focus of most human service workers in every subspecialty; the core functions will embody the attributes of the generic human services field.

Human Service Workers as Agents of Change: Do They Help or Heal?

For almost 200 years, there has been an increasing emphasis on the notion that *deviant* or problem behavior is the result of a disease process in either the physical or the psychological realm. In fact, many consider disruptions in psychological processes to be a function of an underlying physical disorder. The implications of such an approach are numerous. If problem behavior *is* a function of a physical disease, such behavior should be treated, the deliverers of service should be medical personnel, services should be delivered in medical settings (hospitals), and the goal should be cure. Not only should the behavior (symptoms) be changed, treatment should continue until the underlying physical process is modified until it is within normal limits. Patients should be *healed*. They will no longer commit crimes, be mentally ill, be mentally retarded, sexually molest children; rather, they will obey laws, be satisfied, work, learn, and so forth.

The human services model does not totally reject this medical model, since there are obvious values in many of its treatments and since there *are* behavior disorders that result from underlying physical causes. However, in a very real sense, human services expands the range of effective interventions, focusing particularly on types of interventions that have been relatively neglected because of what might be considered an overemphasis on the medical approach to psychological and behavior problems. Human services focuses on *helping* rather than *healing*.

The overall objective of the helping model is either to maintain and support the consumers in their own communities or to create new communities for individuals who have become so unlinked from the mainstream that they have no identifiable community. For the individual client-consumer, meeting this overall objective might well involve dealing with a variety of subsystems (Hansell, 1976).

1. Biochemical and informational supplies: food, oxygen, and a variety of information.
2. A clear concept of self-identity, held with conviction.
3. Persons, at least one (the helper), in persisting, interdependent contact, occasionally approaching intimacy.
4. Groups, at least one, composed of individuals who regard this person as a member.
5. Roles, at least one, which offer a context for achieving dignity and self-esteem through performance.
6. Money or purchasing power to participate in an exchange of goods and services in a society specialized for such exchanges.
7. A comprehensive system of meaning, a satisfying set of notions that clarify experience and define ambiguous events.

Individuals who need assistance generally have a multitude of problems: medical, psychological, behavioral, educational, social, and environmental. A human service worker must act as a psychosocial helper if an adequate impact is to be made on the client's problem network. The worker must deal with clients' feelings in a psychotherapeutic manner but also link the clients with the appropriate services and perhaps even change their life space. A client may need medication, a new job or public financial assistance, a place to live, a structured shelter-care setting, introduction to a peer support system, vocational training, education, or hospitalization.

Of major importance for human services is the ability to identify clients' needs and problems and then to provide the resources to meet the needs and solve the problems personally, by using existing institutions, or by developing new institutions. Human service workers are crisis managers. They know who the current service providers are: physicians, mental health professionals, ministers, bartenders, hairdressers, lawyers, police, parole officers, grandparents, college students, and so forth. They use peer therapists such as Alcoholics Anonymous, ex-offenders, ex-addicts, and others. They set up entirely new systems such as lodging programs for migrant workers or the urban homeless. Human service workers also help people help themselves. Rather than always doing *for* clients, they enable clients to do for themselves (Pearlman and Edwards, 1982). Once clients can become their own advocates, they develop the type of empowerment that the nondisadvantaged have (Rose and Black, 1985). To the degree that this can be accomplished, human services can have a major impact on social problems (Pinderhughes, 1983).

Obviously, any individual human service worker cannot be all things to all people. The preceding paragraphs, however, should give insight into the workers' range of activities. The substantive aspects of the field span this range of strategies and allow a wide variability in the actual roles human service workers perform.

Human Service Workers: What They Really Do

People new to the field frequently ask, "But what do human service workers *do?*" As has been pointed out, they do many things. Human service workers are employed in schools for the retarded, prisons, special education programs, primary grade schools, mental hospitals, mental health centers, foster care and adoption agencies, courts, preschool day care centers, public welfare agencies, crisis counseling centers, rape clinics, and hotline services. They are given a variety of titles: outreach worker, family specialist, behavior technician, mental health worker, human service worker, income maintenance worker, counselor, caseworker, social services worker, youth development specialist, community service worker, social welfare assistant, community development worker, rural development assistant, nutrition aide, and health education assistant (Brawley, 1982, 1986).

To get a feeling for what human service workers *do*, however, takes more than just listing where they work or what they are called. The examples that follow will provide more concrete details on how some human service workers spend their time. Many more examples can be found in Collins (1973a) and in Alley et al. (1979b).

Barb

■ ■ Barb is around forty-five years old and is the director of a cooperative nursery school. Although she hasn't finished her associate of arts degree, she keeps working at it and plans to graduate as a child care worker someday. Those who know her know that in terms of competence she doesn't really need that piece of paper. Barb is simply very good at working with children and their parents, not only because she has the natural ability for it but because she's done a lot of learning on her own.

Her day is fairly busy. Early in the morning she sets up materials for the kids to use that day, plans activities with the four mothers who will help her with the twenty children, and assigns the mothers to specific tasks. As the children arrive, Barb greets them and gets them involved in an activity until the morning program starts. Unlike some nursery schools, this is a low-pressure program that is very flexible in terms of demands.

Barb feels that the most important part of the program is balancing between helping the children develop their creativity and sense of who they are and the requirements that people place on children to be nice and to share and cooperate. Each day, says Barb, has at least one crisis. "Most of these crises center around anger," says Barb, "or around hurt feelings. It's really important to help the children express their feelings fully, but in such a way that they don't really hurt others. It's important for kids to learn that they can be angry without hitting, and that they're still worthwhile even when they do make a mistake. That's the big thing, letting them know that they're all worthwhile."

After cleaning up the rooms, Barb ends her day by planning special events, ordering supplies, and planning parent-staff meetings.

Art

■ ■ Art is a twenty-three-year-old human service worker who works in a gas station. However, this gas station is unlike most others: it's leased and operated by a midwestern state hospital. Although it provides all the regular services to its customers, its main purpose is to train patients from the state hospital for employment after they are discharged.

So while Art pumps gas, changes oil, and does all the other things a regular gas station attendant does, he also trains his clients to do those same things, and as he says, "That's the most important part, the other stuff is just a means to an end. I really feel good about it when one of these guys gets a job as a pump jockey in one of the other stations in town." Art is a one-on-one teacher and trainer; in addition, he spends at least one day a week formally advocating for his clients. He goes to all the surrounding gas stations trying to persuade the managers to hire men he has trained. Sometimes he's successful and sometimes not, but as his relationship grows with the area service station managers, more of Art's clients are getting jobs.

"What's important about this," says Art, "is that if these guys have jobs when they get discharged, they're less likely to have problems again. It boosts their self-concept to know they can work like anybody else, and they have less time on their hands to worry about their problems. Besides, if they're working, they won't have as much time to do something screwy."

Phil

■ ■ Phil is twenty-six years old and is a human service worker in a juvenile correctional facility. His main job is to counsel kids who have gotten into trouble with the police. The counseling is usually on a one-to-one basis, and Phil is mainly interested in developing a trust relationship with his clients. He explores why they got into trouble, what happened afterward, how they feel about it, how things are going in their relationships with the other boys, and what they'll do when they get out.

"The important thing is that they know I'm on their side—that they can trust me," says Phil. "I really care about what happens to them. Brother! You ought to see some of the crap these guys have had to put up with. It's unbelievable. A lot of my time is spent talking with my case load, but a lot of it is being involved with their day-to-day activities. We play ball together, eat together, go on trips together. I enjoy it. But mostly we talk. The one thing I don't like is the paperwork—there's too much of it. This form to fill out, that form to fill out. It's a pain in the butt."

Trish

■ ■ Trish is twenty-seven years old. After obtaining a master's degree in human services, she began working in a rape counseling center. Her main role is counseling women who have been raped, in terms of their feelings about the rape and about the reactions to them from others. Most of her time is spent in one-to-one counseling, but she also sees married couples, runs a group, and does community education.

"Women who have been raped need a lot of help to get over it. They bury a lot of their feelings," says Trish, "and they need to get them out on the table, look at them, deal with them, and then get on with life. Mainly I help them get those feelings out and work them through. They feel a lot better after being able to talk about it. Some of the problems are really severe before they come in. They may be afraid to leave their home, they may feel ashamed when they go to work, and often there are problems with their husbands if they're married. It's really a kind of crisis counseling that I do. Besides that, of course, I'm working with the police department in terms of how they treat rape victims. It's been an educational experience *both* for the police and for me. Now when there's a rape case, we get called right away, and I or one of the other counselors goes over right away to act as a friend for the victim. It makes a big difference."

Trish is now faced with a major decision. She has been offered the recently vacated position of executive director of the counseling center. She would like the promotion and the new challenge, but is worried that she will miss the direct contact with clients that her current role involves.

Dorrie

■ ■ Dorrie is a twenty-nine-year-old human services worker in a state hospital for the mentally ill. She has an A.A. degree from a human services program, which she obtained by going to evening classes while working full time. Dorrie is a hard worker on the day shift. She does a variety of things, including serving food to the patients at mealtime, maintaining a case load, and doing treatment.

Says Dorrie, "A lot of the things that I do are routine but important, like filling out forms, but what I really like is working directly with the patients. They're really interesting what with all the strange things they do. Of course, most of the time they're not that different from anybody else.

"I do a lot of activity work, trips, crafts, games, and cards, but I guess the thing I like the best is doing the behavioral treatment programs. I develop them myself, with the help of the unit psychologist, and then do them. Since I really like it, I've taken a lot of training in it, so I know what I'm doing. The way it works is that I identify a problem behavior that needs to change, like yelling, and then work out a reinforcement program that will substitute a more acceptable behavior, like conversation in a normal tone. Then we reward the acceptable behavior when it occurs with goodies like candy and cigarettes or social reinforcement like attention, and punish the unacceptable behavior by ignoring it or withholding reinforcement.

"The other really important thing I do is that I have a case load of six patients. I'm responsible for knowing everything there is to know about those six people, including what we know about their past life, family, problems, current behavior, treatment plan, and everything else. Where that's really important is in the weekly team meetings where we review all the cases and make decisions about passes, treatment plans, and discharges."

Lynn

■ ■ Lynn is forty years old and has been a human service worker since the late 1960s. She began her career as a psychiatric aide at a mental hospital after graduating from high school, worked for several years, and then went to college full time to obtain a degree in English literature. After graduation from college, she returned to the mental hospital to work as a bachelor's level mental health worker, becoming a ward manager after several years.

Since that time, she has received numerous promotions for her competence and on her own has obtained formal training as an administrator. She now is the director of a forty-bed residential program for developmentally disabled (mentally retarded) clients. She currently has almost no client contact, focusing mainly on administrative matters.

"My main function is administrative and supervisory," says Lynn. "I'm a member of the executive committee of our facility, and so am involved in a great deal of decision making regarding the total facility. I'm involved in budget development, personnel issues, physical plant concerns, and all the other problems inherent in running a large facility. In terms of the supervisory and programmatic issues, I supervise a staff of almost forty, and I'm involved with such issues as hiring, direct supervision, disciplinary actions, and sometimes firing.

"A major responsibility that I have, of course, is for the smooth functioning of the habilitation program for our residents. I don't do a lot of direct work with residents, though, and most of my time is spent in meetings with staff or other administrators."

Jorge

■ ■ Jorge is twenty-eight years old, a graduate from an A.A. degree human services program who works in a Latino community referral center. His main role is to provide assistance to members of the Latino community who are having difficulty.

Jorge says, "I do *everything*, or at least it seems like it! People come in with all sorts of problems; some speak no English, and they all need assistance of some kind. My main job is to link them with the services they need, and sometimes I follow through as an interpreter. To do my job, I have to know all the resources that are available, and that covers the well-child clinic, legal aid, public welfare, employment opportunities, the mental health clinic, and the state hospital. Although some of the people who come to our center are really messed up, most just do need a little support and a lot of information.

"Most of my time is spent in information counseling, and hooking people up to the proper resources so that they can deal with their problems. It's really rewarding when we do follow-up and find out that folks are doing okay. Right now I've got a special community action project going that I really enjoy. It means a little extra time, but it gives me the opportunity to get around the city and let people know what we're doing. It seems to be working too, since we've had people coming in who said they've heard about us that way."

These examples begin to provide a sense of the type of jobs human service workers hold and the range of activities in which they engage. It is clear from these examples that human service workers encounter a broad range of clientele whom they assist in a variety of ways. The seven individuals who have been described perform, in one way or another, most of the activities that have been identified in studies such as that done by the Southern Regional Education Board.

If one concept is common to all these examples, it is most likely that they are agents of *change*. Wherever human service workers are employed, whatever they do, they seem to be commonly engaged in attempts to generate change: change in their clients' behavior, change in the behavior of others toward their clients, or change in larger social systems, such as agencies, communities, or other major sociopolitical systems (Perls, 1979).

Competence and Credentialing

Are human service workers competent? *Competence* is the overall ability to function satisfactorily in a given role or job. It involves having many competencies—skills or characteristics necessary for carrying out a discrete portion of a job that can be operationally defined and assessed. The question of competence of human service workers can be looked at from several perspectives. We can assess an individual worker in regard to specific skills, or

As human service workers, teachers do more than impart information. Through active communication, they teach skills in developing positive relationships.

we can assess workers as a group in reference to other professional groups. Although individual skills are important, the most important issue at this point is the overall competence of human service workers as a group. Do they do as well as the professional disciplines in providing human services? The answer is a qualified but resounding yes.

Human service workers do not do some things as well as trained professionals from other specialty disciplines. For example, human service workers are not as good as physicians at diagnosing and prescribing treatment for medical problems. They are not as good at giving and interpreting psychological tests as psychologists. However, human service workers do seem to be as good at those activities which both they and the disciplinary professionals are trained for and do.

The fact that human service workers can provide helping services that are as effective as the same services given by disciplinary professionals has been documented consistently for over twenty years. In the early 1960s, however, the issue had not yet been resolved. Many professionals in the helping services believed that individuals with no graduate training could not provide services as well as the services that M.S.W. social workers, Ph.D.

psychologists, and M.D. physicians could provide. Undoubtedly some still feel that way.

Gartner (1979) and Durlak (1979) have surveyed a number of evaluation programs that have assessed the effectiveness of human service workers. Of the hundreds of studies surveyed, almost all showed that human service workers were as effective or more effective than traditional professionals. A few studies can be used as examples. One of the earliest studies of human service counseling was completed in the mid-1960s. Truax (1969) compared nonprofessionals who had 100 hours of training in counseling to clinical psychology graduate-level students and to experienced therapists. An evaluation of the three groups' effectiveness with 150 chronic, hospitalized schizophrenics demonstrated that the nonprofessionals provided counseling that was only slightly less effective than that provided by the professionals and was considerably above the counseling provided at graduate student level. In a client population of drug addicts, a more recent study found that ex-addict nonprofessionals and non-ex-addict nonprofessionals were as effective in therapeutic counseling as traditional professional counselors (Aiken, Lo Sciuto, and Ausetts, 1984). Many other studies have found strikingly similar results.

Brown (1974) suggests that nonprofessionals are effective counselors partly because they are selected on the basis of personal characteristics that are important for effective helping rather than on characteristics important for success in graduate school. Success in graduate school requires drive, single-mindedness, and a focus on abstract concepts. Human service workers may have these qualities; they also have "a capacity for empathy, warmth, sensitivity in interpersonal relations, high self-confidence and self-regard, and the ability to accept people with values different from their own" (Brown, 1974).

The effectiveness of human service entry-level professionals as classroom educators has been amply demonstrated. Kaplan (1977) reported on a major evaluation study of nearly 20,000 human service entry-level professionals working in classrooms in 132 school systems in 48 states from 1969 to 1976. Children who had been assigned to classrooms with human service workers did better on standard reading and math tests after their experience than students in classes where human service workers were not used. Another study (Costa, 1975) demonstrated that human service workers who later qualified for teaching licenses (by obtaining further education) had more positive attitudes toward children and received better performance ratings than teachers who had not been human service workers. In addition, their classes performed better than the classes of traditional teachers.

The demonstrated effectiveness of human service workers in a variety of settings has helped broaden their acceptance as competent "new" professionals. In fact, the demonstrated competence of nontraditionally trained human service workers has contributed to a belief that such workers should no longer be referred to as *nonprofessionals, subprofessionals,* or even *para-*

professionals. Of these three terms, paraprofessional is perhaps the least offensive (Perls, 1978), although it is still subject to some criticism. A much preferred term that is now coming into use is *entry-level professional.* It appears likely that the terms nonprofessional, subprofessional, or paraprofessional will be used less once some form of credentialing becomes standard for human service workers.

Credentialing

Are credentials really necessary? If human service workers are to be formally *recognized* as functional, competent professionals in their own right, a credentialing or certification process is probably necessary (Peter, 1984). The traditional professions are credentialed by their graduate education (and academic degrees), by state government licensing exams, and by membership in certifying organizations. There may ultimately be similar advanced graduate programs in the generic field of human services. There already are, of course, hundreds of A.A. and B.A. degree programs and a few master's-level programs in interdisciplinary human services (Clubok, 1984). Some states already certify some types of paraprofessionals.

There are currently two organizations exploring or working on the issue of credentialing processes for human service entry-level professionals: the National Organization for Human Service Education and the Council for Standards in Human Service Education. Both have been mentioned previously in other contexts.

The National Organization for Human Service Education (NOHSE) was founded in 1975 in response to a need perceived by professional care providers and legislators for improved methods of human service delivery. With the support of the National Institute of Mental Health and the Southern Regional Education Board, NOHSE focused its energies on developing and strengthening human service education programs at the associate, bachelor's, master's, and doctoral levels.

The current purposes of the organization are: (1) to provide a medium for cooperation and communication among human service organizations and individual practitioners; (2) to foster excellence in teaching, research, and curriculum development for improving the education of human service delivery personnel; (3) to encourage, support, and assist the development of local, state, and national organizations of human services; and (4) to sponsor conferences, institutes, and symposia that foster creative approaches to meeting human service needs.

Members of NOHSE are drawn from diverse educational and professional backgrounds that include corrections, mental health, child care, social services, human resource management, gerontology, developmental disabilities, addictions, recreation, and education. Membership is open to human service educators, students, field work supervisors, direct care professionals, and administrators. Five regional organizations are affiliated with NOHSE; they include the New England Organization of Human Service Education, Mid-Atlantic Consortium for Human Services, Southern Organization for Human Services, Midwest Organization for Human Service Education, and Northwest Organization for Human Service Education. NOHSE is closely allied with the Council for Standards in Human Service Education.

The Council for Standards in Human Service Education was established in 1979 to give focus and direction to education and training in mental health and human services throughout the country. The council exists to help human service educators and college administrators who are interested in achieving maximum educational effectiveness, and to give formal recognition and approval to programs whose competence warrants public and professional confidence. While the council's major aim is to assist educational institutions in improving the quality and relevance of their mental health/human service training programs, it is expected that employers, public and voluntary agencies, faculty, and students will seek the council's help in identifying quality training programs.

The council's approval process is designed to assist programs in self-study, evaluation, and continual improvement and to produce new, creative approaches to the preparation of human service practitioners at the undergraduate level. Validated national standards serve as the base for guiding and reviewing programs; council approval attests to a program's compliance with these standards.

In addition to maintaining training program standards and assessing applicant programs against these criteria, the council provides information and technical assistance to help programs make necessary modifications or improvements. It advises and informs education boards, program directors, and college administrators. The council maintains a network of resource persons, including educators, administrators, and evaluators, and cooperates in sponsoring regional technical assistance workshops.

The National Organization for Human Service Education and the Council for Standards in Human Service Education agreed in the fall of 1985 to sponsor jointly a group to examine the issues inherent in certification of human service workers (Macht, 1986). There is little doubt that certification or credentialing is on the horizon for human service workers. Its exact form remains to be seen.

Summary

1. Human services is a new field and has not yet attained recognition as a full-fledged profession. But there are signs that such recognition is growing.

2. The need to specify the activities of the human service field has led to a number of studies that have attempted to identify the functional tasks and roles of human service workers. One study identified thirteen functional roles that can be organized as follows:

    Linkage/advocacy
      Outreach worker
      Broker
      Advocate
      Mobilizer
    Treatment/planning
      Behavior changer
      Caregiver
      Assistant to specialist
    Administration management
      Evaluator
      Data manager
      Administrator
      Consultant
      Community planner
    Therapeutic environment control
      Teacher-educator

3. Human service focuses on the relatively neglected aspects of human problems and their effects on clients' existence. The human service worker must be a psychosocial helper dealing with the complete person—his or her internal environment and external environment.

4. Human service agencies focus on clients' psychological well-being but also are concerned with the clients' physical well-being, financial resources, and social relationships. Workers in this field are concerned with how these factors can be altered to help clients enter or reenter the mainstream of functional adjustment.

5. It is often difficult to translate general descriptions of the roles of the human service worker into concrete notions of what human service workers really do. Seven examples have been given of actual human service workers.

6. Evaluative research has clearly demonstrated that human service workers are as effective as traditionally trained professionals in providing a range of generic helping services.

7. Full "official" acceptance of human service workers as entry-level professionals rather than as nonprofessionals or paraprofessionals may not occur until some formal process of credentialing is developed. A number of national organizations are trying to develop a credentialing process.

8. Many people in the field, including many traditionally trained professionals, accept human service workers as professionals in the true sense of the term: qualified members of a specific field who are very experienced and skilled and who function competently.

Discussion Questions

1. Why can we consider human services as a profession?

2. What thirteen functional roles of human service workers were identified by SREB? What four clusters were they later grouped into?

3. List the five characteristics of the generalist.

4. What might be the advantages of the generalist approach? The specialist approach?

5. Should human service workers focus on helping or healing?

Learning Experiences

1. Ask several community members whom they would ask to help a depressed relative: a psychiatrist, a psychologist, a social worker, or a human services worker.

2. Interview several community human service workers to find out which of the SREB functional roles they perform. What additional things do they do?

3. Start thinking about which of these roles *you* would like to fulfill .

4. See how many distinct human service jobs you can identify in your community.

Endnotes

1. "Roles and Functions for Different Levels of Mental Health Workers." Atlanta: Southern Regional Education Board, 1969, pp. 29–30. Reprinted by permission of Southern Regional Education Board, Atlanta, Georgia.

2. "Roles and Functions for Different Levels of Mental Health Workers." Atlanta: Southern Regional Education Board, 1969, p. 34. Reprinted by permission of Southern Regional Education Board, Atlanta, Georgia.

Recommended Readings

Collins, A. H. *The Human Services: An Introduction*. Indianapolis: The Odyssey Press, a Division of Bobbs-Merrill Company, 1973.

Russo, J. R. *Serving and Surviving as a Human Service Worker*. Monterey, Calif.: Brooks/Cole, 1980.

Simons, R., and Aigner, S. *Practice Principles: A Problem Solving Approach to Social Work*. New York: Macmillan, 1985.

Taylor, J. B., and Randolf, J. *Community Worker*. New York: Jason Aronson, 1975.

4

Indigenous Workers
and Parahelpers

- Are there advantages to the use of indigenous workers and parahelpers?
- What is an indigenous worker?
- Who are parahelpers?
- What are some functions of indigenous workers and parahelpers?

Chapter 2 presented a role description of the human service worker developed by the Southern Regional Education Board. The major focus was on the career worker who is attached to a formal agency, such as a mental health center, juvenile detention center, state hospital, neighborhood service center, mental retardation facility, or child care center. In addition to persons who are so identified, and overlapping in function with them, are two groups of persons who have been called *indigenous workers* and *parahelpers*. Although these categories are not really distinct from each other, they will be treated separately for the purpose of discussion. The services provided by these persons clearly represent a major emphasis of the human services concept, particularly in their innovative character.

The use of both indigenous workers and parahelpers originally grew out of the realization that there would never be enough traditional professionals to provide the required services. Additionally, a body of evidence has accumulated that strongly suggests the advantages of using such workers in the human services (Gartner, 1971; Gartner and Riessman, 1982; James, 1979; Kestenbaum and Bar-On, 1982; Nash, Lifton, and Smith, 1978; Smith and Meyer, 1981).

The indigenous worker or the parahelper has the advantage of relating to the needy as peers rather than as outsiders. These workers tend to share the values, customs, language, and problems of the client group, which puts them in a better position to understand real-life problems and gain the clients' trust (see Bokan and Campbell, 1984; Westermeyer, 1987).

In many cases, the indigenous worker and the parahelper have specific skills or attributes that the professional human service worker may not have. Blum (1966) reports that such a group had an "exceptional ability to reach out and establish initial contacts with clients whom professional social workers were unable to reach." Meyer (1969) has stated that "The strength of the nonprofessional as a link stems from his double position as a member of the community and its groups, on the one hand, and a member of the agency, on the other hand." For both indigenous workers and parahelpers, the bridging function is often a major advantage.

Not all indigenous workers make a career out of human services. Many, however, do. Often such individuals are employed through an antipoverty program; they discover that helping others brings meaning to their own existence, in addition to the financial rewards of employment (Riessman, 1965). Indigenous workers become career human service workers at a point of transition in self-perception. That transition involves seeing their helping activities as an important part of their long-term self-perception, and seeing themselves as having a career orientation of helping others, rather than just performing a job. In the next section, Laura Hines's first-person account illustrates the transition from indigenous worker to career human services worker.

The Indigenous Worker

The indigenous worker is an individual employed by an agency from a particular subcultural group that the agency serves. The individual is almost always initially untrained, may have been unemployed, and is trained by the agency to do one particular job. Common subcultural groups from which indigenous workers have been selected are Latinos, Chicanos, blacks, American Indians, and Asians. The following first-person account by Laura Hines (1970) is representative of the indigenous worker concept as applied in a metropolitan mental health center.

A Nonprofessional Discusses Her Role
in Mental Health

■ ■ My name is Laura Hines; I am a forty-one-year-old black woman with a family. At fifteen years of age, I came out of school to go to work to help my family. Most of my twenty-six years of employment I have spent as a waitress, not staying on a job long enough to get a vacation. Before I came to the center to work, I had also been trained through the state employment office to be a sewing machine operator. This was a boring job to me because you were required to sit at a machine all day. I only lasted on this job for three months.

There were many jobs being created by different agencies that were listed in the antipoverty offices, so I thought that I would apply for a job. After being interviewed there they sent me to the little neighborhood schools. I was hired as a home and school coordinator. This job was temporary and lasted only three months.

After the job terminated, I returned to the antipoverty office to see if there were any more openings. They told me that the community mental health center was going to conduct a survey of the North Philadelphia area and that they were going to hire people to work as census takers. I applied at the center, was interviewed and hired. On October 10, 1966, training began. Training consisted of interview techniques. We spent two weeks of training and then the frustration began (census taking).

Learning to be a mental health assistant

In early 1967, I moved from census taker to mental health assistant 1. I had ten weeks of full-time training that consisted of seminars dealing with psychiatric and social concepts. The training consisted of lectures, reading, and paperwork. It was given by professional staff from the center—psychiatrists, a psychologist, a social worker, and a nurse.

My knowledge of mental health or mental illness was very limited when I first came to the center; limited to the extent that all the people in the community who acted queer or whose behavior was not as I thought it should be, I thought of as crazy. After being in class for a short while I saw that people who were not able to function were not crazy but people who needed help. Being directly from the community that the center was going to serve, and wanting to help people, and hoping that I could, I was willing and hoping that I could learn what was about to be taught at the center. I was hoping that with this teaching I could be very effective in my community.

Learning to become a mental health assistant was a frustrating experience for me. It was made as simple as possible but I still had a tough time getting adjusted. There were nights that I hardly slept, thinking of tomorrow when class would resume. It was hard for me to adjust because I never liked school anyway, and I had been out of it for so long. But I was able to adjust with the help of the training director, who was nice but stern. For example, each week she insisted upon your learning to use ten words that were unfamiliar to you. I had to learn how to pronounce them, spell them correctly, and use them in a sentence (which I thought was very useless). It proved to be quite useful in work when talking with different people in other agencies about patients who were in some way connected with their agency.

The director of the program also was a very stern person but one who made every effort to make his teaching as simple as possible for all the trainees; describing symptoms, problems, medication, colors of medication, effectiveness, etc. Some days I came away from class feeling like a medical student, and some days I came away feeling like a social worker. I had to take this learning, put it together, and make it work.

During my clinical work I have been supervised at different times by a social worker, a psychiatrist, or a psychologist. My supervision by the social worker was quite rewarding. His supervision also included formal teaching such as group therapy concepts and family dynamics. We exchanged experiences and gained knowledge and also techniques involved in working with other agencies. In contrast to this social worker, most professionals, I think, have not listened to people such as myself, mostly because they do not understand what we are saying: More sensitive people are needed to work in the poor sections. Workers are needed who will put their hands on people and can make some changes in their lives.

Having been taught all I know about mental illness by a psychiatrist, I felt as though any psychiatrist could teach and support people with less education than they. But I learned how different psychiatrists could be when I started in our psychosocial clinic and had a psychiatrist for a supervisor. He made me feel less important and needed than I had felt from the beginning of my training. My ideas were not accepted as good ideas but as useless thoughts. He did not realize that if we worked together and worked hard, we would be able to be effective and do a great job together for the people that we serve. He should not have let differences in theories or methods prevent him from working with me. Together we could plan and maybe initiate the needed change in our area and also try to create solutions to some problems. But as I worked on, my perception of professionals changed some from my first thoughts. To some extent some professionals still relate to you on a professional-nonprofessional level and do not want to learn your ways of thinking.

Clinic work and home visits

All patients are given an appointment by the receptionist, and a mental health assistant is then assigned to the patient. Whether in the clinic or on a home visit on my first contact, an intake is done. This consists of obtaining social and clinical data and getting any other information that is available from other agencies or other family members. I record all information in patients' charts. also notify referring agencies that the person has reached us. In other words, I am responsible for the patients' care. I also make periodic home visits; I check on patients' medication and I make home visits to people who do not attend the clinic regularly. I also help people to secure welfare, help them in getting housing, and arrange for psychiatric evaluation, psychological testing, social work consultation, etc. I record all contacts, visits, and phone calls. I discuss and determine with my supervisor termination of patients and I am able to make some very good decisions about how I am going to work with them.

One factor that contributes to rapid patient service is my approach: That is, when people come into the clinic, I try to pinpoint the problem and get right to work on it. That way the problems get solved and my case load does not build up. There are many problems in this area that may be related to mental health but are more social. These factors are often diagnosed as mental illness when this is not the case. It has been proven through the center and the mental health assistant that a person diagnosed as psychotic has been able to function in the community with follow-up care. People who have been confined in institutions for many years have been able to come home to live with their families or in some cases to live in boarding homes where they must to some degree be able to take care of themselves. . . .

Groups for children and patients

I am the primary therapist with three groups. One group consists of six preadolescents, all boys who spend from one hour to an hour and one-half, one day a week, in the group. The first half hour consists of play therapy. The other hour is spent in discussing their relationships with each other and with their parents (which is a very big issue) most of the time. Most of the sessions are taped and these tapes are used only for supervision. Most preadolescents are never heard or really ever listened to. We first talk about their reasons for being in the clinic; the reasons are often different than what the school referral has stated.

I decided that I would then start a parent group and called the parents together to tell them about my plans. They all agreed to be part of the group for a trial. Well, this has worked out fine. The parents are really interested in the future of their children and the attendance is good. Each week all of the children and the parents are there, staying sometimes longer than the time we had planned.

I have also developed a group for adolescent girls that also meets once a week. Most of these girls, when they first came to us, were having problems relating to their parents and teachers. In some way most of these girls have shown more interest in themselves since being part of the group. I do not think that these youngsters have ever had anyone who would listen to them. Most youngsters have many fears and concerns about themselves but are afraid to talk about it. All of them have similar problems. They share experiences and in some cases provide good solutions for each other.

Neighborhood outreach

One question that always comes up is Does a mental health assistant do therapy? I feel that when a person comes into the office to sit and talk with me, that in itself is therapeutic. As my case load began to climb, I became aware of my ability and was able to make diagnoses, recommend treatment, and also set up goals for the person that I was seeing. Here I was with five months of formal training, and functioning as though the training had been longer, feeling very important and very needed.

There are people who do not like to work in their own neighborhood, but I do. My neighbors in many cases have come to me for some kind of information. There was a neighbor who had been in a private sanitarium for some five or six years, who returned home only to find out that her daughter, who was twenty-three years old, had a tumor on the brain and had to have an operation. After the operation the mother was in a state of depression, not doing anything for herself, not even combing her hair. The minute you began to talk to this woman she would burst into uncontrollable tears and cry for at least ten or fifteen minutes. After she stopped crying, she would want to talk about her children and her husband not getting along with each other.

I took it upon myself to become her therapist and, using my training and my clinical experience, I began to work with this woman and her family in the evening. I was able to spend at least two hours with this family and to sit and talk with them. I took this family all the way back to when they had gotten married and was able to bring them up to the present date. During the sessions I wondered if I was doing the right thing, because at times it was interesting and sometimes it was frightening. This had not been a happy marriage, but the woman never had revealed this to her mate. It was a matter of days before I could see any progress in what I was attempting to do. The woman was able to come out of this depression, began to take care of her husband, and also was able to visit her daughter in the hospital. Since this breakdown, this woman has been able to survive and function very well, with her daughter having to go into the hospital for five more operations.

After the daughter was discharged from the hospital, she also was very depressed. I talked to the neurosurgeon, told him that I was a mental health assistant and that I worked at the community health center. I told him how important it was that she be seen by someone, that until this point I had played a very important part in this family's life, and that I would like to continue. He thought this was a very good idea. I spent many tearful days with this young lady. One night we sat up most of the night just talking about her and her life, and how she had been mixed up from school days. I also was able to use my homemaking skills with this family. I would help this mother plan her day, because she had a lot to do in one day with a twenty-three-year-old who came home almost a vegetable. Now the mother is able to take care of her daughter, husband, and do her household chores without any help from me. The daughter has gone back to work, and the mother looks forward to my stopping by every Friday evening.

Homemaking services
During the survey I was almost shocked to see how some people kept their homes and their children, and I wanted to do something about this. I brought this back to the center, and I was given the responsibility of developing a homemaking service. There are a few agencies that use the service in the needed way, but most agencies are afraid to really deal with the "nitty gritty" of the problems that exist in the poor areas. They do things that only create more problems. Rehabilitating houses and not rehabilitating people is a most unrealistic thing. They are only building more ghettos. Also there is no service available to people who are in a depressed stage or even going through a crisis, not able to take care of their family. We do not have any kind of service to keep this family together.

When a mother comes into the crisis center, maybe to be admitted to some psychiatric setting for a week or ten days, her family (children) in most cases have to be separated by placing the children in a sheltering agency or foster home. The children then become emotionally upset, and the mother may not respond to treatment. The children are placed in separate homes, different schools, with different playmates, but most of all with different parents. Then the child begins to act out in school.

Also, older people who are able to function but are not able to cook or do their own errands (pay their bills) can become even less able to function when these kinds of pressures remain. I have a patient seventy years old who through her lifetime has only had trouble. She had five children who were physically and mentally normal but had a child during her menopause who was born retarded. Right after the child was born her husband died. This woman kept her child with her because she was alone. The other children had begun to marry and were leaving home. This child has never been in school but yet she is a wonderful housekeeper. The mother has had several breakdowns and has been hospitalized on several occasions. She is now incapacitated and her daughter is going downhill. With my visits it makes things different. There seems to be only one answer, and that is to put this woman in a home or to hospitalize her. But my answer is that if there was a service available, such as homemaking, for this family they could be kept together. At this point, we consider two people as constituting a family, mother and daughter.

"Total community" services

I guess you are wondering if my training affected me as a person and if it affected my home life. Well, it has had an awful lot to do with the reason that my family is together. My husband helped me a lot during training. As time went on and people in my neighborhood were coming to me for all kinds of help he saw some positive results and also became proud of me. I have all kinds of contacts in my area, from the police to the man who will drive people to the hospital during emergencies.

I think that at this point the mental health center has been good for the community. It has taken people from the community, such as myself, and trained them to help others in the community. I feel as though my role is a good role for people who are in the community. But by the same token, people in the community think the center should be doing more, such as coping with agencies that seem to create mental health problems (schools, welfare, etc.). This is where I become confused about mental health centers and their responsibility to the community. I do not believe that mental health centers can take care of all of society's problems.

I do believe that the center provides good care for people in the community who are mentally ill, but it should do more than this. It should try to change some of the agencies to make them less harmful to people. From my understanding of the mental health legislation the centers have to be clinically oriented. I do not think that this should be in the direction for mental health centers operating within areas deprived socioeconomically. In view of my own experiences, I am led to believe that much more emphasis should be placed on higher quality education and vocational training for the hard-core unemployed. We should also work toward providing more adequate housing and consumer education, both of which could be provided through our homemaking service. We should improve medical care offered to the poor, both in attitudes and quality. There should be an emphasis placed on better police-community relationships in the poor areas. There should be more community people involved in the operation of stations in their own communities.

I recognize that these are the needs of the total community, not only of patients. But if they could be resolved, then many problems presented in clinics would not appear. If centers do not concentrate on these goals, and if they cannot see what is really creating mental illness, then there is no relevance for them to mental health. Unless all mental health centers try to provide the kinds of "total community" services that I have mentioned, legislators will never understand and appropriate the kind of funds that such an approach demands.[1]

Mrs. Hines's account of becoming an indigenous human service worker is typical and illustrates how the bridging function can operate. In addition, she demonstrates the wide range of functions that a nonprofessional can serve in such settings. It becomes clear that the indigenous worker rapidly becomes a full-fledged human services worker who just happens to have the advantage of being from the same subcultural group as the prospective clients.

Parahelpers such as this senior citizen volunteer offer a variety of services to the needy, including a warm, caring relationship.

The Parahelpers

A major human services system resource appears to be individuals in the community who already supply informal helping services to persons in need or those who have the potential for doing so. Until recently, such community resources have remained relatively untapped, but more efforts are being expended in the direction of their utilization (Beitman, 1982; Buckley, 1985; Craighead and Mercatoris, 1973). In many cases, such persons are identical to the indigenous worker in that they share subcultural beliefs and values with the person in need. The major difference is that they are usually not *formally* employed by a human service system to provide helping services. The range of parahelpers is broad, including ministers, police, teachers, bartenders, hairdressers, baby-sitters, retired persons, relatives, neighbors, college students, and folk healers. The types of services such persons can provide vary from information giving and referral to major therapeutic interventions.

That parahelpers can provide major human service assistance is relatively well accepted. The major issue today involves the creative use of these persons in programs that work. The following examples show how some types of parahelpers are used.

Beauticians/Bartenders Learn
Mental Health Helper Role

■ ■ Students in a Grand Forks, North Dakota, beauty college got a taste of their future roles as unofficial mental health aides during a "people helpers' workshop" sponsored by the Grand Forks Mental Health and Retardation Center.

"In most American communities, people with emotional problems can easily seek help from an agency or therapist," says Pam McLean, center staff member, who supervised the student beauticians' workshop. "But in North Dakota, with its many small isolated communities, this is not always feasible. To help solve the problem, the North Dakota Mental Health Association suggested a program that would enlist the aid of beauticians as mental health helpers."

Not long after the association publicized its program, the director of a local beauty college called the mental health center and asked for help in setting up such a course for its thirty students, as well as three faculty members. "It was important to include the faculty members in the sessions," Ms. McLean says, "because they have everyday contact with the students and are able to carry over into the classroom what we discuss in the workshop."

Ms. McLean designed a six-week course, with the group meeting for two hours each week. The first meeting, which was lecture style, was not as successful as the later ones, which directly involved the students in role playing and small group discussions, Ms. McLean says. Communication, the role of a beautician, aspects of mental health vs. mental illness, and community resources available for referral were some of the topics discussed. In addition to Ms. McLean, a group therapist and the consultation and education specialist from the mental health center participated in the course.

Participants completed evaluation sheets at the group's final meeting: "I didn't realize how important I could be to a customer"; "Now I understand the importance of good listening"; "I didn't know there were so many resources in this area"; and "I understand better the feelings of people in need of help" were some of the students' comments. Ms. McLean plans to do a follow-up evaluation six months after the end of the course, and is investigating the possibility of setting up similar workshops for bartenders and practicing beauticians.[2]

Calming Family Crises

■ ■ Before they go on patrol, police student officers in New York City learn how to deal with family quarrels. Except for traffic accidents, these incidents are what police deal with most. They are also dangerous: Most of the aggravated assaults in FBI statistics occur during family quarrels. So police learn techniques like separating the combatants, getting them to sit down, and asking if they (the officers) may smoke. The purpose in all this is to cool off the quarrel and avert the chance of violence.

For practice, student officers watch professional police officers simulate family fights. (The dramatizations are based on actual incidents.) A pair of police stay offstage—not seeing what's happening—until they are called. Then they walk in and try to make sense of what has been going on—just what they have to do in real life. They get the couple to talk and try to get their minds off the fight, while at the same time checking for possible weapons and keeping in view of each other.

Other training methods include lectures, field trips, practice in effective listening, and workshops to sensitize police to their own values and automatic responses.

The New York City program stems from a demonstration project conducted by Dr. Morton Bard, a professor of psychology who has also been a policeman, in 1967–69. Bard gave eighteen officers in one precinct a 160-hour training course, using the methods described above. Then the officers put those methods into practice, meeting in groups during the same time to talk about crisis intervention and their own assumptions about family relations.

In a four-month evaluation period, the number of assaults in cases where the unit intervened decreased. Moreover, no homicides occurred, and none of the police were injured. Because of the project's success, all recruits now get training in family crisis intervention.

Versions of the program have been adopted in Louisville, Kentucky, where police sometimes complete their mediation by suggesting professional counseling; Charlotte, North Carolina; and Miami Beach. Pilot programs are starting in other cities as well. The training is usually done by university psychologists or human relations experts, but counseling professionals from mental health centers might be equally appropriate leaders.

Another police training program was conducted by Edward Glaser of the Human Interaction Research Institute, Los Angeles, for Redondo Beach, California, police. He found that simulations were the most effective training technique. "Simulations involve the officers' interest, both as performers and as audience. If videotape is added, an officer can observe what he actually is doing, without having to have it pointed out by an instructor, whose comments may be interpreted as critical, particularly if he suggests ways the officer should change his actions or demeanor.

"Viewing simulations on videotape with the sound turned off is a particularly effective tool. Once the men are aware of what they are doing, an expert in body language can provide them with a repertory of ways of moving—to appear intimidating, when this seems appropriate, or to appear calming, reassuring, and firm, which is appropriate when dealing with emotionally upset participants in a family dispute.

"Lecture material can be effective when it is nondirective. Topics dealing with psychology—of youth, of age, of family problems in general—are well received. Information on techniques of intervention, being implicitly directive, is much less well received."[3]

Texas Trims Some Red Tape

■ ■ The sixty-eight-year-old black woman—let's call her Eloise Denton—was severely depressed. She didn't need a psychiatrist to tell her that much. For days she stayed inside her small frame house near a noisy Houston freeway and watched the cars go by. She didn't bother to change her dirty nightgown because, she said, "There's no one who cares what I look like." She cooked a thin chicken broth for herself and not much else. "Food is expensive," she complained, "and anyway my dentures are hurting so there's not much I can eat."

Most of the day Mrs. Denton simply stared at the ceiling or out of the window. "If I had new glasses, I could read the newspaper, I guess, but glasses are expensive," she said. "Besides, there isn't much that interests an old lady like me."

Mrs Denton's husband died six months ago. She felt alone and isolated without him. Her Social Security payments had been cut in half since he died, and she worried a lot about money. Her daughter tried to help out, but she didn't have much money left over from her own family expenses. She also complained that her mother was unpleasant to be around. "When I visit her she makes me feel that I'm just not there," she said.

When someone suggested that her mother see a psychiatrist, she laughed. "Don't you think she's a little old for that?" she asked. "My mother's not crazy, she's sad and poor. What's a psychiatrist going to do about it?" Nevertheless, she was persuaded to call the geriatric clinic at the Texas Research Institute of Mental Sciences. Within a week the clinic had sent Mrs. Lenora Driver, seventy-four, a black outreach worker, into Mrs. Denton's home to see if she could be of any help.

"You've come because you think I'm crazy," said Mrs. Denton to the outreach worker. "No," said Mrs. Driver, "I've come because I have lots of information I think will be of interest to you."

Mrs. Driver was a walking encyclopedia of information that was of interest to Mrs. Denton. She told her where she could get new glasses free, what clinic offered dental care free, which forms to fill out to get supplemental Social Security income payments. She told her about the local nutrition center, one of a number of county-run senior citizen activity centers where free lunches are served, and where she would meet other people her age who sew, knit, play dominoes, watch television, and plan group outings. Mrs. Driver explained the bus routes or walking directions to all the places she mentioned.

In a couple of months Mrs. Denton seemed transformed. She could see the stitches on a bright red scarf she was knitting. She could chew the chicken in her soup. She was neither alone nor lonely at the nutrition center. She never had to see a psychiatrist, but if her depression had persisted, Mrs. Driver would have arranged for that, too.

Mrs. Driver and ten coworkers are part of an outreach program developed by the Geriatric Services Section of the Texas Research Institute of Mental Sciences, better known by its acronym, TRIMS. TRIMS is the primary research and training facility of the Texas Department of Mental Health and Retardation and its patient care center in Houston; it provides psychiatric services and counseling to people of all ages. The outreach program for older people, which was created gradually over the last few years is fundamental to the TRIMS multidisciplinary mental health model for geriatric services. Each of the outreach workers is responsible for Harris County (Houston) neighborhoods, whose populations vary between 35,000 and 400,000. They think of themselves as advocates for the elderly.

In a two-week training course, followed by weekly training meetings at TRIMS, the outreach workers learn about federal, state, and local programs for old people—Social Security supplements, food stamps, nutrition programs, special medical and dental care services. The only criteria for the outreach workers are that they be able to read and write and enjoy older people. They range in age from twenty-three to seventy-four.

Most of them grew up in the neighborhoods they now serve, and know the indigenous landmarks and language. Spanish-speaking neighborhoods have Spanish-speaking outreach workers.

Once a week Mrs. Driver sits at a small table in one of her local nutrition centers and offers a sympathetic ear and indispensable information. She helps the old people at the senior citizens' center interpret the muddled bureaucratic language, written in fine print which old eyes may be unable to decipher, on the many forms they have to fill out to get benefits. She also helps them telephone special clinics and agencies for appointments. At other times she visits people in their houses or tracks down agency programs. She checks to see if the solutions she suggested worked. She works six hours a day, five days a week, on a salary so modest that she needs other sources of income. A retired woman herself, she likes her reclaimed sense of usefulness.[4]

These brief program descriptions depict the use of beauticians, police officers, and an elderly woman as parahelpers. These programs range from Texas to New York to North Dakota. Similar programs are in operation in most areas of the country, particularly in large metropolitan areas. In addition to the people described above, other types of parahelpers, such as families of penal offenders, "foster grandparents," teenage volunteers, daytime baby-sitters for working mothers, and faith healers, are common.

It should be obvious that parahelpers are of critical importance to the maximum use of resources. Since parahelpers can provide valuable services with the proper training, and since most operate on a volunteer basis, it seems most feasible to use such services in the human service system.

Summary

1. Indigenous workers are people employed by an agency who share the subcultural values of all or part of the agency's clientele. Common subcultural groups from which indigenous workers have been selected are Hispanics, blacks, American Indians, and Asians.

2. Parahelpers are individuals in the community who supply or have the potential to supply informal helping services to people in need. Parahelpers are not usually formally employed to provide helping services but do so in the context of other employment as in the case of a police officer or minister.

3. The use of indigenous workers and parahelpers grew out of the realization that there would never be enough traditional professionals to provide the required services and a growing awareness that the subcultural values and customs shared between indigenous workers and clients could facilitate the helping role.

4. A number of examples are given here of parahelpers, including beauticians, police officers, and an elderly woman.

Discussion Questions

1. What are the advantages of using indigenous workers and parahelpers?
2. What would be a good way to use indigenous workers and parahelpers?
3. How much supervision should such workers have?

Learning Experiences

1. Interview an indigenous worker and find out what he or she does.
2. Interview a bartender, beautician, or police officer. Find out if people tell them their problems, what the problems are, and what the parahelper does about it, if anything.

Endnotes

1. L. Hines. "A Nonprofessional Discusses Her Role in Mental Health." *American Journal of Psychiatry* 126:10 (1970): 1467–1472. Copyright (c) 1970, the American Psychiatric Association. Reprinted by permission.

2. Reprinted by permission from *Innovations* (Vol. 2, No. 2, Summer, 1975), p. 30, published by the American Institutes for Research, P.O. Box 1113, Palo Alto, CA 94302, under a collaborative grant from the National Institute of Mental Health.

3. Reprinted by permission from *Innovations* (Vol. 2, No. 1, Winter, 1975), pp. 23–24, published by the American Institutes for Research, P.O. Box 1113, Palo Alto, CA 94302, under a collaborative grant from the National Institute of Mental Health.

4. By Suzanne Fields. Reprinted by permission from *Innovations* (Vol. 4, No. 1, Spring, 1977), pp. 19–20, published by the American Institutes for Research, P.O. Box 1113, Palo Alto, CA 94302, under a collaborative grant from the National Institute of Mental Health.

Recommended Readings

Guerney, B. (ed.). *Psychotherapeutic Agents: New Roles for Nonprofessionals, Parents, and Teachers.* New York: Holt, Rinehart and Winston, 1969.

Guerney, L., and Moore, L. "Phone Friend: A Prevention-Oriented Service for Latchkey Children." *Children Today* 12 (1983).

Riessman, F. "The Helper-Therapy Principle." *Social Work* 10 (1965).

5

Human Services:
Defining Problems and Causes

- What type of problems should human services target?
- What is meant by *problem behavior*, or *deviance*?
- How is problem behavior defined from an intrapersonal perspective, or as a result of an individual's psychological maladaptation?
- How is problem behavior defined from an environmental, or extrapersonal, perspective?
- What are the major viewpoints about the causes of problem behavior?

In its broadest sense, the term *human services* can be viewed as encompassing all helping services that are aimed at dealing with every human problem. As young as the field of human services is, one can still find published material that suggests that *all* of humanity's problems are the province of the human service worker. The range of issues addressed in the literature has included physical health, crime, education, poverty, homelessness, aging, drug abuse, severe mental disorder, mental retardation, depression, loneliness, and shyness, among many others. A comprehensive list could go on for many pages.

Should we define human services so broadly that the field includes every problem that people have? To do so does not appear either useful or functional. We live in a world of limited resources, and it seems important to focus on a more limited set of issues in order to maximize our impact. One possible way of defining the focus of the new field of human services is in terms of problem severity. The more severe the problem and the greater the risk to the individual, the more likely the problem falls into the human services sector.

Human services should deal with problems of psychological or social *survival* rather than problems of satisfaction. The client is generally not the middle-class educated person who is experiencing problems of dissatisfaction and unhappiness. Rather, clients have such massive problems of survival that if they reach the level of adjustment of having only problems of dissatisfaction or loneliness, we feel we have helped them join the mainstream.

Problems of survival are problems that threaten clients' psychological, social, or economic existence and in some cases may threaten the continued existence of their lives or the lives of others. The target groups of human services include those people who:

1. Cannot maintain contact with reality. They hallucinate (see and hear things that are not really there), have unrealistic suspicions about others, are confused about cause-and-effect relationships, and so on.
2. Violate significant cultural norms. They show no responsibility for their dependents, abandon spouses, abuse drugs, or engage in disruptive sexual practices.
3. Violate major laws or repetitively violate minor laws. They may steal, embezzle, or shoplift.
4. Are self-destructive. They are suicidal, mutilate their bodies, become alcoholics, and so on.
5. Are destructive of others. They may kill, assault, or rape.
6. Cannot maintain their own welfare. They do not care for their physical health, are infirm, are homeless, or are social isolates.

Some target groups may be defined by behaviors that are not accepted by the broader society. For example, they may have hallucinations, take drugs, attempt suicide, fail to hold a job, lead a life of crime, kill their spouses, abuse their children, or have an incestuous relationship with a child.

However, some target groups may be defined simply by the facts of their existence, over which they have little control. For example, they may be young children or they may be elderly; they may be members of a persecuted racial or religious minority; they may be poor; they may be homeless; they may be laid off from work; they may be disabled. These groups may receive a special societal response because we think they are more at risk than other groups. When individuals in these target groups also manifest problem behaviors, society has a traditional institutional response: commitment to a mental hospital, public welfare, placement in a foster home or nursing home, prison, job training, or remedial education. In effect, society defines such cases as problems to which societal responses are imperative.

In other times or in other places, people with problems of psychological or social survival have not been seen as requiring help. A homeless child in the streets of Bombay, India, or Rio de Janeiro, Brazil, is an all too common occurrence; and there are few formal helping services for such children. In the United States, however, a major effort is made to provide social services for such children. We have deemed child homelessness as unacceptable in our culture (Bassuk and Rubin, 1987). Lest we feel too smug, however, we should be aware that the recognition or definition of a problem does not necessarily result in adequate handling of the problem in our society. Although we provide services for young homeless children in this country, adolescent children who are homeless (that is, the 1.2 million teenage runaways in the United States) have few helping services available to them (Hersch, 1988). Defining a condition or behavior as a "problem" is only one step in a lengthy process of conceptionalization that may lead to a formal societal response. It is, of course, a very important step.

Defining Problem Behavior/Deviance

Perspectives for determining whether a behavior or problem requires a helping response may differ widely. We may take an *intrapersonal perspective*, in which we see the problem as being defined primarily by inner aspects of the individual. In contrast, we may take an *extrapersonal perspective*, in which we see problem behavior as being defined by the environment. In each perspective there are a number of ways of defining *problem behavior*:

Intrapersonal
1. Use of biological norms
2. Comparison with an optimal psychological state
3. Assessment of personal discomfort

Extrapersonal
1. Comparison with statistical norms
2. Comparison with cultural and societal standards of behavior

The intrapersonal perspective

Biological norms
Among those who propose that deviant or problematic behavior is a disease, the concept of biological norms is extremely important. Basically, the approach assumes that deviance is a function of biological structural formations or their functions. Adherents of this approach would not necessarily say that a *particular* abnormal behavior is related to one specific function or structure (although that remains a possibility) but rather that the usual biological system defines a potential *range* of "normal" behaviors. Bateson (1987), for example, discusses how the emerging abilities of a child might result from an interplay between the child's genes and existing environmental conditions. Obviously, the biological perspective involves the consideration of genetic abnormality as a possible underlying biological factor in the structure or function of a person's brain, with a corresponding impact on behavior (Andreasen, 1984).

Although much investigation has been done recently on the structure and function of the brain, it seems unlikely that in the near future a useful biological definition of normal or abnormal behavior will be developed. The biological normative approach has at least two major weaknesses: (1) It is too reductionistic; it reduces the mental and behavioral to physical issues without considering other factors such as environment, and (2) it does not adequately take into account the vast individual differences in the range of structure and function among "normal" persons (Offer and Sabshin, 1974).

The optimal psychological state

A common concept in the helping professions is that there is some ideal psychological state that is or should be normal (Sabshin, 1989). This psychological ideal includes concepts of adequacy, maturity, actualization, and productivity. An individual who does not match this ideal, by definition, has a problem. The various descriptions of the ideal psychological state vary from theorist to theorist, but most have a number of common elements. One of the most popular is that of Abraham Maslow.

Maslow proposes that the differences between normal and abnormal persons are differences in degree only and that normality relates to cultural adaptation. He lists ten criteria or signs of normal psychological functioning (Maslow and Mittelman, 1951):

1. Adequate feeling of security
2. Adequate spontaneity and emotionality
3. Efficient contact with reality
4. Adequate bodily desires and the ability to gratify them
5. Adequate self-knowledge
6. Integration and consistency of personality
7. Adequate life goals
8. Ability to learn from experience
9. Ability to satisfy the requirements of the group
10. Adequate emancipation from the group or culture

The major criticisms that can be leveled against such definitions of normality are that they are based on value judgments of the theorists and especially that they are unrealistic. If one accepts this normal functioning as the goal of human services, the client population may well consist of the social majority. How many of us meet all ten criteria of Maslow or those of the other theorists who have developed similarly comprehensive definitions of "good" psychological functioning?

Personal discomfort

Many individuals define or identify *themselves* as problematic. Usually this identification relates to a subjective sense of personal discomfort. Very often, such individuals perceive themselves as falling short of some idealized state similar to that described above. Of course, if one does not achieve an idealized level of functioning but does not *care*, one is unlikely to be discomforted by that fact. However, when people feel they should be happier, less depressed, calmer, or more (or less) independent, their subjective distress may become great enough to result in a self-perception of being abnormal, or different from most other people. This subjective evaluation may lead to the persons' presenting themselves to a human services worker for help, and the label of abnormality may become formalized.

This self-definition of abnormality rests on a belief that one's feelings, thoughts, or behaviors are not right and involves personal value judgments. The casual observer may not label these individuals as abnormal and would probably do so only after extended discussions with them. In more extreme examples, the personal discomfort may be manifested in outward behavior. The individual who subjectively experiences depression may, for example, begin having difficulty concentrating at work or doing the housekeeping or may burst into tears when talking to friends or acquaintances.

However, some individuals manifest troublesome behavior that disturbs *others* more than it disturbs themselves. The concept of personal discomfort does not fit such persons. For example, juvenile gang members are often quite satisfied with their behavior. The victims of their aggression or criminal behaviors are the ones who identify them as needing to be changed. Thus, the gang members' "problem" is defined from an extrapersonal perspective.

The extrapersonal perspective

Statistical norms

In the statistical approach to the definition of problems, normality is what is average; deviance is behavior that falls outside of what is considered usual. To use this approach, one must make the assumption that the behavior being considered is distributed on the normal, or bell-shaped, curve (Figure 5-1). Most biological and many psychological or social traits appear to be distributed in such a manner in the general population (height, weight, intelligence, economic level, etc.). To use the example of intelligence, *normal* is considered to be the central section of the IQ curve (an IQ of 85 to 115). At both ends of the curve are the abnormal or deviant scores, mental deficiency (IQ of 69 or less) and the very superior (IQ of 130 and above) (Wechsler, 1958).

Several problems exist with the use of statistical norms in the definition of deviant, abnormal, or problematic behavior. Since the approach is based on the incidence of behavior within a population, any frequent behavior is considered normal. However, that would make poverty normal in many third world countries even though it is obviously a problem. A second difficulty is that cutoff points are drawn arbitrarily, and people falling on either side of the line are thought of differently. For example, a person with an IQ of 69 could often be institutionalized in most states; a person with an IQ of 71

Figure 5-1 *Normal probability curve with Wechsler IQ equivalents.*

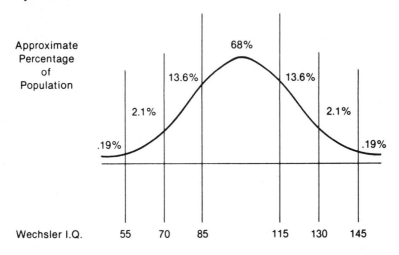

often would not, even though there might be little real difference in their functioning. Finally, there is some question as to whether many behaviors are actually normally (in the statistical sense) distributed.

Cultural/societal norms

Norms are standards of behavior that are maintained by individuals and groups. The norms held by an individual are usually (some would say always) determined by the referent groups to which one belongs and by which one is accepted. Each individual belongs to many referent groups: family, friends, gangs, clubs, profession, race, sex, age, culture, country, and so forth. From the cultural-societal perspective, normality is behavior that fits in with these normative standards of the culture or society. *Deviance* is behavior that varies sufficiently from the norms of a group so that if known, it would become a defensible or legitimate basis for negative sanctions in informal social interaction or by official agencies of the society (Wood, 1974).

Negative sanctions occur in the form of formal punishment if the norm is a law, or in the informal reactions of others if the norm is a "rule." Scheff (1984) used the term *residual rule breaking* to apply to deviance that is not formally proscribed but that violates implicit social norms (for example, mental illness). Scheff suggests that there is a lot of residual rule breaking, that it has diverse causes, and that much residual rule breaking is of no social significance and is therefore ignored. Occasionally, however, others invoke socially shared ideas of (for example) mental disorder as the explanation for the residual rule breaking and so label the person who is deviating, who may, because of being vulnerable or suggestible, accept the label, make it a part of his or her self-image, conform to it, and be rewarded for conformity. The person actually starts to conform to the socially shared idea of *mental illness behaviors*, and thus is defined as mentally ill in his or her own view and the view of others.

In other cases, behavior that is *syntonic* (acceptable and valued) to a small culture (perhaps a delinquent gang) may violate the norms of the main culture. For example, the use and sale of illegal drugs such as cocaine constitutes a violation of our cultural norms. However, within the subculture of those who abuse or distribute illegal drugs drug use and trafficking is accepted behavior. This type of subculturally promoted behavior to a great extent explains the performance of many criminal acts and the failure of correctional systems.

The structure of society (its norms) determines its culture, and culture determines the thought processes of individuals (Eaton, 1986). Based on this approach, then, an individual who is deviant is one who does not abide by the norms of society, and one who abides by the norms of society is not deviant but normal. Criticisms of this approach to the definition of deviance include the concern that a society's *norms* may in themselves be deviant or unacceptable. For example, the persecution and genocide of Jews in Nazi Germany became a norm of that society, yet most of us would not accept such behavior as normal. In that particular culture, the person who did *not* relate to Jews in a prejudicial manner was deviant and obviously (from that perspective) needed to be helped to overcome his or her problems. To those of us outside of that short-lived culture, the idea is repugnant. Another culture whose norms seem unacceptable to most of us is that of some Middle Eastern Moslem extremists. In those groups of terrorists, suicidal attacks on others, in which the attacker has no chance to survive, are accepted, even encouraged, by the referent group. It becomes obvious that in defining deviant behavior, the definer's values must be taken into consideration, as must the values of the culture to which he or she belongs. To a very real extent, we are culture-bound.

Causality of Problem Behavior/Deviance

Some would argue that one must know the cause of problem behavior to deal with it effectively. Others would say that cause is not important; rather, what one must understand is how to change behavior regardless of its causality. Although in many cases one can alter the behavior of individuals and groups without knowing cause-and-effect relationships, it seems important for human service workers to have some sense of possible causal systems if for no other reason than to provide a perspective out of which to operate.

Four major current approaches exist in the conceptualization of causes of problem behavior or deviance. The first three approaches fall within the intrapersonal perspective: (1) the organic, (2) the psychodynamic, and (3) the psychological, including Rogerian theory and learning theory. The fourth approach, falling within the extrapersonal perspective, is the cultural/societal conception of causality. Although each approach has adherents who rigidly reject the others, most helping professionals would acknowledge that the evidence supporting any one approach over the others is not overwhelming. The specific causalities of the various human service problems remain open to question and investigation. It remains to be seen whether any one approach will prove superior over the others in a functional sense or whether causality is some function of all four issues acting in an interrelationship.

The intrapersonal perspective

Organic causality

The organic approach proposes that a person's behavior, particularly deviant or abnormal behavior, is a function of physical causes such as genetic makeup, brain chemistry, infection, toxins, brain trauma (tumors, a blow to the head), and so on. The abnormal individual is as sick as a person who has cancer, pneumonia, or heart disease, and it is considered likely that a medical treatment can be found that will cure or arrest the disease process. A great deal of research is under way in this model, and impressive evidence indicates a biological component in at least the more severe disorders (Eysenck and Eysenck, 1985; Gottesman, 1990).

Organic causality can illustrate how a physiological disorder can influence behavior and create a human services problem. It is estimated that by the year 2000 about 4 million Americans over the age of sixty-five will have a disorder called senile dementia, Alzheimer's type, or *Alzheimer's disease* (Shodell, 1984). In this disorder, for an unknown reason, there are degenerative changes in brain fibers. When a victim of this disease is autopsied, there is a plainly visible shrinkage of parts of the brain. The person has clearly suffered from an organic disease process. However, during the victim's later years, the symptoms of the problem are mainly behavioral. A person with this disorder suffers from memory problems, emotional irritability, difficulty in concentration, neglect of personal hygiene, poor judgment, and general intellectual decline. The following case illustrates the gradual onset and progressive decline that is the result of an organically caused disorder leading to a variety of human service needs.

■ ■ Joan lived a normal life as a wife, homemaker, and mother until her late fifties. Her husband and two daughters described her as a friendly, warm, and quiet woman. At the age of fifty-eight, she seemed to become depressed, apathetic, and forgetful. A particularly disturbing behavior consisted of wandering away from home and entering nearby houses unannounced and uninvited. Her husband and daughters took her to a local hospital for evaluation; she was diagnosed as having an anxious depression and released. Joan's confusion and disorientation became worse during the next few months. Her housework and personal hygiene suffered, and she had to be constantly supervised. A readmission to the medical hospital and extensive tests revealed mild diffuse atrophy of the brain, and she was finally diagnosed as having senile Alzheimer's disease.

Her continued deterioration required that Joan be placed in a state mental hospital. The next four years were marked by increasing immediate and long-term memory deficits, confusion, disorientation, and emotional outbursts. Her judgment suffered, she began to take others' possessions for her own, she constantly paced or slept in a ward chair, and her rambling speech became incomprehensible. She could (or would) no longer dress herself or bathe.

As two more years passed, Joan became incontinent and no longer fed herself. When fed by others, she would spit out the food. Lack of nourishment led to a physical decline, and she was fed through a tube. Joan's motor coordination became poor, her movements were slow, and her vocalization consisted of unintelligible crying noises.

Joan was finally placed in a custodial nursing home. She cannot stand unsupported, is totally nonverbal, and has a vacant wide-eyed expression. She continues to be tube-fed and her basic needs are cared for. Joan is now sixty-nine years old; she has declined for ten years.

The emotional and behavioral problems of senile dementia, Alzheimer's type, appear to be directly due to an organic cause, yet there is no effective organic treatment. Most people with this disorder spend their declining years in nursing homes and require primarily a human services approach to treatment until care must be mainly physical.

Organic explanations may be advanced for other more common behaviors. For example, some individuals do well in school; others do not. Some experts believe the critical factor in school performance is intelligence and that intellectual potential is primarily inherited (Scarr, 1975); they believe, in fact, that genetic potential is the most important factor in one's intellectual ability. Others strongly dispute the position that intelligence or intellectual potential and thus school performance, is the result primarily of genetic influence. They take a strong position that environmental factors are most important. It is an ongoing controversy which will not be soon resolved (Snyderman and Rothman, 1988). Another common problem for which an organic explanation is being proposed is severe depression. Some researchers have identified a possible genetic fault which may contribute to the severe depression seen in some of the 13 million depressed Americans (Nadi, Nurnberger, and Gershon, 1984). These preliminary findings have raised the hope that potential severe depression sufferers could be identified and treated before the depression begins.

There is no question that a number of severe behavior disorders have organic causes; however, in terms of incidence in our society, they are relatively rare. We do see individuals who are dangerously violent because of brain tumors, old people with strange behavior because of cerebral arteriosclerosis, and the like. In addition, we know that certain drugs modify the behavior by affecting brain chemistry. We cannot deny the importance of organic factors; however, at the same time, the evidence indicates that organic factors alone are not sufficient to explain all problem behavior.

Psychodynamic causality

The Freudian psychodynamic approach is a major alternative to the organic concept of causality. It is similar to the organic approach in that persons who have problems in living or who behave deviantly are seen as sick. They behave as they do because of unconscious motivation and are prisoners of early formative experiences. Freud considered human beings to be motivated unconsciously by the desire for pleasure and the avoidance of pain. Unconscious demands and reality are usually in conflict, and to cope, a person's thinking operates on primary and secondary levels. Primary process thinking is primitive, operating on the pleasure principle, and it embodies the base instincts and needs of the id. Secondary process thinking consists of the reality forces that inhibit and constrain the base drives.

Freud proposed three components of personality: id, ego, and superego (Figure 5-2). The *id* is the pleasure-oriented source of psychic energy, totally unconscious. It consists of the instincts, drives, and libido or sexual energy of the personality. The *ego* serves as the mediator between inner drives and outer reality. Its functions include perception, memory, judgment, conscious thought, and action. A strong ego deals with the dangerous id impulses and threats from the external environment. A major function of the ego is *reality testing*, or separating fact from fantasy. If this function is impaired, primary process thinking can break through unmediated by the ego, and the individual may behave in a *psychotic* manner. The *superego* is a function of the personality that introjects or internalizes the parental and societal moral teachings. If effectively internalized, it becomes the personality's "police officer" or conscience and is self-critical and prohibitive, controlling sexual and aggressive impulses.

A major emphasis of psychodynamics is on the development of personality through psychosexual stages. At birth the child has libido or sexual energy, the discharge of which is pleasurable and the blocking of which causes tension. The discharge of this energy focuses on different erogenous zones—oral, anal, phallic, and genital—during various developmental periods. The *oral stage* consists of the first several years of life when the mouth is the primary area of gratification. The *anal stage* occurs around the third and fourth year of life when the retention or expulsion of feces is the focus of concern, attention, and pleasure. During the *phallic stage*, the genital area becomes sensitized, and the child and parents must deal with the Oedipus (or Electra) complex, when the child becomes emotionally attached to the parent of the opposite sex and hostile toward the parent of the same sex. Depending on how this attachment and hostility are resolved, the child's adult sexual relationship will be normal or abnormal. The phallic stage is followed by a period of latency, a nonsexual stage of development which is a result of

Figure 5-2 *Functions of the id, ego, and superego.*

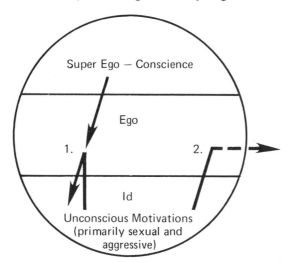

1. Some unconscious impulses are totally unacceptable. The superego blocks their expression and pushes them back into the unconscious.
2. Unconscious impulses that are not totally unacceptable can be expressed after they are modified by the ego. The ego thus acts as a mediator between instinctual drives and the environment.

repression. The *genital stage* occurs during adolescence when a person's libido becomes channeled into love of others rather than love of self.

According to Freud, everyone goes through the stages of development and has to resolve conflicts at each level. Individuals who have problems in living have failed to complete the task successfully because of either excessive frustration or overgratification at particular stages. If the conflicts are not resolved, fixation may occur, and the adult, under stress, will regress to the unresolved conflict, displaying symptoms of that stage of behavior.

This perspective on human behavior may be clearer if we consider an example. Human service workers often must deal with individuals who have become dependent on a chemical substance, such as alcohol. The psychoanalytic conception of alcoholism asserts that alcoholics are fixated at the oral stage of development. During those first few years of life, the individual who later becomes an alcoholic was either frustrated or overgratified by the parents. Because the mouth is the primary area of gratification during the oral stage, this frustration or overgratification results in an oral fixation. As an adult, the individual finds a sense of relief in oral behavior. The alcoholic is thus an individual who in the face of stress regresses to an oral behavior (drinking) because it reduces anxiety, just as the bottle or breast did during early infancy.

Psychodynamic formulations have been proposed as the cause of virtually all types of behavior: alcoholism, sexual offenses, criminal acts, delinquency, suicide, borderline psychotic states, and a host of others. Some recent evidence exists for the validity of the approach (Silverman, 1976), but a great deal of evidence has been presented that questions the validity of psychoanalytic theory (Eysenck, 1966).

Psychological causality

Although the psychodynamic concepts are a subgroup of psychological theory, they have been treated separately because of their strong association with the medical model. The two major concepts of psychological causality that will be dealt with here are the self theory of Carl Rogers and learning theory.

Rogerian theory Rogerian theory views humans from a basically positive perspective. It proposes that the newborn infant or young child has organismic wisdom. The young infant knows what is good for itself; its behaviors, feelings, and thoughts are congruent. As the child develops, society, in the person of the parents or caretakers, begins to put conditions on the child's worth. The child strives for self-actualization, but the conditions of worth ("If you get angry, you're not lovable," for example) may generate a defeating self-concept.

In essence, Rogers proposes that behavior is a function of how one sees one's "self." The self-concept develops out of one's interaction with the environment in the process of self-actualization, the basic motive of existence. In this process, the self may introject the values of others or perceive those values in a distorted fashion. Since the self strives for consistency, experiences that are not consistent with the self-structure are perceived as threats. When the mind blocks awareness of significant sensory and visceral experiences, they are not symbolized and integrated into the self; hence, psychological tension occurs and may lead to maladjustment. The more such experiences occur, the more rigidly the self-structure is organized as a defense against the threat and the greater the loss of contact with reality. The person becomes more and more maladjusted in a vicious spiral.

As people grow into adulthood, they have many experiences that are incorporated into their self-concepts. If, for example, individuals have a number of failure experiences while growing up, they may develop a self-perception of inadequacy. We all fail sometimes, of course, but when these failures become very important because of the values of others (such as parents) they can color our overall valuation of ourselves. If parents focus on their children's failures, those children as adults may have such a strong self-image of failure that they will not even see their own successes. A self-image of inadequacy may lead to behavior that is inadequate or to the avoidance of even attempts to try things at which the person might fail. The individual does not try very hard to succeed because he or she knows that failure will result. The less the individual tries to succeed, the more failures occur, and the self-image of inadequacy is confirmed. The individual becomes inadequate as time passes because of the self-image.

Self theorists reject the unwieldy character of the psychodynamic formulation and argue that self theory can account for most forms of behavior, including the extremely deviant. In a five-year study, Rogers and others worked with schizophrenics in a state mental hospital (Rogers et al., 1967) and claimed good results. However, they found the need to be much more active and directive when working with such persons. Many of the critics of psychodynamics have included self theories in their criticisms (Eysenck, 1966; Rimland, 1969; Wood, 1974). The major criticism of the self theory of causality (and also of psychodynamic causality) is that there is little hard evidence that such theories have a real relationship with behavior. It is particularly difficult to understand how this theory relates to the development of severe behavior disorders such as schizophrenia.

Learning theory The second major psychological approach to causality is that of the learning theorists, who can be classified as behaviorists. In essence, this view maintains that deviant or unadaptive behavior is learned through the normal learning process and is simply an exaggeration of normal behavior. Behavior is seen as a response to external and internal stimulation. However, a number of theorists insist that simple stimulus-response (S-R) relationships are not all that are involved with behavior. Maher (1966) suggests that behavior is a function of the combination of three sources: (1) past learning in relation to similar circumstances, (2) current motivational states and their attendant effect on sensitivity to the environment, and (3) individual biological differences, either genetic or resulting from physiological disorders.

Eysenck makes a strong case for a biological predisposition toward the learning of a range of maladaptive responses. Both Eysenck and Yates (1970) emphasize that major disturbances (such as psychoses) have a perceptual-neurological component that interferes with data processing and that learning and motivation figure into treatment. In addition, it is commonly accepted that many of the so-called symptoms of major disturbances *are* the result of learning. The implication of this position is, of course, that while behavioral therapy cannot "cure" the psychotic condition or predisposition, it can modify many or most of the deviant behaviors manifested by persons with such predispositions. Not all behaviorists would agree with this position, however, and many would take the position that extremely deviant behaviors, such as the psychoses, are a function purely of S-R learning or operant conditioning.

Current-day theorists and practitioners have expanded the scope of behavioral explanations of problem behavior to include cognitive factors such as thoughts, talking to oneself, mental images, self-evaluation, feelings, memories, and beliefs. They have developed a cognitive learning approach. Cognitive learning theorists believe that simple stimulus-response learning is important, but that to explain fully why certain behavior occurs requires taking into account a person's inner experiences or cognitions.

Physical or psychological neglect and abuse can lead to many childhood disorders. The effects can remain in adulthood.

Variables seen as important include: (1) encoding—how people selectively attend to specific aspects of their environment; (2) expectancies—what outcomes people expect, in terms of both what their behavior can achieve and what they expect to be the results of events in their environment; (3) the values that people attach to outcomes; and (4) the goals and standards that people set for themselves.

The increasing emphasis on the cognitive factors in learned behavior has resulted in a more comprehensive view of behavior on the part of many learning theorists. Bandura (1978, 1982), for example, sees behavior as due to a process of reciprocal determinism. Specific acts or ways of behaving that have been learned through reinforcement are influenced by the environment and cognitions; behaviors act on the environment and also influence cognition; and cognitions affect how people perceive the environment and how they behave (see Figure 5-3). Under certain circumstances, one factor may clearly dominate the others, but usually cognitions, strengths of learned behaviors, and environment are all factors that must be considered if one is to understand why people behave in particular ways.

The major criticisms of the learning or behaviorist approach to causality follow:

1. Except for the cognitive approach, it is too simplistic, in that it usually ignores the problem of a person's experiences, of who and what the person is; that is, the behaviorist treats the mind as a mysterious "black box."
2. It assumes that a particular behavior change is accomplished by applying a certain behavior principle because the original behavior was learned through a similar principle. It is unwarranted to assume that a behavioral principle is responsible for developing a particular abnormal behavior simply because the later application of the principle can change the behavior.
3. Only symptoms are dealt with, not the true underlying "cause," and symptom substitution will result.

On the other side of the issue, however, is a massive amount of evidence that indicates that the therapy based on this theory of causality is dem-

Figure 5-3 *Reciprocal determinism.*

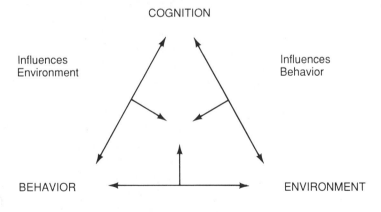

COGNITION

Influences
Environment

Influences
Behavior

BEHAVIOR

ENVIRONMENT

Influences
Cognition

onstrably effective in dealing with an extremely wide range of behaviors: enuresis, stuttering, phobias, obsessions, compulsions, delinquency, psychopathy, criminality, sexual disorders, alcoholism, drug addiction, retardation, mutism, delusions, hallucinations, regression, suicide threats, incontinence, violence, and disturbances of children. Also, this theory can be used in a wide variety of settings: schools, mental hospitals, mental health centers, general hospitals, and the home. In Chapter 8 we'll see some of the ways in which human service workers make use of the behavioral approach.

The extrapersonal perspective

Cultural/societal causality

This approach suggests that maladaptive behaviors are an aspect of achieved or granted social or cultural roles. The approach is similar to learning theory but differs in that it emphasizes the consideration of role structure rather than principles of learning. Sarbin (1968) identifies three critical dimensions of social identity (role functioning that answers the question, Who am I?): (1) the status dimension, (2) the value dimension, and (3) the involvement dimension.

Granted roles (age, sex, kinship, and so on) carry relatively neutral status; achieved roles can carry low or high status. The value continuum is different for the performance or nonperformance of roles at different points of the status dimension. Nonperformance of achieved roles (baseball player, musician) tends to be neutrally valued, while proper performance of achieved roles is positively valued. For example, if one is unable to play a musical instrument (the achieved role of "musician"), little issue is generally made of it (unless, of course, one is trying to be a professional musician). However, if one can play a musical instrument well, status is gained. Nonperformance of ascribed or granted roles (husband, male, female, child, etc.) is given a strongly negative value, while proper performance is neutral. Poor performance of roles that are ascribed or granted generally results in formal or informal social sanctions. An irresponsible or abusing husband, a homosexual, or a disobedient, disrespectful child is viewed as violating the norms of our culture and faces negative sanctions from others. On the other hand, acceptable behavior in these granted roles is simply expected, and when it occurs no special consequences will follow. The involvement dimension is determined in two ways: (1) the amount of time a person devotes to a particular role enactment and (2) the degree of organismic energy expended. Involvement in achieved roles is usually variable, depending on time and place, while involvement in ascribed roles is usually high and consistent.

Most deviant roles (delinquent, crazy person, crook, retardate, street person, bum) are ascribed; that is, a person is assigned that role by society. Certain behaviors are seen by observers (members of society) as characteristics of the deviant role. When a person exhibits some of these role characteristics, the person often is perceived as belonging to the class of people given that role label. The unemployed man who is unkempt and is found sleeping in a building doorway or train station may be assigned to the class of "vagrants" or "bums." Such a man may then confirm the role label by thinking of himself in those terms. When people act toward him as if he *were* a vagrant or bum, he begins to self-identify in that role and may become locked into behaving even more like his conception of how a vagrant is expected to act. Thus, he is subtly pushed toward taking on the ascribed role (Eaton, 1986). The social conditions that led to the development of the deviant role hinder the individual in using techniques that would help him break out of the deviant role behavior.

Critical to this definition of causality is the concept that social conditions lead to maladaptive roles. Certainly, there is no doubt that adverse social conditions can lead to problematic behavior or life-styles. We can, for example, consider life in the inner-city ghetto. It is not surprising that lifelong ghetto dwellers do not meet middle-class expectations of normal behavior. As children, their predominant role models are adults who may be unemployed, who may use drugs, and who often receive some form of social welfare. Minor and major illegal activities are common. Schools are agencies of social control rather than institutions of education. With so many problematic role models, what is really surprising is that so many people can surmount their role training in the inner city and become part of the mainstream.

Another example of problematic roles is in the area of criminality. This approach suggests that the *role* of "criminal" is a product of society. Social conditions are the stimulus for a response labeled "criminal." Once the person is so labeled, the individual enters into a role structure supported (often inadvertently) by the behavior of others, such as police, corrections workers, parole officers, judges, lawyers, cellmates, and the general populace. Given this situation, deviant roles would be very difficult to change unless the individual were relocated in a setting that did not support the deviancy and would lead to the development of techniques for dealing with the psychological strain resulting from a life of denigration.

While a number of other concepts fit under the cultural/societal approach to deviance, the notion that problem behavior is a function of cultural or societal organization is common to all of them. What is different about this approach is that it minimizes examining the individual and emphasizes examining the societal or cultural environment. If the root problems of a culture or society can be eliminated, it proposes, there should be a decrease in the individual deviance seen in the members of the culture or society.

There are two major concerns about this approach: (1) It does not seem to be easily utilized for explaining extreme deviance of individuals, and (2) it seems to accept the norms of the parent culture as the appropriate standard for assessment of deviance, when some would argue that a wider frame of reference is necessary. Although significant problems exist for the use of this approach as a causal theory, an abundance of evidence indicates that cultural and societal factors are highly important in the development of problem behavior (Grier and Cobbs, 1968; Krassner, 1986; Scheff, 1984; Srole et al., 1978; Zimbardo, 1970).

The Life Matrix

Human behavior, both functional and dysfunctional, is clearly the result of *something;* it has meaning, purpose, and goals. The preceding surveys of approaches to defining behavior and of concepts of causality demonstrate that no one concept is superior as the *prime* explanation of problem behavior.

For the human service worker, it seems most functional to think of specific human behaviors as the functions of networks of issues. Behavior is the function of the life matrix in which people exist (Figure 5-4), a combination of physical, psychological, and environmental issues. The life matrix would include people's organic makeup, psychodynamic character, self-concept, learning, the cultural or societal complex in which they live, their physical environment, and any particular stress events that they experience.

Any individual's behavior at a particular time may be a predominant function of one of the factors (for example, a high-stress event or a brain tumor). However, in most cases, behaviors are a function of the total matrix of internal and external forces operating on the individual.

It is fairly obvious that each of the approaches to defining causality has its strong points and evidence in its favor. Perhaps, however, the best conclusion to be drawn is that we shall have to wait for any final answer. Unfortunately, the need to provide services cannot be postponed until we know the "true" cause of all human problems. For this reason, it seems most reasonable for human services systems to be broadly based in dealing with those in need. We cannot afford to be dogmatic.

Whether the problems are a result of biological, psychological, or social causation is important in terms of determining strategies for dealing with them, but the evidence in most problems of survival suggests that some combination of two or more factors causes the person's difficulty.

We shall survey the techniques most commonly used with persons who have difficulty in society: the kinds of clients most likely to relate to a human service system. Even though some of the strategies based on the concepts of causality introduced in this chapter would be used only by a specialist (for example, a physician or psychologist), human service workers must be familiar with these techniques in order to know both their usefulness and their limitations. With this familiarity, they gain the expertise needed to make rational referrals and recommendations.

Figure 5-4 Behavior as a function of the life matrix.

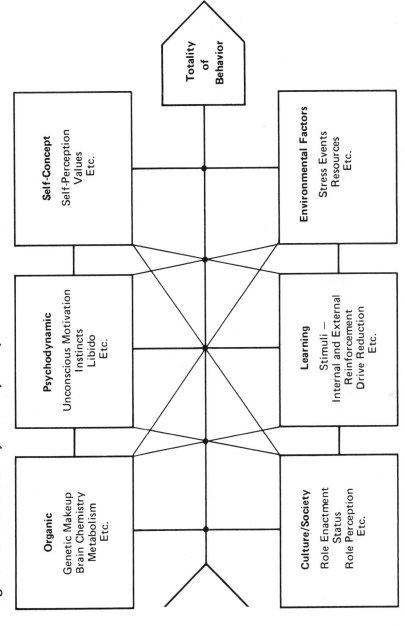

Totality
of
Behavior

Self-Concept
Self-Perception
Values
Etc.

Environmental Factors
Stress Events
Resources
Etc.

Psychodynamic
Unconscious Motivation
Instincts
Libido
Etc.

Learning
Stimuli —
Internal and External
Reinforcement
Drive Reduction
Etc.

Organic
Genetic Makeup
Brain Chemistry
Metabolism
Etc.

Culture/Society
Role Enactment
Status
Role Perception
Etc.

Summary

1. Human services is concerned with problems of psychological or social survival rather than problems of satisfaction. Its goal is to help the disadvantaged join the mainstream.

2. Problem behavior or deviance can be defined from several different perspectives. Intrapersonal perspectives focus on inner or personal aspects of the individual, including (a) biological norms, (b) comparison to an optimal psychological state, and (c) assessment of personal discomfort.

3. From an extrapersonal perspective, the definition of problem behavior or deviance focuses on environmental or social factors. The definition is based on (a) comparison to a statistical norm or (b) comparison to cultural/societal standards of behavior.

4. Four major approaches exist in the conceptualization of causes of human behavior: (a) organic, (b) psychodynamic, (c) psychological, and (d) cultural/societal.

5. The organic approach focuses on physiological causes of human behavior. It has been criticized for being too limited.

6. The psychodramatic approach, as illustrated by Freudian theory, focuses on unconscious motivation and early childhood psychosexual development. Psychoanalytic theories are difficult to support scientifically.

7. Psychological theories of causality are illustrated by Rogerian theory and learning theory. Rogerian theory emphasizes the development of the self-concept and its importance in determining behavior. Like psychoanalytic theory, it is difficult to support using scientific methodology. Learning theory suggests that problem behaviors are learned according to the same principles that govern the learning of all other behaviors. This model has been criticized as too simplistic to explain complex behavior.

8. The extrapersonal perspective of causality focuses on the impact of culture and society. It is concerned with external factors in the development of human service problems. There are several concerns about this approach, including the following: (a) It does not seem very useful for explaining individual cases of extreme problem behavior, and (b) some cultures or societies may have norms that promote problem behavior in a wide segment of the population.

9. Human behavior can best be viewed from an integrated perspective. Behavior results from a life matrix that includes organic or biologic factors, psychodynamic character, self-concept, learned behavior, and socioculturally influenced roles.

Discussion Questions

1. List the human problems you think should be the primary concern of human service workers.

2. List the human problems you think should be only of secondary concern to human service workers.

3. What issues should be considered in attempting to define whether a particular behavior or situation is a problem involving human services?

4. How would *you* define *normality?*

5. What criticisms might arise in regard to the concept of the life matrix?

Learning Experiences

1. Using each of the most common approaches to defining abnormality (biological norms, optimum psychological state, personal discomfort, statistical norms, and cultural/societal norms), try to identify a personal behavior that you or an acquaintance exhibits that each of these approaches would define as abnormal (one behavior for each approach).

2. As in Learning Experience 1, use the approaches to identify behaviors described in your community newspaper.

3. Think about your own life matrix and try to describe it in writing as fully as you can.

Recommended Readings

Eaton, W. W. *The Sociology of Mental Disorders.* (2d Ed.) New York: Praeger, 1986.

Mehr, J. *Abnormal Psychology.* New York: Holt, Rinehart and Winston, 1983.

Offer, D., and Sabshin, M. *Normality.* New York: Basic Books, 1974.

Scheff, T. *Being Mentally Ill: A Sociological Theory.* (2d Ed.) Chicago: Aldine Publishing, 1984.

6

Human Service Boundaries: Special Populations, Special Systems

- What special populations and service systems fall within the boundaries of human services?
- Why are children particularly at risk for the development of problems?
- Why are the elderly at risk for the development of problems?
- How serious a problem is drug abuse?
- What types of human service programs are available for the mentally retarded?
- What service systems are available for people with mental health problems?
- What are the goals of the correctional system in dealing with criminal offenders?
- How does poverty relate to human service problems?

Human service workers are involved in providing many forms of assistance to a broad range of people. Individuals receiving human services fall into many categories and have many different problems. Some groups of people have been identified as needing services because we believe that some special degree of vulnerability puts them at risk for developing problems. Examples of these types of groups include children, the elderly, and the poor. Others receive services because our society has traditionally perceived them as requiring a formalized response and has created systems for the provision of those services. Examples here include people who abuse chemical substances, the mentally retarded, people who have severe mental disorders, and lawbreakers.

Through the first half of this century, many of the helping systems had a primarily exclusionary focus. Disadvantaged people or people with severe problems often were excluded from community life. The organized formal responses of society toward people with human service problems frequently consisted of institutionalization. Children without parents were placed in foundling homes or orphanages. Juveniles in trouble with the law were routinely placed in youth detention facilities. The mentally ill were kept in mental hospitals in remote rural areas, far from their relatives' communities. The mentally retarded were put in residential schools far from their homes.

Institutionalization was the social response even to some medical illnesses. For example, before an effective treatment was developed for tuberculosis, people with this disease were sequestered in residential sanatoriums operated by state or county governments. The disease was considered too contagious to be treated in community hospitals; thus, willing or not, those afflicted were segregated from friends and family for long periods while the disease was active.

In the past twenty-five to thirty years there has been a distinct change in attitude about the value of excluding people from their communities because of behavioral, emotional, social, or economic problems. Workers in the helping professions have begun to realize that the process of exclusion of a person from the community in order to provide services has many negative effects. In this context community does not simply refer to a geographical place of residence but also refers to a social support network of loved ones, relatives, friends, coworkers, and employers who care about and can provide support for an individual. Recognition of the negative effects of exclusion from supportive social networks has led to the development of a strong emphasis on community-oriented helping programs. The boundaries of human services are inclusionary rather than exclusionary, integrative rather than segregative.

The boundaries of human services have been drawn very broadly and include a great variety of helping programs. The diversity of populations and programs that fall into the boundaries of human services allows the human service worker to focus on any one of a number of specialty areas when considering long-range career planning.

Some of the areas of special focus in human services revolve around special populations, and others center on the formal systems that have been developed to provide services to people with certain kinds of problems. This chapter will introduce some of the special populations and special systems that fall into the boundaries of human services.

Problems and Services
for Children and Adolescents

Human service workers see children and adolescents as being particularly at risk for the development of problems. Children lack many of the coping skills that are developed by adults and thus are more sensitive to the negative effects of events such as family disruptions, physical illness, the stresses of school, and poverty environments. Children undergo a process of change and development from birth to adulthood during which they learn many behaviors and skills, develop a self-concept, and create a style of life that may be adaptive or may result in problems in adulthood. The process of development is neither a simple nor an easy task.

The difficulties of human development are illustrated by estimates of the number of children who have significant psychological problems. In the United States today, perhaps 6 to 7 million children between the ages of five and nineteen have emotional problems that interfere with their learning in school and require human services interventions. For some children and adolescents these emotional problems are so distressing that they feel there is little point in continuing to live. About 6,000 children or adolescents (usually the latter) kill themselves each year in the United States, and as many as 2 million unsuccessfully attempt suicide every twelve months (Grimes, 1986). Another growing and often unrecognized and unaddressed problem is teenage runaways. There may be as many as 1.2 million adolescents who have run away from home and live a hand-to-mouth existence daily on the streets of major cities. Most are not boldly seeking adventure and challenge but are victims of dysfunctional families and are fleeing from stressful environments. Only about half have any realistic prospect of ever returning home to live. Of the remainder, about 300,000 are hard-core homeless. Thirty-six percent of all runaways are fleeing physical and sexual abuse; 44 percent are running away from other severe long-term crises such as drug-abusing, alcoholic parents or stepfamily crises; and 20 percent from short-term crises such as divorce, sickness, death, or school problems. Approximately 70 percent of the runaways who come to emergency shelters have been severely physically abused or sexually molested. Many of the children are "throwaways," kicked out because family resources are inadequate, or because a parent cannot accept a son or daughter who is gay, or perhaps just because a parent "can't handle" the adolescent (Hersch, 1988).

Equally important though less dramatic are the millions of children who spend their childhood in the squalor of disadvantaged urban or rural environments. Almost one in three of these children will have significant emotional or behavioral problems. They lack proper food, clothing, education, and physical health care. Without human service assistance, a disproportionate number of these children will do poorly in school, be unemployed (and perhaps unemployable) as adults, end up in prison, abuse drugs or alcohol, and experience a number of other life problems at a higher frequency than children who have had the good fortune to be raised in more positive settings.

The increased risk of disturbed functioning that children and adolescents from all levels of society face has led to the development of many human service programs that focus on enhancing young people's developmental environments. Human service workers in such programs may do many different things, depending on the particular focus of the program, as illustrated in the following examples.

1. *Well-child clinics.* Physical well-being is a critical factor in childhood. In well-child clinics, the focus is on preventive health care for infants and children and on training mothers to provide adequate physical and emotional care for their children. In many well-child clinics, as in other human service settings, human service workers (child care workers) are an important element in the teaching of child management and functioning as family change agents (Dangel and Polster, 1988; Garland, 1987).

> The Human Service health worker . . . has incorporated into her role some of the functions of the public health nurse, the lawyer, the social worker, the physician, and the health educator. . . . The worker's base is the health center, but much of her time is involved in making home visits in the community. . . . She is assigned from 40 to 60 families. . . . Daily activities . . . include a variety of health education, patient care, and social advocacy activities. She instructs the new mother how to bathe and feed the baby, and is alert to household hazards such as fire traps and broken paint on walls. In her training, strong emphasis is placed on patient education, case finding, the preventive aspects of medical care, and the emotional factors influencing illness. (Wise, 1968)

2. *Education.* Socially, emotionally, and physically deprived children often have serious difficulty in educational settings. The area of preschool and primary school education is one in which large numbers of human service workers provide a variety of remedial experiences to children who need special help. Major federally funded programs for early intervention such as Head Start and day care programs have provided such services to millions of disadvantaged children (Zigler, 1985).

Human service workers in educational settings are often called teacher or classroom aides. Working alongside the classroom teacher, they provide individualized instruction and activities for needy students. They often work with the most difficult students in remedial teaching. Human service workers in the school system also engage in counseling programs for students in some settings, do outreach work with truant children, run adult education programs, and do many nonteaching tasks that would otherwise be done by regular teachers. Formal jobs for human service workers have increased dramatically in school systems. In 1968, there were about 35,000 paid human service workers employed by school districts and more than 45,000 in Head Start programs (Gartner, 1971). By the end of the 1970s those figures increased ten fold; they have remained at that level in the 1980s (Zigler, 1985).

3. *Children and family services.* State governments fund programs that specialize in the detection of problems and provision of services for children

in families in which the emotional and physical well-being of the child is at risk. In Illinois, for example, this social service system is called the Department of Children and Family Services (DCFS). A major problem that agencies such as this confront is child abuse. Situations involving the abuse of children can range from home environments in which the basic physical needs of the child are neglected (lack of nutritious food, heat, and clothing) to those in which children are psychologically abused, those in which children are sexually abused, and those in which children are repeatedly severely physically injured by parents or other caretakers (Walker, Bonner, and Kaufman, 1987).

The incidence of child abuse or neglect is staggering and the reported cases have increased astoundingly in recent years. It is not clear if the increase is due to an increase in actual abuse and neglect over the years or due to improved case findings and reporting by state agencies. Today the annual incidence of reported cases is over two million per year according to the American Humane Association. The majority of these reported cases involve neglect rather than direct physical abuse. Yet each year thousands of children die from physical abuse by their parents or caretakers and tens of thousands are seriously injured.

Agencies such as Illinois's DCFS may provide home visits, counseling, and case follow-ups to such problem families and in extreme cases may remove endangered or neglected children from the custody of parents. In such situations the children are placed in foster homes. These foster homes consist of families who either volunteer or are paid to take in neglected children and provide them with a physically safe and emotionally secure environment. Such placements are usually temporary while the child's legal parents receive counseling or other services that will help them be "fit" parents. Group homes are another kind of temporary placement. A group home is generally operated as a formal agency with a human services staff that cares for children in a group setting. The staff of a group home requires special training and preparation for dealing with needy children in such a setting (Maier, 1987). Foster home parents are sometimes formal human service workers, and even when they are not, they at least receive some formal training. The first-line case managers who work in children and family agencies are human service workers with two- or four-year college degrees rather than traditional professionals.

The type of intervention that may be required when a parent or caretaker lacks appropriate parenting skills is illustrated in the case of Mrs. B. In this example, a human service worker (in the agency, called a parent aide) provides a variety of services aimed at improving the parenting and caretaking skills of a mother, in order to deal with an identified problem for a child.

The Case of Mrs. B.

■ ■ At the time she was referred to the program, Mrs. B., twenty-seven years old, had one two-and-a-half-year-old daughter at home and another, five months old, who had been placed in state foster care because of suspected child abuse. Mrs. B. had been separated from her husband for two months and was feeling depressed and hopeless. She had essentially no child management skills and felt overwhelmed by the idea of parenting two children. Her two-and-a-half-year-old was very active and demanding, had temper tantrums, and was lagging in speech development. The household was unsanitary and disorganized.

The aide was requested to model appropriate parenting and help Mrs. B. develop the time and home management skills that would enable her to regain custody of her baby. Mrs. B. was willing to have the parent aide service but was skeptical about what would be accomplished. One of the first suggestions the aide made was that Mrs. B. and the aide spend one of the two weekly appointments visiting the baby. This way, the aide could witness the interaction between mother and child. At first, there was little evidence of bonding between the two and Mrs. B. seemed uncomfortable handling the baby. The aide discovered that Mrs. B.'s mother had cared for the older girl until she was a year old, so Mrs. B. had had no real experience mothering an infant.

The initial goals of the case were directed at increasing Mrs. B.'s ability to mother the older child and maintain a clean, safe environment for both children. When the goals were reviewed after nine weeks, some progress had been made. It was decided to extend the original goals for another contract period and establish new goals centering on Mrs. B.'s developing the skills necessary to care for the baby. During these first two contract periods, the situation was complicated by the indefinite state of Mrs. B.'s marriage, the unpredictable involvement of her husband, and extended, interfering visits by her mother, her brother, and her brother's partner. All of this was confusing to Mrs. B., who wasn't sure what she wanted and was reluctant to assume responsibility for herself and her family.

During the second contract period, she made great strides, and the decision was made to return the baby to her care. This was done on a graduated basis, with progressively longer visits preceding the final return. With the return of the baby, the decision was made to extend the service for one more contract period, with the aide visiting only once weekly so that Mrs. B. would have support during the transition period. Two months later, Mrs. B.'s divorce was finalized and she was granted custody of both children.

When the service was terminated, both the aide and clinician stated that Mrs. B. was still prone to feeling overwhelmed at times when she felt isolated. The aide supported Mrs. B.'s acting on her own, so that her self-reliance would grow. While progress was made in this area, Mrs. B. was still unsure of herself as a single parent when the service ended. In the year since then, she has maintained custody and her periodic correspondence with the aide has indicated that she is continuing to expand her abilities to parent her children.

The aide's aim was to help Mrs. B. develop enough skills to continue developing her independence. This case required that the aide work with a complete social service team. During the course of service, the aide was involved with eleven collateral persons, including lawyers, state workers, a visiting nurse, and school personnel.[1]

This example of the human service problems of childhood and the types of services provided only scratches the surface of the many problems and services that exist for this particular population. Childhood is not the idyllic

The physical, economic, and social losses of many of the elderly leave them particularly vulnerable to psychological disorders such as depression.

period we often think it is. Programs for children are thought to be very important since adequate services for a troubled child may allow that child to develop into a healthy, functional adult.

Problems and Services for the Elderly

The elderly accounted for about 12 percent of the population of the United States in 1988, which meant that some 28 million people in the United States were sixty-five years of age or over (News and Notes, 1987). Because of declining birthrates and increased life span, some projections have been made that in another fifteen years, as much as 20 percent of the population may be over age sixty-five. Human service programs focusing on the problems of the elderly will obviously be even more important by the turn of the century.

Many factors come together to make the elderly a group at risk for human service problems. Many elderly live a life of loss: loss of physical stamina, loss of health, loss of friends, loss of loved ones through death, and loss of income (one-third of older Americans live at or below the poverty level) (Krause, 1987). Their roles in life change. They are no longer breadwinners, and their children are now independent adults. Rather than taking care of others, they often need to be taken care of. In our culture, old age carries a stigma of fading worth. The physical and psychological losses of old age take a heavy emotional toll. Many older Americans are lonely, depressed, and frightened. Some have serious problems of mental deterioration leading to confusion, memory loss, and odd behavior.

Growing recognition of and sensitivity to the plight of the elderly has led to the development of community human service programs for this population. These programs, often called senior citizen centers, provide social, nutritional, and health programs for their participants. Human service workers in such programs often engage in outreach activities to encourage seniors to come to the center or may regularly call on homebound clients.

Many older Americans are physically or psychologically unable to continue to live independently. In the United States, these individuals often find themselves spending their remaining years in nursing homes. Unfortunately, the quality of care in many of these homes is poor, although some are very good. However good the care may be, though, they are still institutions. A major problem in these settings is the lack of social involvement and the routine days that the elderly must confront (Gutheil, 1985). Some homes have begun to make major strides in creating a more psychosocially positive atmosphere.

There is a growing recognition of a need for more small, community-oriented homes rather than the large impersonal nursing homes that are currently so common (Weihl, 1981). The positive effects of innovative programs in nursing homes are demonstrated clearly in the following excerpt (Fields, 1977).

Bright autumn sunlight floods through the windows, softened only by opaque curtains that suffuse the room in a warm cocoon of rosy-gray light. A dozen old men and women sit in a circle in the center of the room, their strong Scandinavian features chiseled in soft relief by the subdued sunlight. Some are in wheelchairs, others snuggled deep into cushions and sofas. Some are blind. Others are deaf. All have dressed—or have been dressed—with great care, and here and there a withered hand smoothes a wrinkle or brushes a strand of thin, silky hair back into place.

No one moves much, but everyone sits alert, dead still in anticipation. The scene is in slow motion: even the rhythm of the labored breathing is in quarter time.

The door of an elevator across the room flies open and ancient eyes look up, startled, at the explosion of bright color, darting motion, and yelps of youthful enthusiasm suddenly released to cascade into the room.

"Grandpa Olson!"

"Grandma Larsen!"

"Uncle Eric!"

Guided by a teacher from their nearby nursery school, the children skip boisterously around the circle, shaking hands and occasionally exchanging little hugs. Finally, with greetings finished, the teacher settles the children into their places among the old folks.

"Today," says the teacher, "we're going to color cards with autumn leaves, using our red, brown, yellow, and orange crayons." Tiny hands reach for sheets of paper and bright sticks of color, and several children then take their places shyly in the laps of grateful "grandmothers" and "grandfathers." Others take places in the center of the circle, channeling their energy into their drawing and coloring. The room is electric with color, sound, movement.

When the coloring is finished, the teacher has something else for them. "Lots and lots of leaves that fell from the trees are hidden inside the room," she explains. In fact, some of the leaves are hidden on grandpa and grandma—in pockets, on hats, between the spokes of the wheels of their chairs. Quickly, the children are chirping with excitement, scurrying around the room with the industry of cardinals chasing squirrels through a garden of elms.

Before young and old tire of this game, the teacher has less strenuous fun. It's a quiz, with the old people watching as amused arbiters.

"What's today?" the teacher asks.

"Thursday."

"What month?"

"October."

"What season?" There's a pause, and old eyes twinkle as the pause lengthens.

"Is it winter?"

"Yes!"

Grandma Olofson can no longer contain her amusement—nor can she restrain her impulse to act as a teacher. Her voice cracks with gentle laughter.

"No, it isn't," she says. "It's autumn, the season of the falling leaves."

"And where are we?" the teacher asks.

"Ebenezer!" cries a little boy in a blue corduroy jumper. "Ebenezer Nursing Home."

"Right!" the teacher tells him. The boy is pleased, and shows it with a smile that spreads across his face. The teacher starts a song; soon young and old are singing together, shrill tenors and mumbling baritones and basso profundos.

"If you're happy and you know it," cries the teacher, "clap your hands." Two dozen hands smack in unison. "If you're happy and you know it, tap your feet." Two dozen feet tap a bright staccato on the floor; across the room, an old man with mirth in his eyes taps out a shaky accompaniment with a cane.

The last notes of the song die, and the children begin picking up caps and coats and gloves. Another round of tiny hugs and whispered confidences, and the children walk out to the elevator. The room falls quiet, settling back to silent warmth rocked by the fading vibrations of the morning's merriment.[2]

Drug Abuse: The Problem and Human Services

Many chemical substances have significant effects on the behavior, thinking processes, and emotions of human beings. Some of these substances have long histories of social use and abuse. A few of the more important substances are listed in Table 6-1, along with their immediate effects and the symptoms of overdose. When an individual uses these types of drugs frequently, a physical or psychological dependence may develop. The individual becomes a drug abuser. The person must take the drug either to avoid painful or unpleasant physical withdrawal symptoms or to avoid unpleasant psychological experiences.

The most abused drug is alcohol. Around 18 million Americans are problem drinkers; that is, alcohol use causes them significant problems in living. Unfortunately, the large majority of problem drinkers do not recognize their problems with alcohol abuse and do not seek treatment. Since the late 1970s, though, the numbers of people in treatment and the number of treatment programs have increased substantially. The number of alcoholism and other drug treatment programs increased from 465 in 1978 to 829 in 1984, an increase of 78 percent. On any one day about 210,000 people with alcoholism and 90,000 people who abuse other drugs are in treatment. In 1984 approximately 1,000,000 people were hospitalized for short-term treatment for alcoholism (Secretary of Health and Human Services, 1987).

In the past thirty years, the incidence of cocaine abuse has soared dramatically. It is estimated that five million U.S. citizens use cocaine regularly, and one million are significantly dependent on it. For many years it was believed that cocaine use did not cause a physical dependence like alcohol and heroin, but experts today have determined that cocaine is in fact physically addictive (Franklin, 1990). In the mid 1980s a new form of cocaine called "crack" became common on the streets. This crystallized form of the white cocaine powder sells relatively cheaply and has introduced cocaine addiction into the lower socioeconomic classes. Cocaine in its powdered form is quite expensive and had been a drug more common to the well-to-do. Crack cocaine rapidly produces an intense high that is relatively short term, and this, combined with its low price, results in a drug that is ranked as more addictive than heroin. Heroin abuse is a serious problem for about 300,000 Ameri-

Table 6-1 *Some commonly abused substances and their effects.*

Drug	Effect	Overdose effects
Alcohol	1. Initial sense of stimulation 2. Loss of judgment 3. Poor coordination 4. Loss of peripheral vision	1. Disorientation 2. Depressed breathing 3. Coma 4. Possible death
Heroin	1. Euphoria 2. Floating feeling 3. Drowsiness 4. Constricted pupils	1. Coma 2. Convulsions 3. Depressed breathing 4. Possible death
Tranquilizer	1. Sense of relaxation 2. Drowsiness 3. Slowed reflexes 4. Impaired sensation	1. Stupor 2. Coma 3. Death
Marijuana	1. Mild euphoria 2. Relaxed inhibitions 3. Large doses lead to hallucinations and impaired sensation	1. Disorientation 2. Agitation 3. Severe hallucinations 4. Paranoid suspicions
Cocaine	1. Intense euphoria 2. Increased energy 3. Heightened alertness 4. Labile emotions	1. Anxiety 2. Confusion 3. Cocaine psychosis 4. Violence

	Number of persons with drug problem or illegally using*
Alcohol	18 million problem drinkers
Heroin	300,000 to 600,000 addicts
Tranquilizer	300,000 addicts
Marijuana	22 million users
Cocaine	5.8 million users

* Source: National Clearinghouse for Drug Abuse Information, 5600 Fishers Lane, Rockville, MD.

cans (some estimates say 600,000). The incidence of abuse of other drugs is less well known, although it is believed to be high (Kornetsky, 1976).

Drug abuse, a serious problem in its own right, is associated with many other problems. For example, alcohol abuse by pregnant women may lead to fetal alcohol syndrome in their children. This syndrome includes possible physical birth defects and mental retardation. In recent years, the increase in crack cocaine addiction among pregnant women has resulted in the births of many thousands of infants who are addicted at birth and must experience drug withdrawal immediately after birth. These children have been noted to be in generally poor physical health and to have a variety of behavioral deficits when compared to children born to nonaddicted mothers (Chasnoff and Schnoll, 1987). The alarming increase in infants born of addicted mothers are likely to present a new population needing human services in the years to come.

The incidence of abuse of drugs is particularly high among the urban disadvantaged, although the abuse of drugs has become much more common throughout all strata of society. With the exception of alcohol, the social use of most drugs is illegal, and thus drug abusers frequently have problems with criminal convictions. Contrary to popular belief, however, drug users do not necessarily engage in acts of criminal violence because they are high on drugs. Addicts (especially heroin addicts) do have a higher rate of criminal behavior than nonaddicts primarily because of their efforts to obtain money to buy the illegal drugs. In today's marketplace, a typical heroin addict requires $200 to $300 a day to support the addiction. That kind of money is hard to come by except through illegal activity.

Chronic drug abuse has a variety of negative consequences, depending on the particular substance used. Most addicts experience serious deterioration in personal relationships, problems in maintaining job functioning, and related health problems. Some drugs (alcohol, for example) can damage brain tissue and lead to significant mental deterioration, as illustrated in the following case.

■ ■ Mr. Wells is a fifty-five-year-old man who has been a chronic alcoholic for at least fourteen years. He has recently stopped drinking and experienced withdrawal symptoms. As he began to recover from the withdrawal symptoms, Mr. Wells displayed signs of significant brain damage from the long-term effects of alcohol abuse. His memory for recent events is extremely poor, and he fills the gaps with fabrications that he believes are the truth. He is disoriented in relation to time and does not know what year it is. When asked to subtract 7 from 100 successively, i.e., 93, 86, 79, and so on, his responses were 93, 89, 72. . . . His intellectual impairment and faulty memory present a serious impediment to his return to occupational employment.

The serious, sometimes life-threatening effects of drug abuse are considered a major social problem in the United States, and a large number of human service workers are employed in agencies that treat substance abusers. Workers in these types of programs perform many functions: counseling, group problem solving, family counseling, outreach, community education, employment linkage, referral to other services, and administration (Alley et al., 1979b).

Three major types of services are available for substance abusers: methadone maintenance programs for heroin abusers, and self-help programs and therapeutic community programs for abusers of all types.

Heroin abuse is often treated in methadone maintenance programs. Methadone is a drug that substitutes for heroin. It does not produce the psychological effects of heroin but prevents the physiological symptoms of withdrawal. The focus of these programs is on the maintenance of individuals on methadone in order that they will not need to use heroin. Ideally, while in such a maintenance program the individual is provided with other rehabilitation services.

Although self-help groups are available for addicts of all types (McAuliffe and Ch'ien, 1986), the best example of an addicts' self-help group is Alcoholics Anonymous (AA). Today there are over 40,000 different AA groups in the world. Basically, AA is a self-help organization that focuses on helping members to: (1) admit they have a drinking problem, (2) make amends for the problems they have caused, and (3) commit themselves to a "higher power" (which some choose to call God). AA has abstinence as a goal, and members try "one day at a time" to accept that they can never drink again. Members stand ready to provide support to those in crisis, and to help each other avoid the bottle and learn to live by new rules. The approach is reported to be more successful than traditional professional approaches, and tens of thousands of people have been helped by this organization. However, the structure of AA, with its lack of membership lists and case history files, prevents accurate evaluation of its effectiveness. AA's effectiveness must be taken on faith, an important ingredient in its overall approach.

Therapeutic communities are oriented around drug-free treatment of addicts in residential programs. The therapeutic community philosophy is that treatment should be aimed at modifying negative patterns of behavior, thinking, and feeling that lead people to use drugs, and that treatment should encourage responsible, drug-free life-styles (DeLeon and Ziegenfuss, 1986). Participation, which is voluntary, includes confrontation of "addict behavior" in group settings. The confrontation is often brutal (perhaps necessarily so) and demanding of a change of life-style. This approach has been relatively successful with addicts who stay with the programs. However, dropout rates for these types of programs appear high (DeLeon and Schwartz, 1986). A major evaluation of therapeutic communities and methadone maintenance programs (Bale et al., 1980) found that participants who had been in therapeutic communities longer than seven weeks or who were continuing in methadone maintenance were more likely to be working or attending school, and less likely to be in jail, using heroin, or convicted of a serious crime than those who had only been detoxified. However, Bale et al. found that therapeutic communities had a dropout rate of 61 percent; methadone programs had a dropout rate of 69 percent. Only 18 percent of the patients assigned to the therapeutic communities actually entered treatment, and only 30 percent of those assigned to the methadone program actually entered treatment. Of the total addict populations surveyed, only 10.3 percent entered and stayed in treatment for the recommended length of time. The data clearly suggest that although these two treatments are somewhat successful, the large majority of addicts either will not or cannot take advantage of them. Until some way is found to maintain addicts in treatment, the dropout rates of over 90 percent in some programs will prevent real impact on the addiction problem through these types of approaches.

The challenge for human services is to find effective approaches for dealing with addictions of all types and to integrate approaches such as Alcoholics Anonymous and therapeutic communities into the wider human services network (Nebelkopf, 1986).

Mental Retardation Services

There may be as many as 6 million mentally retarded citizens in the United States. Approximately 900,000 children with mental retardation between the ages of three and twenty-one years are being served in public schools under the requirements of Public Law 94–142, the Education of the Handicapped Act of 1975 (Schroeder, Schroeder, and Landesman, 1987). This important act codifies six principles for the education of the handicapped.

1. The principle of zero reject holds that schools must provide free special education and related services for all handicapped children between three and twenty-one years, except in states that serve only children aged five to eighteen years. Not only are special education needs to be met, but extracurricular services such as counseling sessions, athletics, transportation, health services, recreation, and special interest groups and clubs are to be provided for these youngsters. No children can be rejected from these services.

2. The second principle, nondiscriminatory evaluation, requires initially determining what a child can do, rather than merely what he or she cannot do. An interdisciplinary team approach is mandated and evaluation must consider, if appropriate, the child's health, vision, hearing, social and emotional status, general intelligence, academic performance, communicative status, and motor abilities.

3. The third principle focuses on an individualized education program (IEP) that must be written for each child. The IEP must include specific details about (a) what is to be taught, (b) how this will be taught, and (c) the way progress will be measured.

4. The fourth principle—that of least restrictive environment (LRE)—states that handicapped children should be educated with nonhandicapped children to the maximum extent appropriate. Knowledge of the school environment and of the various classrooms in the school is vital to planning effective placements. Even more important is awareness of issues relating to social acceptance, peer pressure, self-esteem, and social learning.

5. The principle of due process is intended to ensure fairness of educational decisions and to assign accountability and responsibility to professionals while assuring that the rights of the child and parents are not violated.

6. Parental participation is a separate principle. It recognizes that parents are among the most important teachers in a child's life and that their involvement in their handicapped child's education can no longer be denied. Parents have access to all records and information generated by the schools.

Unfortunately, some mentally retarded citizens are so disabled, either by their level of retardation or by associated behavior problems, that they simply cannot be placed in a regular school or other community setting. Of these, about 100,000 are residents of government-operated residential institutions.

Four levels of mental retardation are commonly described: mild, moderate, severe, and profound. The great majority of the mentally retarded fall into the higher intellectual levels of moderate and mild. Those who are moderately retarded require some supervision and assistance but can often live outside of institutions in group homes. The mildly retarded often can live independently and work at unskilled jobs. Those who are severely or profoundly retarded require constant care and supervision, as illustrated in the following example.

■ ■ Alberta is severely retarded. The highest score she has ever attained is an IQ of 27 on the Stanford-Binet intelligence scale. Now forty-seven years old, she has been a resident of a state school for the retarded since the age of eleven. She was institutionalized when her mother became ill and could no longer care for her at home. Her mother died when Alberta was twelve, and she has not seen her father since he remarried when she was thirteen.

Alberta was born with a disorder called phenylketonuria. This defect of recessive genes results in mental retardation unless the child is provided with a special diet from birth onwards. The disorder was first identified in 1934, but by the time it was widely known, it was too late to treat Alberta. Intensive training since childhood has enabled Alberta to talk in simple sentences and to make her wants known. Continuing supervision ensures that Alberta washes and bathes regularly and, with some help, dresses herself. She enjoys watching television, particularly action-filled cartoons. Alberta has tried doing simple tasks in the school's workshop, but she cannot attend to a single task long enough to be productive. A major current problem for Alberta is that she is self-mutilative. She hits herself in the head rapidly with her closed fist and picks and scratches at her arms and legs. She may go months at a time with open sores from the picking and scratching.

The following features of Alberta's case are typical of a severely retarded individual:

1. There is clearly impaired development in infancy or early childhood.
2. Usually a genetic or other obvious organic cause such as physical injury, infection, or metabolic disorder is found.
3. Usually these individuals can profit only from lengthy training in self-care skills and habit training.
4. Parents have major difficulty managing the individual in the home, and usually must place the child in an organized institutional setting where almost constant supervision is available.
5. Social adaption skills are minimal even in adulthood, and major behavior problems may occur.

The incidence of severe and profound retardation is equivalent across all socioeconomic levels. But, as in many human service problems, the problem of mental retardation at the mild and moderate levels occurs with greater frequency among the socioeconomically disadvantaged. The greater incidence of mild and moderate retardation in the lower socioeconomic levels supports the idea that although some retardation is due to organic causes, much of the mental retardation in our society is due to cultural-familial causes. That is, it is due to a combination of sociocultural deprivation and genetic predisposition.

The mentally retarded citizen faces more problems than learning and functioning at a lowered intellectual level. At the levels of severe and profound retardation, there are often physical disabilities and deformities associated with the retardation. At all levels of retardation, these individuals must face a lifelong public stigma that influences how they are viewed by both professionals and laypersons (Bogdan and Taylor, 1976). They encounter problems in school, family, and employment. They have difficulty avoiding dependence and have impaired coping skills. The mentally retarded often experience crises when facing developmental milestones that normal people handle with much less difficulty, such as starting school or the birth of a sibling. The mentally retarded person experiences anxiety, depression, and a sense of loss, brought on by incomplete mastery of these milestones and the unmet need to develop greater independence and autonomy (Gilson and Levitas, 1987).

Program delivery systems for the mentally retarded have changed in recent years, illustrating the movement toward community-based programs in human services. The number of residents in state-operated "schools" for the retarded decreased from 139,000 in 1980 to a projected 100,000 in the middle to late 1980s (Braddock, 1981). In 1990 it appears that estimate was optimistic. The current census in state-operated "schools" is about 120,000. However, the population does continue to decline, and in the last 10 years more than 40 developmental disability institutions have been closed in the United States (Braddock, 1990). The retarded who are leaving these residential institutions and many who in the past would have been admitted to them are finding services offered in community settings. For example, the residential needs of many retarded people are now being met by small group homes of fifteen people or fewer in community settings (NARF, 1983). In the ten-year period from 1970 to 1980, the number of these community residential settings increased 900 percent to over 6,000 homes. These community homes now serve almost 60,000 mentally retarded people, and it is estimated that another 55,000 could benefit if more homes were available (Janicki, Mayeda, and Epple, 1983). Life in group homes for the mentally retarded is believed to be a positive experience since it provides a more normal environment than an institutional setting (Blake, 1985/86). Unfortunately, there continues to be some prejudice against group homes on the part of communities when they find out that such a home is to be opened. Since more group homes are needed, one of the areas of focus for human service workers in the field of mental retardation will be to develop strategies for obtaining community support for the opening of additional group homes (Hogan, 1986).

The development of the community group homes has been paralleled by the development of other types of community services. One involves the provision of employment training and productive paid work for mentally retarded adults. Many retarded adults have the potential to be self-supporting or contribute to their support, but for many years this potential was unrealized. However, there has been dramatic growth in sheltered workshops in which the retarded can be trained to engage in productive work for pay. Between 1972 and 1979, the number of these workshops expanded 600 percent, and they now provide training and employment for 100,000 mentally retarded citizens (McLeod, 1985). These sheltered workshops are concerned with more than developing job skills. Most also offer or link clients with counseling services. We are now finally beginning to address the emotional needs of retarded citizens (Turkington, 1984).

Mental Health Problems and Service Systems

Many of the problems dealt with by human service workers have traditionally been seen as mental health problems. Some observers have described the mental health service system as the octopus of human services, with tentacles everywhere.

When behavioral problems are defined as having organic or intrapsychic causes, the mental health system is usually the provider of services. These services may be provided by traditional professionals such as psychiatrists, psychologists, or social workers in private practice or in publicly funded systems. The public systems include county, state, and federal mental hospitals and comprehensive community mental health centers. Mental hospitals provide services to individuals with behavioral disorders. They have a special responsibility to provide care and security for people who are dangerous to themselves or others as a result of psychological dysfunction. Comprehensive community mental health centers often provide short-term inpatient care, but most of their services are on an outpatient basis. These centers offer many services that are helpful to people who have not been traditionally seen as having mental disorders. They offer crisis counseling, marital therapy, family therapy and consultation, and education services.

As in other human service subsystems, emphasis on community-based services has grown in the mental health sector. The population in mental institutions dropped from almost 600,000 in 1955 to 110,000 in 1990 (Torrey, 1989). Many who might have spent most of their lives in mental hospitals live in sheltered settings in the community and receive services from a variety of community-based programs, in addition to mental health centers (Segal and Aviram, 1978).

A significant problem for the provision of community services for those who are labeled mentally ill has to do with the stigma attached to mental illness. While seven out of ten Americans have come to believe that mental illness is on the rise (with one out of three people knowing an acquaintance or family member who has been treated for it) much misinformation is common. The proposed development of community residential treatment programs often runs into the NIMBY (Not in my backyard) phenomenon. Many people think the development of community programs is a good idea until one is proposed for their neighborhood. They then fight to keep it out because they fear what it might do to their property values, and the supposed "dangers" for their children of having the mentally ill near their homes (Program on Chronic Mental Illness; National Survey, 1990).

Unfortunately, the push to deinstitutionalize persons who in the past would have been kept in mental hospitals has created a new human services problem. The need for community services has far outstripped the available resources. Many mentally disturbed individuals have become homeless street people, particularly in large cities. There are as many as 2 million homeless people in the United States, and of these, 50 percent may have severe, persistent mental disorders, as well as drug and alcohol abuse (Cordes, 1984). Many of the seriously mentally ill are also locked away in jails and prisons. They are often charged with minor crimes simply to get them off the street. For example, one individual in Illinois was arrested and charged with stealing a $1.88 item from a store and to date has spent over six months in a moderate security setting because he is not fit to stand trial due to his mental illness. It is estimated that between 35,000 to 150,000 jail and prison inmates are seriously mentally ill (Torrey, 1989). Few receive appropriate treatment for their mental illness. Many simply move between jail and the streets where they become homeless again, and back to jail when their behavior comes in conflict with the law. The recognition of the plight of the homeless mentally ill, and of homeless people in general, will—it is hoped—lead to the development of more human service programs for these individuals (Youngstrom, 1990).

Some attention does seem to be being paid to the issue of the homeless. In 1987 Public Law 100–77 established federal funding for two-year programs to provide housing, health care, and emergency assistance for the homeless, including the homeless mentally ill. The appropriation of $355 million included $32.5 million in grants to states for services for the homeless mentally ill (New Law, 1987). Simply providing money, however, is not enough. While deinstitutionalization has worked in the sense of increasing the freedom of ex–mental patients and new homeless mentally ill, we must now help these people deal with the risks of freedom. There is more to a successful community support system than a collection of programs. In each system, planners and clinicians must analyze the total system design in terms of ease of engagement and continuity of services (Minkoff, 1987). The increased funding will do little good if the homeless mentally ill do not have easy access to it or interest and motivation in using the services.

Correctional Systems

Crime is a major social problem in the United States. Until recently, each year saw significant increases in reported crimes. Studies demonstrated that as many as one of every two teenage boys has engaged in delinquent behavior (Farrington, 1979). Although fewer adults engage in illegal behavior, crime still poses a serious problem for society. In 1982, in spite of a decrease in reported crimes in the preceding two-year period, 8 million people were arrested and held in jail; almost an equal number were released during the year. By the end of 1984, more than 2.6 million Americans, one in every sixty-five adults, were in prison, on probation, or on parole (U.S. Department of Justice, 1983, 1984). At the beginning of 1990 over 700,000 people were inmates in federal and state prisons, and county jails (Church, 1990). In the past ten years the most rapidly growing segment of the correctional population has been women. The population of females in jails and prisons has tripled in the 1980s, and in 1989 alone, rose twenty two percent. This increase in the female correctional population is due mainly to arrest and conviction for drug related offenses. Women in jail and prison have special problems including the fact that 80 percent of them are mothers, and of those, 85 percent have custody of their children. Today's jails and prisons are ill equipped to deal with the problems of female inmates. The dramatic increase in population has placed a severe strain on correctional facilities oriented towards dealing with male inmates.

The worker in the field of corrections may focus on crime prevention, rehabilitation of offenders, or both. Prevention often involves working with juvenile offenders to get them off the route to becoming adult criminals. It may also involve more indirect efforts such as working with street gangs to redirect their activities into legal community-supportive behaviors. Even more indirect are attempts to modify the social ills, such as poverty, that increase the likelihood of criminal activity.

Rehabilitation of offenders can occur through a number of systems. Human service workers in probation and parole systems deal with people who are under the supervision of the court after committing a crime. In probation the convicted person is not imprisoned but is placed under the supervision of a worker whose duty is to counsel, broker services, and supervise the individual's behavior in the community. Probation can, in the event of a lack of success, require that the individual be returned to court for sentencing to imprisonment. Parole is a similar process that occurs after an individual has spent some part of the court sentence in prison. The person is given an early but supervised release that has the goals of reintegration into the community and future compliance with the law. The parolee is under the guidance of a parole officer (a human servicer worker), who provides counseling and referral to necessary services. Parole failure also can lead to reimprisonment while the individual serves out the sentence.

Although progress has not been as widespread as in other areas, there has been a growing emphasis on community services in corrections (see Chapter 14).

Imprisonment has at least three goals: rehabilitation, punishment, and deterrence. Of these, only rehabilitation is a service provided for the offender; punishment and deterrence are services for society. Within most prisons, human services are relatively scarce. Prisons are oriented more toward containing criminals than toward rehabilitating them. The penitentiary has always been, in practice, a custodial institution. Custody is a part of the heritage of the prison, with or without an agenda of human services reform. This reflects the prison's ancient origins as a vehicle for exclusion and containment of society's rejects (Johnson, 1987). Thus, a custodial reality forms the backdrop for any rehabilitative services that are provided. Some services do exist, however: Human service workers provide work-training programs, education, counseling, and recreational services, among others. Unfortunately, only slightly more than 12 percent of employees in such facilities have human service–oriented duties (Clare and Kramer, 1976). Most employees are concerned with security. The impact of a human services perspective in correctional institutions is only beginning to be felt.

The Poor

Who are the 31 million poor? When one thinks about the poor, the usual image that arises is of a person who has no money and who either ekes out an existence by panhandling or lives on welfare monies. There is a fair percentage of moneyless people (often homeless street people) who do not receive any welfare money. The nonworking poor who live exclusively on welfare comprise about 4 million U.S. citizens.

In 1989, 12 million people, one out of every 20 U.S. residents, lived below *half* the poverty line. This is an increase of nearly 45 percent from 1979, when unemployment was roughly the same as in 1990. The poor became even poorer during that 10 years. This "hyper-poor" 12 million people included almost 5 million children, lived in mostly single-parent female-headed families, were 61 percent white and 35 percent black, and only *two* out of five received welfare benefits. Even among the hyper-poor, forty-six percent of the households have some earnings, yet still cannot break the $6,000.00 per year total income mark (Whitman, 1990).

There are another 7 million Americans who work full or part time who still are unable to earn enough to break out of the upper ranks of the poor. These are the "hidden poor," employed yet poverty-stricken (Whitman et al., 1988). The hard-core inner-city poor make up only 7 percent of the nation's poor. Sixty percent of all able-bodied poor adults work and are evenly divided between urban and rural areas. In the economy of 1990, a family of four with work income of $12,675 was below the poverty line.

The Homeless

Over the past decade, homelessness has gained a great deal of popular attention. Prior to 1980 most Americans would have asserted that very few people were homeless, living in the streets. The last time homelessness was emphasized as a problem was during the Great Depression of the 1930s when it was estimated that between 200,000 and 1.5 million people were homeless (Rossi, 1990). After that time, the number of homeless declined drastically and in the 1950s consisted primarily of older men living in skid row areas of large urban cities. It was predicted that homelessness would virtually disappear by the 1970s. However, in the 80s homelessness has risen dramatically and at least 250,000, to as many as 3 million people, are homeless during the year in the U.S. (Ropers, 1988; Rossi, 1990). The Urban Institute has concluded that on any given night between 567,000 and 600,000 people are homeless (Burt and Cohen, 1989).

When the new homeless of the 1980s and 90s are compared to the homeless of the 1950s and 60s some important differences are found. Few of the old homeless had to sleep in the streets, while today it is common. Today's homeless include many more women and an increasing number of families with children. About half of the homeless of the mid-century were often employed at least intermittently. Of today's homeless, only about 3 percent work steadily and 39 percent work intermittently. Income for today's homeless in one study was about $1,200.00 per year (Rossi, 1990). The low income level is a serious problem since few homeless receive welfare payments due to the lack of a permanent address. Given these income levels, it is no mystery why the homeless are without shelter. Their incomes simply do not let them compete effectively in the housing market, even on the lowest end. The only way most homeless people can survive at all is to use shelters for a free place to sleep, food kitchens and soup lines for free meals, free community health clinics and emergency rooms for medical care, and the clothing distribution depots for something to put on their backs. That the homeless survive at all is a tribute to the many charitable organizations that provide these and other essential commodities and services.

Like the old homeless, the new have high levels of disabilities, including chronic mental illness (33%), acute alcoholism (33%), serious criminal records (20%), and serious physical disabilities (25%). Seventy-five percent have one or more of the disabilities mentioned (Levine and Rog, 1990).

Poverty: A Common Denominator

Not every human service client is poor, nor does being poor necessarily mean that a person requires services beyond financial assistance. However, human service problems are significantly more frequent among people who live in poverty. There is a greater incidence of problems for children, such as poor health, behavior disturbances, poor school functioning, parental abuse, and mental retardation. The elderly poor have more survival problems than the middle- or upper-class aged who have pensions and caring, intact families. The poor are more likely to abuse chemical substances, such as alcohol, perhaps to escape from the harsh realities of poverty. Major psychiatric disorders are more frequently diagnosed among the poor, who are more likely to require hospitalization in public mental hospitals than are people from higher socioeconomic classes. Criminal convictions are more likely among the poor, and the victims of criminals are most often poor people.

Poverty does not cause all the human service problems. It appears to cause some, and it certainly is a contributing factor in many. Some human service problems may lead to poverty for some individuals. It is a complicated relationship. However, whatever the relationship, poverty has a severe impact on human functioning, and human service workers have to confront the problem of poverty in their clients. Its eradication is unlikely, and even if that could be accomplished, it would not solve most human service problems. However, programs that focus on the elimination of poverty for individuals or groups are within the boundaries of human services.

Many human service systems have been established with the goal of reducing poverty and its impact in the United States. These include portions of the Social Security Administration, aid to families with dependent children, state-funded public aid, and Medicare-Medicaid. Some types of social welfare programs focus on providing financial aid to poor people. Other human service programs provide assistance to people by educating or training them for paid employment and by finding them jobs. The following example from Collins (1973a) gives some idea of the benefits that such programs can provide.

> Outside the July sun gilded the boarded-up stores, the rotting tenements, and the empty lots where the sun only adds a stench to the scenery. . . .
> Inside, on the ground floor of the modern neighborhood manpower service center . . . more than a hundred black and latin teenagers

crammed themselves into every inch of space, hoping for a summer job.

The Center is a place of hope. On one wall the faces of Malcolm, Althea Gibson, Martin Luther King and other negro heroes, stare gently or fiercely out from a map of the U.S. on which they are superimposed. A handscrawled poster advertises city university reading courses tied in with the Center's program for Brownsville dropouts.

In a Peanuts cartoon someone has tacked up, you sense the empathy of the young staff, mostly Brownsvillians themselves who, through in-service university training and experience in trying to awaken stifled ambitions, have become sophisticated vocational counselors at 22 and 26. The cartoon says, "There's no heavier burden than a great potential."

By the end of the week, they would have matched more than 1,000 teenagers with jobs in parks, hospitals, city office buildings and other sites that would supply job experience and a paycheck. . . .

But the Center's main responsibility is not the summer teenagers. It is a whole community festering in poverty and running out of hope.

Like most New York ghettoes, Brownsville is filled with young people who die early inside. They were poorly taught or saw too little value in schooling to stay; they have no marketable skills; they have felt the lash of job discrimination; they have given up looking for decent jobs.

At the rate of about 70 a week, the Brownsville Manpower Service Center seeks them out (or they walk in), tests them, finds remedial programs and training slots for them, counsels them, encourages them to speak about their hopes, refers them to jobs, follows them up, gets some of them into college. And obviously cares.

One such Brownsville manpower worker is 26-year-old Carol . . . a totally-involved dynamo with a college degree whose whiteness nobody on the largely black staff seems to pay any attention to. She is Supervisor of Regular Placement and Intake and talks about her work this way.

"We try to work with them where they're at—vocationally, educationally, and psychologically. One of the hardest things is to get these kids to tell you what they really want. At first they all say they want to be auto mechanics. They're afraid to want to be something else. How can you think you want to be a doctor when you've been raised here? In counseling, some of them discover they don't want to lug garbage, and maybe they don't have to.

"Everybody on the staff has somebody special he keeps tabs on. Mine is Sheila. I think about her when I get discouraged.

"Sheila's 19 now. She first showed up about a year ago in the same blue jeans and sandals she wore for months after that. I couldn't believe anyone as tiny as she could be such a rough little kid. She was raised by an aunt after her parents died and she'd been sick a good bit of her life with epilepsy and a rare blood disease. But she was determined to get off welfare. She couldn't stand being dependent, even with a two-year-old child to raise. She used to say, 'It just mess me up.'

"She was almost too far behind to do anything with. She was reading at the third grade level, but she was a firecracker and bright. We got her into a night math and reading program and she pulled herself up several grades in no time.

"You couldn't tell her there was anything she couldn't do. . . .

"Well, she finally decided on clerical work and I arranged for her to be interviewed for our Wall Street training program. Not long before, she'd lost out on a part-time job because she showed up in blue jeans. This time I called the Department of Social Services and got her some clothing money and made her come in here before the interview to pass muster. She really looked swell. And she felt swell. She kept hugging this wooly coat she'd bought.

"I got a call later from the woman at Wall Street. Sheila had kept the coat buttoned up tight all during the testing. The lady caught her fanning herself in the hall later with the lapels of the coat and told her she didn't have to worry that she was wearing an old dress. She was being accepted.

"The woman said to me, 'Her reading's a grade low but she's got so much spunk we've got to take her.'

"Now she's almost got her high school equivalency, and she's being accepted into City University's SEEK program. I still keep tabs on her, but I think this kid is going to do all right."[3]

The Multiproblem Client

In the helping professions, we often talk about specific problems and the services that have been organized to deal with them: child abuse treatment, education, alcoholism, mental retardation, crime, delinquency, depression, suicide, and poverty.

We do that, perhaps, because it simplifies the issues and makes them easier to understand. But in another way it hampers our understanding if it oversimplifies the issues and leads to a fragmentation of service systems. The typical human service client rarely has only one problem. It is more likely that the individual has interlocking problems that must all be dealt with. For example, a typical client might be poor, depressed, unemployed, and abusing alcohol; be in an unstable marriage; have a mentally retarded child; and have another child in trouble with the law. Another client might be an ex-convict who is abusing his wife and having trouble in his job. A third might be poor, old, in ill health, and wandering the streets. Whichever service system the human service worker is employed in or whichever special population is being worked with, the clients are likely to have problems that extend to the broad boundaries of human services.

Summary

1. Over the past several decades there has been a distinct change in the helping services from an exclusionary/segregating attitude to an inclusionary/integrating attitude. The negative effects of excluding people in need from supportive social networks are being combated by means of an increased emphasis on community-based human services.

2. Children are viewed by human service workers as being particularly at risk. The types of services and service systems available for children and their families include well-child clinics, educational services, and state and community protective service agencies.

3. The elderly constitute a growing segment of the population that may reach 20 percent by the year 2000. The physical, social, and psychological losses experienced by many elderly people make them vulnerable to many problems; thus, the elderly require extensive helping services.

4. Human service programs for those who abuse legal or illegal chemical substances must address the physical, social, and psychological problems associated with this phenomenon. The major types of services available for substance abusers include methadone programs, self-help programs like AA, and therapeutic community programs.

5. Partly in response to legislation such as Public Law 94–142, community services for the mentally retarded have been growing at an astounding rate. These programs focus on maximizing the potential for self-support of mentally retarded citizens and have contributed to a decline in institutional populations.

6. The mental health system is another area in which deinstitutionalization and community services have become a major aspect of human services. The homeless mentally ill present a problem that has resulted from a lack of sufficient resources for community services. The provision of effective services for this group will require an even greater emphasis on community programs.

7. Crime is a major social problem, as illustrated by about 700,000 people held in jails and prisons. The goals of the correctional system are rehabilitation, punishment, and deterrence. Community human service programs in corrections focus on rehabilitation.

8. Poverty may be considered a common denominator for human service clients. Although not all clients are poor, those who are show a greater incidence of problems. Many human service systems address the problem of poverty directly, and all systems serve clients who are poverty-stricken.

9. The typical human service client has multiple problems that cut across systems of categorization. These needs determine the broad boundaries of human services.

Discussion Questions

1. Why is it important for human services to take a community-based approach?

2. Why are children identified as being particularly at risk for human service problems?

3. Why are there so many elderly people who are poor?

4. Why is alcohol the most abused drug?

5. What factors about life in the lower socioeconomic levels might contribute to the higher incidence of mild and moderate mental retardation at those levels?

6. The mental health system has been called the "octopus" of human services. Why might it have become involved with so many types of human problems?

7. Why does the correctional system emphasize punishment more than rehabilitation?

8. What do we mean by defining poverty as a common denominator in human service problems?

Learning Experiences

1. Attend a special education class at a local primary school.

2. Volunteer at a nursing home for the elderly.

3. Monitor your drug intake for one week. Do not forget that coffee, tea, and some soft drinks contain caffeine (a stimulant drug) and that cigarettes contain nicotine.

4. Find out if there are any community retardation facilities in your locality. Visit one if you can.

5. Find out whether there are services for homeless street people in your community.

6. Visit your local city or county jail or find out the location and size of each of your state's prisons. Do they have any human service programs?

Endnotes

1. From K. Miller, E. Fein, G. W. Howe, C. P. Gaudio, and G. V. Bishop. "Time-Limited, Goal Focused Parent Aide Services." *Social Casework* (65: 8), 1984, p. 476. Reprinted by permission of the publisher, Family Service America.

2. Reprinted by permission from *Innovations*, Vol. 4, No. 1, p. 4, published by the American Institutes for Research, P.O. Box 1113, Palo Alto, CA 94302, under a collaborative grant from the National Institute of Mental Health.

3. Collins, A. H. *The Human Services: An Introduction*. Indianapolis: The Odyssey Press, 1973. Reprinted by permission of the publisher, The Bobbs-Merrill Co., Inc., pp. 159–161.

Recommended Readings

Evans, D. P. *The Lives of Mentally Retarded People*. Boulder, Colo.: Westview Press, 1983.

Harrington, M. *The Other America*. New York: Macmillan, 1962.

Kozol, J. *Rachel and Her Children: Homeless Families in America*. New York: Crown, 1987.

Lamb, H. R. *The Homeless Mentally Ill*. Washington, D.C.: American Psychiatric Association, 1984.

MacLeod, C. *Horatio Alger, Farewell*. New York: Seaview Books, 1980.

Roberts, A. (ed.). *Social Work in Juvenile and Criminal Justice Settings*. Springfield, Ill.: Charles C. Thomas, 1983.

7

Medical/Psychiatric Approaches and the Person in Need

- Why is a basic understanding of the medical/psychiatric model important?
- What are the primary assumptions of the medical/psychiatric model?
- What are some of the common treatment strategies of the medical/psychiatric model?

Medical and psychiatric problems are among the most frequent and costly problems impacting on people in need. Approximately $400 billion is spent on health care each year in the United States (Edelstein and Michelson, 1986). Thus, it is not surprising that the medical/psychiatric model is one of the most common models for conceptualizing human problems and for dealing with people in need.

There are actually at least two medically oriented models. The strict medical approach deals with people who have problems related directly to physical health. When one has a health problem, such as appendicitis or a broken leg, one seeks help from physicians and other caregivers who specialize in this approach. The other approach, the psychiatric approach, consists of the application of a medically oriented view to a wider spectrum of behavioral, emotional, or cognitive problems. It is this approach that has had the greatest impact on human services. Many professionals from social work, psychology, and other human service fields, in addition to physicians and nurses, function in accordance with medical/psychiatric assumptions.

Returning for a moment to the strict medical approach, it is important to recognize that even acute or chronic medical disorders have human service implications. Physical illnesses (especially when they are severe or devastating) can result in psychological, social, and economic problems for the individual; and these problems are usually not addressed by the purely medical specialists who treat the physical aspects of the disorder. The nonphysical problems associated with physical diseases often fall within the boundaries of the human service field and are dealt with by human service workers.

AIDS: Physical Disease—
Human Service Issue

A modern-day disease that illustrates these issues is Acquired Immune Deficiency Syndrome, or AIDS. AIDS is a viral disease affecting the immune system of the body. The immune system is our defense against diseases, and if it is impaired it allows otherwise controllable infections to invade the body and cause additional disease. At the current time there is no effective treatment for AIDS. It leads to death due to massive infection such as pneumonia, or due to tuberculosis or diseases like cancer.

The first cases of AIDS were reported in this country in 1981, and it has since become a major public health issue. To date, over 125,000 U.S. citizens have developed AIDS and about 78,000 have died (Gavzer, 1990). Many more (up to one million according to the Center for Disease Control) have tested positive for the HIV virus but have not yet developed symptoms. By the end of 1991 an estimated 270,000 cases of AIDS will have occurred, and 179,000 deaths are expected (Koop, 1986).

The AIDS epidemic, while strictly speaking it is a medical crisis, has an indirect bearing on human services in two ways. First, AIDS is most common among homosexuals and intravenous drug users, although heterosexuals and non–drug users can also develop the disorder. AIDS spreads because of *behaviors* that result in the sharing of bodily fluids; for example, homosexual intercourse and the use of contaminated needles by drug users. Thus, in order to slow down the spread of AIDS, people must change their behavior. Both homosexuals and IV drug users will have to be much more cautious in their behavior in order to avoid infection. Human service workers will contribute in this area by providing education on prevention for these special groups. The second area in which AIDS impacts on human service workers is in the later stages of this disease. AIDS patients and their families and friends require human service support by human service counselors and volunteers (Lopez and Getzel, 1987; Wiener, 1986). the types of services needed by persons with AIDS include (Leukefeld, 1989):

- *Housing:* The stigma of AIDS and people's fear of becoming infected makes it difficult for AIDS infected people to find adequate affordable housing.
- *Income maintenance:* The loss of income from being unable to work and the costs of treatment are financially devastating.

- *Long term and hospice care:* People with AIDS often have no one to care for them as they become more and more disabled.
- *Child care:* Mothers with AIDS or mothers of children with AIDS often need assistance in care for their children either when the mother is hospitalized or disabled or when the child is disabled at home.
- *Legal assistance:* Help will be needed at a minimum in preparing for financial matters after death.
- *Medical care:* As a debilitating, fatal disease, AIDS requires major medical interventions.
- *Counseling and mental health services:* People with AIDS need assistance in dealing with their debilitation and impending death. Some will develop AIDS dementia, an organic brain disorder due to destruction of brain tissue and may need residential care for that problem.

As the numbers of persons with AIDS increases, more and more human service workers will find themselves working with AIDS victims (O'Hara and Stangler, 1986). Human service workers who come in contact with AIDS infected clients will have to deal with their own fears and anxieties about the risk of becoming infected themselves (Wallack, 1989). Even among physicians and nurses who could be expected to be well informed, fear that they would become infected was present in about 25 percent of those surveyed. In fact, very few health care professionals have developed AIDS due to treating AIDS infected patients. Human service workers will have to become better educated in regard to this disease in order to understand the plight of AIDS infected people, to help their clients who are at risk for AIDS, or who have already been infected, and to understand their own feelings and fears about the risk of becoming infected and the relationship of those fears and feelings to the factual risks.

Facts about AIDS

1. There is no known risk of non–sexually related infection from casual contact.
2. Health workers who are exposed to AIDS patients' blood, stool, and other bodily fluids have not become infected unless they received a needle stick from a contaminated needle. There were only forty such cases by 1991.
3. Risks of infection increase if
   a. You are homosexual and do not know if your partners are free of infection.
   b. You are heterosexual and you have multiple sexual partners whose history you do not know.
   c. You have even microscopic tears in the tissues of the penis, vagina, or rectum and engage in sexual behavior with a partner who is infected and contacts those areas.
   d. You frequent female or male prostitutes.
   e. You share intravenous drug needles with others.

4. Risks are minimized if
   a. You have had a monogamous sexual relationship for five years.
   b. A rubber (condom) is used during intercourse.
   c. Intravenous injections are done *only* with sterile needles.
5. There is no risk
   a. In casual nonsexual social contact with an AIDS infected person.
   b. In 94,449 blood transfusions out of 100,000.
   c. In caring for a person who has AIDS.
   d. In having contact with one of the few children who have AIDS who are in school settings.

In contrast to the medical approach, the psychiatric approach is likely to enter into human service work on a frequent basis. Many of the people in need of human service help will have had and will continue to have contact with traditional professionals or service systems that are oriented to the psychiatric approach. It is only in the past twenty to twenty-five years that a growing criticism of this approach has developed. In spite of this criticism, the model remains extremely widespread. In fact, even the language of some human service systems reflects the medical/psychiatric model; for example, problem behavior may be called *pathology,* may be grouped according to *symptoms,* may be classified in a process called *diagnosis,* and may be changed in a process called *therapy* (Maher, 1966).

The widespread acceptance of the psychiatric model makes it critical for human service workers to have a basic understanding of the model's assumptions, philosophy, concepts, and approaches to persons in need. Whatever the setting in which human service workers are employed—schools, prisons, mental retardation facilities, mental hospitals, neighborhood service centers, public aid departments, or community mental health centers—they will encounter and work alongside persons who are strongly influenced by the medical/psychiatric model. The human service worker must be able to assess adequately the pros and cons of this particular approach to persons in need.

One of many specific examples of the involvement of the medical/psychiatric model approach in nonmedical settings occurred in my experience several years ago. In a large midwestern city, a state employment office frequently had difficulty maintaining its clients in jobs. Many of the clients had difficulty dealing with job interviews, and once placed, many were quickly fired or quit. The clients often responded to these events with emotional reactions such as anxiety, anger, sadness, and guilt. The frequent response of the employment counselor was to refer them to a local mental health clinic to straighten out their "problems." Once at the clinic, the clients were most often seen quickly by a physician whose prime response was to prescribe a tranquilizing drug so that they would not "get upset" on the job. In effect, a medical/psychiatric model approach became a primary tool of the employment counselor.

The Basics of the
Medical/Psychiatric Model

We have seen how both medical problems and a psychiatrically oriented approach impact the human services worker. Let's consider the *medical/psychiatric model* as a unified mindset. The primary assumption of the medical/psychiatric model is, of course, that abnormal behavior is a function of a disease process; that is, people behave abnormally or deviantly because of some disturbance of their body which then affects their psychological processes and behavior. The physical disturbance is usually considered the result of one or more of the following problems: genetic inheritance, biochemical metabolism, or brain tissue damage. While little hard evidence exists for the application of this model to the complete range of human behavior problems, there are many disorders that have documentable physical causes and fit the disease model.

The best examples of disorders that fit the medical/psychiatric model are inherited disorders such as Huntington's chorea and many forms of mental retardation, and the disorders of aging, such as Alzheimer's disease or arteriosclerosis (hardening of the arteries), which lead to changes in behavior that are often called senility. Some other personality changes have been demonstrated to be a function of physical destruction of brain tissue caused by tumors, high fever, syphilis, or a severe head injury, as illustrated in the example of Bob.

■ ■ At age twenty-three, Bob was involved in an auto accident that resulted in the destruction of one-fourth of his frontal lobes, damage to the motor cortex, and a two-month coma. Before the accident, he had a factory job and was engaged to be married. After his primary recovery, he received intensive physical therapy for approximately six months at a rehabilitation hospital. However, Bob's brain damage resulted in major deficits in speech, coordination, and ambulation. Over the next ten years Bob had numerous hospitalizations in state mental hospitals, usually with a diagnosis of "organic brain syndrome without psychosis." Between hospitalizations, Bob lived in various nursing homes. His admissions to the mental hospitals were precipitated by "combative" behavior. Nursing home and hospital staff members assumed Bob's combative behavior to be due to his impulsivity and a "lack of control of rage" resulting from his organic damage.

Bob's problem was clearly physical in origin—actual damage to a part of his brain—and was appropriately treated from a medical perspective. Yet in the end Bob was also helped by a human service approach that did not use the medical perspective.

When seen, Bob was a patient on a medical unit because of his physical infirmity. He spent all his time in a wheelchair; his speech was difficult to understand; and his motor movements were relatively uncoordinated. His "extremely combative" problem behavior consisted of knocking down infirm patients and trying to punch staff. This behavior was subsequent to his various demands for constant attention not being met.

A human service worker instituted a simple behavioral program with Bob. Bob was informed that knocking down other patients and punching staff would result in the loss of privileges. He was also told that the absence of such behavior would result in his receiving a cigarette every thirty minutes, and that one full day of no violence would be reinforced by a thirty-minute meeting with a human service worker (who happened to be a young attractive female). When the program began, Bob's average frequency of violence was between five and six incidents daily. Within five weeks, no incidents were occurring.

After the aggression disappeared, the human service worker began a similar reinforcement program to encourage Bob to take physical therapy, to practice rehabilitation exercises, and later to practice walking. In four months, Bob was able to walk with crutches, something he had not done for several years. His heightened ability to control his temper, and his physical improvement, allowed him, at the age of thirty-six, to leave the state hospital to live in a long-term community care facility, where he made a good adjustment.

For many years, Bob's use of a wheelchair and his combative behavior were presumed to be due to irreversible organic brain damage. Some of his problems, such as his speech deficit and some motor uncoordination, were certainly due to such damage, and continued to be a problem even after contact with the human service worker. However, his aggressive behavior and inability to walk responded to a specific human services approach: behavioral treatment. Certainly, organic disorders such as Bob's original brain damage are appropriately the province of the medical/psychiatric model, but many human service workers are concerned with the model's wider application to problem behaviors, since little evidence exists that they do have a physical cause.

The argument that disturbed behavior has a physical cause has often been based on the development of physical techniques that change the behavior in question, rather than on more basic proof that an underlying physical cause exists. In fact, in almost all cases of medical treatment for behavioral or psychological disorder, there exists little proven explanation of why the treatment works. As we shall see, this is the case in the drug therapies, electroconvulsive therapy, and lithium therapy.

The basic assumptions of the medical/psychiatric model have been criticized by a variety of authors (Bloom, 1965; Buss, 1966; Mehr, 1983; Sarason and Ganzer, 1968) and can be summarized as follows:

1. Behavioral and psychological disturbances are diseases that have a consistent etiology, cause, and outcome.
2. The diseases have an organic basis.
3. The underlying disease is manifested in symptoms, and changing the symptoms does not cure the disease.
4. Responsibility for the disease symptoms (behavior) is attributed to the disease, not to the person who has it.

5. Cure is a complex process that is a function of treatment administered by highly trained professionals who have medical training or by people who are supervised by physicians.

If eventually these assumptions turn out to be fact (which I consider very unlikely), in the future treatment will ultimately be medical in nature and may include techniques such as eugenics (sterilization of persons carrying "bad" genes), chemotherapy (administration of behavior-changing drugs), surgery (removal of damaged brain tissue), or electroconvulsive therapy (modification of brain function through the application of electrical current).

However, in no way does the evidence support such a dogmatic acceptance of the medical/psychiatric model as is common today. It is obvious, though, that a number of "medical" treatments exist that are very effective in changing behavior. Hence, human service workers must be pragmatists; that is, while they may be critical of the medical/psychiatric model, they cannot afford to reject treatments that seem to work.

Common Treatment Strategies
of the Medical/Psychiatric Model

It is interesting to note that many of the major psychiatric treatment strategies developed not as a result of intensive research efforts but as a result of accidental observations. Insulin shock therapy (a common convulsive therapy before electroconvulsive treatment), for example, was discovered by Dr. H. Steck in Switzerland when he noticed that the insulin he had administered to his patients to increase their appetite had a positive effect on their mental condition. This discovery was followed by the work of Dr. Manfred Sakel, who in 1938 accidentally induced a coma in a psychiatric patient whom he was treating with insulin and then noticed that after recovery from the coma, the patient's psychotic symptoms were lessened. Following the publication of Sakel's results, the treatment became common throughout Europe and the United States (Valenstein, 1973).

The later convulsive treatments of metrazol shock and electroshock therapy were based on the mistaken notion that schizophrenia and epilepsy are biologically antagonistic, meaning they cannot both exist in the same person. More recent evidence refutes this idea. It was this belief that led Ugo Cerletti, an Italian psychiatrist, to begin inducing convulsions in human beings using electric current. More recently, in the 1950s, the development of modern chemotherapy was a function of physicians noting the general quieting effect of a drug, reserpine, on patients to whom it was given for high blood pressure.

Although by and large discovered accidentally, the medical treatments of disturbed behavior remain extremely common and well accepted. Great efforts are being expended in research to determine how and why these processes work. Many questions still remain unanswered, however, and the best we can say is that some of the treatments work, and work well, on certain types of disorders. The medical/psychiatric model treatments with which the human service worker should be familiar are electroconvulsive therapy and chemotherapy (because of their frequent usage) and psychosurgery (because of its reappearance and the criticisms that are being leveled at it).

Electroconvulsive therapy

Electroconvulsive therapy (ECT), sometimes known as electroshock therapy, is a relatively uncommon psychiatric treatment today. Only about 60,000 to 100,000 people receive ECT per year, a sharp decline from twenty to thirty years ago, when about twice as many people received the treatment each year (Sackeim, 1985). ECT is usually given in an inpatient setting but sometimes is administered on an outpatient basis. In its early history, it was a very dangerous treatment since the convulsions it generated were of such proportions that subjects sometimes broke or dislocated arms, legs, and backs while undergoing treatment. Today, however, the seizures are softened by the injection of muscle relaxant drugs, and the dangers have been minimized.

The subject lies prone, electrodes are placed on the temples, and a 0.1- to 0.5-second dose of 70 to 130 volts is given. The subject immediately becomes unconscious. With the use of a muscle relaxant, the seizure is only slightly noticeable as tremors in the hands and feet. After the treatment, there is a period of confusion on the part of the subjects, and they may lose memory of events immediately preceding the treatment. Treatments are usually given several times a week until the problem behaviors lessen. Maximum benefit is usually obtained in five to ten treatments during a period of two to three weeks.

Electroconvulsive therapy is reported to work particularly well in people who are depressed when there is no evidence of external precipitants for depression, such as loss of a job or divorce. It is particularly well regarded by many physicians in the treatment of depressions occurring during middle age and in depressions that are part of the manic-depressive syndrome. Successful use of ECT for a recurrent depression is illustrated in the case of April.

■ ■ April, a forty-two-year-old homemaker and mother of four children, had a history of repeated depressions since the age of twenty-eight. She had been in psychotherapy for years and had also been treated with antidepressant medication with little or no benefit. Her depression finally became so severe that April required inpatient treatment.

April described her depressive experience as being "like living in a black hole." Her appetite had disappeared and she had lost twenty-five pounds; her sleep was disturbed; she could no longer concentrate on her housework or reading. April was obsessed with the idea that she had ruined the lives of her family, was racked with guilt, and had threatened suicide. After seven treatments of ECT, April recovered completely from her depression, returned home, and was linked with a community mental health center for follow-up by a psychiatrist and a human services case manager.

A great deal of negative feeling toward electroconvulsive therapy exists among human service workers, owing in part to the abuses of the treatment in the early and mid-1960s. Since alternatives were lacking until then, electroconvulsive therapy often was used routinely on a broad variety of disorders with very poor results. Today, the use of ECT is very closely monitored and reviewed in order to prevent the kinds of abuses that were more common thirty years ago (Sakauye, 1986). Unfortunately, because of the common misperception about the dangers of ECT, the pendulum may now have swung too far, and people who could benefit from this treatment may now find it hard to obtain.

The chemotherapies

The most pervasive of the medical/psychiatric model approaches to people in need is the use of chemotherapy (drug treatment), which includes the minor and major tranquilizers, the antidepressants, and lithium carbonate therapy. Although a number of chemotherapies have been used for a very long time, such as the barbiturates and bromides, the widespread use of mind-affecting chemicals dates mainly from the 1950s and the introduction of new minor and major tranquilizers and antidepressants. These new drugs have the effect of modifying affective (emotional) states without massively decreasing cognitive functioning. Several of the more widely used minor and major tranquilizers and antidepressants are given with their generic (chemical family) and trade names in Table 7-1.

Table 7-1 *Major chemotherapeutic drugs.*

Category	Generic name	Trade name
Tranquilizers		
Minor	Meprobamate	Miltown, Equanil
	Diazepam	Valium
	Chlordiazepoxide	Librium
Major	Chlorpromazine	Thorazine
	Thioridazine	Mellaril
	Trifluoperazine	Stelazine
Antidepressants		
MAO inhibitors	Phenelzine	Nardil
	Tranylcypromine	Parnate
Tricyclics	Imipramine	Tofranil
	Doxepin	Sinequan
	Amitriptyline	Elavil

Minor tranquilizers

The minor tranquilizers are frequently used to reduce anxiety that is less than disabling. Physicians commonly prescribe these drugs for individuals who are tense, anxious, or mildly depressed. The first of the tranquilizers to be discovered and patented was meprobamate (1952). Many others quickly followed, and their use expanded to such an extent that today one out of seven Americans is estimated to be using such drugs frequently. The evidence indicates that these drugs are quite effective in reducing the obvious symptoms of anxiety. However, their widespread use has been criticized as merely covering symptoms and not helping the person deal with problems constructively.

Major tranquilizers

The major tranquilizers, also known as the antipsychotics, have been developed from a class of drugs known as the phenothiazines. The first of these drugs, chlorpromazine (sold under the brand name of Thorazine), was introduced in Europe in 1950. The drug was first introduced in the United States in the mid-1950s and quickly became a primary medical/psychiatric model treatment in private and public mental hospitals. Later it was used with discharged hospital patients on an outpatient basis and with the patients of psychiatrists in private settings.

The use of the antipsychotic drugs is considered by the National Institute of Mental Health (1975) to be one of the two major advances in the treatment of disturbed persons in the last twenty-five years. The drugs in effect mask or cover the stranger patterns of behavior of seriously disturbed persons. Target behaviors that are likely to improve while the drug is being used include combativeness; tension; hyperactivity; hostility; negativism; hallucinations; poor sleep, dress, and appetite; acute delusions; and sociability. Behaviors that are less likely to improve include lack of insight, poor judgment, poor memory, and lack of orientation.

Much of the credit (or blame) for the tremendous decrease in mental hospital populations since the mid-1950s must go to the antipsychotic drugs. The reduction in severely disturbed behaviors has encouraged many helping professionals to accept the notion that many hospitalized patients could live in the community. However, in order to maintain the behavioral changes resulting from the use of these drugs, patients must continue to take them on a long-term maintenance basis. Unfortunately, many people released from hospitals as a result of the positive effects of the drugs tend not to continue to take them. This results in the strange behavior reoccurring shortly after their return to the community, which often requires rehospitalization. In this sense, the drugs are only a temporary measure, although apparently a valuable one. The antipsychotic drugs do *not* cure the major behavior disorders, nor are they usually able to turn a poorly adjusted, severely disturbed person into a well-adjusted, well-functioning community member.

Table 7-2 presents some of the more likely side effects of the minor and major tranquilizers and antidepressants. Unfortunately, many of the long-

Table 7-2 *Some side effects of psychoactive drugs.*

Tranquilizers		Antidepressants	
Minor	Major	Tricyclics	Monoamine oxidase inhibitors
Drowsiness	Drowsiness	Dry mouth	Constipation
Dependence	Dryness of	Constipation	Gastrointestinal
Slurred speech	mouth	Dizziness	disturbance
Nausea and	Blurred near	Weight gain	Blurred vision
vomiting	vision	Headache	Dizziness
Tachycardia	Constipation	Insomnia	Weight gain
Confusion	Nausea and	Gastrointestinal	Sexual disturbance
Depression	vomiting	disturbance	Drowsiness
	Weight gain	Agitation	Insomnia
	Impotence	Parkinsonism	Agitation
	Menstrual	reaction	Confusion
	irregularity		
	Glaucoma		
	Allergic reaction		
	Hyperglycemia		
	Lowered seizure		
	threshold		
	Parkinsonism		
	reaction		
	Tardive dyskinesia		

term effects of the drugs are not yet known, but obviously some of the side effects listed are very severe. In particular, with the major tranquilizers, a disorder called tardive dyskinesia sometimes occurs in persons who take the drugs over long periods of time. This disorder, believed to be usually irreversible, consists of repetitive involuntary facial movements such as smacking and licking of the lips, sucking movements, chewing movements, rolling and protrusion of the tongue, blinking, grotesque grimaces, spastic facial distortions, and body movements such as jerking of the fingers, ankles, and toes and contractions of neck and back muscles. Other major side effects resulting from long-term use of the major tranquilizers may be discovered in the near future. We now have people who have been taking the drugs continuously since their introduction more than thirty years ago, and who run a very high risk of dangerous long-term side effects.

Antidepressants

Both classes of antidepressants—tricyclics and monoamine oxidase inhibitors (MAO inhibitors)—were developed for use on other disorders, but when their mood-elevating properties were noted, they began to be used on individuals experiencing depression. The tricyclics seem to be quite effective in combat-

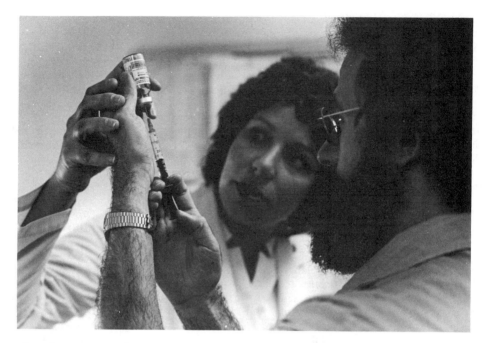

A major treatment approach of the medical model involves medication.

ing endogenous depressions, that is, depressions for which there is no observable external stimulus (Lapolla and Jones, 1970). Less evidence exists for the general utility of the MAO inhibitors, which seem to work on a lower percentage of people. Since they are tricky to use safely—requiring special dietary adjustments—their popularity is limited.

Lithium carbonate therapy

Although its use was reported as early as 1949 by Dr. J. F. Cade in Australia, lithium has only recently become a relatively available treatment. Before the late 1960s, this highly dangerous drug could not be monitored effectively in the subject's blood, and since the dangerously poisonous levels are close to the required therapeutic levels, many subjects experienced severe side effects. It was not until 1970 that lithium was available for general prescription use in the United States (Kornetsky, 1976). However, since the blood levels of lithium can now be monitored quite accurately, the treatment has become more common.

The use of lithium seems particularly worthwhile in people who behave in a manner that has been called manic-depressive, or manic type. Manic individuals are characterized by excessive elation, irritability, talkativeness, accelerated speech and motor activity, and rapidly changing ideas. They often become caught up in wild ventures, squander their resources, alienate family and friends, and often lose their jobs. When this disorder is diagnosed by a physician who uses lithium, he or she will prescribe approximately 1,800 milligrams of lithium carbonate per day until the subject's blood lithium reaches the required therapeutic level. Once the therapeutic level is reached, approximately 80 percent of the subjects show a distinct improvement. They are no longer highly elated or irritable, are calmer and more concerned with day-to-day functioning, and no longer believe they can do everything they desire. Once the behavior is modified, the subject is usually kept on a maintenance dosage to prevent a recurrence.

To date, little good evidence exists to prove exactly why lithium has this effect. The most that can be said is that it does alter brain chemistry in some manner that affects people who behave in a manic pattern. Unfortunately, the use of lithium is spreading rapidly in the treatment of other disorders in spite of the lack of evidence for its usefulness other than in manic behavior. It has already been used with poor results in the treatment of people who have schizophrenia, emotionally unstable personalities, alcoholism, or premenstrual tension and with hyperactive children.

Common usages of drug therapy

Although only the minor and major tranquilizers and antidepressants have been dealt with specifically, many additional types of chemotherapy exist, such as the use of antabuse with alcoholics, methadone for heroin withdrawal, and Ritalin for hyperactive children. Mental health, of course, is the system in which chemotherapy is most common. It has been estimated that over 85 percent of inpatients in mental hospitals are on one or more of the psychoactive medications. Also, both psychiatrists and general practitioners routinely prescribe the minor tranquilizers. In both adult and juvenile corrections systems, psychoactive drugs frequently are given to troublemakers. The drugs are less frequently used in mental retardation facilities but still are common. Even in child care and primary education facilities, the use of drugs, particularly Ritalin, is common in controlling disorderly or hyperactive behavior. It has been estimated that 500,000 to 1 million children are taking medications like Ritalin (Bruck, 1976).

Psychosurgery

Although relatively infrequent today, psychosurgery was popularized as a treatment in the 1940s and 1950s, when 40,000 to 50,000 lobotomies are estimated to have been performed in the United States. With the advent of chemotherapy, psychosurgery became much less popular, and increasing criticism of the technique led to a severe reduction in the number of such operations. However, in the early 1970s there was a renewed interest in the technique, and an increasing number of the operations have been performed on a variety of subjects, accompanied by a great deal of new criticism (Breggin, 1973). The evidence supporting psychosurgery is somewhat questionable, but there is relative agreement on the possibility of severe side effects.

Basically, psychosurgery consists of cutting or destroying the nerve fibers connecting various parts of the brain. It has most often been used as a manner of controlling behavior in extremely violent, aggressive, and dangerous persons with whom nothing else has worked. Unfortunately, once the operation is performed it is irreversible, and a number of side effects frequently appear, including lethargy, childlike behavior, poor judgment, irresponsibility, and vulgar, profane behavior.

Much criticism has centered on the use of psychosurgery on persons without their informed consent, most notably in the corrections system. As a result of this criticism, a moratorium on psychosurgery was instituted in 1974 by the Department of Health, Education and Welfare. However, the moratorium was lifted two years later, in September 1976, after a report from a federal commission that concluded that "the 'common belief' that all forms of psychosurgery are unsafe and ineffective 'has been rebutted. A large proportion of patients—about half' . . . found relief for their 'disabling emotional disorders' "(Cohn, 1976).

Many human service workers feel that psychosurgery embodies the major flaws of the medical/psychiatric model. These flaws include the assumptions (1) that a deviant behavior has an organic cause (a malfunction of brain tissue), (2) that a medical treatment can be developed (in this case, surgery), and (3) that the disease can be cured. What may be particularly of concern to human service workers is the apparent assumption that the end (socially acceptable behavior) justifies the means (destruction of brain tissue).

Prospects for the Medical/Psychiatric Model

As has been noted, the medical/psychiatric model remains a major force in dealing with people in need. Most research on human problems occurs in this model since relatively ample funds are available to its adherents. The drug industry is a multibillion dollar concern, and the American Medical Association is the most powerful of the professional organizations. Many medical/psychiatric model theories have been advanced to account for human behavior, and we can expect many more to be developed. However, the theories *remain* theories. It is not likely that conclusive proofs of these theories will be found in our lifetime, owing to the complexity of human behavior.

Summary

1. There are two medically oriented models. The medical approach deals with the physical ailments to which all people are subject. The medical/psychiatric model deals with behavioral, emotional, and cognitive problems that fall in the area of human services.

2. Medical/psychiatric approaches have been used in systems as diverse as corrections, child care, early education, mental health, public welfare, and mental retardation.

3. The primary assumptions of the medical/psychiatric model are as follows:
   a. Disturbed people suffer from a disease.
   b. Diseases have an organic basis.
   c. A disease is manifested in symptoms, and changing the symptoms does not cure the disease.
   d. Responsibility for behavior is attributed to the disease, not to the person.
   e. Cure is a complex function of treatment delivered by highly trained professionals.

4. While many human service workers strongly question these medical/psychiatric assumptions, the pragmatic human service worker cannot dogmatically reject medical/psychiatric treatment. Human service workers must assess these treatments objectively and maintain an awareness of their limitations and benefits, because they often must work with followers of the medical/psychiatric model in many settings.

5. The common treatments of the medical/psychiatric model include electroconvulsive therapy and chemotherapy. Electroconvulsive therapy is an effective treatment of severe depression. However, severe side effects that were common in the early years of its use, and the abuse of the treatment in later years, have elicited strong criticism of the technique.

6. The chemotherapies include the minor and major tranquilizers (antipsychotic drugs) and lithium carbonate. Each of the chemotherapies has its effective uses. But one significant problem with them is that they may produce unpleasant or even dangerous side effects.

7. Psychosurgery consists of the severing of neural connections in the brain. Previously used to control unwanted behavior such as aggression, the technique is infrequently used today and is generally viewed as an unacceptable approach by most human service workers.

8. The medical/psychiatric model is a major force in dealing with people in need. It is, however, unlikely that the medical/psychiatric model theories will be fully confirmed in our lifetime.

Discussion Questions

1. Why does the human service worker need to understand the medical/psychiatric model?

2. What are the basic assumptions of the medical/psychiatric model?

3. What might account for the negative feelings that many human service workers have toward the medical/psychiatric model?

Learning Experiences

1. Watch a "doctor" program on television. What does it communicate about the medical/psychiatric model?

2. Ask your acquaintances their opinions about their doctors or about doctors in general.

3. Find out the degree of involvement of physicians in local human service programs in your community.

Recommended Readings

Gorenstein, E. E. "Debating Mental Illness—Implications for Science, Medicine, and Social Policy." *American Psychologist*, 39 (1984).

Sarason, I., and Ganzer, V. "Concerning the Medical Model." *American Psychologist* 23 (1968).

8

Behavioral Approaches and the Person in Need

- What are the classical and operant learning models of human behavior?
- How may disordered behavior be learned?
- What is systematic desensitization?
- How does a token economy help change behavior?
- What is cognitive behavioral therapy?

The behavioral therapies are among the most recent approaches to people in need in that their use has increased greatly since the 1960s. As we saw in Chapter 2, their historical development can be traced as far back as Ivan Sechenov, the Russian physiologist, in the mid- to late 1800s, and Ivan Pavlov's classic experiments on conditioning around the turn of the century. However, major application of its concepts began in the 1950s through the work of Joseph Wolpe and Arnold Lazarus in South Africa, Hans Eysenck in England, and B. F. Skinner and Julian Rotter in the United States (Goldfried and Davison, 1976). For the purpose of introduction, certain common themes can be identified which are hallmarks of behaviorally oriented approaches, and which help to distinguish these approaches from other theoretical orientations.

1. The emphasis is on measurable current behavior and its impact on the environment, or on the impact of environment on the measurable behavior. Behavior is defined as physical actions, current emotions, or specific cognitions (thoughts).

2. Specific behaviors, emotions, or cognitions, once they are identified, may be modified by concrete actions of the person or others that can be clearly or objectively defined.

3. It is assumed that changed behaviors, emotions, or cognitions will affect the client's adjustment; that is, the removal of socially maladaptive or distressing personal behaviors, or the acquisition of positive social responses, will lead to reinforcing feedback from the person's interpersonal environment or to self-reinforcement by the person.

The behavioral approaches are based primarily on theories of learned behavior. The behaviorist takes the position that all (or nearly all) of people's thoughts, feelings, and behaviors are a result of learning and that established principles determine how the learning process works. Differences between human beings are seen as the result of the individuals' having learned different behavioral, emotional, or cognitive responses to their environments.

Four Models of Learned Behavior

Although many detailed theories exist on how learning takes place, the following generalizations help provide an overview of the process. Behavior can be considered to be either patterned or random. Most human behavior, however, seems to be patterned or goal-directed; that is, it represents a purposeful attempt to obtain something. The goal may be to satisfy physiological needs, such as food, water, and air, or to satisfy secondary needs that have been learned, such as needs for social approval, material objects, or attention. Disagreement exists between theorists as to whether some needs are instinctive (inborn), and, if so, which ones.

Many models have contributed to the development of behavioral approaches but four major conceptualizations can be used as examples (Black and Bruce, 1989). They are the classical, operant, social, and cognitive models. In the *classical model* shown in Figure 8-1, a stimulus (s) causes an unconditioned response (UCR). For example, food shown to a hungry animal causes the subject to salivate. A second stimulus, such as a bell, light, or gesture, is then paired with the original stimulus through closeness in time or distance, and with great frequency. It then becomes associated with the original stimulus (food) and with the unconditioned response (salivation), to the extent that the existence of the second stimulus (bell) elicits the response (salivation), which is then considered to be *conditioned*. One ends up with what appears to be a very strange situation in which the ringing of a bell causes salivation.

The *operant model* developed by B. F. Skinner is concerned more with the consequences of a response than with the initial stimulus. It takes the approach that all behaviors have consequences on the environment and that the consequences reinforce the response (make it more likely to occur), maintain it, or extinguish it (make it less likely to occur). The consequences of a response may appear to be unpleasant from a commonsense viewpoint but still may reinforce behavior. For example, most parents react very negatively

Figure 8-1 *The classical conditioning model.*

Original Situation

S₁ ──────────────→ R₁
(Food)   (Salivation)

Paired Stimulus Situation

S₁ + S₂ ──────────────→ R₁
(Food) (Bell)   (Salivation)

Post-Conditioning Situation

S₂ ──────────────→ R₂
(Bell)   (Salivation)

S₁ = Unconditioned stimulus (UCS)
S₂ = Conditioned stimulus (CS)
R₁ = Unconditioned response (UCR)
R₂ = Conditioned response (CR)

to a child's temper tantrums, but frequently the negative reactions do nothing in terms of stopping the child's tantrums. On the other hand, if temper tantrums are ignored, they often decrease in frequency. To explain this, one could suggest that the temper tantrum response is reinforced by the attention of the parent given to the child even if the attention is punitive. This might be obvious in a situation in which the parents usually ignore the children when they are quiet and occupied in a positive activity. In effect, children may learn that a major way to obtain meaningful extended responses from the parent is to create a scene.

The operant behaviorist, however, is less concerned with determining the causality of behavior than with determining how to change its consequences in order to increase or decrease its frequency. Along this line, much of the interest of Skinnerians has been in the area of reinforcement schedules—determining whether behavior should be reinforced every time it occurs, every second or third time, or on a number of other variable schedules. The main interest is, of course, to determine the most potent approach to changing learned behavior. For a beginning understanding of the behavioral approach to persons in need, several additional concepts must be considered (see Table 8-1). *Generalization* is the tendency to perform a response in a new setting because of the setting's similarity to the one in which the response was learned, with the likelihood of the response's occurring being proportional to the degree of similarity between settings. For example, a child is bitten by an angry dog. For quite some time after the experience, the child probably will generalize a fear of all dogs, even those which behave in a friendly manner.

Table 8-1 *Behavioral concepts.*

| Concept | Process | | |
	Event or behavior	Consequence	Outcome
Generalization	Child bitten by dog	Emotional reaction	Fear generalizes to all dogs
Discrimination	General fear of dogs	Encounters friendly dogs (wagging tail, etc.)	Fears snarling dogs or does not fear friendly dogs (discriminates)
Punishment	Child swears at parent	Parent slaps	Swearing decreases
Positive reinforcement	Temper tantrum	Parental attention	More tantrums
Withdrawal of positive reinforcement	Child swears at parent	Parent takes toys away	Swearing decreases
Negative reinforcement	Child picks up clothes	Parent doesn't nag	Picking up clothing occurs more often
Extinction	Temper tantrum	Parent ignores tantrum	Tantrums decrease

Discrimination is the learning of different responses to two or more similar but distinct stimuli because of the different consequences associated with each one. Using the previous example, the child bitten by an aggressive dog first may become frightened by dogs in general. The child may then learn to discriminate between dogs that appear menacing (growling, barking, baring teeth) and those that appear friendly (wagging the tail, etc.). The child will fear the first and approach the second.

Punishment is the presentation of an unpleasant or aversive stimulus in order to decrease a particular behavior. Just as the absence of reinforcement (reward) leads to a decrease in a behavior (extinction), the occurrence of an unpleasant stimulus leads to the suppression of a behavior. For example, a child who slaps a parent is likely to receive an immediate unpleasant response (a spanking), which will, other things being equal, reduce the likelihood of that behavior's recurring.

Positive reinforcement is any consequence of a behavior which increases the probability of a behavior occurring more frequently. As noted previously, a positive reinforcer may appear to be unpleasant, although most positive reinforcers are pleasant events or things, such as money, candy, praise, status, attention, and so on.

Withdrawal of positive reinforcement occurs when a behavior occurs and the usual reinforcement is not offered or is taken away. This is a common strategy in everyday life. A child misbehaves, and he or she is not allowed the reinforcement of watching television.

Negative reinforcement is a somewhat tricky concept. It means that the probability of a behavior is increased by the termination of an aversive (unpleasant or painful) stimulus. For example, a child constantly drops his or her clothing on the floor wherever the clothes are taken off. The parent continually nags the child about this behavior (nagging is the aversive stimulus). Finally, the child does pick up some articles of clothing and puts them in their proper place, and the parent doesn't nag (termination of the aversive stimulus). The termination of the aversive stimulus is a reinforcer since it increases the probability of a behavior (picking up clothing), but it is negative (something is subtracted; i.e., the aversive stimulus). Therefore, it is called "negative" reinforcement.

Extinction is the absence of reinforcement. If a behavior is being reinforced, and the reinforcement stops, eventually the behavior will occur less often and, if the reinforcement does not occur for a long enough period, the behavior will disappear completely.

While these concepts or procedures appear relatively simple, their effective use requires a great deal of attention to detail and consistency in application. The operant behavior must be clearly defined, the steps leading to change must be clearly specified, and the reinforcement approach must be consistently applied.

Social and cognitive models of learned behavior accept many of the theories of the classical and operant models; their contributions to the understanding of learned behavior have been primarily additive. Social learning theorists such as Albert Bandura (1977, 1982) have stressed the importance of both environmental reinforcers and internal processes. For example, people seem to be able to learn without external reinforcers in a process called modeling or observational learning. The process occurs because people make a mental or cognitive image of behavior that later can be copied in physical behavior. In this process, trial and error play a negligible role, although reinforced practice refines the behavioral skills. Social learning theorists believe that the complexity of human behavior precludes the shaping of each single response through differential reinforcement. In their view, some other learning processes, such as modeling, must be operative. Cognitive learning theorists go even farther in emphasizing the importance of internal processes in learning. Theorists such as Donald Meichenbaum (1977) emphasize the importance of cognitive events that influence behavior, such as thoughts, talking to oneself, mental images, self-evaluations, feelings, memories, and beliefs. The views of social and cognitive learning theorists have led to a more integrated perspective on human learned behavior. One way of describing this theory is as a process of reciprocal determinism. Specific behaviors learned through reinforcement are influenced by the environment and influence cognition, and cognitions affect how people perceive the environment and behave. Thus, human behavior is viewed as the result of both internal and external factors that influence people according to established principles of learning.

A range of concepts fall under the label of behavioral approaches. In the material that follows, we shall see in addition that a great variety of techniques have been brought together under the terms *behavior therapy* and *behavior modification*. In spite of this variety, a number of specific unifying characteristics of the techniques have been identified by several authors. Davison and Stuart have compiled a list of fairly representative unifying characteristics:

1. The focal behavioral techniques have been derived from or are consistent with research in experimental and social psychology.
2. Their intrinsic goal is the alleviation of human suffering and the enhancement of human functioning.
3. When responsibly practiced, the techniques always involve a systematic evaluation of treatment outcome using single-subject or group designs.
4. They typically involve reeducational efforts intended to facilitate improved functioning as measured by increased skill, independence, and satisfaction.
5. The practice of behavior therapy is typically guided by a contractual agreement between client and therapist specifying the goals and methods of intervention.[1]

The Development of Disordered Behavior

In the framework of the behaviorist, abnormal, deviant, or disordered behavior is "learned," just as is normal behavior. There is little need for concepts such as mental illness, the unconscious, transference neurosis, or repression. Individuals in need are not conceptualized as sick, they simply are engaging in a behavior or group of behaviors that they or others have identified as problematic. Such problem behaviors have been experimentally created in subjects by a number of researchers, beginning with Watson and Rayner (1920), who reproduced the prototype of the phobia in a laboratory setting.

A number of examples can be given as illustrations of how disordered behavior can be thought of as learned. In Watson and Rayner's famous experiment during the 1920s an eleven-month-old boy named Albert was presented with a white rat, to which he showed no fear response. Subsequently when he was given the white rat, an extremely loud, sudden noise was made, with the effect that "the infant jumped violently and fell forward, burying his face in the mattress." Within a small number of such pairings of the white rat and the unpleasant stimulus of the loud noise, the presentation of the white rat alone led the infant to react in a terrified manner. Later investigation revealed that Albert's fear had generalized to rabbits, dogs, and fur coats, and his fear continued after one month with no intervening presentation of the rat or other furry objects. This basic situation is considered one prototype of phobia development.

An additional example of the development of deviant behavior through learning can be seen in the area of crime and delinquency. Many criminals or delinquents spend their lives in an environment that supports criminal behavior. They are reinforced by the material rewards of their activities (money, possessions) and by the social approval of associates and friends. But what about the delinquent who comes from a "good" family in the middle or upper class? Here also delinquency may be a rewarding behavior in that it is certainly a powerful attention-getting device for individuals who feel neglected by their parents. It is, of course, not that simple. In fact, in most cases of delinquent behavior, one must consider the complete variety of behaviors that have been reinforced in a family setting for many years.

To date, behavioral explanations have been proposed and utilized in the treatment of a broad spectrum of problems, including anxiety, passivity, obsessive-compulsive disorders, depression, alcoholism, criminal behavior, severe mental disorder, and problematic behaviors in the elderly (Becker, Heimberg, and Bellack, 1987; Cohen, 1985; Goldfried and Davison, 1976; Hussain and Davis, 1985; Stravynski, Grey, and Elie, 1987). A variety of behavioral treatments have been developed to deal with such disorders, and a high level of treatment effectiveness has been reported. Space limitations preclude examining the full spectrum of techniques; however, a representative sample of the current behavioral approaches are described in the section that follows.

Representative Behavioral Treatment Approaches

Two general classes of behavioral treatment approaches have been developed. Techniques exist that focus on dealing specifically with problems that an *individual* experiences, such as a phobia, passivity, obsessive behavior, obesity, or self-mutilating behavior. Also, techniques have been developed for dealing with problems from a *group-system* focus, such as "token economies" in institutional settings.

Individually focused programs

Systematic desensitization
Systematic desensitization is a treatment technique designed to help a client overcome irrational fear (phobia) or anxiety reactions to objects or situations. Phobic reactions are presumed to be a result of some traumatic experience in a situation or with an object similar to the one that precipitates the later reaction. In the case of Albert, the original phobic stimulus was a white rat, but the reaction later generalized to a fear of furry objects. Usually the degree of fear or anxiety experienced is directly related to quantitative aspects of the

situation: the closer to it, the greater the fear. Phobias can be quite disabling. For example, individuals who have a strong fear of elevators would be very disabled if fear prevented them from getting to their workplace on the twenty-fifth floor of an office building.

The process of systematic desensitization is based on the inability of an individual to be both anxious and relaxed at the same time. The goal is to enable the individual to be relaxed (a competing response) rather than anxious in the presence of the phobia situation. Wolpe (1961), an early proponent of the approach, proposes that a response (relaxation) that inhibits anxiety in the presence of the phobic stimulus will weaken the connection between the stimulus and anxiety. This is called the principle of *reciprocal inhibition.*

Treatment of a phobia begins with training in relaxation and the development of an anxiety hierarchy. The client learns progressive deep relaxation through a process of alternately tensing and relaxing muscle groups. This enables the client to discriminate between feelings of tension and relaxation so that he or she can learn to relax more completely. The training occurs, of course, under the supervision of the therapist but is structured so that the client can practice the procedure at home.

Along with the relaxation training, the therapist and client create an anxiety hierarchy. The client describes a wide variety of situations related to the phobia and then subjectively rates them according to the degree of distress caused by each one. Ordinarily, twenty to thirty situations are described and ranked from least distressful to most distressful. An individual phobic to dogs, for example, might rank looking at a picture of a puppy as least distressful and standing next to a snarling German shepherd as most distressful, with twenty items ranked between them according to level of distress.

Once the relaxation process is learned and the hierarchy created, the process of desensitization begins. The therapist asks the client to imagine the hierarchy stimuli, beginning with the least distressful. At the point at which tension begins to develop, the client engages in the relaxation procedure to dissipate the anxiety. Repeated presentation of the imagined stimulus with no evoked anxiety decreases its tension-eliciting potential. As the stimulus is counterconditioned, the process generalizes to other stimuli of the hierarchy. The process then moves on to the next higher level of the hierarchy.

After a number of desensitization sessions, the client can ordinarily move up to the highest levels of the hierarchy without experiencing any anxiety. Ultimately, the individual can confront the real-life situations without experiencing the original phobic response. Some therapists, however, believe that the desensitization does not necessarily generalize to the real-life setting. They believe that the therapist must continue to take clients one step farther, that is, accompany them into the actual concrete situation and continue desensitization at that point.

Impressive success rates have been reported with the use of this technique to treat phobias. Wolpe (1961) reports that 91 percent of clients were significantly improved after approximately eleven or twelve sessions. In a study on college students who were phobic to public speaking, systematic desensitization proved more effective than attention placebos and insight therapy, and the results were maintained in a two-year follow-up study (Paul, 1967). Systematic desensitization has become a common technique among behaviorists for the treatment of a wide variety of anxiety- and stress-related disorders. The technique can be used as effectively by paraprofessionals as by professionals (Shelton and Peterson, 1978).

Operant approaches to an individual problem

As described previously, the operant approach is concerned with the effects or consequences of behaviors on the environment. Treatment involves controlling the consequences of a behavior in an attempt to change that behavior. Through the control of the consequences (rewards), the behavior can be modified. The process is best illustrated through a case example. A famous case illustrating these principles has been reported by Bachrach, Erwin, and Mohr (1965) and deals with the disorder known as anorexia nervosa.

Before implementing a behavioral program, the therapist must obtain information about problem behaviors, possible reinforcers, and the clients' goals for the treatment.

Anorexia nervosa consists of an extreme refusal to eat or the regurgitation of food to the extent that a severe weight loss occurs. In extreme situations, the problem can become life-threatening. Individuals have been known to become so weakened as to die from complications of the debilitation. In the case being described, the patient, at the age of thirty-seven, had slowly lost weight during a period of seventeen years, reducing from a weight of 118 pounds to 47 pounds at the point of hospitalization. On admission, she was completely weakened, suffered from severe malnutrition, and could not stand erect without assistance. A complete physical examination revealed no physiological cause for her inability to eat; instead, it seemed to be psychologically determined.

The treatment program was based on the assumption that her inability (or refusal) to eat was a result of her noneating behavior being *rewarded* (reinforced) by family, friends, and medical staff in previous situations. She was obtaining immediate gains (attention, pity, solicitude) that were more rewarding than the negative consequences of her behavior in terms of ill health. Treatment consisted of placing her in a room devoid of all previous sources of reward. There were no magazines, no radio, no television, no books, and no one to chat with. The restoration of all these pleasant activities became *contingent* on her engaging in eating behavior.

The therapist aimed to shape the patient's behavior specifically in the direction of eating. To do this, the therapist broke the process into steps: (1) presenting food, (2) touching a utensil (fork, spoon, etc.), (3) picking up a utensil, (4) picking up food with a utensil, (5) placing food in mouth, (6) chewing, (7) swallowing, and (8) eating increasing amounts of food. At each step the patient was rewarded by social contact, watching television, praise, or some other desirable (for her) reinforcement. Following implementation of the program, the patient was soon eating normally and the reinforcers became contingent on weight gain. By the end of the program, the patient's weight had increased to eighty-eight pounds.

Another operant approach is used in dealing with children who have a problem controlling aggression. Patterson (1971) has become known for his work in this area, especially since aggressive behavior in children is seen by school officials and parents as a particularly important problem. In Patterson's program, parents are taught to observe and record both the child's problem behavior (aggression) and the parents' own reaction to it. It usually turns out that the parents attend more to the disruptions than to the positive behaviors in which the child engages.

In the next phase of the program, the parents are taught how to change the contingencies of the child's behavior. That is, they are taught to react differently to the aggression. Frequently, as simple a change as ignoring the aggression and emphatically rewarding competing behaviors (such as cooperative play) will result in eliminating or decreasing the aggression. Programs such as Patterson's have been remarkably successful in a variety of settings. In his original work, Patterson reported that the frequency of aggressive behavior was reduced 60 percent in children treated by the method. Of particular interest for the human service worker is the fact that the actual treatment was administered by the parents and, in other similar programs, by classroom teachers rather than by a formally trained therapist.

Cognitive-behavioral approaches

Cognitive-behavioral therapists attempt to improve the client's awareness of negative self-statements. They focus on teaching the client to use problem-solving and coping skills. Three factors are focused on: (1) the person's behaviors and the reactions they elicit; (2) the person's internal speech, or what he or she says to him- or herself before, during, and following the behavior; and (3) the cognitive factors (feelings, beliefs, and attitudes) that give rise to the person's internal dialogue.

At the beginning of cognitive-behavioral therapy, the therapist encourages the client to become a self-observer. The client must identify problem behaviors, thoughts, and reactions in need of change. In the second phase, the client is helped to create new cognitions, especially inner speech or self-talk, that are incompatible with the old self-defeating cognitions. In the third phase, the client is trained to produce new behaviors, first in the therapy session and then in the everyday world. As the client's new behaviors are trained and practiced, the therapist reinforces them and the new inner speech. The extensive rehearsal of new behaviors distinguishes this approach from simple "positive thinking." Without extensive reinforced practice, thinking positively is unlikely to have a powerful effect on behavior. Table 8-2 lists some examples of positive self-talk used in the training of clients who need help in dealing with stress.

Group-system focused programs

Token economies

If one asked who should receive the most credit for the development of the token economy concept, it is likely that Theodoro Ayllon and Nathan Azrin would receive the honor. Even though others had considered the issues before, Ayllon and Azrin seem to be the first to have mounted a full-scale project. As early as 1961, they initiated a token economy program at Anna State Hospital in Illinois (Ayllon and Azrin, 1968). Since that time, the concept has grown in popularity, and token economies now can be found in an astonishingly wide variety of institutional settings.

The token economy is a system for redesigning total environments to make them supportive of positive or socially desirable behaviors, and capable of extinguishing negative, maladaptive, or socially undesirable behaviors. The initial project of Ayllon and Azrin was to redesign a total ward environment in a mental hospital. Other workers have since designed and implemented token economies in settings such as correctional facilities, juvenile detention settings, and a host of other types of institutional facilities.

Table 8-2 *Self-talk rehearsed in cognitive-behavioral therapy for dealing with stress.*

Preparing for stress

What is it I have to do?
I can develop a plan to deal with it.
Just think about what I can do about it. That's better than getting anxious.
No negative self-statements: Just think rationally.
Don't worry: Worry won't help anything.
Maybe what I think is anxiety is eagerness to confront the stress.

Confronting and handling stress

Just "psych" myself up.
I can convince myself to do it. I can reason my fear away.
One step at a time: I can handle the situation.
Don't think about fear; just think about what I have to do. Stay relevant.
This anxiety is what the therapist said I would feel. It's a reminder to use my coping exercises.
This tenseness can be an ally: a cue to cope.
Relax; I'm in control. Take a slow deep breath.

Dealing with the feeling of being overwhelmed

When fear comes, just pause.
Keep the focus on the present; what is it I have to do?
I should expect my fear to rise.
Don't try to eliminate fear totally; just keep it manageable.

Reinforcing self-statements

It worked; I did it.
Wait until I tell my therapist about this.
It wasn't as bad as I expected.
I made more out of my fear than it was worth.
My damn ideas—they're the problem. When I control them, I control my fear.
I can be pleased with the progress I'm making.
I did it!

The worker develops the token economy by identifying desired behaviors ranging from those of quite low level (such as brushing teeth, combing hair, dressing, wearing clothes, proper toileting, and eating with utensils) to those of a higher level (such as attending meetings, performing work activities, holding logical conversations, and other activities that make up responsible behavior). A reward system is then set up in which engaging in a desired behavior entitles the subject to an immediate reward of a plastic token or paper chit that is redeemable for material goods such as clothing, magazines, toilet articles, food, drink, or a variety of other items, including special privileges. In addition, a system of fines is organized through which the subject may lose tokens for engaging in inappropriate behavior (which is specifically defined) or failing to perform a required task.

One may argue that such systems of reward and punishment have existed before in institutional settings. That is true, but the major differentiation between the primitive, personalistic systems that existed previously and the token economy is the tremendous emphasis on detail, specificity, and particularly *consistency* in the token economy programs. Such a brief presentation can hardly do justice to the involved intricacies of the token economy. Interested students may refer to the many published works that deal with this subject in depth. It can be reported, however, that as a management system, the token economy has no equal. Impressive evidence exists indicating that a wide variety of strange and bizarre behaviors can be extinguished through its use (Kazdin, 1982).

Token economies are particularly useful in working with people who have been institutionalized for many years and have lost most of the self-care skills one takes for granted, including personal hygiene behaviors, eating with a fork and knife, wearing clothing, and appropriate toileting. Programs that combine token reinforcements with training in social skills may be particularly beneficial. Such training involves direct instruction, modeling, performance feedback, and role-playing experiences. It has been effective even with severely disturbed psychiatric patients (Matson and Zeiss, 1978). When such group programs are combined with individual treatment focusing on the problem behaviors of individuals, dramatic changes can occur in behavior. However, the extent to which such programs can stimulate massive changes in the most disabling problems of institutionalized people is not known. A token economy program, no matter how sophisticated, is unlikely to change a chronic psychotic into a pillar of the community or a longtime criminal into a law-abiding citizen.

Other group approaches

In addition to token economies, which use an operant behavioral approach, the cognitive-behavioral approaches have been used more widely in recent years to deal with persons in groups (Thyer, 1988; Upper and Ross, 1985). For example, Nardone, Tryon, and O'Connor (1986) have reported on a cognitive-behavioral group treatment for reducing impulsive-aggressive behavior in adolescent boys in a residential setting. Ten boys were treated in two groups (five boys in each group) for thirteen sessions over six weeks. Each session was fifty minutes. The first five minutes consisted of an orientation period in which three rules were covered: (1) don't hurt yourself, (2) don't hurt others, and (3) don't damage property. The next ten minutes were spent in a relaxation exercise. The following ten minutes was "talk time." The therapist taught the boys problem-solving skills in a picture story format: (1) defining the problem, (2) developing plans or solutions, (3) acting on plans and solution, and (4) evaluating the outcome of the action taken. The next twenty-minute period was devoted to a group game or project designed to elicit situations like those presented in "talk time." The therapist spent the final five minutes reviewing the hour with each boy and giving reward points for positive behavior which could be exchanged for tangible reinforcers. During the last two weeks, boys could pool their reward points to obtain a group trip (disco roller skating), to emphasize the consequences of each boy's behavior for the group as a whole.

During the course of the project, the frequency of impulsive-aggressive behavior on the part of the boys declined dramatically. During a follow-up period, the therapist discovered, however, that the positive gains slowly eroded and had disappeared within five weeks. This finding emphasizes the need for maintenance reinforcement programs following active behavior therapy programs. The need for follow-up intervention is a common finding with many behavioral approaches.

The Effectiveness of Behavioral Strategies

To some extent, the effectiveness of the behavioral strategies has been considered in the description of the various modalities in this chapter. A number of texts, including Franks (1969), Goldfried and Davison (1976), and Wolpe (1981) offer more substantive considerations of their effectiveness. A major asset of the behavioral strategies is that a majority of their proponents are thoroughly indoctrinated in the scientific method and tend to be extremely concerned with proving whether the techniques work. This has led to a situation in which a large number of highly controlled studies preponderantly support the claims of significant behavior change resulting from the techniques. These results are in relatively sharp contrast to the usually anecdotal evaluations of the intrapsychic strategies.

Common criticisms

The behavioral approaches are not without critics, however. Franks (1969) presents the most frequently leveled criticisms of the behavioral approaches as follows:

1. Treating the patient's overt behavioral symptoms is superficial. The underlying cause remains.
2. The token economy and other behavioral approaches *cannot*, by their nature, change the underlying causes of disruptive behavior.
3. The effects of behavioral approaches are not likely to be lasting because of their superficiality; the modified behavior will return.

4. Behavior therapy may cause symptom substitution. Since the underlying cause remains, another symptom will develop that will manifest the deeper pathology.

Such criticisms are representative of the problems encountered when persons of differing assumption networks (such as psychotherapeutic versus behavioral) examine each other's work. In this case, the reply of the behaviorist to such criticisms would be simply that they have no impact since they are all predicated on the existence of a concept (underlying cause) that the behaviorist rejects as nonexistent.

The effectiveness of the behavioral approaches seems well documented, particularly in instances where a client has a behavior problem that we know can be modified by the use of behavioral techniques. In situations in which the clients' problems seem more global and less easily compartmentalized, other forms of intervention may be more appropriate.

Summary

1. The behavioral approaches to people in need are among the most recently developed therapies. They are concerned more with observable behavior than with underlying causes. Human problems are viewed as primarily learned behavior patterns.

2. If the reinforcement contingencies are modified or counterresponses to learned behavior are conditioned, problem behavior can be extinguished or modified in positive patterns, or entirely new behaviors can be created.

3. Four major conceptualizations of learned behavior have been developed: classical learning theory, operant learning theory, social learning theory, and cognitive learning theory.

4. Several major concepts important in learning theory have been introduced: conditioning, reinforcement, generalization, discrimination, and punishment.

5. Systematic desensitization can be applied effectively to individuals. It has been used successfully in helping clients overcome irrational fears or anxiety reactions.

6. The operant approaches to individual behavioral problems involve controlling the reinforcers in a person's environment. Through control of the reinforcers or modification of the consequences of behavior, the behavior can be changed.

7. Cognitive-behavioral interventions focus on changing behavior through changing cognitive events such as feelings and thoughts in addition to reinforcing actual behaviors.

8. The token economy is a group-focused behavioral approach. It is a system for redesigning total environments. In token economies, a system of rewards for desirable behaviors and fines for undesired behaviors is maintained consistently.

9. In recent years, the cognitive-behavioral approaches have been used with persons in groups with some reasonable success.

10. The behavioral approaches have been effective in helping human service clients. They seem to be efficient.

Discussion Questions

1. How are the behavioral strategies different from the intrapsychic strategies?

2. Which learning model seems more relevant to human behavior: classical, operant, social, or cognitive? Why?

3. How is behavior learned?

4. How is problem behavior changed through behavioral strategies?

5. Discuss the concept that "the world is an unplanned token economy."

6. What are the common criticisms of behavioral strategies?

Learning Experiences

1. Try to identify learned behaviors in your pet. For example, does your dog bother you when you eat?

2. Can you think of behaviors you engage in because they are reinforced?

3. Develop a plan for changing a specific behavior of an acquaintance. Don't try it unless you have your instructor's approval.

Endnote

1. G. Davison and R. Stuart. "Behavior Therapy and Civil Liberties." *American Psychologist*, Vol. 30 (July), p. 755, 1975. Reprinted by permission, American Psychological Association.

Recommended Readings

Bellack, A. S., and Hersen, M. (eds.). *Dictionary of Behavior Therapy Techniques.* Elmsford, N.Y.: Pergamon Press, 1985.

Fuoco, F. J.; Naster, B. J.; Vernon, J. B.; Morely, R. T.; and Middleton, J. F. *Behavioral Procedures for a Psychiatric Unit and Halfway House.* New York: Van Nostrand Reinhold, 1985.

Hersen, M., and Bellack, A. S. (eds.). *Behavioral Assessment: A Practical Handbook.* New York: Pergamon Press, 1976.

Kazdin, A. E. *Behavior Modification in Applied Settings* (4th ed.) Pacific Grove, Calif.: Brooks/Cole, 1989.

McGee, J. J.; Menolascino, F. J.; Hobbs, D. C.; and Menousek, P. E. *Gentle Teaching: A Non-Aversive Approach to Helping Persons with Mental Retardation.* New York: Human Sciences Press, 1987.

Meichenbaum, D. *Cognitive-Behavior Modification: An Integrated Approach.* New York: Plenum, 1977.

Sundel, M., and Sundel, S. *Behavior Modification in the Human Services.* New York: John Wiley and Sons, 1975.

9

Psychotherapy
and the Person in Need

- What are the basic assumptions of the psychotherapeutic approaches to human problems?
- What are the common components of the different types of psychotherapy?
- What are the basic concepts of psychoanalysis?
- What are the characteristics of client-centered therapy?
- Are there advantages to group psychotherapy?
- What is family therapy?
- Does psychotherapy work?

Psychotherapeutic approaches assume that a large proportion of people's problems result from the internal psychology (thinking and emotion) of the individual. Within this broad generalization there are a variety of approaches to and ideas about human behavior, from psychoanalysis to gestalt theory. Taking into consideration the major approaches and their many variations as well as the numerous less common approaches, literally hundreds of different systems exist. Even though many different approaches have been developed, most hold a similar set of assumptions. The following six assumptions constitute the basic framework out of which adherents of these approaches function:

1. Psychological distress or behavioral disturbance is a function of problems in the subject's personality structure.
2. The function of internal psychological processes is more important in determining behavior than the subject's current environment.

3. Usually, past experiences are more important than current experiences in determining behavior or personality because of either the sheer amount of past experiences or the special significance of past experiences, particularly those of childhood.
4. Behavior is overdetermined; that is, the basic personality structure (including problem areas) is so powerful that individual acts of will that focus on changing ingrained patterns (such as New Year's resolutions) are ineffective.
5. There is an optimum personality structure that allows individuals to deal effectively with the environment in a manner that maintains an optimal level of satisfaction.
6. If individuals have not reached the optimal level of personality structure and are experiencing difficulties, they often can be helped to grow through a process of relating to a trained helper who understands human development. This relationship process is almost always verbal.

The helping process these approaches use is called *psychotherapy*. Even though the various subsystems differ in their theoretical formulations of behavior and therapeutic approaches, a number of common elements are apparent.

Two major continuums on which the approaches range are the degree of directiveness and the degree of intensiveness of the process. Psychoanalysis, for example, is considered to be a directive therapy. The determination of issues, such as the content of therapy, its length, and its goals, is more the province of the therapist than of the subject (the therapist directs the client). On the other hand, Rogerian client-centered therapy is nondirective; the client or subject has a greater influence in determining its content, length, and goals (the therapist is more a helper than a healer). In addition to the directiveness continuum, one can describe the difference in intensity of the various processes, ranging from five-times-a-week sessions as in traditional psychoanalysis to once-a-week sessions as in most client-centered processes. Despite such differences, certain common elements do appear. Harper (1960) summarizes the common components of psychotherapy along the following lines.

1. One or more persons (clients) have some awareness of neglected or mishandled life problems.
2. One or more persons (therapists) exist with relative lack of disturbance who perceive the distress of the clients and believe themselves capable of helping the clients reduce distress.
3. There is a positive regard of client for therapist and vice versa.
4. The therapist has understanding of and empathy for the client.
5. The client perceives the positive regard for and empathic understanding of him or her by the therapist.

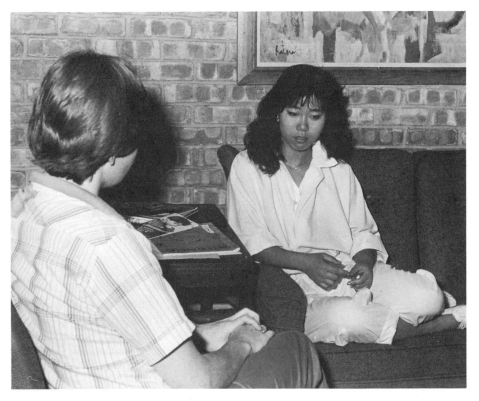

The one-to-one therapeutic relationship is an important tool in human services.

6. The therapist provides corrective information for the client regarding his or her environment.
7. The therapist assists the client in achieving a better self-evaluation.
8. The therapist provides a setting in which the client can experience emotional venting (catharsis).
9. There is a gradually increasing number of tasks for the client to perform between therapy sessions in terms of applying new information about him- or herself and his or her environment.
10. There is a gradual process by which the client learns to become independent of the therapist.

With so many varieties of psychotherapy in existence, it would be impossible to deal with each in depth. In the following pages, let's examine two major approaches—psychoanalysis and Rogerian client-centered therapy. We'll also describe briefly a number of newer approaches and consider several structural variations such as group and family therapy.

Psychoanalysis

Even though there are only about 2,500 members of the American Psychoanalytic Association, there may be as many as 10,000 practicing analysts in the United States (Fine, 1973). Psychoanalysis is the grandfather of the current psychotherapies. It dates from its origination by Sigmund Freud in the 1890s and grew out of Freud's work on conversion hysteria with his colleague Josef Breuer. Freud and Breuer began by using hypnosis, under which they observed that patients could remember early events of their lives that they could not recall in a waking state and that they could then integrate into their personality with a relieving of symptoms soon following.

Freud later abandoned hypnosis for a technique called *free association* (Freud, 1953–1964). In this technique, patients say whatever comes into their minds without concern for its relevance. No limits are put on what they talk about. In this process, the early experiences of patients and their deeper attitudes and ideas are revealed to themselves and to the analyst. As free association continues, the analyst is particularly concerned about childhood experiences that determine later personality reactions and about the unconscious mind—that part of the mind into which the memory of many early experiences are pushed out of awareness, particularly painful experiences, and from which they still have an effect in determining reaction patterns of the individual. In psychoanalysis, the ability of patients to be "well" comes through their awareness of the unconscious forces in their personalities and their ability to bring those forces into an orderly arrangement so that they have control over them.

Somewhat similar to free association is the study of dreams. Freud assumed that ego defenses are lowered during sleep, allowing repressed material to be expressed symbolically in dream content. The materials are expressed in disguised symbolism since the repressed material is very threatening to the conscious mind. The analyst's role is to assist patients in interpreting the true meaning of the dream symbols.

As unconscious material appears, both in free association and in dreams, the analyst uses the technique of interpretation. Since the goal is to help patients face their repressed and emotionally laden conflicts, the analyst begins to point out to patients the underlying sources of resistance to awareness. If the interpretations are correct and appropriately timed, patients can begin to examine their problems from the perspective of their current reality. They can begin to realize that they no longer must fear their impulses, and this realization leads to a further relaxation of defenses.

Psychoanalysis makes use of *transference*. Transference is the tendency, considered to exist in all human beings, to relate or transfer the emotions and attitudes that have developed in personality growth to people in the present-day, immediate environment. The simplest example is the person with unresolved childhood difficulties in dealing with a parent, who transfers these residual feelings onto current authority figures such as bosses, teachers, police, and others and behaves toward them as he or she did toward the parent. The transference feelings that the patient experiences toward the analyst, both positive and negative, are strong motivations for the patient. The analyst uses these positive feelings to promote change and interprets the negative feelings to assist patients in understanding their origin in early life experiences. As patients begin to understand the origin of these negative feelings, they can work toward making the feelings more positive.

A major aspect of the analysis is the reenactment of previously repressed childhood experiences and feelings as remembered by patients, with a related high degree of emotional tension. The discharge of these repressed emotions and the development of *insight* (understanding of their infantile origin) is called *abreaction*. The reexperiencing of the emotions and the development of insight under the direction of the analyst are considered major factors in the development of personality changes.

In the following excerpt from Wolberg (1977), an analyst deals with transference feeling in the patient. Through judicious questioning and interpretation by the analyst, the patient suddenly discovers something about how her early childhood experiences and feelings influence her current behavior and feelings.

Patient: I want to talk about my feelings about you.

Therapist: Mm hmm.

Patient: You sit here, a permissive person who lets me go on. I want to do something now, but I'm afraid you will be disappointed in me if I upset the apple cart, if I explode. I think we are too nice to each other. I'm ready not to be nice. My greatest fear of you is that you are potentially going to be severe with me if I let loose. Also, I fear I will let you down by not performing well, by not being nice. I feel I will gain your disapproval and yet I see you don't condemn and don't criticize. It is still important to me to gain a nod from you or a smile. (*Pause.*)

Therapist: It sounds as if you would like to let loose with me, but you are afraid of what my response would be. (*Summarizing and restating.*)

Patient: I get so excited by what is happening here, I feel I'm being held back by needing to be nice. I'd like to blast loose sometimes, but I don't dare.

Therapist: Because you fear my reaction?

Patient: The worst thing would be that you wouldn't like me. You wouldn't speak to me friendly; you wouldn't smile; you'd feel you can't treat me and discharge me from treatment. But I know this isn't so, I know it.

Therapist: Where do you think these attitudes come from?

Patient: When I was nine years old, I read a lot about great men in history. I'd quote them and be dramatic. I'd want a sword at my side; I'd dress like an Indian. Mother would scold me. Don't frown, don't talk so much. Sit on your hands, over and over again. I did all kinds of things. I was a naughty child. She told me I'd be hurt. Then at fourteen I fell off a horse and broke my back. I had to be in bed. Mother then told me on the day I went riding not to, that I'd get hurt because the ground was frozen. I was a stubborn, self-willed child. Then I went against her will and suffered an accident that changed my life, a fractured back. Her attitude was, "I told you so." I was put in a cast and kept in bed for months.

Therapist: You were punished, so to speak, by this accident.

Patient: But I gained attention and love from mother for the first time. I felt so good. I'm ashamed to tell you this. Before I healed I opened the cast and tried to walk to make myself sick again so I could stay in bed longer. (*Pause.*)

Therapist: How does that connect up with your impulses to be sick now and stay in bed so much? (*The patient has these tendencies, of which she is ashamed.*)

Patient: Oh . . . (*Pause.*)

Therapist: What do you think?

Patient: Oh, my God, how infantile, how ungrown up (*pause*), it must be so. I want people to love me and be sorry for me. Oh, my God. How completely childish. It is, is that. My mother must have ignored me when I was little, and I wanted so to be loved. (*This sounds like insight.*)

Therapist: So that it may have been threatening to go back to being self-willed and unloved after you got out of the cast. (*Interpretation.*) Perhaps if you go back to being stubborn with me, you would be returning to how you were before; that is, active, stubborn, but unloved.

Patient: (*Excitedly.*) And, therefore, losing your love. I need you, but after all you aren't going to reject me. The pattern is so established now that the threat of the loss of love is too overwhelming with everybody, and I've got to keep myself from acting selfish or angry.[1]

The course of analysis is, however, by no means smooth. Usually the symptoms that lead persons to seek help exist as defenses against underlying anxieties, fears of involvement with others, and fears of really knowing oneself. As the process of free association occurs, patients begin to learn about themselves. They defend against this exposure (to the therapist and to themselves) through forces that tend to slow and thus prevent their growing awareness of their internal processes. The analyst must be aware of such resistances and help patients overcome them.

As resistances are overcome and treatment continues, patients become increasingly aware of their immaturities and begin to attempt to change with the support of the analyst. It is assumed that at some level even resistant patients desire to be better. In fact, the desire to improve is considered a universal trait. The healthy parts of patients' personalities are used at this point as strengths to rely on as new behavior patterns are attempted.

In effect, psychoanalysis is a process involving a gradual breaking down of the personality and a rebuilding of it in changed patterns at the same time. Patients come to understand the structure of their makeup, their relationships with others become more clear, and their efforts to achieve a more functional life-style begin. The analyst holds a mirror to the patients, helping them adopt more mature reaction patterns, interpreting their motivations and the composition of their maladaptations, and assisting in their attempts to change.

Rogers's Client-Centered Therapy

Carl Rogers's system of therapy is intimately tied to the notion that each individual has basic potentialities for growth and development. The major role of the therapist is to provide an atmosphere in which the client can engage in self-examination, achieve self-understanding, and reorganize perceptions of the world and his or her place in it. Particularly important in understanding behavior is the concept of the phenomenological field. Each person has such a field, which is an understanding of events as that person *perceives* them. An individual's behavior is a reaction to that field as it is uniquely perceived. The field includes self-concepts, experiences, and perceptions, which are admitted to awareness. When the organism denies to awareness the significant experiences (thoughts, feelings, behaviors) that do not fit the self-concept, psychological tension arises, and the experiences are disowned. It is this lack of fit between what a person *is*, *thinks* he or she is, and *would like to be* that causes individuals to be distressed and to need help.

For Rogers, the most appropriate source of information about the patient is the patient's self-report. Rogers rejects the notion that true motivation is unconscious and unavailable to self-awareness. Rogerians place little emphasis on dreams, slips of the tongue, and free association. Rather than being concerned with the symbolism of what the client says, the Rogerian is more concerned with creating an atmosphere that is nonthreatening, in which the client can self-explore and try new behavior without fear of rejection or ridicule. The *relationship* is more critical than what is said, and the therapist must have empathy and positive regard for the client and must be genuine.

In addition to empathy, genuineness, and positive regard, certain characteristic activities of Rogerian therapists (Harper, 1960) include:

1. The therapist makes strong, consistent efforts to understand the client's content of speech and feelings as conveyed by words, gestures, and expressions.
2. The therapist makes an effort to communicate this understanding to the client by words or by a general attitude of acceptance.
3. There is an occasional presentation of a condensation or synthesis of expressed feelings.
4. There are occasional statements on the nature and limits of the therapeutic relationship, the participants' expectations of the situation, and the therapist's confidence in the ability of the patient to handle his or her problems.
5. Question answering and data giving are denied when they seem likely to increase the patient's dependency.
6. Interpretations are avoided unless they are summary in nature.
7. The therapist does not try to promote insight directly, give advice, praise, blame, teach, or otherwise direct the client.

Client-centered therapy is a process of disorganization and reorganization of the self. The primary goal is to assist clients in developing a more accurate conception of a much wider range of sensory experiences based on their own system of values rather than on a system of values borrowed from parents or other significant figures. Clients are able in effect to take themselves apart and put themselves back together in a more functional structure, because their contradictory attitudes and behaviors are completely accepted by the therapist.

The experiences of the clients during client-centered therapy are illustrated in the following comments by people who have actually experienced sessions with a client-centered therapist.

Exploring Oneself

■ ■ At first the inconsistencies between what I felt about myself (and said in the counseling session) and what I thought about myself were the most annoying. Later, inconsistencies between one interview and another bothered me much more. I was enjoying the feeling of being honest for the first time, and I didn't like this apparent evidence of untruth.

Discovering Denied Attitudes

■ ■ I began to think and actually admit things to myself that I had never considered admitting before. I began to see just what was at the root of all my actions. Why I was so often likely to cover up what I had done with excuses.

Reorganization of the Self

■ ■ Now, after four visits, I have a much clearer picture of my self and my future. It makes me feel a little depressed and disappointed, but on the other hand, it has taken me out of the dark, the load seems a lot lighter now, that is I can see my way now, I know what I want to do, I know about what I can do so now that I can see my goal, I will be able to work a whole lot easier at my own level.

Experiencing Progress

■ ■ It's wonderful how relaxed I can get talking about ideas I couldn't even think about last year, things that just require saying, getting rid of. Last year I kept thinking what a pleasant way out illness would be. This year in my daydreams when the same thing happens I say, "Hell, no, that's not what I want."

Putting it Together

■ ■ You know, it seems as if all the energy that went into holding the arbitrary pattern [of problem behavior] together was quite unnecessary—a waste. You think you have to make the pattern yourself; but there are so many pieces, and it's so hard to see where they fit. Sometimes you put them in the wrong place, and the more pieces misfitted, the more effort it takes to hold them in place, until at last you are so tired that even that awful confusion is better than holding on any longer. Then you discover that left to themselves the jumbled pieces fall quite naturally into their own places, and a living pattern emerges without any effort at all on your part. Your job [in therapy] is just to discover it, and in the course of that, you will find yourself and your own place. Looks as if the whole of life is pretty nondirective, doesn't it? You must even let your own experience tell you its own meaning: The minute you tell it what it means, you get antagonism and you are at war with yourself.[2]

From these client reports, the process of client-centered, or nondirective, therapy can be summarized as a series of progressive stages. At first the client is enabled to explore the discrepancies among his or her words, attitudes, feelings, and behaviors. Then the client begins to discover aspects of himself or herself that have been denied to conscious awareness. With the nonjudgmental, caring support of the therapist, the client then begins to reorganize his or her experiences into a new and more functional self-concept and discovers that progress is being made. The client finally has new adaptive skills that will help make future behaviors and experiences more satisfying and productive. Rogers et al. (1967) characterize the essence of the therapeutic process as follows:

As he finds someone listening to him with consistent acceptance while he expresses his thoughts and feelings, the client, little by little, becomes increasingly able to listen to communications from within himself; he becomes able to realize that he is angry, or that he is frightened, or that he is experiencing feelings of love. Gradually, he becomes able to listen to feelings within himself which have previously seemed so bizarre, so terrible, or so disorganizing that they have been shut off completely from conscious awareness. As he reveals these hidden and "awful" aspects of himself, he finds that the therapist's regard for him remains unshaken. And, slowly, he moves toward adopting the same attitude toward himself, toward accepting himself in the process of becoming. Finally, as the client is able to listen to more of himself, he moves toward greater congruence, toward expressing all of himself more openly. He is, at last, free to change and grow in the directions which are natural to the human organism.

Rogers (1957) has described what he feels are the necessary and sufficient conditions to bring about personality change:

1. A psychological contract must be present; that is, both the client and the therapist must be aware of the presence of each other.
2. The client senses a difference between his or her experiences and his or her self-concept.
3. The therapist's experiences support his or her own self-concept.
4. The therapist experiences unconditional positive regard for the client.
5. The therapist experiences an empathic understanding of the client's percepts of his or her own experiences and tries to communicate this empathy to the client.
6. The client *experiences* the therapist as being empathic and having positive regard.

If these six conditions are met, effective psychotherapy can occur, according to Rogerian therapists. However, most therapists operating from differing viewpoints would disagree that these conditions alone are *sufficient*.

Client-centered therapy has become quite popular since its inception in the late 1940s. Harper (1960) suggests a number of reasons: It fits our democratic tradition since the client is treated as an equal; it appeals to the inexperienced therapist because of its apparent (and deceptive) simplicity; it promises to be a quicker route to personality change than psychoanalysis; and finally, it is American in origin rather than foreign. In Chapter 10, it will be seen that client-centered therapy has contributed much to the human services approach.

Alternative Psychotherapies

The psychotherapies to be described in this section are *alternatives* in the sense that they appear to have fewer followers among the helping professions than the two major approaches that have just been described. The alternative approaches are no less complicated, well developed, or conceptualized than any other, nor do they promise to be any less effective than psychoanalysis or client-centered therapy.

Transactional analysis

Developed by Eric Berne (1966) as an outgrowth of his experience in group psychotherapy during World War II, the basic concepts of transactional analysis (TA) were first formally published in 1957. The major focus of TA is on an approach to interactional psychology—an approach centering on the interaction processes between two or more persons. As a therapy, it is a contractual form of treatment in which individuals specify as clearly as possible what they want to achieve in the therapeutic relationship. The therapists accept or reject the contract depending on whether they think it likely that assistance can be provided.

The therapist is an expert in structural analysis, transactional analysis, and script analysis. *Structural analysis* is a fundamental system for describing and analyzing the three basic ego states: parent, adult, and child. Major communication and interaction problems can exist when different states of the egos of different persons determine the content of messages (see Figure 9-1).

For example, as indicated by the solid lines in Figure 9-1, appropriate communication at the adult level would be as follows.

Initiation: "Let's go to the movies." (adult to adult)

Response: "Okay, that would be fun." (adult to adult)

Distorted (crossed) communication or interaction, as indicated by the dotted lines, would be:

Initiation: "Let's go to the movies." (adult to adult)

Response: "All you ever think about is goofing off." (parent to child)

The analysis of such transactions between persons is, of course, *transactional analysis*. Transactions can be grouped in the categories of (1) withdrawal, (2) ritual, (3) pastimes, (4) games, (5) activities, and (6) intimacy. The purpose of transaction is considered to be the satisfaction of needs such as the need for strokes (unit of recognition), the need for structuring time, and the need for excitement. The needs can be satisfied through the six types of transactions; however, the lower-numbered ones are safer, whereas the higher-numbered ones not only are more risky in that they demand more vulnerability to others, they also satisfy more effectively. According to Berne's theory, transactional analysis attempts to give the client the opportunity to *choose* his or her type of transactions.

Script analysis is a process of assessing the predominant themes in a person's life. A "life script" manifests a decision made by the person as to how he or she spends his or her life. The decision, however, is usually made at an early age, without conscious awareness, and based on simplistic or

Figure 9-1 *Transactional ego states.*

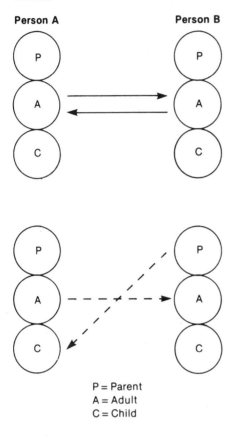

Person A   Person B

P = Parent
A = Adult
C = Child

distorted data. The determinants of the life script include how the person sees and values himself or herself and others in terms of "OK-ness." The TA analyst attempts to assist the client in getting free from self-defeating *scripts* and developing an autonomous self-chosen lifestyle that can flexibly be changed at any time to a more interesting and rewarding pattern and that allows true intimacy with another person.

Transactional analysis as a total system uses many techniques common to most forms of therapy: querying, reflection, self-analysis, interpretation, modeling, owning up to behavior, homework assignments, and reinforcing (stroking) of positive behavior. Its particular uniqueness includes its emphasis on the group technique and its particular pop language: *parent, adult,* and *child* for ego states; *scripts;* and the names of the "games" that people play, such as *rapo* and *kick-me.* Its use of everyday language and pop terms has made its concepts extremely well accepted and widely popular.

Gestalt therapy

Gestalt therapy is the creation of Frederick Perls, a physician-psychologist whose concepts were developed in the mid-1960s. It is a highly experiential approach with little theory, at times seeming very philosophical in its premises. A colleague of Perls, Walter Kempler (1973), exemplifies this approach in his description of *man:*

> Man may be seen as a momentary precipitation at the vortex of a transient eddy of energy, in the enormous and incomprehensible sea of energy we call the universe. . . . Could man order his energy like gravity, magnetic flow, or the laser phenomenon, we might expect him to disappear from tangible view and exist exclusively as the powerful force that is now only his inherent potential.

The therapeutic process in this system is focused entirely on the here and now. The gestalt therapist cares little for historical or past data about the client. The total focus is on the relationship between the therapist and client and the client's inherent potential for actualization. Problems are seen as being caused by one part of the client's personality refusing to accept another part. Positive change occurs when the two parts recognize and come to appreciate each other to the point where they have no conflict or dissatisfaction. To be able to persuade the patient to confront his or her discordant elements, the therapist must have no internal discord.

The major factor for the therapist is to be able to identify the patient's opposing elements and to then get the patient actively to engage the opposites in order to bring them to a resolution. The therapist's attributes are concepts similar to those held by Rogerians: positive regard, empathy, and genuineness. However, a major difference in approaches is the gestalt therapist's willingness to *judge* and the patient's presumed expectation of *being* judged. An approval-disapproval continuum develops in which the patient discovers valued behaviors and is helped to relinquish disvalued behaviors. The basic mechanism of this type of therapy is the creation of a situation in which the patient can show himself or herself to another in order to be able to "find" himself or herself.

Rational-emotive therapy

The originator of rational-emotive therapy was Albert Ellis, who was trained as a psychoanalyst in the 1940s. His rational-emotive therapy (RET) is one of the most popular alternative psychotherapies in the Western world today (D'Zurilla, 1990). Ellis came to believe that for people to live fully productive lives, they would have to give up a number of deep-seated biosocially learned irrational *ideas*. Ellis felt that the irrational ideas were not effectively dealt with through the existing psychotherapies. In fact, he felt that the existing psychotherapies only helped the client live with the underlying irrationalities. What would work better, Ellis thought, was an active-directive, cognitive-emotive-behavioristic attack on the major self-defeating irrational value systems of the client.

Ellis (1973) presents eight main propositions of rational-emotive therapy:

1. The human being is born with a potential to be uniquely rational and straight-thinking as well as a tendency to be a uniquely irrational and crooked-thinking creature.
2. An individual's tendency to irrational thinking, self-damaging habituations, wishful thinking, and intolerance is frequently exacerbated by the culture, and the family group in particular, especially during childhood, when one is most vulnerable to outside influences.
3. People tend to perceive, think, emote, and behave simultaneously and interactionally. They are, therefore, at one and the same time cognitive, conative (emotional), and motoric.
4. Therapies that are highly cognitive, active-directive, homework-assigning, and discipline-oriented are likely to be more effective, usually in a significantly briefer period of time and with fewer sessions, than other therapies.
5. The rational-emotive therapist does not believe that a deep or warm relationship between the counselor and counselee is either a necessary or a sufficient condition for personality change.
6. The rational-emotive therapist uses a variety of techniques with a client—including role playing, assertion training, desensitization, humor, operant conditioning, suggestion, support, etc.
7. Serious emotional problems stem from magical, empirically unvalidatable thinking, and if these disturbance-creating ideas are vigorously and persistently disputed by a rigorous application of the principles of logico-empirical thinking, they can almost invariably be eliminated and will cease to occur.
8. Ordinary psychological insight does not lead to major personality change, since at best it only helps people see that they do have emotional problems and that these problems have dynamic antecedents, presumably in childhood.

The rational-emotive therapist attacks the disturbed individual's irrational position in two main ways. The therapist (1) serves as a counterpropagandist, directly contradicting and denying the irrationalities the client keeps perpetuating, and (2) encourages, persuades, and sometimes commands the client to engage in activities that will support the destruction of the irrationalities. The focus of the therapy is not only to help the client develop insight into the early causes of the behavior and come to understand that disturbances are reinforced through a tendency to think irrationally but also to demonstrate that the client must rethink irrational beliefs in order to change behavior.

Reality therapy

Reality therapy was developed in the late 1950s and early 1960s by the psychiatrist William Glasser (1965). Glasser's work, initially with young offenders, led him to the conclusion that until clients accept responsibility for their behavior, little change can occur. The basic premise of reality therapy is that most people with difficulties deny reality and behave irresponsibly. The reality therapists use their relationships with clients as a tool to assist the clients in becoming responsible, owning their own behavior.

Glasser's theory is based on the concept that the one prime need in all people, no matter what their culture, is the need for identity, for uniqueness. This identity, in addition, must have meaning in relation to others and usually takes form as either seeing oneself as being successful in life or seeing oneself as a failure. This failure identity, feels Glasser, is a function of not being responsible for one's own behavior. It is through relationships with others that the identity sense grows and through positive-valued relationships in particular that the sense of identity can change in positive directions.

In reality therapy, the relationship (1) is personal and caring, (2) focuses on present behavior rather than on feelings, (3) focuses on the present circumstances rather than on past history, (4) includes value judgments on the part of the therapist and the client as to what is "good" behavior, (5) includes planning for changing failure behavior to success behavior, (6) focuses on client commitment, (7) accepts no excuses, and (8) accepts no punishment systems. The therapist is very active and directive, much like the rational-emotive therapist, but with a very commonsensical approach. Much of the process consists of setting limits, examining facts, arguing constructively, and engaging in confrontation. The goal of therapy is to help clients become increasingly responsible, able to resolve crises and adjustment problems through the acceptance of responsibility, and able to fulfill needs without hurting themselves or others.

Structural Variations of the Psychotherapeutic Approaches

The six systems of psychotherapy that have been presented vary greatly in a broad range of areas, including their conceptions of the basic nature of human beings, why people behave as they do, and how to intervene specifically in order to change them. Yet they maintain the common elements presented earlier in the chapter. As they have been described, the focus has been mainly on the one-to-one verbal relationship between client and therapist. However, a complete introduction to these approaches must also consider certain structural variations on psychotherapy: group and family therapy. In either variation, the underlying theoretical framework may be any one of the systems already described or virtually any other system. Significant differences, however, do exist between these variations and the process that occurs in individual psychotherapy. It is the differences that will be focused on here.

Group psychotherapy

The development and use of group psychotherapy has been traced back to the early 1900s, when group treatment was used by the physician Joseph Pratt in the treatment of emotional aspects of pulmonary tuberculosis (Harper, 1960). It was not, however, until the post–World War II years that its use became more common. Part of its popularity, of course, comes from its obvious efficiency—the therapist can work with ten to twelve clients in a session rather than just one. Proponents of the group psychotherapy model, however, focus more on the unique influences of the group process on individuals as a rationale for its use than on the issue of its efficiency (Yalom, 1985).

Even though group therapists may have a formal background in any of the theoretical systems, most would concur on the specific advantages of the group setting. To begin with, in the group, the individual soon discovers that he or she is not alone with problems, that others have problems as severe. Each individual is encouraged to express himself or herself freely, often finding reassurance that he or she is "not too bad." By being able to share problems with others, the individuals not only experience an emotional catharsis or ventilation but also discover that rejection and ridicule are not necessarily a result of openness. Rather than being sanctioned positively or negatively, personal behaviors are analyzed by both the therapist and other group members in terms of their problem components and the difficulties they may cause.

A major force in group psychotherapy is the impact of peer pressure and support as manifested in group standards and values. An incorporation of group standards often neutralizes the individual's self-oriented needs. The therapist sees to it that the standards of the group are not self-defeating and that adaptive patterns become part of the group norm. However, within the norm of the group, the individual is encouraged to behave "naturally," that is, without excessive restraint. The person may be competitive, aggressive, submissive, withdrawing, or dominant, for example, so that the group becomes a laboratory for behavior that can then be examined by the members and the therapist.

When problem behaviors are expressed, they are open to interpretation and analysis by the therapist *and* other group members. A major advantage of group treatment is this possibility of a client's behavior's being interpreted and analyzed by more than one person. It is less easy for a client to reject an interpretation or analysis when a number of group members agree that it is correct and provide feedback than when just one person (the therapist in one-to-one psychotherapy) presents it. In addition, the individual has the support of a number of persons rather than just one for changes in behavior.

A major consequence of group therapy is considered to be the possibility of vicarious learning. The group member can learn how emotional processes function by observing how others react and solve problems and often seems to be able to apply these observations personally. Clients in the group setting have reported that even though they may have sat through several sessions without verbally participating, they were experiencing the group ebb and flow and were learning about themselves and experiencing change.

To summarize, group psychotherapy provides a laboratory under the guidance of a trained leader in which the clients may do the following:

1. Discover that their problems are neither unique nor "bad."
2. Become involved with others while being supported.
3. Reduce tension and anxiety through ventilation.
4. Study their own behavior in relation to others in order to gain insight and understanding.
5. Receive strong support in their efforts to change self-defeating behavior.
6. See themselves as others really see them, not as they *imagine* others see them.
7. Have a chance to receive the intrinsic reward of helping others.
8. Practice and develop positive self-supporting behavior.

Family therapy

Family therapy is a relatively recent phenomenon that became common in the late 1950s and early 1960s. It is partially an outgrowth of the observation that family members have tremendous influence on what the client does and is able to do outside the therapy session. It is particularly apparent that the functioning of persons in need is intimately tied to family relationships, and in many cases the clients' problems cannot be effectively dealt with in isolation from the family environment. To deal with this issue, a number of therapists began to see total families. It was soon discovered that the family must often be conceptualized as a unit, that an individual's problem behaviors are often an acting out of interactional problems in the family. A particularly striking observation is that often when the identified client becomes more appropriately adjusted, another member of the family begins manifesting problem behavior as if to replace the original member's disturbances.

As early as the mid-1950s, Jackson (1957) introduced the term *family homeostasis* to refer to the activities of families operating as a unit in order to maintain a balance in relationships. When family relationships are distorted, disturbed, or pained, members often take on themselves the task of maintaining the family unit by engaging in distorted behavior that acts to cover the family's real problems. The distortions of behavior that appear can be so bizarre as to be labeled *psychotic*. In fact, one theory of the causality of schizophrenia is based on the concept of distorted family communication as the prime factor in the development of these types of seriously disturbed lifestyles.

Even though the specific activities of family therapists may be influenced by the theoretical framework to which the therapists adhere, the common tie is the emphasis on intercommunication between family members. The therapist most often meets the family as a unit with no members excluded from the session. The therapist explores the structure and function of the family, acting as a resource person who is relatively objective. Therapists act as models of communication, teaching the members to communicate directly with no hidden meanings or secret agendas, clarifying incongruities, and confronting double messages. As communication systems in the family become clarified, the family can begin to give up covert or hidden agendas and learn to tolerate differences without fear of disaster (Satir, 1964). The members (particularly the identified patient) then can begin to give up the distorted behavior patterns that caused the original identification of one member as being disturbed.

Evaluating the Effectiveness of the Psychotherapuetic Approaches

Do the psychotherapeutic strategies work? If one were to ask any practicing psychotherapist, the answer would certainly be in the affirmative. Many questions do exist, however, and many criticisms have been leveled at these processes. Foremost of the critics has been Hans Eysenck (1966), who surveyed the available literature on evaluating psychotherapy and came to a number of conclusions.

Eysenck found that most of the studies he surveyed had negative or equivocal results. Many indicated that people who were treated with psychotherapy for psychological problems did not improve any more than people who received no treatment. He also found that people who were treated with behavior therapy based on learning theory improved significantly more and more rapidly than those treated with verbal psychotherapy.

Most recent criticisms of the effectiveness of psychotherapy are based on this 1966 study. However, Eysenck has received considerable criticism in regard to the methodological soundness of his study. More recent evidence based on controlled quantitative studies (Meltzoff and Kornreich, 1970; Sloane et al., 1975; Smith, Glass, and Miller, 1980) indicates that there are significantly more changes in persons who are treated than in those who receive no treatment. In addition, these researchers point out that of seventy controlled studies available when Eysenck drew his conclusions, he included only eleven, and that if he had included all seventy, his conclusions would have been reversed.

One recently reported major long-term study of psychotherapy spanned the years from 1954 to 1982. It examined the effects of psychoanalysis and other less intense types of psychotherapy on the lives of forty-two people (Wallerstein, 1986). This study found that therapy had a significant impact on most of the forty-two people and that the effects lasted many years. In addition, the study indicates that in most cases, supportive (less intense) therapies like client-centered counseling were as effective as depth psychoanalysis. The study suggests that psychoanalysis has a narrower therapeutic role than previously thought and is most appropriate for the less seriously disturbed person.

The issue of the effectiveness of psychotherapeutic approaches is nowhere near a dead one. The final accounting will have to wait for a greater sophistication in research techniques in terms of the definition of problem behaviors and the control of additional variables. Until that time, human service workers will have to rely on their own judgment and experiences in determining the value of the verbal psychotherapies. What does seem clear in the final analysis is that when most psychotherapies work, they work best with the population for which they were designed: reasonably intelligent, often introspective, usually middle-class individuals who can deal with or have the potential to deal with their problems on a verbal-emotional level. Psychotherapy is less likely to work well with individuals who are not highly verbal or introspective, who need to work out their problems by *doing* something rather than by talking about them.

Summary

1. Psychotherapeutic approaches are based on the assumption that many problems result from defects in the internal psychological functioning of the individual.

2. A number of different theories of psychotherapy exist. While there are substantial differences among the psychotherapeutic approaches, they also share a number of common elements.

3. The oldest of the psychotherapies is psychoanalysis. It is intensive and directive. Important concepts and techniques include free association, transference, and abreaction.

4. Rogerian client-centered therapy is nondirective and rejects the importance of unconscious motivation. It focuses on the importance of the self-concept. It attempts to create a therapeutic atmosphere of nonjudgmental acceptance. The therapist must have empathy, genuineness, and unconditional positive regard for the client.

5. Transactional analysis focuses on the interactions between two or more persons. Important concepts include structural analysis, script analysis, and games.

6. Gestalt therapy focuses on the here and now of the client and avoids dealing with the past. It emphasizes helping the client to be in touch with all aspects of his or her personality.

7. Rational-emotive therapy focuses on changing the irrational beliefs of troubled persons. It is active and directive, often involving confrontation and persuasion.

8. Reality therapy emphasizes the need for clients to become responsible for their own behavior and the importance of developing a success identity rather than a failure identity.

9. The structural variations in psychotherapy include group psychotherapy and family therapy. Therapists of all theoretical orientations use these methods.

10. The effectiveness of psychotherapy has been debated for years. Recent evidence indicates that there are significantly more positive changes in persons who have had psychotherapy than in those who have not.

Discussion Questions

1. What are the six basic assumptions of the intrapsychic strategies?

2. What disadvantages can you identify in the psychoanalytic approach in terms of using it with human service clients? What advantages?

3. What advantages can you see in the use of transactional analysis?

4. What advantages are there for group psychotherapy over individual psychotherapy?

Learning Experiences

1. Try to describe a period in your life when you experienced a transference relationship with someone.

2. Try to recollect an early childhood experience that seems important to the way you behave now.

3. Try to describe a communication experience using the parent-adult-child model of transactional analysis.

4. Reflect on how it feels to talk about your problems to someone.

5. Observe group behaviors. For example, have you noticed how you and your classmates tend to sit in the same desk in a classroom almost all semester? Why haven't you moved around?

6. Identify and list the rituals you engage in. (For example, ask others, "How are you?" What happens when they don't answer, "Fine"?)

7. Identify an event that caused an upset in your family's homeostasis (balance). What effect did it have? How was it resolved?

Endnotes

1. Wolberg, L. R. *The Technique of Psychotherapy*. 3d ed. New York: Grune & Stratton, Inc., 1977, pp. 560–561. Reprinted by permission.
2. From Carl R. Rogers: *Client-Centered Therapy*. Copyright (c) 1951, renewed 1979 by Houghton Mifflin Company. Used by permission.

Recommended Readings

Corsini, R. (ed.). *Current Psychotherapies*. Itasca, Ill.: T. E. Peacock, 1973.

Haveliwala, Y. A.; Scheflen, A. E.; and Ashcraft, N. *Common Sense in Therapy: A Handbook for the Mental Health Worker*. New York: Brunner-Mazel, 1979.

Hergenhahn, B. R. *An Introduction to Theories of Personality*. Englewood Cliffs, N.J.: Prentice-Hall, 1984.

Lindner, R. *The Fifty-Minute Hour*. New York: Rinehart and Co., 1955.

Wolberg, L. R. The *Technique of Psychotherapy*, 3d ed. New York: Grune & Stratton, 1977.

Yalom, I. D. *The Theory and Practice of Group Psychotherapy*, 3d ed. New York: Basic Books, 1985.

10

Integrating Contemporary Strategies, Personal Relationship Skills, and the Supervisory Process

- How do human service workers integrate the contemporary strategies into their work?
- What is meant by *personal relationship skills?*
- What attitudes, values, and feelings are important in personal relationship skills?
- Do verbal communication techniques enhance the helping relationship?
- How do people express themselves without using words?
- How do human service workers enhance their skills once they are employed?

The contemporary strategies have much to offer the person in need. Many individuals have benefited or can benefit from medical/psychiatric treatment, behavior therapy, and psychotherapy. For some, these approaches are sufficient for dealing with their problems; for many others, much more in the way of human service alternatives is required.

In some settings, human service workers work with other professionals whose primary role is to engage in the contemporary strategies. Human service workers in these settings may or may not be encouraged to use aspects of those strategies in their work. A more probable situation is one in which the contemporary strategies are used and the human service worker begins to use some aspects of one or more of the approaches through experience, training, and supervision. The human service worker may be employed in a setting that does not offer medical/psychiatric approaches, psychotherapy, or behavior therapy, yet the worker who has some understanding of the contemporary approaches of medical/psychiatric treatment, behavior therapy, and psychotherapy may have an advantage in terms of understanding the clients.

In the material that follows, a number of examples will illustrate how the human service worker may become involved in the use of medical/psychiatric, behavioral, and psychotherapeutic approaches in human service settings. The importance of some elements of the psychotherapeutic approach to all human service activities will also be identified. The human service worker has one particular tool, always available, that can be of great assistance in his or her work: personal relationship skills. Like all tools, these skills must be developed through training and maintained through supervision.

Using Contemporary Strategies

Medical/psychiatric approaches

The human service worker is unlikely to implement medical or psychiatric treatment directly. An individual who has career goals in these areas usually trains in medicine and becomes a physician, nurse, practical nurse, physical therapist, or medical technician or enters another medically oriented field. In some settings, however, a human service worker may have a close working relationship with such individuals and may deal with clients who are receiving medical treatments for physical or emotional problems. Such settings include support groups for persons with chronic medical disorders, nursing homes, private or public mental hospitals, senior citizen centers, and community mental health centers. In these settings, the human service worker may need a basic understanding of the medical problems of the client, the medical treatment being rendered, and the impact of the medical problem and its treatment on the client's life.

Individuals with physical illnesses often can benefit from human service approaches. Helping ill or recovering clients, human service workers, like the one described below, need to become knowledgeable about medical disorders and treatment.

▪ ▪ Pat Richards is a human service worker at a multiservice community center whose work required her to become familiar with a particular physical disease, its treatments, and its end results. Over a period of a few years, several of the center's clients and one staff member developed cancer and were treated with surgery and chemotherapy at a local hospital. From a medical perspective the treatment and medical management of these individuals was as good as could be expected. However, it seemed to several staff members that the people who had been stricken with the disease were receiving little support in dealing with the emotional and psychological problems of having cancer and living with its aftermath.

Discussions about the need for support services began to take place among the staff members and led to the center director making contact with the hospital. After much planning, the hospital and the community center announced that a joint project would be initiated. Two support groups would be run, one for cancer victims and one for victims and their family members.

Pat Richards, through training, experience, and supervision, had over the years become a good group leader. In addition, she had had direct experience with the emotional and psychological ravages of cancer and its treatment since her eldest sister had been treated for breast cancer. The center director selected Pat as one of the leaders of the support group, and she was enthused about the opportunity.

Planning, organizing, and leading the cancer support groups with a nurse co-leader from the cancer treatment unit was as much an educational experience as a work experience, particularly in the beginning. Pat found that she needed to learn a great deal about various types of cancer, their treatments, the side effects of treatments, and people's psychological reactions to the illness and treatment. Her nurse co-leader was a great help, but Pat also did a lot of reading at the library, made contact with the American Cancer Society, and visited a similar support group in another city.

This groundwork helped Pat understand the pain, concerns, and fears that the participants in the group were experiencing and talking about. It provided a base of knowledge on which to build as Pat learned about the members of the group, and it helped her communicate to the group members that she could really hear what they were saying about their difficult and frightening experience.

Pat did not start out in human services with the idea of spending a substantial part of her time working with people with medical problems. She has found, however, that she is becoming a lay expert on a set of medical problems and treatments. She does not do medical treatment, but she does have to integrate her human services work with approaches based on the medical model.

More commonly, psychiatric approaches are an integral part of a human service system. Many human service workers are employed in community mental health centers, public mental hospitals, or other agencies where clients are treated for emotional or behavioral disorders with medical/psychiatric approaches such as chemotherapy. Knowledge of the purpose, effects, and side effects of such treatments can be helpful in dealing with these clients.

■ ■ Carmen Villalobos is a human services caseworker for a state department of children and family services. Her agency is responsible for the identification, protection, and monitoring of children in families in which child abuse or neglect has occurred. Carmen's role includes making outreach field visits to families in which abuse or neglect has occurred in the past, partly to monitor the welfare of the child but also to provide assistance and support to the parent.

Carmen's case load includes a single-parent family consisting of a mother, Joan Mitchell, and her children, Ricky, age twelve, and Lisa, age nine. The location of the father is unknown. Three years earlier Joan had been charged with child neglect. Intervention at that time revealed that the children were being neglected but not physically abused. Ricky had missed an extreme amount of school, leading to the discovery of the problem. The home was unheated, the children were unfed and dirty, and Joan appeared very withdrawn and disturbed. Joan's relatives in another city were contacted and temporarily took in Ricky and Lisa. They encouraged Joan to admit herself to a psychiatric unit in a general hospital.

After Joan was admitted to the psychiatric unit, she was diagnosed as suffering from acute schizophrenia. She was treated with short-term psychotherapy and chemotherapy and within seventeen days was discharged as recovered. She was very much her old self again. At discharge, Joan was referred to a local mental health center for outpatient treatment. Within two months her children returned to live with her.

Joan continued going to the mental health center once a week for psychotherapy and once a month to see a psychiatrist about maintenance medication. After a year she dropped psychotherapy but continued to go for medication. In addition, Joan and the children were visited regularly by a caseworker from Carmen's agency.

Carmen Villalobos "inherited" Joan, Ricky, and Lisa from the original caseworker somewhat less than two years ago. About six months ago, Carmen became aware of a change in Joan during visits to Joan's apartment. Joan complained of being drowsy and sleeping too much and of always having a dry mouth. She wondered aloud if the medication she was getting was doing any good or was making her sick. Carmen suggested that Joan check it out the next time she went to the mental health center.

A month later, as Carmen was arriving at Joan's apartment, she was already thinking about the last visit. In reviewing her notes, she realized that Joan's drowsiness and dry mouth were side effects of Thorazine, which she was receiving at the mental health center. Carmen wondered how Joan was doing this time.

Unfortunately, Joan was not doing very well. She was reluctant to let Carmen in but finally did so. Carmen found that Joan was very withdrawn. The apartment was in disorder, dirty dishes were in the sink, apparently from a number of meals, and unbagged garbage was lying about the kitchen. Both Ricky and Lisa were home on a school day. At first Joan seemed unwilling to talk to Carmen, but Carmen was able to draw her out.

Carmen's suspicions were confirmed. The side effects of the Thorazine had become so unpleasant for Joan that she had completely stopped taking the medication. She also had missed an appointment with the psychiatrist at the mental health center. The deterioration in Joan's behavior, the withdrawal, and the neglect in homemaking and parenting skills constituted an early sign that Joan's disorder was appearing again. Carmen's knowledge of schizophrenia, the effects of Thorazine, and the side effects of medication helped her understand how to help Joan.

Because of her longstanding positive relationship with Joan, Carmen was able to persuade her to go to the mental health center immediately. There, in a session with the center psychiatrist, Carmen was able to act knowledgeably as Joan's advocate and explain the problem with side effects and the changes in Joan's behavior. The psychiatrist was able to administer a fast-acting antipsychotic drug and prescribe a medication with less noticeable side effects.

For the next few weeks, Carmen increased the frequency of her visits. Joan, taking her medication again, became progressively less withdrawn and disorganized. Within a month, she was back to normal and was determined to continue her monthly medication reviews with the psychiatrist at the mental health center.

The agency that employs Carmen Villalobos does not use medical/psychiatric approaches in its delivery of services, yet many of its clients are being treated medically or psychiatrically. Carmen Villalobos's ability to deliver human services was enhanced by the integration of her knowledge of medical/psychiatric approaches into her day-to-day functioning.

Many human service workers are employed in settings where specific medical or psychiatric knowledge is not necessary. Pat Richards and Carmen Villalobos found that they needed to know more about some aspects of medicine or psychiatry than they had expected. Both knew from their training when it was necessary to find out more. In both cases, the needs of their clients dictated the specific knowledge and skills Pat and Carmen developed.

Behavioral approaches

In the past two decades, the application of behavior therapy has become quite widespread. In many settings it is conducted or supervised primarily by professional psychologists with master's or doctoral degrees. In other settings the implementation is conducted by individuals with generic human services training supervised by these types of professionals or by experienced human services workers.

Human service systems in which behavioral therapy is used include public school programs for emotionally handicapped children, residential programs for the mentally retarded, residential and outpatient programs for children identified as mentally ill, and juvenile and adult corrections facilities. The success of these programs in diminishing the intensity and frequency of problem behaviors and in helping people develop more functional new behaviors is likely to lead to greater use of such approaches in a variety of agencies.

■ ■ Pauline Erickson is a graduate of an associate of arts degree human services program in child development. She works as an instructional aide with Kathy Turner, a special education instructor, in a public school. The classroom has five children who have behavior problems that prevent their being taught in a regular classroom. The children need more individual attention than would be possible in a class of twenty-five to thirty children.

One of the five children with whom Pauline works is Billy Keller. Billy is a nine-year-old who among other problems is hyperactive. He is extremely active and impulsive, and his motor coordination is below average. He finds it difficult to sit still and concentrate, squirms in his chair, taps his feet, talks loudly to children during class, and often gets up and moves about the classroom instead of listening to the teacher or studying. In spite of his average intelligence, it is hard for Billy to make progress in class because of these behaviors, which also disrupt the general progress of the whole class.

In order to help Billy change his behavior, Pauline, with her supervisor, Kathy, met with the school psychologist. After several meetings they decided to implement a behavior therapy program modeled after one developed by Nathan Azrin (Azrin and Powers, 1975). The behaviors they targeted for change were inappropriate speaking out in class and leaving the seat without permission.

Since in this classroom the school day was broken down into twenty-five-minute class sessions and five-minute recesses, they decided that the first step would be to use verbal reminders and loss of recess as a consequence for rule breaking. At the beginning of each class session Billy would be reminded not to speak inappropriately and to stay in his seat. If he behaved acceptably, he would be given verbal praise at the end of the class. If he spoke out or left his seat, he would be told to stay in the room during recess. Pauline, Kathy, and the school psychologist agreed that Pauline would make this behavioral program her special task for several weeks.

On a Friday Pauline observed Billy and recorded how often he disrupted the class by engaging in the two behaviors. It happened twenty-two times. The following Monday morning Pauline told Billy about the program and the consequences if he disrupted class. By the end of that week, it was obvious that the program was helping: Billy was down to six disruptions a day. That Friday, Pauline, Kathy, and the school psychologist met again and decided to add another step. After each class period in which Billy did not speak out of turn or leave his desk without permission, Pauline would post a large gold star next to his name on the bulletin board. At the end of the day, Billy would be able to take a gold star home to his mother if he earned stars in more than half the sessions. Once again, Pauline would take responsibility for the program.

The following Monday, Pauline explained the addition to the program to Billy. By the week's end, Billy was down to three disruptions a day. After another week he was taking a gold star home almost every day. On some days there were one or two disruptions; on other days, none. More important, Billy's schoolwork was showing a noticeable improvement. Over the course of the year, Pauline and Kathy were able to fade the program. Billy eventually maintained his progress without losing recesses and toward the end of the year did not need gold stars to maintain the behavior.

The behavioral program of punishment and positive reinforcement had worked. Pauline and Kathy have been able to use the same approach with other children in the years since they tried it with Billy, with equal success in most instances.

In many human service settings, behavioral approaches may meet one client's particular needs, whereas other approaches may meet the needs of clients with different problems. For example, one child in Pauline Erickson's classroom was in play therapy with a child psychologist. Another child who, like Billy, had been identified as hyperactive was receiving a medication called methylphenidate that seemed to reduce the problem behaviors. Pauline

Human service workers' knowledge of psychotherapeutic approaches such as play therapy can often be applied in other settings, such as teaching the mentally retarded.

integrated a behavioral approach into her work because one of the people she wanted to help could benefit from it.

In many human service systems, behavioral strategies are the primary approach. Human service workers who obtain employment in some residential settings often must integrate the behavioral approaches into their work with all their clients.

■ ■ Joe Benson works in a juvenile corrections facility that provides residential services for young offenders, that is, a live-in setting for boys who have usually had multiple run-ins with the law. These boys have been arrested and tried in juvenile court for offenses ranging from homicide and major theft to multiple offenses of a less serious nature.

In his four-year human services degree program, Joe Benson took several courses that dealt with principles of learned behavior and behavior therapy. Joe's knowledge of behavioral approaches has helped him in his work, since the correctional facility program involves a token economy.

Joe works from 7 A.M. to 3 P.M in a cottage that houses eight boys in their early teens. The token economy provides a structure for their group life. In this token economy a variety of positive, or prosocial, behaviors are identified. When the boys engage in these behaviors they earn tokens, called "units," that they can redeem for commodities such as candy, soft drinks, and snacks and items such as clothing, combs, and radios. The units also can be redeemed for privileges such as attendance at movies or other special activities. The prosocial behaviors for which the boys earn these units include rising on time in the morning, making one's bed, good grooming, being prompt, attending counselor sessions, attending school, and helping other students. Thus, the units earned act as positive reinforcement for appropriate behavior.

The units also are used to apply punishment or withdrawal of positive reinforcement. Boys who do not engage in prosocial behavior are not positively reinforced; if they engage in unacceptable behavior, they may have units taken away (they are fined). Unacceptable behaviors that result in fines include foul language, stealing, and fighting.

Joe's duties as a cottage worker are varied. He is involved in counseling the boys under his supervision regarding their day-to-day behavior, their fears and concerns, and their general adjustment to the correctional facility. He also organizes and participates in daily recreational activities. However, the behavioral token economy provides the underlying structure for the group life of the eight boys in Joe's cottage.

When a new boy joins the cottage group, Joe explains the rules and the token system of reinforcers or fines. Joe observes the new boy for several weeks and identifies any particular problems and assets. This data-collection period provides the information for designing an individual program for the boy. In consultation with his supervisor, a psychologist, Joe then develops an individual behavioral program for that boy, involving a plan for reinforcing desirable behaviors and setting up consequences for unacceptable or problem behaviors.

Once an individual plan is developed, Joe collects data on the frequency of the positive and problem behaviors. While this process goes on, it provides the data that determine whether Joe gives units to the boys as reinforcers or administers fines. Joe also keeps records of the units given, taken away, and spent and notes whether the behaviors change for the better or worse. Joe has found that over a period of time the token economy has had a significant effect on promoting the development of prosocial behavior and reducing problem behaviors.

Joe Benson and the other human service workers at his facility have integrated behavioral therapy into their work with all cottage residents. The correctional facility also requires that Joe and his coworkers be able to interact with the clients as group leaders, activity workers, and counselors. They must be able to relate to the boys in an understanding, caring manner so that each boy realizes that he is seen as a unique individual rather than an object to be manipulated.

Human service workers employed in settings that place a major emphasis on behavioral approaches obviously need to develop skills relevant to their approaches. They must understand the basic principles of learned behavior and concepts such as positive reinforcement, punishment, and negative reinforcement. Like Joe Benson, some human service workers develop a basic understanding of the behavioral approaches through college courses. Many others develop these skills through on-the-job or in-service training.

Psychotherapeutic approaches

Psychotherapy has been viewed traditionally as a treatment process in which a highly credentialed, trained, and experienced professional develops a helping relationship with a psychologically or emotionally troubled client. The psychotherapist typically engages in a verbal process with the client in order to uncover the psychological causes of the troubles and helps the client change his or her problematic ways of thinking, feeling, and behaving. This treatment process usually occurs on a one-to-one or small-group basis.

For years the practice of psychotherapy was primarily limited to several professional groups. Psychoanalysts, some psychiatrists, clinical psychologists, and M.S.W. social workers were the primary providers. In the private, fee-for-service sector this is still basically the case. Traditional professional training and degrees are required for licensure or certification for the provision of psychotherapy for a fee in all states.

Within human service agencies the situation is somewhat different. For the past twenty-five years nontraditional workers have engaged in activities ranging from one-to-one intensive psychoanalytically oriented psychotherapy and client-centered counseling to the informal or formal application of psychotherapy principles in a variety of helping relationships. These activities are often called *counseling* to indicate that they are not as intensive as psychotherapy. In practice, a human service counselor may achieve the same ends as a professionally educated and trained psychotherapist (Brown, 1974; Hattie, Sharpley, and Rogers, 1984).

■ ■ Fred Zimmerman is an alcoholism counselor at a community alcohol and drug abuse agency. He obtained an associate of arts degree in human services in 1973, worked for several years, and returned to a university to obtain a bachelor's degree with a focus on addiction counseling. Since his graduation in 1978 he has worked full-time at the same agency.

Fred deals with recovering alcoholics. His case load consists of both inpatients and outpatients. He spends his day doing counseling with individuals on a one-to-one basis, and three times a week he leads a group session with about six members.

The basic philosophy of Fred's agency is that alcohol and drug addictions develop because people discover that chemicals help them avoid the painful realities of living. They feel better when they take drugs or use alcohol. Later, the alcohol or drug use causes problems in living, but the addictive process makes stopping very difficult. The agency's treatment approach is first to find out why clients started abusing drugs (that is, what problems the drugs solved) and then to help the clients change so that they can solve these problems in more adaptive ways. One treatment vehicle that is used to achieve these goals is psychotherapy.

When Fred does psychotherapy with an agency client, he thinks of it as having three phases. In the beginning phase, Fred develops a relationship with the client. During these opening sessions he gets to know the client, the client's life problems, and the client's addiction problems in some detail. The client also gets to know Fred very well. It is important that the client begin to see Fred as someone who wants to help, who cares about the client, and who *can* help.

During the middle phase, Fred creates an atmosphere of trust and acceptance in which the client can reveal his or her needs, fears, and deepest problems. It is a time when the client can risk change by giving up old behavior patterns and trying new ones. Fred sees this as the most difficult period for the client, who often experiences emotional turmoil. The final phase of treatment is termination. If all has gone as desired, a close relationship has developed between the client and Fred, and the client has been able to change significantly. Now the client must deal with his or her feelings about leaving therapy. At this point the client is often fearful or anxious about leaving the relationship and becoming independent. During the termination phase Fred helps the client deal successfully with those feelings.

Fred's work as a psychotherapist requires a number of skills that must be learned and practiced. He learned some of the basic skills in his human service education program but has also had a lot of training at the agency. He continues to be supervised weekly by a more experienced psychotherapist. Fred has become very good at listening. He listens not only to the words of the clients but also for the feelings underlying the words. He also "listens" to nonverbal communication. For example, a client may say, "I'm feeling fine," but her behavior may say that she is anxious or angry.

Fred also has become good at communicating. In psychotherapy that means much more than being a good speaker and transmitting information. Fred can respond to clients' words and feelings in a way that tells them that Fred understands what they are saying and feeling. He can reflect back what clients say so that they know whether he understands them. He has learned to confront clients when their actions do not match their words or feelings. Fred also has become skilled at interpretation. He is able to interpret the clients' behavior, words, or feelings in ways that help the clients gain new understanding into why they feel or behave in particular ways. Often when the clients gain new understanding, they change established problem behaviors.

Fred's listening and communication skills constitute a major part of his ability to do psychotherapy. His knowledge of addiction and its causes and of the problems of alcoholics is also important. Equally important is the fact that Fred cares about his clients. He is able to feel nonpossessive warmth toward them. He accepts them as they are; he does not demand that they be something else but is willing to help them change if they wish. Fred is able to be empathic. He can put himself into the clients' shoes and see the world through their eyes, however bleak that view might be.

Fred also has an air of genuineness. He is not a phony. He is able to reveal his true feelings, and his true feelings are expressed in his behavior. He has no need to manipulate clients or pretend to be something he is not.

Some of the settings in which human service workers may function as psychotherapists are obvious. In public mental hospitals or mental health centers, clients frequently have problems that require psychotherapy. Many human service workers in such settings may be trained to function as psychotherapists or counselors in addition to their other duties. Workers in crisis centers with phone hotlines for people with emotional problems may also need formal psychotherapeutic skills.

In other human service settings, the workers may not have to provide formal psychotherapy. However, the ability to use effective personal helping skills based on general psychotherapeutic principles is likely to be important. The human service worker in a correctional facility, rehabilitation workshop, preschool, senior citizen center, rape counseling center, or public aid office will encounter people in need for whom a helping relationship based on psychotherapeutic principles will be helpful.

Most college or university education programs in human services do not train graduates to be psychotherapists. Surprisingly, the same can be said about most graduate programs for traditional professionals. Psychiatrists and clinical psychologists, for example, may take a college course or two on the principles of psychotherapy. However, traditional professionals usually learn to do psychotherapy as apprentices to more experienced psychotherapists during an internship or residency after they have received a graduate degree. Fred Zimmerman became a psychotherapist through much the same process. He learned by doing psychotherapy under the supervision and training of an experienced psychotherapist at his agency.

In human service agencies that do not offer formal psychotherapy, the integration of some of the principles and skills of the psychotherapeutic approach may still be useful. Even when clients' needs consist of such things as housing, money, medical care, job training, or education, clients will enter into a personal relationship with a human services provider that is often very important in finding solutions.

■ ■ After graduating from a two-year associate of arts degree program in human services, Irene Thomas found employment directing an activity program in a county nursing home. It was challenging and rewarding to work with the elderly people who needed the support services of the county residence. Most of the residents seemed to respond very favorably to the activities Irene organized and to her relationship with them.

Irene remembers one resident who needed individual attention. Mrs. Wilson was seventy-six years old and widowed. Her son and daughter-in-law had brought her to the county home because she could no longer maintain herself in her apartment and needed a limited amount of nursing care for a chronic illness.

Mrs. Wilson did not seem to adapt to the home. She stayed by herself in her room, staring out the window. She refused to be involved in activities. The nursing staff described her as angry, critical, and complaining. When Mrs. Wilson's son and daughter-in-law would visit, she would berate them for putting her in the home, beg tearfully for them to take her out, or sit without speaking.

Irene began to drop by Mrs. Wilson's room several times a day. For weeks Mrs. Wilson had little to say, and Irene would just sit quietly with her. On occasion Irene would tell Mrs. Wilson that she enjoyed sitting quietly with her. Soon Mrs. Wilson began to talk about her life with her husband and how much she missed him. Irene reflected those feelings back to Mrs. Wilson and shared how she felt about losing people she had known. Mrs. Wilson began to share more of her life with Irene. They talked about the meaning of friends, home, and family. Irene's genuine interest in Mrs. Wilson helped Mrs. Wilson share her fears, concerns, interests, and beliefs.

Irene and Mrs. Wilson began to talk about what it meant for a person to have to go to a nursing home. Mrs. Wilson was able to share her feelings of abandonment and her anger toward her son and daughter-in-law. Yet talking about these things with Irene helped Mrs. Wilson sort out her mixed feelings, and she soon was able to talk about how much she loved her son, his wife, and their children.

The growing relationship between Mrs. Wilson and Irene seemed to help Mrs. Wilson see the nursing home as a friendlier place. With Irene's urging, she began to get more involved in the activities and made friends with the other residents. The nursing staff began to notice that Mrs. Wilson was more talkative and friendly and complained less. Mrs. Wilson began to relate more positively to her son and daughter-in-law again.

For the next several years, Irene continued her relationship with Mrs. Wilson. Each respected the other, and Mrs. Wilson knew that Irene could understand her feelings. It seemed to Mrs. Wilson that often, after she had talked to Irene, she had a better grasp of how she really felt about things. Mrs. Wilson never really did like being in a nursing home, but Irene helped her make the best of the situation.

The relationship between Irene and Mrs. Wilson was not psychotherapy. Irene used her personal relationship skills to create an atmosphere in which Mrs. Wilson could examine her situation and change her way of dealing with it. But Irene Thomas was more than a friend who sympathized with Mrs. Wilson's plight and took her side. Irene in fact took no sides. She did not support Mrs. Wilson's early attitudes about how terrible it was to be put in the home and how terrible the son and daughter-in-law were to do that to her. Irene did show that she understood how Mrs. Wilson felt and that she cared about her, and she helped her see things from a different perspective.

Using Personal Relationship Skills

A common thread runs through the case examples provided in this chapter. Although each human service worker described is unique and although each works in a different setting with different roles and functions, all use effective personal relationship skills in their work.

What characterizes effective personal relationship skills? Although the question cannot be answered in absolute terms, sufficient study, research, and experience in psychotherapy suggest what some of the important factors may be (Danish and Hauer, 1973; Truax and Carkuff, 1967; Zingale, 1985). Effective personal relationship skills can be divided into two broad categories: being (Moustakas, 1986) and doing. Being refers to the attitudes, values, and feelings a human service worker holds that color his or her actions. Doing refers to the observable skills or activities that enhance relationships. Both, of course, are intimately related.

Being

You probably encountered people whom you found easy to talk to, whom you felt cared about you, who accepted you as you are with all your faults and strengths, and who valued your uniqueness rather than what you have, who you know, or what your social status is. Such individuals have developed a sense of being that helps them develop positive relationships with others. Some develop this sense naturally; others have to work to achieve it. To a greater or lesser extent, the human service workers described in this chapter have developed this quality.

For the human service worker, three aspects of this sense of being have been identified as being particularly important: warmth, empathy, and genuineness. These terms are used to describe interrelated and overlapping attributes that are sometimes called the Truax triad, named for a counselor who emphasized their importance (Truax and Carkuff, 1967). These will be described separately, but are closely related and interdependent (see Figure 10-1).

Figure 10-1 *The Truax triad: distinct but overlapping attributes of being.*

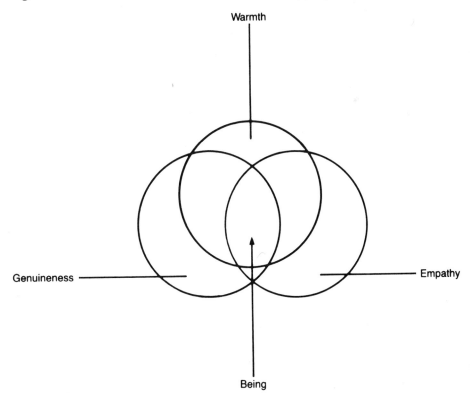

Warmth

Warmth is a fuzzy concept. It consists of a subtle communication of tender, caring feelings. People who lack warmth are described as cold, uncaring, or uninvolved. Thus, warmth implies involvement. The expression of warmth requires a nonjudgmental attitude and an avoidance of blaming. Warmth involves acceptance of the equal worth of others. It is necessary for a sense of closeness toward others and the ability to be open and revealing of oneself to others. The feelings of warmth one has toward others are most fruitful when they are nonpossessive. Possessive warmth may occur when one person maintains a relationship with another in order to manipulate that person or to meet his or her own needs rather than the needs of the other. Nonpossessive warmth entails a feeling of caring and concern without placing conditions on the relationship.

Empathy

People often want to help others out of sympathy, which is sorrow over the distress and misfortune of others. Empathic feeling goes a step farther. Rather than feeling *for* someone, empathy means feeling *with* someone. The empathic process in helping relationships has been described as having four aspects (Marcia, 1987):

1. *Identification*—paying attention to another and allowing oneself to become absorbed in contemplation of that person.
2. *Incorporation*—making the other's experience one's own via internalizing the other.
3. *Reverberation*—experiencing the other's experience while simultaneously attending to one's own cognitive and affective associations to that experience.
4. *Detachment*—moving back from the merged inner relationship to a position of separate identity, which permits a response to be made that reflects both understanding of others as well as separateness from them.

Empathy has often been described as walking in another's shoes. Empathy involves experiencing another's point of view, experiences, and feelings. Empathy allows one to know the world as another knows it. To the extent that one can do this, one's understanding becomes deeper. To the degree that one has empathic understanding of another human being, one is more able to accept that person. Empathic feelings, acceptance, and openness are reflected in behavior and allow others to feel that one understands them.

Genuineness

Being genuine means that what a person says, does, or thinks reflects what that person actually feels. It is a condition of congruence between all aspects of the individual. To be genuine requires that the human service worker be aware of his or her feelings and accept them. It involves the ability to express these feelings accurately in words and behavior. It also, however, requires the maturity and skills to be able to express these feelings in the context of a warm and empathic relationship. Genuineness helps differentiate between feelings that are appropriately due to relationships and feelings that derive from one's inaccurate perceptions.

Is being all that it takes?
Warmth, empathy, and genuineness are described as critical aspects of helping relationships. Some experts go so far as to suggest that if these three characteristics are present, effective helping relationships will develop naturally. There is some research to support this view. In one study, researchers selected college students who were experiencing anxiety, depression, and a sense of isolation (Strupp and Hadley, 1979). The students were assigned for counseling to experienced psychoanalytically oriented psychotherapists, trained experientially oriented psychotherapists, or untrained therapists. The study also compared the students with a waiting-list control group selected from the same student sample. The "untrained" therapists were college professors with no special knowledge or training in human services. They were selected because they were reputed to be interested in and available to students with problems and had been described as warm, caring, and trustworthy.

The study found that the students who had received counseling had improved more than the students in the control group. More important, the students seen by the untrained but warm, caring, and trustworthy professors had improved as much as those seen by highly trained specialists.

Although some research and a great deal of practical experience suggest that things such as warmth, empathy, and genuineness are important factors in effective helping relationships, other factors also may be important. Before any conclusions can be drawn in this regard, we must await further study (Frank, 1979). In the meantime the development of the ability to be warm, empathic, and genuine will continue to be important for human service workers.

Doing

We have seen that warmth, empathy, and genuineness are important qualities of effective personal relationship skills. These factors constitute personal attributes of human service workers that are expressed in the things they do. In later chapters, we shall examine many of the things human service workers do. Within the specific context of one-to-one personal relationship skills, though, there are a number of things worth identifying.

The doing skills that enhance personal relationships involve a particular way of communicating. In typical social intercourse, communicating most often involves a sharing of data or information. Although information sharing is often important in human services, a deeper form of communication is more desirable: the expressive communication of understanding, caring, warmth, empathy, and genuineness. The vehicles for this expressive form of communications include paraphrasing, reflection, confrontation, and interpretation, as well as nonverbal communication. Before we consider these techniques, a word of caution is in order. Techniques such as these cannot be learned through reading any more than warmth, empathy, and genuineness can. They *can* be learned, but it takes supervised practice.

Paraphrasing

Paraphrasing is putting a person's words into a new form in order to clarify what has been said. It may involve simply repeating a word or phrase that captures the essence of the communication or using entirely new words.

> *Client:* Sometimes I feel like I'm being choked. There's too many demands that people are putting on me. I can't swallow them fast enough.
>
> *Counselor:* Choked? (Repeating the client.) Like you're being force-fed. (Restating, substituting new word.)

The repetition of important, emotion-filled words or the rephrasing of the content of the communication serves two functions. First, it communicates to the client that he or she has been heard and encourages him or her to continue. Second, it gives the client the opportunity to correct the counselor if the counselor has missed the meaning of the communication.

Reflection

Reflection involves the identification and expression of the client's feelings. If the client's feelings are reflected back to the client, those feelings will be brought to the forefront of the client's awareness. Becoming more aware, the client is more likely to be enabled to deal with those feelings.

> *Client:* Things just don't seem to be going right. I'm in a dead-end job, I can't seem to concentrate on my studies. . . . I just don't know how to grab a hold of things.
>
> *Counselor:* Feeling trapped and helpless.

A client's feelings may at times be obvious both to the client and to the human service worker. At other times the person may be less aware of the feelings that he or she is experiencing and that are influencing behavior. When the counselor is able to "hear" between the lines and accurately reflect those feelings back to the client, the client often perceives that he or she is deeply understood. The client is encouraged to look more closely at himself or herself. This opens the possibility of exploring the relationship between the new feelings of awareness and the client's behavior. Through this process, reflection increases the consistency between what the client feels and the client's words and behavior. Reflection has the potential of increasing congruence and genuineness.

Confrontation

Confrontation involves bringing the client face to face with his or her denials, discrepancies between feelings and behavior, or unpleasant realities. Since many clients also deny their strengths and assets, confrontation is also used to help them recognize these positive aspects of themselves. The purpose of confrontation is not to attack but to push the client toward self-awareness and change within a supportive atmosphere.

> *Client:* Well, that last job I got canned from . . . I couldn't get along with the foreman. Nobody could. He had some kind of problem.
>
> *Counselor:* But the others didn't get fired. *You* did. How's that similar to the other jobs you lost?

Confrontation is a risky technique when used improperly or to excess. If the client feels attacked or demeaned, he or she may feel alienated from the human service worker. Confrontations that are improperly timed or too aggressive may undo previous progress in the development of a helping relationship. Confrontation is a device that must be used sparingly and within a supportive atmosphere.

Interpretation

Interpretation involves the human service worker in a process of placing the client's communication and behavior in a broader or different framework. It is an attempt to enable the client to see his or her behavior from a different perspective. Effective interpretation results in new self-understanding for the client, and that understanding may help the client see underlying motivations for particular behaviors or reasons for particular feelings. Effective interpretation requires that the human service worker have a deep and accurate understanding of the client.

> *Client:* God, what is it with me? Every time I get involved with a guy, he's married to somebody else!
>
> *Counselor:* You know, Judy, that's one way of protecting yourself from a relationship that can grow.
>
> *Client:* Huh! Yeah, I see it. If a guy was single, I'd have to take responsibility for the long term! Wow, that's something to chew on!

When interpretations are appropriately timed and based on an accurate understanding of the client's reasons for behavior, the client is able to integrate the counselor's views into his or her own self-perceptions. The resulting change in the client's self-perception allows the client to "try on" new ways of behaving or feeling with the continued support of the counselor. The ability to make effective interpretations requires substantial training and experience.

Nonverbal communication

The personal relationship skills discussed so far have been described as verbal processes of communication. Another significant aspect of communication involves nonverbal behavior. All people can communicate volumes about themselves and their reactions to others without the need for spoken dialogue. Sensitivity to our own and others' nonverbal communication can facilitate the development of effective helping skills. The reverse is also true. If one is not aware of nonverbal communications, one may transmit incomplete or even discrepant messages.

Some forms of nonverbal communication are obvious. The clenched hand with thumb up in the air or pointing down to indicate that things are good or bad is a case in point. Arms spread wide and extended toward a person represent an invitation to closeness. The arm stretched toward a person with the palm upraised indicates that the other person should stop or stay distant. Such gestures often cut across cultural boundaries.

Posture and body movement may communicate feelings that cannot be expressed verbally, perhaps even things of which a person is not consciously aware. A slouching posture may indicate depression, hopelessness, or disinterest on the part of a client. The counselor who sits leaning slightly toward the client communicates interest. The client who sits stiffly and rigidly may be unaware of his or her own tension and discomfort, but the observant counselor still can "hear" the communication and respond to it. Squirming, tapping fingers, wringing hands, pacing, and rocking the body are all behaviors that carry messages about the feelings and attitudes of clients and counselors.

The face is one of the most expressive body parts. People communicate joy, concern, fear, anxiety, anger, and depression through facial movement. Smiles, frowns, widened eyes, a dropped jaw, narrowed eyes, tears, and slack features all contain messages that must be heard and reflected, perhaps confronted and interpreted.

The human service worker who is sensitive to both verbal and nonverbal communications has a greater opportunity fully to understand a client. The counselor who is aware of his or her own nonverbal communications is able to have a greater degree of awareness of his or her own feelings about the client. A nonverbally aware counselor can also use nonverbal communication to respond to the client.

Client: (Enters room with a bounce in his walk and a beaming smile.) Hi, John!

Counselor: Hi, Bob. You seem to be feeling *up* this morning.

Client: (While discussing his relationship with his wife, begins to slouch forward, drops his head, and stares at the floor.)

Counselor: Jim, you're beginning to look pretty sad. How do you feel?

Client: (In the middle of a session, talks about a painful, emotional interaction with her husband. Her voice trails off.)

Counselor: (Leans forward and nods in an understanding manner.)

Client: (Exhales breath heavily, looks at counselor, and in a tremulous voice continues to talk about feelings.)

Client: I really have a hard time speaking up in meetings at work. Everyone else seems to have something to say, but I . . . I . . . I don't think people pay much attention when I talk.

Counselor: (While the client talks, furtively glances at the clock on the wall. Although neither is consciously aware of it, the counselor is not involved with the client, the client doesn't feel like he is being heard, and the nonverbal behavior of the counselor shuts off the client. The session lurches to a strained conclusion with both parties feeling uncomfortable and unsure why they feel that way.)

Nonverbal communication can both add to and detract from personal relationships. All people are aware to some degree of their own and others' nonverbal messages. Through training and experience, human service workers can improve their sensitivity to these messages. As one's awareness increases, personal relationship skills are enhanced.

Developing personal relationship skills

It may seem that developing effective skills requires attributes that are difficult to describe, much less develop. Let us briefly look at them again:

Being
Warmth
Empathy
Genuineness

Doing
Paraphrasing
Reflection
Confrontation
Interpretation
Nonverbal communication

Does acquiring these attributes and skills seem an insurmountable task? As they begin their careers, many human service workers wonder whether they will be able to achieve an adequate level of functioning in these areas. Be assured that most do. One should also realize that reading about these attributes in a book does not prepare a person to employ effective personal relationship skills. How are such skills developed?

Each human service worker brings something with him or her into the field. Each brings a desire to be involved, along with many motives, beliefs, attitudes, and feelings. Many aspects of one's self are strengths; others are weaknesses. It is on this foundation—the personal equation factor—that human services training builds.

Effective personal relationship skills are developed through experiential training and supervision. A college-level human service program will teach students the basic knowledge required in human services. In addition, some courses involve actual practice of personal relationship skills. Such practice usually involves events such as role playing and supervised feedback aimed at increasing warmth, empathy, genuineness, and communication skills. No one expects the novice to have all these attributes and skills fully formed and ready to go.

The development of personal relationship skills is an ongoing process. After completing college training, human service workers find employment in settings that usually require supervision. It is exceedingly rare for inexperienced or even experienced human service workers to be thrown into a situation where they must rely only on their own resources. Under the supervision of more experienced professionals, human service workers can continue the process of developing and sharpening personal relationship skills.

Who Helps the Helper? Supervision and Teamwork

For some period of time, the novice and even the experienced human service worker can expect to function under the supervision of a more experienced professional. The focus of the supervision, its intensity, and the nature of the supervisor vary from setting to setting. To a great extent these aspects depend on the type of agency, the needs of the client population, the approaches used to deal with the clients' needs, and the training of the supervisors.

The professionals who have the role of supervisors come from many disciplines, including education, social work, psychiatry, and psychology (see Table 10-1). And since the generic human services field has been growing for almost a quarter of a century, there are now many supervisors who began as human services professionals. In some settings the novice is supervised by both a traditionally trained specialist and a senior human services worker.

Supervision for the beginning human service worker generally falls into three categories: housekeeping factors, role-specific factors, and personal relationship skills. Housekeeping factors include things such as use of time. The supervisor deals with such issues as worker absenteeism, tardiness, keeping

Table 10-1 *Examples of supervisors of human service workers.*

Discipline	Education and training	Settings
Educator	Bachelor's or master's degree in education or special education, practice teaching, supervised practice	Schools, preschools, special education programs, mental retardation programs
Psychiatrist	Medical degree (M.D.), psychiatric internship, psychiatric residency	Mental health clinics, mental hospitals
Psychologist	Doctorate in philosophy (Ph.D.), doctorate in psychology (Psy.D.), or master's in psychology, plus one year internship	Mental health clinics, mental hospitals, school systems, mental retardation programs
Social worker	Master of social work degree (M.S.W.), bachelor of social work (B.S.W.), plus practicum training	Mental health clinics, mental hospitals, family service agencies, wide variety of human service settings
Activity therapist	Bachelor's or master's degrees in activity therapy (A.T.), recreation therapy, and so forth; practicum experience	Work rehabilitation programs, mental hospitals, mental retardation programs
Human service worker	Associate of arts, bachelor's degree, or master's degree in human services program, plus experience	Virtually all human service settings

appointments, and other factors that are important in any type of employment. Role-specific factors are things relevant to a particular job in a particular agency. The supervisor may be concerned with, and give guidance on, the worker's understanding of the specific knowledge and needed skills. Behavior therapy, group dynamics, brokering, outreach, interviewing, activity therapies, and data collection are a few examples of the functions in this category on which supervisors may focus. In terms of relationship skills, supervisors often provide guidance and feedback on the human service worker's warmth, empathy, and genuineness with clients and on the effectiveness of the worker's verbal and nonverbal communication.

Many of the issues in effective personal relationship skills are relevant to making good use of supervisory sessions. The effective supervisor acts as a role model; warmth, empathy, and genuineness are attributes that the good supervisor should express toward the supervisee. As in the counseling relationship, growth is promoted by an atmosphere of acceptance, involvement, and concern. The supervisor should also engage in effective communication, giving the supervisee clear feedback on strengths and weaknesses, positive behaviors, and errors in a supportive atmosphere.

The human service worker has an equal responsibility for making the supervisory relationship work. In order to benefit from supervision, it is important to be as self-disclosing and open about oneself as possible. Being supervised is an active rather than passive process. Employees who cover their mistakes will not be able to discover better ways of functioning. The most functional approach to receiving supervision is to adopt the attitude that behavior can be openly examined and modified. Human service workers who are helped by a supervisor to be aware of their own motives or behaviors have the opportunity to enhance their skills (Atwood, 1986).

Whether a novice or an expert, the human service worker usually does not work in isolation but as a member of a team that is a highly organized group of specialists or a looser group of generalists. Whatever the type of team, the members have the opportunity to develop a mutual support system. Like formal supervision, membership in a team provides a vehicle for enhancing skills. People can learn from peers and coworkers just as they learn from experts. To the extent that people can share their experiences, are self-disclosing, and listen to others, they can grow and develop as human service workers.

While the supervisory relationship is usually positive and helpful, on occasion a human service worker may find him or herself with a supervisor who does not provide the supervision which is needed, or with whom a serious personality conflict develops. At times this type of situation can be resolved by the efforts of the two persons to deal with the situation. But what of the human service worker who has this type of problem with a supervisor and who has been unsuccessful in resolving it with that supervisor? At the least the human service worker should discuss his or her situation with peers for the support they can provide, and must seriously consider taking the problem to a higher level of the organization (i.e. his or her supervisor's, supervisor). Additional strategies for dealing with this type of situation, and other personal problems that human service workers face, such as handling personal values when working with clients, professional stress, burnout, and a variety of ethical issues are covered in specific detail in an excellent text by Schneider-Corey and Corey (1989) titled *Becoming a Helper*.

Summary

1. Human service workers often are employed in settings in which the contemporary strategies constitute major treatment approaches. At times human service workers use one or more of these approaches in their work.

2. In working with clients with medical or psychiatric problems, human service workers may need to be familiar with medical or psychiatric symptoms, treatments, and the side effects of these treatments.

3. Behavior therapy is applied to a wide variety of client problems in many human service settings. The human service worker often implements behavioral programs in these settings.

4. Some human service workers engage in intensive individual psychotherapy. Many more use the principles and skills of the psychotherapeutic approach in counseling clients and developing effective personal relationship skills.

5. Effective personal relationship skills fall into two broad categories: being and doing. Being refers to the attitudes, values, and feelings that have an impact on human relationships. Doing refers to observable skills or activities that enhance relationships.

6. Three aspects of being that have been identified as important are warmth, empathy, and genuineness. Warmth consists of the expression of tender, caring feelings and implies the ability to be involved with others. Empathy refers to the ability to "tune in" to another's point of view, feelings, and experience. Genuineness refers to congruence between behavior, feelings, words, and thoughts. Warmth, empathy, and genuineness are interrelated and important in forming effective helping relationships.

7. "Doing" skills involve particular communication techniques that enhance the expression and reception of information and feelings. These techniques include paraphrasing, reflection, confrontation, interpretation, and nonverbal behavior.

8. Effective personal relationship skills develop primarily through experiential learning and supervision. They cannot be learned through reading.

9. Novice and experienced human service workers both can expect to be supervised by more experienced professionals. These supervisors may be traditionally trained specialists or more experienced human service workers.

10. Supervision usually deals with three categories of functioning. Housekeeping factors include routine issues such as employee use of time. Role-specific factors are specific to a particular job. Relationship factors are warmth, empathy, genuineness, and communication.

11. The supervisory relationship focuses on enhancing the supervisee's functioning. Ideally, supervisor and employee collaborate to increase the employee's awareness of personal strengths and weaknesses.

Discussion Questions

1. Is it necessary for human service workers to understand the contemporary strategies?

2. Should every human service worker be required to demonstrate competence in the relevant skills of each of the strategies?

3. Are warmth, empathy, and genuineness absolutely necessary for a person to work effectively in human services?

4. What might be an appropriate way of dealing with a supervisor with whom it seems impossible to develop a working relationship?

Learning Experiences

1. Listen to the content of your conversations with others. How much is focused on information transmission? How much on feelings?

2. Since paraphrasing is nonthreatening, practice the technique in daily conversations. Do not overdo it; a little bit goes a long way. Does it facilitate an interchange that clarifies what people say?

3. With another student, spend some time observing people's nonverbal behavior in different settings (in the classroom, cafeteria, or student union). Share your impressions about what the nonverbal behavior might mean in terms of people's communicated feelings.

4. In your interactions with others, try to analyze how their verbalizations and nonverbal behaviors are affecting you.

Recommended Readings

Bergantino, L. *Psychotherapy, Insight, and Style: The Existential Moment.* Boston: Allyn and Bacon, 1981.

Okun, B. F. *Effective Helping, Interviewing and Counseling Techniques.* (3d Ed.) Monterey, Calif.: Brooks/Cole, 1987.

Schneider-Corey, M. and Corey, G. *Becoming a Helper.* Pacific Grove, Calif.: Brooks/Cole, 1989.

Schulman, E. *Intervention in Human Services.* St. Louis: C. V. Mosby, 1974.

Truax, C. B., and Carkuff, R. R. *Toward Effective Counseling and Psychotherapy.* Chicago: Aldine Publishing, 1967.

11

Problem Assessment, Planning, Brokering

- Why is it important to make an accurate assessment of a client's presenting problem?
- What general principles govern the assessment and planning process?
- What type of assessment data should be gathered from clients?
- What is linkage, or brokering, of services?

The human services deal with a wide variety of people problems, and no single treatment, technique, or program can meet the needs of all persons. Specific problems require specific solutions or responses, and before a solution or response can be provided, the problem must be identified accurately. The human service worker must sort out the important problem or problems that the people in need are experiencing and link them to the appropriate services or experiences that will assist the clients in changing themselves or their environment. To list all the problems a human service worker will encounter is virtually impossible, but a number of illustrative problems can be presented to sensitize the worker to the types of issues in question.

Typical Problems Seen by Human Service Workers

1. *Problems of personal dissatisfaction.* Large numbers of individuals from all classes of society suffer from a sense of personal dissatisfaction. That is, they feel incomplete, unhappy, aimless, anxious, and lost. They are not "making it." It is not unusual for such persons to walk into a human service center seeking relief.

■ ■ Betty Wilson is a forty-two-year-old mother of three. For several years she has felt a lack of fulfillment in her life. Her relationship with her husband seems routine, and he seems more involved with his work and friends than with

209

Betty and the children. For about six months Betty has felt increasingly depressed about her life. No one seems to care how she feels, and she spends a lot of time tearfully recollecting "better times." Her painful feelings have become so pronounced that she has talked about them with her minister. He suggested that she make an appointment at a community women's center to talk to a counselor.

2. *Problems of isolation.* A major problem for human service workers is the social isolation of many individuals: the elderly in retirement homes, ex–mental patients in sheltered-care homes, and vagrants in skid row transient hotels, among others. The extract below is an example.

■ ■ Ethel Warren is seventy-one years old. Her husband died three years ago, and her children live in distant cities. Ethel lives alone in a two-room flat in a large rundown urban apartment building. Her friends are long gone, and she sees no one but the clerk at the grocery store. Ethel feels lonely and uncared for. She is frightened of going out because of the dangers of her neighborhood. Her days are bleak and uninteresting, each blending into another. Ethel often wishes that death would overtake her.

3. *Problems of poverty.* It has been estimated that there are approximately 20 million people living below the poverty level in the United States (Whitman et al., 1988). Most human service programs thus require tax support in order to serve this needy group. When poverty strikes, there are often associated psychological experiences of distress and turmoil.

■ ■ John Selton is twenty-eight and unemployed. He was laid off from his job at a Detroit automaker and drove to Dallas, Texas, because he heard that work was available in the sunbelt. His grade school education and lack of technical skills did not make him a good candidate for employment, and he now lives in his car in a tent city along a ravine outside Dallas. He survives on handouts from a charity group and feels demeaned and desperate.

4. *Problems of addiction.* Alcoholics and drug abusers are commonly seen as clients at human service centers, as indicated below.

■ ■ Miguel Hernandez is thirty-two years old and is separated from his wife and two children. He is on his third job in seven months as a manual laborer. Miguel has lost his family and his jobs because of excessive drinking. Most of his paycheck is spent in bars. In the past half year he has been arrested four times for drunk and disorderly conduct. On the verge of being fired again for drinking on the job, Miguel still denies that he has a problem with alcohol abuse.

5. *Problems of crisis.* Individuals experiencing a crisis often become human service clients. Loss of a loved one through death, divorce, or abandonment; loss of a job; or any number of severe stress situations can lead to an inability to cope with day-to-day events, as depicted below.

■ ■ Mary Jo Brandt is a young farm widow whose husband recently died from a heart attack. Mary Jo is losing the heavily mortgaged farm to foreclosure by the bank. She has trouble sleeping and caring for her school-age children. Mary Jo feels guilty over her inability to function but is unable to keep from slipping into inactivity and depression. She feels that things are hopeless and does not know where to turn for help.

6. *Problems of severely disruptive behavior.* Many people end up in human service settings because they engage in extremely disruptive behavior that is not the result of a crisis experience but is long-standing in nature. Ordinarily these problems are categorized as neuroses or psychoses.

■ ■ Larry Teal is twenty-three years old. His middle-class parents are extremely distraught about his behavior. Larry dropped out of college after one semester because he could not handle the work load even though he had been a B student in high school. His behavior has been very strange. He recently was apprehended by the police after creating a disturbance on a city bus. Larry had disrobed in front of the other passengers while screaming that he was the new Christ and that nakedness could open the doors to heaven. When police tried to take him into custody, Larry fought them and claimed that they had been sent by Satan.

In Table 11-1, these typical problem areas are presented with common responses for each problem. Unfortunately, individuals who have only one problem are rarely seen in human service centers; rather, we see multiproblem persons. For example, one might encounter individuals who have lost their jobs because of drunkenness; who have no friends or family, no money, and no place to live; who have bleeding ulcers; and who think everyone is out to get them. In other multiproblem cases, the issues may not be so clear. It becomes the human service worker's responsibility to identify the problems accurately so that appropriate responses can be made.

Table 11-1 *Typical problems and common responses.*

Problem	Response
Personal dissatisfaction	Psychological counseling
Isolation	New social network
Poverty	Public financial assistance
	Vocational training
	Employment counseling
Addiction: alcohol	Alcoholism counseling
	Alcoholics Anonymous
	Residential treatment
Addiction: drugs	Methadone maintenance
	Synanon program
Crisis	Crisis counseling
Severe behavior problems	Medication
	Psychotherapy
	Residential program

The Need

Why is it so critical to identify accurately the problem areas in the multi-problem person? We have already touched briefly on one major reason: the need to tailor services to the problems the client experiences. Not only does it not make good conceptual sense to use, for example, the verbal psychotherapies as a shotgun approach for all human problems, but it is not likely to work. The following example, from Fisher, Mehr, and Truckenbrod (1974), illustrates the results of applying inappropriate services to certain kinds of problems:

A Black Mother

■ ■ A black mother with several children and no husband at home takes her one son to a county hospital clinic for medical care. There she waits her turn, which takes six hours. She has no food for the child, receives curt, ill-mannered treatment from a harried staff, is quickly dismissed by an overworked resident physician, and is told to come back for tests the next day. She explodes—yelling, screaming, and throwing chairs around. The police are called and take her into custody. She is anxious about what will happen to her child, hostile toward the police, begins talking about "Whitey's plot against her." The police take her to the local mental health center because she is a hostile "paranoid." At the clinic, she is seen by a white, middle-class, male psychologist who helps her calm down and sets up an appointment for the next week. She returns at that time and is given a battery of tests, which indicate that she is of nearly average intelligence, verbal, impulsive, suspicious, fears attacks on the integrity of her self-image. The staff feels that she is a possible candidate for individual psychotherapy with the psychologist who has begun to develop a relationship with her.

Therapy begins, one hour a week. The psychologist wants her to talk about her feelings and early life experiences. She wants to talk about her deserting husband, the home she lives in, her children and the possibility that they will get on drugs, the rats in her building, her lack of money, how she has to take the subway across town to the clinic and cannot afford it and ends up walking through dangerous neighborhoods. The psychologist interprets this as resistance to therapy, thinks she is afraid of walking through the "dangerous neighborhoods of her psyche." The sessions continue. The woman's husband shows up at home and moves back in. Welfare workers discover this and discontinue her aid-to-dependent-children (ADC) funds. She is upset and calls her therapist who tells her to talk about it at their next session. He doesn't want the feelings "leaked" over the phone; besides, she might come to depend on the phone calls. The woman is annoyed by the psychologist's response but walks to the clinic for the next session.

During the session, she is keenly interested in getting back on ADC from the welfare department and wants the psychologist to help her. He asks her about her feelings about her husband coming home and suggests that she may lose her welfare support if he does it again. She accuses him of tricking her, of being against her just like the others. In a rage she runs from the office, slamming the door with such force that the glass shatters. She never returns for her sessions, but does, of course, return to the ghetto. The psychologist closes the case with a summary describing her as extremely impulse-ridden, resistant to therapy, lacking in insight, suspicious of those who desire to help her, and paranoidal, with a poor prognosis. Even had he "cured her," the end result would most likely have been the same: she would have returned to the same situation she came from—public aid, dependent children, county hospital clinics, rat-infested rooms, and so forth.

Following her withdrawal from the clinic sessions, angry, hostile, and suspicious, she makes repeated attempts to have her welfare money reinstated. Public aid workers respond to her angry threats and "paranoidal" allegations by having her taken by the police to the state mental hospital. Following an admission examination, which confirms her paranoidal ideation and high level of anger and hostility, she is persuaded to voluntarily sign into the institution and is transferred to a ward. The social worker of the ward subsequently obtains her clinic history folder; as a result of the psychologist's negative remarks in her clinic history, the social worker feels that the patient would not benefit from talking therapies. The patient is placed on tranquilizing drugs and her symptoms are gone in a short time (several months). During the course of her hospitalization, a complete social history is done, which outlines her occupation (none), family relationships (few), and social patterns (lacking). She is not considered a good therapy case, so little more than chemotherapy is tried. She is released and again placed on public aid. Following her release, she gets her children (who stayed with a cousin) and returns to the ghetto. Her environment is now the same as it was prior to hospitalization—the same frustrations, same resources (none), same problem. There is only one change: she is now considered mentally ill, with a poor prognosis.[1]

In a case such as this, an accurate problem-sorting process could well result in a different ending by eliciting different responses to the client's problems. In this example, by applying effective problem assessment, the following problems would be identified and responses made:

■ ■ *Problem*	*Response*
A. Behavior in hospital waiting area	1. This is a system problem, not necessarily a person problem. Change clinic system into a more humanizing approach. 2. County hospital needs staff to respond to crisis when it occurs. Provide intervention.
B. Behavior at mental health center intake	1. Provide crisis response to help person grab hold of self, express immediate feelings (this was done in example).
C. Real-life problems	1. Offer counseling so that she can express and work through her feelings about her situation. 2. Help her work on resolving real problems: a. Finding better housing b. Link with job training program c. Directive counseling in regard to husband d. Link her child to youth program if needed

In effect, this describes problem identification as a process to *expedite linkages*. Effective, accurate problem identification assists the human service worker in directing the client to the appropriate services and resources. Figure 11-1 depicts the flow of clients through a hypothetical human service system based on this triage (sorting out) process.

In this system, the client is first assessed in the triage system. Physical and psychological crises are dealt with first: food, medical problems, money, housing, and crisis feelings. The client then can be linked with psychotherapeutic services if the problem is psychological, with social or environmental support systems if those are sufficient, or with both if necessary. If maximal impact systems are required (such as a residential treatment program), the client can ultimately be linked to those that are appropriate and available. At any point in the system flow, clients can exit if their identified problems have been resolved or can enter new services if new problems appear.

A second rationale for this process involves maximizing resource use and determining priorities. As discussed earlier, funding for human services is not unlimited. At times, the human service worker must make very unpleasant decisions about which of the potential clients should receive the services. Using the common example about the middle-class housewife who is mildly depressed about her place in life and the ghetto mother on public aid, it would seem that it is more critical to provide services to the latter, since the middle-class housewife usually has alternative resources (for example, she may be able to pay for private services). This is not a hard-and-fast statement, of course. Obviously, such decision making must rest on the situations and data of individual cases. One can propose, however, that the greater the need, the more likely that services should be provided.

Principles

A few general principles govern the effective application of the triage process. The following discussion will clarify the importance of each.

1. Not all people are alike; different problems demand different solutions. Even though this principle may seem obvious, in practice the same type of solution (such as psychotherapy) is often applied to widely different problems.

2. The more specific to the problem the solution is, the more effective and efficient it will be. The child who is phobic (frightened and anxious) about going to school usually can be treated more quickly and with better results through a behavior therapy program than through verbal family therapy.

3. The less intrusive the solution, the better. A common occurrence in the identification of problems and their linkage with solutions is a tendency to "oversolve" the problems; that is, the service provider does not let the

Figure 11-1 *Human services flow chart.*

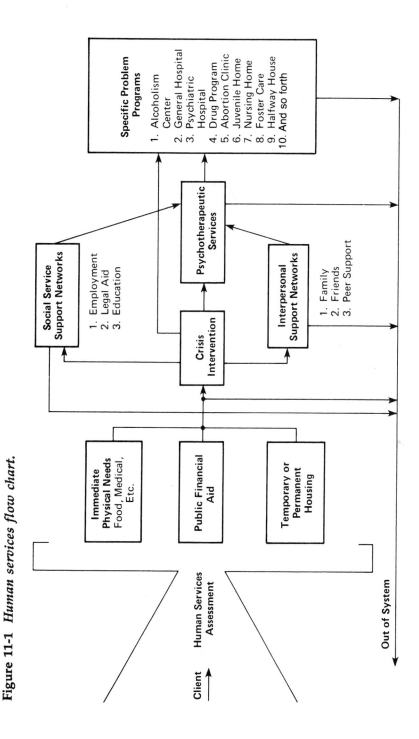

client *go* when the identified problem is solved or handled. Rather than just dealing with the specific problem, the service provider attempts to revamp the psychological and behavioral makeup of the client completely. Such an approach tends to create in clients unnecessary dependency on the services being provided and links clients into the system for an inappropriate length of time. In effect, this principle suggests that only services that are absolutely necessary be provided—if an individual needs a job, help him or her get one but do not attempt to remake personality through psychotherapy.

4. Solutions are more effective if applied soon after the development of the problem. Strong evidence supports this principle (Duggan, 1984; Fraser, 1986; Hansell et al., 1970; Hoff, 1984; Lieb et al., 1973). As time passes after the development of a problem, individuals often develop inappropriate ways of trying to cope. The more they use these inappropriate coping strategies, the more difficult it is for them to change. This principle implies that human service centers should not have waiting lists of clients and that there should be no delays in linking clients to services once the problems have been identified in the triage process.

5. Problems must be identified (assessed) accurately if appropriate solutions and resources are to be linked to the client. The case example presented earlier in this chapter illustrates this principle. Obviously, if one cannot identify the client problem accurately, there is a greater likelihood of offering inappropriate and ineffective services. For example, a chronic alcoholic arrives at a human service intake program having just lost his job. The intake worker accepts that problem at face value and links the client to an employment counselor. The odds are that the problem will be repeated (the client will lose the new job) because the critical issue (the drinking pattern) has not been modified.

When individuals ask for help, there are four basic ways to gather data in order to assess the problem and its severity. The human service worker can (1) ask the client, (2) ask someone who knows the person, (3) observe the client in his or her natural setting, or (4) observe the person in certain standard test situations. By far the most common assessment technique is interviewing the client. The interview generally can be described as a structured conversation that has goals.

In the triage process, the goals are ordinarily to identify the client's problems, determine what factors have led to the development of the problems, and most important, determine the severity of the problems. The interview is important, but it is only one part of the assessment process, which also includes (1) preparation (learning the client's problem); (2) input (data collection, including interviewing, testing, and naturalistic observation); (3) processing (organizing and interpreting the data); and (4) output (decision making, including possibly rejecting clients, referring them, or brokering services) (Sundberg and Tyler, 1962). The interview is so important that numerous human services books devote most of their material to its discussion and

The interview is a primary information-gathering tool of the human service worker.

presentation. Since an intensive treatment of the interview process is not possible here, we must limit ourselves to a broad consideration.

The process of effective interviewing is clearly a skill, the acquisition of which requires hands-on practice, training, supervision, and experience. It cannot be learned from books. What can be considered here is the type of information or data a human service worker may need in order to make reasonable decisions during the triage process. The following outline contains the major types of data human service workers have found helpful in the triage process. Not all the data are necessary in all cases, and the choice of particular areas of data collection for a particular client is dependent on the individual situation.

Client Care Data

I. Current life status
   A. Major life setting. Describe major life systems the client interacts with (work, family, school). How adequately is the client functioning in these systems?

B. Problem behaviors
   1. From the client's perspective, what are the problems?
   2. What do significant others consider to be a problem for the client?
   3. From the human service worker's perspective, what are the problem behaviors?
C. History of presenting problems
   1. A chronological description of the reasons for and events surrounding present status.
   2. Special attention may be paid to the duration and onset of the problems, especially in making efforts to quantify the problems, circumstances, and events in frequency and time.
   3. A brief review of past and present treatment: involvement in social service agency or agencies.
   4. A report of the antecedents to the problem behavior(s) and the subsequent consequences.
   5. What the client has tried to do to solve the problems and how he or she has been coping with them.
D. What does the client want out of this contact?
II. How does the client present him- or herself?
   A. Physically: healthy, sick, attractive, unattractive, slovenly, neat, etc.
   B. Emotionally: depressed, nervous, energetic, angry, quiet, loud, controlled, impulsive, mature, etc.
   C. Client's self-description
   D. Intellectual assets
III. Social determinants
   A. Group membership
      1. Referent groups
      2. Occupational identity
   B. Family
      1. Structure
      2. Relationships
   C. Education
   D. Work
   E. Ecology
      1. Type of community
      2. Community involvement
IV. Major stress and coping
   A. Type of stress
      1. Social
      2. Interpersonal
      3. Situational
      4. Intrapersonal
   B. Current coping styles
      1. Withdrawal
      2. Aggression
      3. Internalization

V. Development
  A. Analysis of the client's significant past experiences that have led to this client's current "being."
VI. The conceptualization
  A. Bring together all the information into a relatively concise conceptualization of the person as he or she is and can be.
VII. The plan
  A. Identify the needed changes in order to assist the client.
    1. Environmental or social
    2. Intrapersonal
  B. Outline the necessary steps to effect the changes, including the linkages to other personnel or agencies.
  C. Develop a criterion for successful implementation of change agentry.

After the human service worker has gathered the critical data and identified the client's problem areas, several important decisions must be made. The first, of course, is whether the client needs the available services. If the client does, the services must be specified, the goals for the services must be defined, and the client must be linked to those services. (In the outline above, this occurs in section VII.) In other words, the human service worker develops a service plan, in writing, that can follow the client along as he or she receives help. Such a plan is important in that it (1) provides a baseline around which services can be organized and (2) specifies desired results so that the human service worker knows whether the original goals are being reached. It is possible and even likely that as the client receives the initially identified services, new data will be discovered or new problems may arise, and the original service plan may be modified.

The final product of the process is the actual linkage or brokering of services for the client. In the ideal system, all services are available under one agency; therefore, the worker can link the client to the needed service with a minimum of effort. Unfortunately, few human service systems are organized in such a manner. Much more commonly, in order to provide needed services for clients, the human service worker must refer them across agency lines. Figure 11-2 illustrates this system, with two hypothetical human service clients: an individual having a psychotic episode (broken line) and an alcoholic (solid line).

In this example (Figure 11-2, the isolated services system), the human services agency staff members function mainly as problem identifiers. Thereafter they serve as advocates and brokers for the client, following the client through the maze of services and assisting the transition between services when such transfers are necessary. Most community service systems function along these lines. Many services are available, but they are functionally isolated from each other. Unfortunately, most communities do not have a central human services agency to play the advocate-broker role for the client. This coordinating role is just now being developed in most communities. It is

Figure 11-2 *Isolated services system.*

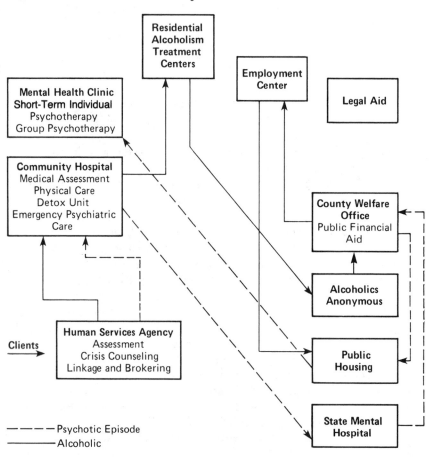

often up to individual human service workers to act as advocate-broker-coordinators for their clients.

Obviously, to function in this role, the workers must *know* their community, know the services available, and know the contact person in the corresponding agencies (Petrie, 1986; Whittaker et al., 1983). Dugger (1975) suggests that human service workers assess the community and develop a community resource directory. Such a directory would contain a list of the resource agencies, the services each provides, and their client requirements, cost, intake process, and contact person. In addition, it might include the informal systems that would benefit the client, such as clubs, organizations, transportation, and recreational systems. Without knowing community resource data, human service workers cannot effectively assist their clients.

Summary

1. Human service workers are confronted with a wide variety of people problems, including personal dissatisfaction, isolation, poverty, addiction, crisis, and severely disruptive behavior.

2. Human services clients often have combinations of problems. It is critical to identify the problems accurately so that appropriate services can be rendered in a manner that maximizes resources.

3. A number of principles have been identified that govern the triage or assessment and linkage process.
   a. Different problems demand different solutions.
   b. Solutions should be specific to the problem.
   c. Solutions should not be intrusive.
   d. Solutions should be rapid.
   e. Assessment should be accurate.

4. The assessment process includes preparation, client input, data processing, and output (decision making).

5. Interviewing is a major assessment technique that must be learned experientially. Many types of information must be obtained in an assessment interview.

6. The client care data gained in the assessment process are used to identify problems or client needs in order to develop an individual services plan that provides the basis for organizing services. The plan specifies desired results so that service delivery can be evaluated.

7. The final product of the assessment and planning process is the actual linkage, or brokering, of services. This often places the human service worker in a coordinating role among various community agencies.

Discussion Questions

1. What types of problems do human service workers encounter?

2. How specifically should problems be identified and assessed?

3. Why is it important to identify problems accurately?

4. What are the principles of assessment, planning, and brokering?

5. Why is it important to have a service plan?

Learning Experiences

1. Practice an assessment interview on a friend with the friend's permission.

2. Develop a hypothetical service plan for a make-believe client (or a real client if you have access to someone and permission to do it).

3. Identify the formal human service resources in your community (hot lines, mental health clinics, and employment offices) by name and address.

Endnote

1. From Walter Fisher, Joseph Mehr, and Philip Truckenbrod. *Human Services: The Third Revolution in Mental Health.* Copyright 1974, by Alfred Publishing Co., Inc. Reprinted by permission of Alfred Publishing Co., Inc.

Recommended Readings

Amidei, N. "How to Be an Advocate in Bad Times." *Public Welfare* 40 (1982).
Cormier, W. H., and Cormier, L. S. *Interviewing Strategies for Helpers: Fundamental Skills and Cognitive-Behavioral Intervention.* (2d Ed.) Monterey, Calif.: Brooks/Cole, 1985.
Schulman, E. *Intervention in Human Services.* Saint Louis: C. V. Mosby, 1974.
Sunley, R. *Advocating Today: A Human Service Practitioner's Handbook.* New York: Family Service America, 1983.

12

Crisis Intervention

- How is a *crisis* defined?
- What are the signs of crisis states?
- What are some examples of common crises?
- What common reactions are seen in major disasters?
- What principles guide most crisis intervention programs?

When people in need seek help, they are often in a state of crisis. Most people have a strong desire to see themselves as being able to handle life's problems without outside assistance. Our culture has given people the expectation that they should be strong, independent, and self-reliant. When one begins to be overwhelmed by difficulties, a common first reaction is to feel that one has let oneself and others down, that one has failed because of personal weakness. Many if not most people are unwilling to reveal that sense of personal weakness to others. To seek out help is often seen as an admission of failure, and many people avoid taking that step until no other solution seems possible.

Unfortunately, when people try to solve serious problems on their own, they are often unsuccessful, and the problems become more severe. As the problems become more complex and disabling, the individual's problem-solving capabilities become even more impaired. Events reach crisis proportions before the individual can admit that he or she needs outside assistance. To deal with the emotional turmoil of people in such crises, a major development has been the crisis intervention programs.

The concept of crisis intervention is an outgrowth of attempts to deal with acute psychological problems resulting from major environmental stress. Much of the early work in crisis intervention was done during World War II, when men experienced a reaction to combat called combat neurosis or battle fatigue. Additional knowledge about reactions to stress and techniques for dealing with crisis experiences were gained from the study of reactions to natural disasters.

Understanding Crisis States

One of the first studies of crisis states was Erich Lindemann's report on the Cocoanut Grove nightclub fire in Boston during 1942, in which 492 people were killed (Lindemann, 1944). Lindemann studied the psychological reactions of the survivors and their families and the reactions of the family members of those who had died. He found that half the families needed psychological help in dealing with their reactions to the loss of loved ones. Lindemann found, as have others, that some people appear to adjust remarkably well shortly after the disaster but that problems surface later on:

> A girl of seventeen lost both parents and her boy friend in the fire and was herself burned severely, with marked involvement of the lungs. Throughout her stay in the hospital her attitude was that of cheerful acceptance without any sign of . . . distress. When she was discharged at the end of three weeks she appeared cheerful, talked rapidly, with a considerable flow of ideas, seemed eager to return home and to assume the role of parent for her two younger siblings. Except for slight feelings of "lonesomeness," she complained of no distress.
>
> This period of griefless acceptance continued for the next two months, even when the household was dispersed and her younger siblings were placed in other homes. Not until the end of the tenth week did she begin to show a true state of grief with marked feelings of depression, intestinal emptiness, tightness in her throat, frequent crying, and vivid preoccupation with her deceased parents. (Lindemann, 1944)

Caplan (1964) defines a *crisis* as "a short period of psychological disequilibrium in a person who confronts a hazardous circumstance that for him constitutes an important problem which he can for the time being neither escape nor solve with his customary problem-solving resources." A major premise of crisis intervention theory is that a crisis can be resolved adaptively or maladaptively, positively or negatively. During the disruption characteristic of the crisis state, individuals are thought to be vulnerable to intervention by others. They are especially sensitive to their own inability to cope and look for ways to reduce their discomfort. If at this point they receive support from a human service worker, their changes can be positive. If, however, alternative coping mechanisms are unavailable, the *disruptive* behaviors of the crisis state can be incorporated into the person's personality structure, and the person may stabilize at a level of functioning that is even less adaptive than the precrisis behavior. Figure 12-1 illustrates this crisis phase sequence.

Figure 12-1 *Crisis phase sequence.*

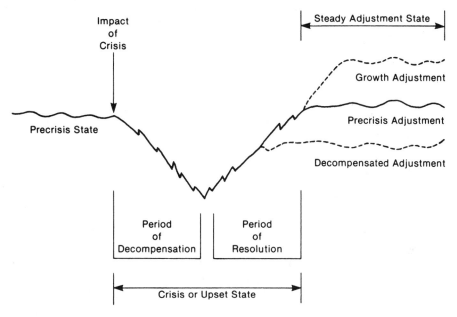

Source: Reproduced with permission of Robert J. Brady Co., Bowie, MD 20715, from 1975 copyrighted work titled, "Emergency Psychiatric Care: Management of Mental Health Crisis."

Before a crisis-producing event occurs, most individuals maintain an adjustment level whose effectiveness varies only slightly from time to time. However, as the crisis makes its impact on the subject, a period of decompensation occurs during which the usual coping mechanisms fail and behavior becomes relatively disorganized and ineffective in solving problems. If this decompensation does not occur, of course, the individual is able to work through the problems and by definition is not in crisis.

Individuals who experience crisis decompensation as a result of stress eventually "bottom out" in the behavioral decline, and since crisis states seem to be self-limiting, they enter a period of crisis resolution. After the resolution, these persons once again enter a steady adjustment state that has only slight variations in levels of effectiveness over a period of time. What is particularly significant about the postcrisis adjustment level is that it may be at a higher-functioning level than the precrisis state, a lower level than the precrisis state, or the same level as the precrisis state.

People who make a moderately successful adjustment to a crisis, who regain their normal coping mechanisms, return to the precrisis level. People who are relatively unable to deal with the crisis and decompensation period and who have few coping mechanisms and resources are likely to end up with a decompensated adjustment level. In other words, they have learned maladaptive responses during the crisis, and afterward they are less able to deal with stress and day-to-day living than they were before. However, people may resolve the crisis state with a growth adjustment and be able to function at an even higher level after the crisis period. For such to occur, the crisis individual usually needs assistance in the form of crisis intervention strategies in order to learn highly adaptive coping techniques. Such coping techniques are, however, self-learned in some instances.

Successful crisis resolution that results in a return to precrisis behavior or a growth adjustment requires (1) correct perception of the situation, furthered by seeking new knowledge and keeping the problem in consciousness, (2) management of emotion through awareness of feelings and verbalizations leading toward tension discharge and mastery, and (3) development of patterns of seeking and using help with actual tasks and feelings by using interpersonal and institutional resources (Rapoport, 1962).

A major element of the crisis state, of course, is the client's *perception* of an event as so extremely stressful that it interferes with the individual's normal coping patterns (Parad and Resnik, 1975). To an objective observer, the stress may appear to be high or low. To most people, high-stress events such as divorce, natural disasters (tornadoes, earthquakes, floods), or the death of a loved one are easily accepted as crisis-developing situations. But even what appear to be relatively low-stress events to an outside observer can be crises for some. What makes an event stressful? The following are four characteristics of stressful events often noted in the literature on stress and coping resources.

1. People feel a sense of loss of control over the events in their lives. They feel helpless to change what is going on or to intervene successfully in the process.
2. There is an anticipation or occurrence of physical or psychological pain. For example, the individual fears being injured or killed (as in a disaster) or is threatened with a loss of self-esteem (as in a divorce).
3. There is a loss of social and emotional support. In a disaster, friends and relatives may be missing or killed. Less dramatic events such as divorce, job loss, or marriage may separate individuals from family members and old friends.
4. The event or some aspect of it is perceived as unpleasant or aversive, and the individual tries actively to avoid it.

Some people appear to be unable to deal with common events such as a child going to school for the first time or a son or daughter marrying and leaving home. For these individuals, these common experiences interact with other variables to fit the four characteristics noted above. Such events *are* able to produce crisis in some individuals as a result of their threat to the *needs* or *goals* of an individual at a particular point in his or her life.

In this vein, Hansell (1976) has proposed that crisis is a result of the threat to certain *essential attachments* that all human beings must make and the individual's inability to cope with that threat. Hansell's seven essential attachments can be paraphrased as follows:

1. *The need to take in supplies.* Certain *supplies* are considered essential to maintaining function (food and water); in addition, we need to be able to take in *information*. Signs of failure: physical malfunction, boredom, and loss of curiosity.
2. *The need to maintain an intimate relationship.* A continuing relationship, someone to share secrets, a sense of closeness to someone, a chance to share deep feelings, sex. Signs of failure: living alone in isolation, minimal companionship, no reports of intimacy, lack of sexual contact.
3. *The need to be part of a peer group.* Referent group and social networks, such as social clubs, work groups, school groups, which can provide daily give and take. Signs of failure: feeling alone, isolated, not feeling part of a group, lack of acquaintances.
4. *The need for a sense of identity.* A clarity of self-definition, a sense of who one is, cherishing one's self-definition. Signs of failure: ambiguity about oneself, disliking oneself.
5. *The need for a sense of competency and esteem.* A feeling of well-being, knowing that one can handle problems. Signs of failure: depression, sense of failure, lack of clear-cut work role, lack of dignity.
6. *The need to be linked to a cash economy.* To have a job, be married to a person who supports his or her mate, be a member of a family, be independently wealthy, receive social security benefits, be on public aid. Signs of failure: no purchasing power, lacking the physical necessities of life, homeless.
7. *The need for a comprehensive system of meaning.* A system for making decisions, setting life priorities, knowing how one fits in. Signs of failure: no pattern to decision making, aimlessness, inability to make choices, a sense of alienation from society.

In Hansell's system, crisis behavior can be the result of the impact of high-stress events on certain attachments (see Figure 12-2). For example, the death of a loved one would impact on the need to maintain an intimate relationship and possibly on the need for a comprehensive system of meaning. Other types of major stress would affect most of the attachments at the same time. The destruction of the city of Armero, Colombia, by a volcanic eruption on November 13, 1985 is an example. In this tragedy, a double eruption of built-up molten rock and trapped gases melted tons of ice and snow that covered the top of the volcanic peak. A steaming, mile-wide avalanche of ash, mud, and rocks roared thirty miles down mountain valleys and buried the city under 50,000 million cubic feet of boiling mud. The catastrophe left

Figure 12-2 *Crisis impacts on the essential attachments.*

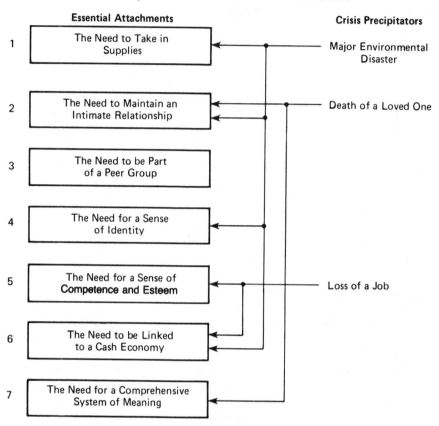

22,000 people dead or missing and thousands injured, orphaned, or homeless (Cohen, 1987).

Another example is the December 1988 earthquake which struck Soviet Armenia (DeAngelis, 1990). An estimated 50,000 were killed and 80,000 injured. A year and a half after the earthquake one 14-year-old girl who was the *only* survivor from her entire school class felt so guilty that she was the only one left alive, she tried to kill herself by throwing herself in front of a car. She is one example of tens of thousands of Soviet Armenians who continue to suffer the psychological, behavioral, and physical effects of the disaster. Because of the overwhelming impact of these types of disaster, a crisis response was generated in all the immediate survivors, no matter how effective their problem-solving abilities prior to the event. In fact, in disasters of this severity, crisis responses often occur in rescuers and human service workers who arrive later to give assistance following the disaster event.

Crisis behavior can also appear under low-stress precipitators, as has been indicated before. In Hansell's system, this would be the result of an individual not having developed to a sufficient extent the seven essential attachments. Such an individual, with weakened attachments, would appear to be crisis-prone (Bassuk and Gerson, 1980).

Signs of Crisis States

Whereas some individuals can withstand more stress than others, all individuals have a breaking point. Whatever the level of stress an individual can withstand, once the stress is great enough to set off a crisis, certain common signs of the crisis experience usually appear:

1. The individual seems preoccupied.
2. Guilt is experienced over the inability to resolve the problem.
3. Hostility is felt toward others or toward the world in general.
4. Physical distress may be experienced: nervousness, stomachaches, inability to sleep, and so on.
5. Established patterns of conduct may change: personal hygiene slips, routines are disrupted.
6. The person may become apathetic.
7. There may be a lot of aimless activity.
8. Relationships with others change; the person may become more dependent or withdrawn.
9. Behavior may appear detrimental to the individual's self-interest.

Parad and Resnik (1975) present similar signs of crisis in terms of the client's *sense* of experience. As they describe it, the client has a sense of:

1. Bewilderment: "I never felt this way before."
2. Danger: "I feel so nervous and scared—something terrible is going to happen."
3. Confusion: "I can't think clearly; my mind isn't working right."
4. Impasse: "I feel stuck; nothing I do seems to help."
5. Desperation: "I've got to do something—don't seem to know what though."
6. Apathy: "Nothing can help me. I'm in a zero situation."
7. Helplessness: "I can't manage this myself. I need help."
8. Urgency: "I need help now."
9. Discomfort: "I feel miserable, so restless and unsettled."[1]

It is not unusual for human service workers to encounter the *same* individual over and over again manifesting the signs of crisis. Parad and Resnik

(1975) have identified a list of problems that may maintain such persons at a point at which they are particularly vulnerable to crisis:

1. Difficulty in learning from experience
2. A history of frequent crises ineffectively resolved because of poor coping ability
3. A history of mental disorder or other serious emotional disturbance
4. Low self-esteem, which may be masked by provocative behavior
5. A tendency toward impulsive *acting-out* behavior (doing without thinking)
6. Marginal income
7. Lack of regular, fulfilling work
8. Unsatisfying marriage and family relations
9. Heavy drinking and/or substance abuse
10. History of numerous accidents
11. Frequent encounters with law enforcement agencies
12. Frequent change in address[2]

Such a list clearly suggests that the more problems individuals have, the less likely they are to be able to handle a crisis situation. In addition, the multiproblem person is less likely to benefit from crisis intervention without additional support systems that can deal with the problems that are of a longer-standing nature.

The Crisis of Major Disasters

It is clear that an overwhelming majority of people exhibit crisis behavior during events such as major disasters. Events that can be considered major disasters include any sudden, unexpected loss of life or damage to property involving relatively large numbers of persons, such as earthquakes, floods, tornadoes, train wrecks, and major aircraft crashes. In the aftermath of such occurrences, the victims manifest a wide variety of problem behaviors that are compounded by the physical security problems of fiscal aid, housing, food, and medical care. How do you imagine you would react in a disaster situation?

Imagine, for example, that on May 18,1980, you are vacationing at a campsite on the slopes of Mount St. Helens in the state of Washington. On that date, a volcanic eruption destroyed a large area of land and forest, killing sixty-three people and injuring others. Many of the dead have never been found. What would it have been like to be there and survive? Imagine yourself there. A deafening roar, the earth shaking, day turning into night from the falling ash, the air almost unbreathable from gases, extreme heat, roads blocked—helpless against the threat of injury or death, you think only of escape. In terror for your life, you and your companions start for safety, which you hope exists miles away through the wilderness. Abandoning your camp, you try to walk out; your car will not run. After marching continuously for thirty-six hours, you yourself are finally found and rescued. But a vivid memory remains of your companions being swept away by a flood of mud as the group tried to cross a ravine, their screams echoing in your ears. You are certain that they are dead and their bodies maimed, but they are never found. Few of us would handle such an experience well; we would manifest crisis behavior almost immediately and for some time afterward.

In one study of the Mount St. Helens disaster, reported in 1989, two rural communities in the Northwest, one of which was affected by the volcanic eruption, were analyzed to determine the lifetime rate of crisis behavior. The lifetime rate was found to be about 3 percent (Shore, Vollmer and Tatum, 1989). The rate for crisis behaviors (also known as *posttraumatic stress disorders*) was found to be substantially higher in those people who had the highest degree of exposure to the volcanic eruption. Other studies have discovered extremely high rates of human service problems in previously emotionally normal people who have been victims of disasters.

Norman Farberow (1977), in a survey of reports on nine major disasters spanning the period from 1971 to 1974, indicates a long list of problems seen by human service workers doing crisis counseling in the period after such disasters. The problems included nightmares, hostility, depression, phobias, guilt feelings, amnesia, eating problems, agitation, immobilization, alcohol intoxication, marital problems, inability to concentrate, and psychosomatic reactions. In one study (Taylor, 1976) of the Xenia, Ohio, tornado disaster, 56 percent of the victims were depressed afterwards, 27 percent had sleeping problems, 19 percent experienced eating problems, 15 percent had psychosomatic difficulties, 25 percent had headaches, 19 percent had respiratory problems, 28 percent reported marital problems, and 81 percent of the children showed greater fear of storms (see Figure 12-3).

The emotional problems experienced by victims of disasters may be quite severe, even when they are not immediately apparent. They may not appear until months after the actual physical disaster. Hartsough (Farberow, 1977) has developed a tentative set of postdisaster phases that identify the sequence of reactions of victims of disaster:

- *Heroic phase:* Most individuals respond to the immediate disaster with positive action to save their own and other lives and property. A sense of shared community and altruism develops that may last up to several weeks. During this phase, many people manifest the initial crisis behavior reactions.
- *Honeymoon phase:* Efforts focus on cleaning up and establishing new sites of residence and are accompanied by a strong sense of shared experi-

Figure 12-3 *Percent of victims showing crisis problems after Xenia, Ohio, tornado.*

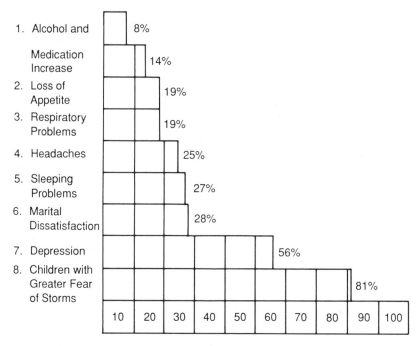

ence. Much help is promised by officials and expected by victims. This phase lasts one week to six months after the disaster, and behavioral problems continue to appear.

- *Disillusionment phase:* From two months to twelve months after the disaster. A loss of the feeling of shared experience and bitterness and anger over the delays or failure in promised aid. Many behavioral problems previously hidden now appear.
- *Reconstruction phase:* From six months to several years following the disaster. Victims realize they need to solve their own problems and attempt to do so; most are successful. Some behavioral problems are still apparent during this phase.

The evidence from studies such as those surveyed by Farberow clearly demonstrates that crisis behavior is a common response to unexpected high-stress events. Efforts must be directed to dealing with these behavioral problems in addition to the life-support problems created by the major disasters. Differences do exist in the levels of stress that are required to produce crisis behavior in different individuals.

Common Crisis Situations

It is relatively easy to understand that a major natural disaster can lead to difficulty in adjustment among its victims. However, even more common events can result in a crisis response among essentially normal people. A variety of events are experienced as more or less stressful by different individuals.

1. *Family and marital problems.* Between 1970 and 1980 there were an estimated 10 million divorces in the United States. A problematic marriage is stressful for both partners and for any children who may be involved. If the marriage is dissolved, the members of the family must deal with new relationships, old and new feelings, and the impact of divorce on self-esteem. Children frequently develop problem behaviors in response to the disruption of family life.

■ ■ At the age of thirty-two, John married Ann, a twenty-nine-year-old schoolteacher. The first year and a half of the marriage appeared to be relatively uneventful. By their second anniversary, things were no longer going well. Ann told John that she felt that the marriage was not working. She felt tied down by John's desire that she spend all her time with him. Ann began going "out with the girls" several times a week. During the next year, Ann and John fought more and more often. As the problems escalated, they finally came to a mutual decision to divorce.

John felt bad about the upcoming divorce. During a separation while waiting for the divorce to become final, he was preoccupied by thoughts of how he had failed as a husband. All he seemed able to do was to think about Ann. As the filing of the final divorce papers came near, he became very depressed. He was unable to complete his work satisfactorily and dropped out of an evening graduate course that he had been taking. His unusual behavior alarmed his parents, who had never seen him become depressed over setbacks before. They encouraged him to enter counseling to "get his head straight." In counseling sessions, John finally expressed his anger at Ann for "dumping him" and his sense of helplessness about the situation: "Nothing I did, none of the changes I made, seemed to make any difference to her."

Over six months John's depression lifted, and he began to date again. He was no longer preoccupied with "what [he] did wrong" in his marriage to Ann. He was again able to work energetically and enthusiastically. Three years later John married again, and he has had a successful relationship with his second wife for the past seven years.

2. *Death of a loved one.* Most people handle this loss reasonably well. They experience sadness and grief, but soon go on to lead their lives as before. At times, though, the loss is accompanied by depression and despair, guilt and anger. These reactions are particularly common when the loved one has died unnaturally (suddenly in an accident, or violently) (Rynearson, 1986). These reactions may interfere with a return to effective functioning.

3. *Criminal victimization.* Millions of individuals are victims of crime each year. People are subjected to muggings, beatings, robbery, burglary, and rape. Some are killed, and their families must deal with that difficult loss. It's hard for anyone to cope with the effects of criminal events. A number of studies have found that after criminal victimization, there is an increase in anxiety, fear, nightmares, anger, social withdrawal, and depression.

Consider an event known as the Chowchilla school bus kidnapping (Terr, 1981). In July 1976, a school bus carrying twenty-six children aged five to fourteen and a bus driver was hijacked by three masked men. The children were driven around for eleven hours in darkened, enclosed vans and then transferred to a truck trailer buried underground. Sixteen hours later, two of the older children were able to dig an escape route. The kidnappers were never caught. Twenty-three of the twenty-six children were studied, and each one manifested disturbed behaviors in the year afterward. Twenty-one developed unusual fears of mundane experiences (e.g., anxiety attacks when riding in the family car) including Mandy and Sammy, described below. All the children feared another kidnapping and became extremely suspicious and frightened of any event that reminded them of the ordeal.

■ ■ Mandy, age seven, twice screamed that her little brother had been kidnapped when he was actually playing next door or trying on clothes in a store dressing room. Exactly one year after the kidnapping, Johnny, age eleven, refused to sleep in his bedroom for many nights because he believed the ceiling was collapsing.

Sammy, age ten, experienced two panicky episodes, according to his mother. "Before Christmas during vacation he was biking with a friend [in the] sandhills. A station wagon, two guys, and a dog were there. He abandoned his bike and ran home. He said he didn't want to be kidnapped again. He cried a lot. I advised him not to panic and run. . . . Just before the fair in May there were strangers on the road, and he gave up biking there and refused to go further."

4. *Employment.* Job stresses may lead to a crisis reaction, but job loss is an even more stressful event. Chronic unemployment often leads to feelings of hopelessness and defeat and apathy. Many people find unemployment compensation or the receipt of welfare to be very damaging to their self-concept.

5. *Retirement.* Although most people look forward to retirement, it can be quite stressful. Retirees often feel useless, engage in boring busywork, and encounter a loss of status and economic support. They often become depressed and anxious. In addition, the elderly must deal with a decline in physical ability, loss of friends and relatives, the threat of sickness, and children who are busy leading their own lives.

The five examples given here of common crisis situations are just a few of the many that could have been used. Human service workers will see people experiencing these types of crises and many others.

Intervening in the Crisis

In crisis counseling, as in all types of counseling situations, client and counselor expectations are of great importance. As Getz et al. (1974) note, "In crisis counseling, if the counselor and client establish the expectation that the client can regain control over himself and his environment, there is an increased opportunity to assist the person in regaining a sense of mastery over what has happened to him." In addition to the expectations, however, a broad range of specific intervention techniques may be brought into play. The intervention may range from advice giving and assertiveness training to ventilation and interpretation of psychodynamic processes.

At times, the crisis intervener is fighting a holding action, trying to maintain an individual until more formal structured intervention can be arranged. The first contact with an individual in crisis is usually by telephone, especially since a number of telephone crisis lines have been organized in major cities. The human service worker who handles calls on a crisis line has a demanding job, as illustrated in the following excerpt.

In recent years, emergency shelters have become a setting for intervention into many types of crises experienced by the homeless.

I settle down at my desk and just then comes the soft chime of the suicide line. As always, I feel the familiar tightening in my throat and a sinking sensation in my stomach.

I answer: "Suicide and Crisis. Can I help you?" I hear a click and then a dial tone. Entry in Log Book: 4:12—Anon. Hung up.

Stephanie hands me a file and says: "Here's one you ought to call back. She gave us permission. Marilyn was pretty worried about her and Marilyn's judgment is sharp."

I skim the file. Evelyn J. is fifty years old, has a husband and two grown sons. Deeply depressed and threatening suicide. Husband harsh and unsympathetic. She calls him "Daddy." She says her poodle is the only one that cares about her anymore and that's all that is keeping her alive. I call the number.

"Mrs. J.? I'm calling from the Suicide and Crisis office. I was just reading your file and I'm a little worried about you. How are you feeling now?"

Her voice is light and airy, in fact unnaturally so. "Oh, really? Isn't that nice!"

I answer, "Is it difficult for you to talk right now? Is there someone there?"

Her response comes in the same light tone. "That's right."

"Okay, Mrs. J. I'd really appreciate it if you would call back when you can. We want to know how you're doing."

"Fine, I'll do that. Goodbye."

Log Book Entry: 4:15—Called Evelyn J. She'll call back.

Betsy has come in by now and we chatter awhile about her date last weekend. Again come the chimes of the suicide phone.

"I'll get it," says Betsy as she settles down at the other desk. It is a student requesting information about our service for a paper he is writing. I do some more filing and chat with Stephanie. Again the phone rings on the second suicide line.

I answer and it is Evelyn J. calling me back. This time there is no airy quality in her voice She is crying softly while she talks to me. She is at the end of her rope. She has tried so hard to please Daddy but nothing she does is right in his eyes. He makes $2,000 a month and won't even buy her a car after all their years of work and struggle for financial independence. The one son at home has turned against her, too, because she has started drinking a little to ease her depression. Only her poodle cares. I find out that Evelyn has a bottle of sleeping pills she is saving for the big step to oblivion, and I urge her to go to a psychiatrist. It seems Daddy doesn't believe in psychiatrists and would never approve. I ask her about menopause symptoms and learn that she is beginning to have them. When I tell her she should go to a gynecologist for hormones, she seems surprised. Daddy doesn't believe in doctors for all that nonsense either. I tell her I'm forty-eight years old and know what I'm talking about; she gets interested and asks about me. I urge her to go to a doctor or therapist or both, regardless of what Daddy thinks. I point out that she has been a doormat long enough.

I tell her: "If he objects, tell him to go to hell!"

This brings a giggle from her and she stops crying.

"Oh, that's so funny! I think I'll just do that." She giggles off and on throughout the rest of our conversation whenever she thinks of the prospect of telling her husband off. She says she will call for an appointment and promises me she will do nothing drastic until I call her again next week. She tells me I'm a darling girl and she's very grateful.

Entry: 4:55—Evelyn J. called back on follow-up. OK for now.[3]

The goal of the first contact, in addition to preventing deterioration in the client, is to obtain a commitment from the client to seek substantial help. Once the client enters into a more formal crisis intervention relationship, we can aim for significant change in the problem behavior.

In general, the crisis counselor provides a setting in which clients can ventilate their feelings, discuss their problems, examine their approaches to the problems, receive feedback (both positive and negative) on their coping methods, receive support in their coping attempts, and obtain resources that will help them solve the current problems and learn better ways of solving future problems. As we have discussed earlier, during a crisis, people seem particularly open to developing new positive response patterns with the proper guidance, in relatively short periods of time. The intervention process is guided by a number of principles embraced by most crisis intervention programs.

1. *Interventions are made with a minimum of delay.* It is generally accepted that crises are self-limiting from a time perspective. The period of crisis (Figure 12.1) is usually four to six weeks in duration. Once the person has reached the postcrisis stage, the pressure to resolve the crisis has dissipated, and the crisis worker is left with little to work with. This fact requires rapid intervention and *no* waiting lists. The effective crisis worker must work fast.

2. *Interventions are time limited.* Most crisis programs adhere to short-term programs for the reason just described. Interventions beyond the crisis phase not only tend to waste resources but also to promote dependency. Referral to other programs is, of course, a separate issue when their purpose is to deal with long-standing problems such as personality malfunction or job training.

3. *The client's social network is used.* Frequently, clients have resources that they have been unable to tap, such as friends, family, employers, and ministers, that can be drawn in to provide support and assistance.

4. *The client is usually seen by more than one worker.* The use of more than one worker helps avoid dependency relationships and brings broader experience to bear on the problem.

5. *Intervention is focused on the current life situation.* Since the disorganized crisis state, during which the client is particularly open to change, often lasts only four to six weeks, the intervention attempts must focus on the current life situation if for no other reason than economy of effort. Yet, since the crisis is generally precipitated by a specific problem situation, it is that problem which must be the focus of problem solution strategies.

6. *Trust and rapport must be established.* In order to develop a working relationship between the worker and the person in crisis, the client must have trust that the worker is operating in the client's best interest, is really concerned, understands the client's problems, and is willing to help.

7. *The client's self-esteem and self-reliance must be supported.* Not only do the crisis workers focus on the client's maladaptive problem-solving efforts, they also reinforce the positive behaviors and aspects of the client. The workers do not solve the client's problem *for* him or her, since this would support the client's personal helplessness and dependency, but instead, they help the *client* to solve them.

The Goal and Setting of Crisis Intervention

Because crisis is often associated with extreme change in interpersonal or environmental functioning, stabilization is a primary goal in crisis intervention (Duggan, 1984). Thus, a primary goal of crisis intervention is emotional-environmental first aid. Its goal is definitely *not* to resolve all the problems of the client. As has been indicated, by its very nature it is time-limited and its effectiveness cannot exceed the crisis experience of the client. During that period, the actual intervention activity may occur in a variety of settings, including the following:

1. The field site of a disaster.
2. Transportation vehicles.
3. The emergency room while the patient waits or receives needed medical care.
4. The walk-in clinic offering crisis counseling to ambulatory patients.
5. Hotlines (or rap lines) offering suicide prevention and other crisis-intervention telephone services to troubled individuals. (These services may be independent of or part of emergency medical services. They rely mainly on telephone counseling by trained volunteers, ideally with professional consultation available on a backup basis.)
6. Mobile services (often called home treatment teams or emergency teams), usually staffed by two or more team members.

Obviously, the first encounter with the crisis client may begin with much of the character of the assessment, planning, and brokering session discussed in Chapter 11. But once the client is identified as being in crisis,

Figure 12-4 The return to assessment, planning, brokering after crisis intervention.

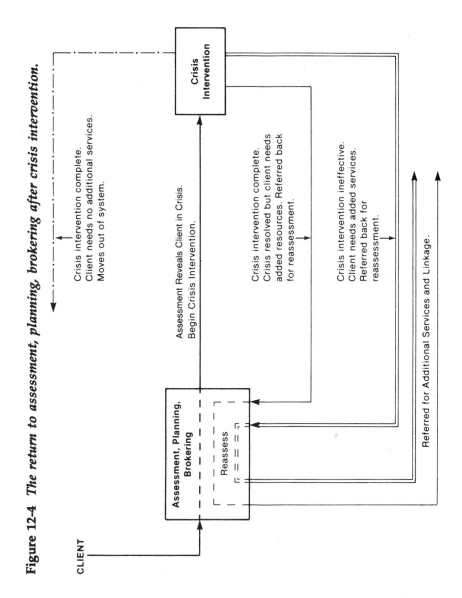

CLIENT

Assessment, Planning, Brokering

Reassess

Crisis Intervention

Crisis intervention complete. Client needs no additional services. Moves out of system.

Assessment Reveals Client in Crisis. Begin Crisis Intervention.

Crisis intervention complete. Crisis resolved but client needs added resources. Referred back for reassessment.

Crisis intervention ineffective. Client needs added services. Referred back for reassessment.

Referred for Additional Services and Linkage.

the concepts discussed in this chapter come into play. However, at the termination of the crisis intervention process, the human service worker returns to the assessment approach: What additional problems does the client have, if any, and what additional services may the client need? Three obvious possibilities exist, as illustrated in Figure 12-4. The client's crisis may be resolved, and no additional services may be necessary. The client's crisis may be resolved, but additional services may be necessary. And the client's crisis may *not* be adaptively resolved, and additional longer-term interventions may be necessary. In succeeding chapters, we shall deal with strategies available for clients with whom crisis intervention was not successful, was not available, or was successful but uncovered further problems in addition to the crisis state.

Summary

1. People in need often postpone seeking help until their problems have reached crisis proportions.

2. Crises usually follow a similar pattern of disorganization of behavior, slow recovery, and reorganization.

3. Individuals usually resolve crises in four to six weeks, reorganizing their behavior at a higher, lower, or equivalent level of functioning compared with the precrisis period.

4. Crisis intervention is employed to assist in the reorganization of behavior at a higher or equivalent level of functioning and to prevent reorganization at a lower level of functioning.

5. Some human service practitioners have identified a crisis-prone type of client whose resources are so limited that the client is likely to experience stress as crisis-provoking.

6. Common signs of crisis states have been identified; they range from preoccupation to behavior that appears detrimental to the person's self-interest and from bewilderment to discomfort.

7. A crisis can be set off in almost any person by extremely stressful events such as natural disasters.

8. Many people respond with a crisis reaction to more common events, such as family dissolution, death of loved ones, criminal victimization, loss of employment, and retirement.

9. A number of principles have been identified under which crisis intervention programs operate, including promptness of service, time limits on treatment, use of social networks, prevention of dependency, focus on

current problems, and development of trust, self-reliance, and self-esteem by the client.

10. Though crisis periods may be resolved effectively, the crisis worker must be alert to longer-term problems and must be prepared to link clients to additional services.

Discussion Questions

1. What is a crisis?

2. What are the nine signs of crisis?

3. What might it take to develop a crisis state in *everyone?*

4. What are the characteristics of a crisis-prone person?

5. What phases do people go through after a major disaster?

6. What are some of the common crises that people experience?

7. What are the principles of crisis intervention programs?

Learning Experiences

1. List the crises you have gone through. How did they affect you?

2. If your community has a crisis intervention program, visit it and find out what kinds of problems it deals with and how it deals with them.

3. Make a list of events that you think could precipitate crisis behavior in yourself.

4. Explain how you usually cope with high stress.

Endnotes

1. H. J. Parad and H. L. P. Resnik, "The Practice of Crisis Intervention in Emergency Care." Reproduced with the permission of the Charles Press Publishers, Bowie, Md. 20715 from their copyrighted work *Emergency Psychiatric Care,* (c) 1975.

2. H. J. Parad and H. L. P. Resnik, "The Practice of Crisis Intervention in Emergency Care." Reproduced with the permission of the Charles Press Publishers, Bowie, Md. 20715 from their copyrighted work *Emergency Psychiatric Care,* (c) 1975.

3. E. Atkinson, "Four Hours on the Suicide Phone." *Bulletin of Suicidology,* No. 7, 1970, pp. 38–39.

Recommended Readings

Getz, W.; Wiessen, A.; Sue, S.; and Ayers, A. *Fundamentals of Crisis Counseling.* Lexington, Mass.: Lexington Books, 1974.

Hoff, L. A. *People in Crisis: Understanding and Helping.* (2d Ed.) Menlo Park, Calif.: Addison-Wesley, 1984.

Reid, W. J., and Epstein, L. *Task-Centered Casework.* New York: Columbia University Press, 1972.

Smith, L. L. "A Review of Crisis Intervention Theory." *Social Casework* 59 (1978).

Williams, T. (ed.). *Post-Traumatic Stress Disorders of the Vietnam Veteran.* Cincinnati: Disabled American Veterans, Inc., 1980.

13

Peer Therapy
and Mutual Self-Help

- What is peer therapy?
- Why is peer therapy effective?
- What are mutual-help or self-help groups?
- What similarities do these groups share?
- What potential hazards exist in the use of mutual-help or self-help groups?

The notion that only highly educated and specially trained professionals from the traditional disciplines of medicine, psychology, and social work can effectively help others is obviously rejected by followers of the human services approach. Elsewhere in this text, we have seen that a wide variety of people can provide helping services under the proper circumstances. A logical extension of this position is the use of the client's peers as helpers as well as the utilization of groups banding together to provide mutual help and support. Even though *peer* ordinarily means "equal," in the context of this chapter we can consider peers to include parents, siblings, employers, and others. *Peer therapy* and *mutual-help therapy* are terms that are often used interchangeably. However, for present purposes, we shall attempt to differentiate the two.

Peer therapy consists of the activities of a naturally significant other from a person's social support network, such as a parent, sibling, close friend, or classmate, that are directed toward developing positive change in the person. *Mutual-help therapy* refers to the activity of two or more otherwise unrelated people who band together for mutual social support in order to receive help *from* others and to provide help *to* others.

Both peer therapy and mutual-help processes utilize social support systems as important factors in their effectiveness. In peer therapy, the social support comes from an existing, naturally occurring support network. In mutual-help groups, a new social support network is developed or made available to a person. The importance of social support networks for effective personal functioning has been touched upon in prior chapters. It remains unclear exactly how social support networks enhance human functioning, but it is obvious that they can have important effects both positive and negative (Hurley, 1988).

When social support networks are intact, people in trouble have others to whom they can turn for help, advice, guidance, and expression of concern. The psychological and social support offered or available from one's social network appears to provide a buffer against stress or the experience of psychological or even physical crises (Stephens et al., 1987; Throits, 1986). For many human service clients, the absence of a viable social support network compounds already present problems or is in itself the problem. It must be recognized, however, that a strong social support network may also have a *negative* influence on a person (Scheffler, 1984). If a person's social support network is dominated by a manipulative or malevolent person, damage can certainly be done. As a case in point, consider the Reverend James Jones, who in the 1970s convinced his flock to leave the United States and emigrate to a compound in South America, and who, not long after, presided over the mass suicide of hundreds of his followers and himself. That particular social network was clearly destructive. This unusually tragic example suggests the possible negative effects of problematic social support networks, which may exist on a smaller, less dramatic scale. The key for human service workers is to be sensitive to the possible negative impacts of social support systems while working to encourage and develop social support networks that will have positive impacts on people.

Peer Therapy

Unless they are extremely isolated and alienated, most individuals have people to whom they have strong bonds. The prime example of such a relationship is that between child and parent. Other examples include the relationships between siblings, spouses, and close friends. In addition, certain types of settings encourage the development of strong attachments that maximize the effects of peer relationships, as in the relationships between barrackmates in the military service, classmates in a schoolroom, or cellmates in prison. Guerney (1969) has termed such relationships between people whose actions are inherently significant to one another's behavior as *symbiotic* and the members as *symbionts*. In this context, he uses the term *symbiotic* to mean a living together of two organisms in a manner that is not disadvantageous to either, or is advantageous or necessary to both.

In peer therapy, the relationship is clearly intended to be advantageous for one member of the peer dyad, and usually is advantageous to both. A significant other interacts with the person in need in such a way as to modify the person's problematic behavior or to provide general support or assistance to help the person meet his or her needs. The distinguishing feature that sets peer therapy apart from other important relationships between significant others is that the peer therapist typically functions under the supervision of, or is trained by, a human service worker who is experienced in the peer therapy approach.

Peer therapy seems to be effective for three reasons:

1. Naturally significant others are usually strongly motivated to learn how to help the person in need change his or her behavior.
2. By virtue of his or her inherent role, the significant other is already linked into the physical and psychosocial need system of the client.
3. Significant others naturally function as models or identification figures for the client.

In the human services, the use of peers as therapists or change agents seems to have the potential to be a powerful, cost-effective approach. By their very nature, peers have strong influences on each other, and their "helping" attempts are usually formalized into their natural relationships.

Peer counseling can be a potent force in human service systems, particularly for adolescents who may feel uncomfortable seeking help from older adult human service workers.

An excellent example of the use of significant others as change agents is in the Regional Intervention Program (RIP) in Nashville, Tennessee. RIP is a professionally administered, parent-operated, therapeutic preschool for children who have severe behavior problems. In this program, parents are trained to act as change agents. Services are free, but once the child has completed the program, each parent must volunteer his or her services to the program for three mornings a week for six months.

The RIP program described below represents programs that use significant others (such as parents) as change agents. It illustrates the helper-therapy principle: Not only does the child's (client's) behavior change, the parent's (helper's) behavior changes positively also.

The Regional Intervention Program:
A Typical RIP Experience

■ ■ Mr. and Mrs. James Pruden with their four-year-old son, Paul, came to RIP at the suggestion of their pediatrician. Paul was unmanageable. Rather than eat he preferred to throw his food on the floor. He still wet his bed. He was reckless with his toys and those of other children, and he had no young friends because he preferred to pinch his playmates instead of play with them. Mr. Pruden blamed Mrs. Pruden for poor management. Mrs. Pruden cried and said she didn't feel the child's behavior was her fault. At the suggestion of her doctor, she had taken a job to "get away" from Paul, but no babysitter could cope with the child either.

A parent "intake worker" interviewed the Prudens with a checklist of questions. She comforted them with the admission that she had been through similar kinds of problems with her daughter and that it sounded as though Paul could be helped by the RIP program if one of his parents could work with the child there at least three mornings a week for several months.

Since Mr. Pruden worked, and Mrs. Pruden had quit her job, it was agreed that Paul and his mother would immediately start in the program. In a few weeks another parent from RIP would visit the Prudens at home to see how things were going there, and then Mr. Pruden could learn directly some of the techniques taught at RIP At the conclusion of the interview, Mr. and Mrs. Pruden watched a twenty-minute movie about RIP which simply explained the program's organization. Paul and his mother returned to RIP the next day to begin the initial observation sessions in the Generalization Training Module for children with behavioral problems.

Behind the one-way mirrors
The Generalization Training Module has a simulated three room apartment—living room, bedroom, and kitchen—where RIP staff can observe a parent with child. Here Paul and his mother were to meet for twenty minutes every day for several months in a highly structured format. Two RIP parents would observe their relationship, systematically rating behaviors that they would interpret for Mrs. Pruden after each session.

In the first session, Mrs. Pruden was asked to play with her child as she would play at home, with one exception. The living room in the apartment had ten toys, and Mrs. Pruden was to change the toy her child was playing with every two minutes. (An observer from behind the window tapped the window with a pencil as a signal that two minutes were up.) Because most children want to keep certain toys for more than two minutes, this procedure brought out Paul's frustrations, and quickly allowed the RIP staff to observe parent-child behavior in frustrating situations.

"Without this kind of specialized procedure," says Judy Horowitz, the professional staff person responsible for the Generalization Training Module, "it might take a long time for Paul to exhibit his typical problems in front of strangers. Instead we try to see the oppositional behavior quickly so we can begin to train the parents quickly."

Paul's frustration level was quickly reached in the first session of toy changes. As toys were taken away he kicked and cried, even threw one toy at his mother. And the greater his aggressive behavior, the more attention, albeit negative, he received from his mother.

In a conference after the first twenty-minute session, Mrs. Pruden was shown the checklist and graph reflecting Paul's aggressive actions, recorded by two observers. In twenty minutes, six kicking tantrums, four punching actions, etc.

"This is what we call 'baseline information,' " says Ms. Horowitz. "After two or three baseline sessions, after we've had a chance to see what is happening between parent and child, we begin to teach a parent new ways of handling her child. We begin to teach some of our 'tricks.' "

RIP's tricks belong to the repertoire of popular procedures used by behavior modification technicians. They are special "interventions that help a parent control a preschooler's behavior," says Ms. Horowitz. "Parents are warned at the outset that they do not provide a cure-all, but if everybody stays healthy, we are reasonably sure that we can help a parent resolve many of the difficulties they are having with their child."

The interventions
A series of mimeographed pamphlets outlining training procedures are given routinely to parents who come to RIP, and videotapes show them how other parents have worked with children with similar problems. The actual learning experience, however, begins in the training sessions in the modules. After the baseline information was obtained, for example, Mrs. Pruden was told that she would be taught the right way to time her attention with her child.

"In your next play session," a trained parent told her, "you are to bring a toy down as you have done before, but this time you must add a definite command as you hand it to Paul. Say to him, 'Now it's time to play with the truck.' You have to tell a child what you want him to do before you can expect him to do it. If Paul listens to you and begins to play with the toy, play with him. Give him lots of attention. We call this 'turning on.' Talk to him, hug him, describe to him what he is doing, talk with him about the toy you are playing with. But if your child does not listen to what you've told him to do, ignore him. We call this 'turning off.' Do not talk to your child. Do not look at him. Don't shake him to make him obey. Simply sit or stand with your back to him and play quietly with the toy. If Paul then comes to you and wants to play with the toy, it's time to turn on and talk to him."

She emphasizes: "This is the general rule: when you like what your child is doing and would like him to do it more often, give him lots of attention. But when you don't like it, ignore him."

To those familiar with behavior modification theory, this may sound elementary. What's stressed at RIP, however, is not theory but experience. Mrs.

Pruden learned the concept of differential reinforcement—rewarding desired behavior and ignoring undesirable behavior—by doing it. And she learned it under the observing eyes of those skilled in the technique.

The Generalization Module is like a laboratory, one mother explains. "We experiment until we find out what works for us."

What works

For the next several sessions, Mrs. Pruden and Paul looked as though they were acting in a melodramatic silent film. Mrs. Pruden would animatedly encourage her son when he played actively, but not aggressively, with his toys. She turned away stonily when he tried to get her attention through tantrums, tears, and toy throwing.

All during these sessions, *raters*—observers with checklists of behavior—were tabulating the kinds of behavior exhibited by Paul from behind the one-way mirror. After a couple of weeks, a graph of Paul's behavior sharply depicted his changing behavior patterns. As a RIP staff person read the graph to Mrs. Pruden, it sounded like a kind of behavioral Dow Jones report: kicking and crying down 50 percent; toy involvement and appropriate behavior up 75 percent.

By the time of this graph report, however, Mrs. Pruden really didn't need the data to know that Paul was getting more manageable. She could see it. But she did need to learn that what she was doing was directly responsible for it. Perhaps, she said, he was just growing out of bad habits.

"It's important at this point," says Ms. Horowitz, "that a parent fully understands and experiences the changed interaction pattern as the reason for a child's improved behavior habits." Thus, in what behaviorists and RIP staff call "reversal" sessions, Mrs. Pruden was instructed to go back to her old ways of dealing with Paul: she was asked to pay lots of attention to him when he cried, and to be passive when he played quietly. In other words, the reinforcement techniques which she had learned were turned around and, consequently, so was Paul.

"It was a nightmare experience," says Mrs. Pruden. "Paul was back to his kicking tantrums in only two reversal sessions. I got the point which I don't think I'll ever forget. Techniques taught to me at RIP had worked in helping Paul become a less hostile, aggressive child." The effects of the reversal sessions were, of course, temporary. The second phase of differential reinforcement was instituted immediately.

After a few months of morning work at RIP, Mrs. Pruden was visited by Vera Britton, a paraprofessional staff person at RIP who also teaches in one of the preschool classes there.

"The home situation is not so structured as RIP," says Mrs. Britton, "and I can help parents generalize what they've learned at RIP in a much more relaxed setting in their own living rooms and kitchens."

Positive reinforcement becomes much more selective after a parent learns the basic behavior modification techniques. As Ms. Horowitz explains, "Nobody is continually reinforced in real life for good social behavior. Nobody gets constant praise or attention every time they behave well. What we call 'intermittent reinforcement,' therefore, is more practical. When you're making dinner, you don't have time to pay constant attention to your child."

The practice of intermittent reinforcement begins behind the one-way mirror where a parent is asked to read a magazine while the child is playing, or she pretends to cook something in the module kitchen. Sometimes RIP arranges to have someone visit the module living room. Mrs. Pruden began to learn intermittent reinforcement when a RIP staff person visited with her in one of the module units. Paul also had a visitor that day; another preschool child came to play with him.

As a child's behavior improves, as Paul's did, the number of weekly sessions behind the one-way mirror is decreased. Habits learned in the training sessions tend to spill over to other activities in the child's life. Paul, for example, suddenly stopped wetting his bed.

In the eight months that Paul spent at RIP, he played in preschool classes after his one-way mirror sessions. First there was the initial intake classroom where he was observed for placement. That was followed by the community classroom which was designed to prepare him for a public school kindergarten. In each of these classes, he participated in routine activities of preschool—coloring, drinking juice, eating cookies, building with blocks. Lots of free time was spent in a big indoor sandbox laden with toys. Classroom teachers continually applied the same kinds of techniques taught to Mrs. Pruden.

Periodically Paul's classroom behavior was rated in checklists similar to the ones used behind the one-way mirrors, so that his aggressive actions toward other children—pinching, biting, kicking—were monitored for change. Raters in the classrooms, as those behind the one-way mirrors, are parents or special education students from local colleges who are getting their practicum experience.

RIP staff, like most behavior modification adherents, insist on the importance of data-based behavioral charts. "Without the charts and graphs," says Principal Vince Parrish, "services to RIP families could deteriorate into the professionals' self-evaluations of 'the good things we do for kids.' "

He admits that there are problems with the data-based system, too. It forces the staff "to allocate much time to training parents in the appreciation and procedures of data taking. Further, master's level personnel must review the data frequently, an act that involves probably ten to fifteen hours per week per resource person. Such review requires a degree of commitment and patience not always found in professionals."[1]

As noted previously, peer therapy is not limited to children and parents. Numerous examples can be given in which peer therapy concepts have been applied to other types of peer relationships. Hawkinshire (1969), for example, discusses the application of peer therapy to criminal offenders. Roy and Sumpter (1983) describe a peer-group program for widows and widowers. Craighead and Mercatoris (1983) have described the use of mentally retarded residents as peer therapists, and Byers-Lang (1984) has reported on the use of peers for building networks for the elderly blind. Even children may be used as peer therapists for other children. Sancilio (1987) describes the use of programmed child-child interactions as a method of intervention in the social and behavioral difficulties of children. In the approach he describes, adults program the interventions of children as peer therapists. The children function as social reinforcers and social initiators in group interactions and social skills training. Sancilio demonstrates that with adult supervision, environments can be changed so that a problem child's peers interact with him or her in such a way as to bring about a desired behavior change.

Common to a majority of such programs is a recognition that the peer therapists must be given assistance in becoming change agents. The prospective peer therapist must be trained for that role. Hawkinshire (1969) has identified a number of issues that must be faced when peers serve as change agents:

1. The peers must be trained in the activities they are to engage in.
2. The peers need at-the-elbow support from the trainer or supervisor so that they can develop confidence in the new behavior and have someone to turn to when problems arise.
3. The peers must have the opportunity to give feedback to the trainer or supervisor in terms of their feelings about what is happening.
4. The peers are most effective when a support group of other peer therapists is available as a source of critique and new ideas.[2]

These four points are certainly not unique to the use of peer therapists, but they are clearly important in the use of any type of change agent. They may, however, have special significance for peers, since peer therapists are often relatively naive in dealing appropriately with the person in need and most likely will initially need extensive assistance and supervision.

Mutual-Help Groups

Two broad functions for mutual-help groups exist. Some mutual-help groups provide support for people who have personal problems, while others provide advocacy for groups of people who view themselves as being disenfranchised from the broader society. The first function has emerged from a concern with the individual problems or behavior of the group members. In contrast, social advocacy groups are marked by a belief system that assumes dysfunctional social structures. Membership consists of committed community activists with a broader, recognized constituency. The emphasis of these groups tends to be on the acquisition of services, resources, and access for their constituencies; and their strategies revolve around changing social, political, economic, and service-delivery systems to obtain equity and control over resources. In this chapter the emphasis will be on mutual-help groups that focus on providing support for people who have personal problems. In actuality, though, most mutual-help groups that focus on personal problems of members, also, to a lesser or greater extent, have a social advocacy function.

Who can benefit from a self-help or mutual-help group? Many people may find that the concern and assistance of their peers in a small-group setting helps them deal with important life problems. The individuals in the examples below represent just a few of the types of people who might benefit.

Margaret and Bill

■ ■ Margaret and Bill are the parents of a young child with cancer. For two years they have shared suffering, dashed hopes, and heartbreak. In spite of caring friends and professional support, they feel alone in their grief.

Jean

■ ■ Jean is a divorced mother who has custody of her three children. She now finds herself overwhelmed by the problems of single parenthood. Her teenage son has become difficult to handle, and she is increasingly discouraged in trying to provide for her children's needs and the demands of her job.

Roger

■ ■ Roger has a serious drinking problem. He has been fired from two jobs in the last year and is deeply in debt. He has lost the respect of his family and friends. He entered treatment at an alcoholism clinic but began to drink again two months after the treatment ended. He realizes that his addiction is ruining his life but feels helpless to control it.

Paul

■ ■ Paul is very bright, but he has a poor opinion of himself because of his stutter. When he sees people with speech problems who are successful, he wonders how they did it.

Marilyn

■ ■ Marilyn's doctors consider her physically recovered from breast surgery, but she cannot escape the feeling that she is disfigured and may develop cancer again. She becomes more and more depressed as she withdraws from friends "who just can't understand."

Jim

■ ■ Jim is a heavy man whose overeating has caused him great personal unhappiness. After years of unsuccessful attempts to control his weight with medical help, fad diets, and pills, he sees himself as a hopeless victim of his own weak will.

To individuals engaged in human service activities, it has become clear that alienation and isolation from significant others is a major factor in the development and maintenance of problem behaviors. Some have gone so far as to suggest that most human service problems are a result of people feeling adrift and unlinked from each other because of the disruption of the traditional institutions of home, family, church, school, and neighborhood (Gendlin, 1970; Hurvitz, 1975; Mowrer, 1971; Van der Avort and Van Harberden, 1985). In what appears to be a response to this situation, in recent years there has been a fantastic growth in what has been called the small-group movement. Gendlin (1970) reports that while these groups have different names, and in some cases deal with very different contents [e.g., religious doubts in a church group, security concerns in a Neighborhood Watch Group], a certain vital group process occurs in all of them: The newcomer finds himself listened to, responded to, discovers that he makes sense, can articulate feelings and reach out to others, be accepted, understood, appreciated, responded to closely.

While the small-group movement includes the formal group-psychotherapy type of group, what may be most significant about it for human services is the growth of mutual-help groups or peer groups (Katz, 1981). Mowrer (1971) considers them to be new primary social institutions. Such groups consist of persons who gather together in a relatively permanent relationship to provide one another with mutual support and assistance in dealing with any one or a number of life's problems. Mowrer distinguishes between two types of mutual-help or peer groups:

Type I—A group of peers in the sense of persons having, for example, comparable professions; similar socioeconomic, sex, or age status; or the "same problem."

Type II—A group of persons who are highly diverse in all their characteristics but who are peers in the sense of being equals, without status or rank, except as special functions may be temporarily assigned to them or in terms of informally recognized group experiences and competence.

A less general categorization of self-help groups would include four subtypes of groups (Schensul and Schensul, 1982).

1. Conduct reorganization or behavioral control (for example, Alcoholics Anonymous).
2. Common predicament (for example, Gray Panthers, a support group for the elderly).
3. Survival or self-esteem (for example, Reach to Recovery, a support group for women who have had mastectomies).
4. Personal growth or self-actualization (for example, Parents without Partners).

Often, mutual or self-help groups do not fit neatly into this type of categorization and their goals or focus may overlap, and there are, of course, alternative models of categorization (Powell, 1987). One such alternative categorization describes four broad categories of groups: those for physical or mental illness, those for reforming addictive behavior, those for coping with a crisis of transition, and those for friends and relatives of the person with the problem (Hurley, 1987).

Gartner and Riessman (1977, 1983), rather than making broad distinctions between types of mutual-help groups, focus on their similarities. They propose that certain features are critical to the identification of groups as of a self-help or mutual-help nature:

1. Self-help groups always involve face-to-face interaction.
2. The origin of self-help groups is usually spontaneous (not set up by some outside group).
3. Personal participation is an extremely important ingredient, as bureaucratization is the enemy of the self-help organization.
4. The members agree on and engage in some actions.
5. Typically, the groups start from a condition of powerlessness.
6. Each group acts as a reference group, a point of connection and identification with others, a base for activity, and a source of ego reinforcement.[3]

By whatever scheme they are categorized, it is characteristic of all these groups that the participants have banded together for mutual help in the sense that they are seeking help in changing themselves or their environments without resorting to outside professional assistance. In fact, many such groups are openly antagonistic or hostile to trained professionals, who have for many years rejected the mutual-help groups as interlopers and amateurs in a highly complex field (Emrick, 1990; Hurley, 1987). This rejection by professionals has weakened dramatically in recent years, mainly because of the persistent success of many of the mutual-help group activities (Chutis, 1983; Toreland and Hacker, 1982). In fact, now the professionals are in some cases being accused of jumping on the mutual-help bandwagon.

To give some sense of the extent of the mutual-help movement, one can use as an example the prototype mutual-help organization, Alcoholics Anonymous. Since it was founded in 1935, Alcoholics Anonymous has grown to an organization with 41,000 chapters and over 800,000 members in the United States and Canada. Worldwide its membership is 1.5 million (Hurley, 1987).

At a 1977 conference sponsored by the National Self-Help Clearinghouse, its codirector, Frank Riessman, reported that there are self-help groups for check bouncers, convicts, crooks, divorcees, suicide attempters, debtors, the unemployed, mistresses, former mental patients, and every disease identified by the World Health Organization.

Mutual-help groups are being developed for new population groups on a constant basis. For example, the past few years have seen the development of self-help groups for mentally retarded citizens as an important new community approach (Browning, Thorin, and Rhoades, 1984). Nationwide there are over 150 self-help groups for the mentally retarded; they focus on activities such as socialization, fund raising, political lobbying, and group advocacy. Across the United States, there are over 500,000 self-help groups of dif-

Table 13-1 *A sampling of mutual-help groups.*

Name	Focus
Candlelighters	Peer support for parents of children with cancer
The Compassionate Friends	Peer support for parents whose children have died
Gamblers Anonymous	Peer support to help people stop gambling
Gray Panthers	Advocacy and support for the elderly
Mended Hearts, Inc.	Peer support for those who have had heart surgery
Narcotics Anonymous	Peer support for recovered drug addicts
National Alliance for the Mentally Ill	Peer support and information about and advocacy for seriously mentally ill people
Overeaters Anonymous	Peer support for overweight people and programs to combat overeating
Parents Anonymous	Peer support and crisis intervention for abusing or ex-abusing parents
Reach to Recovery	Peer support for women who have had mastectomies
Theos Foundation	Peer support for the widowed and their families

ferent types currently in operation, with 12 million members (Hurley, 1987). Obviously, the range of mutual-help groups is quite broad. The boxed examples below are illustrative of the types of mutual or self-help groups in existence or in the process of being developed around the country. An additional sampling of the broad range of targeted issues dealt with in self-help groups is given in Table 13-1.

Self-Help for the Widowed

■ ■ A self-help group for widows and widowers, an outgrowth of a "Workshop for the Widowed" sponsored by the Rockland County (New York) Mental Health Association at the local community college, has been meeting weekly since May, 1974.

The widowed workshop offered each semester at Rockland Community College is one of several programs designed by the association to provide preventive intervention at critical transitional periods in people's lives, according to Pat Thaler, director of the association's Educational Service.

Participants reported that while the workshop was extremely helpful to them in dealing with their new life situation, they wanted to meet with an ongoing group of widowed persons because they felt their problems were quite separate and distinct from those of divorced persons—who have groups such as "Parents Without Partners."

"The Widowed Group" meets each week at the Rockland Community Mental Health Center in Pomona. More than 125 men and women have participated in the program, with each meeting attracting between thirty and forty persons. Membership is limited to those under the age of fifty-five because it is felt that the problems of widowed people in the early and middle adult years are different from those experienced by older individuals who lose their spouses toward the end of the life cycle—the younger widowed have problems related to helping children deal with the death of a parent, untimely loss of a spouse, moving into the world of singles, anger and grief, extrusion by society. Ms. Thaler is consultant to the group, and is the only professional involved. There is no other expense to the association since the group collects dues and is self-sustaining.

"This is a self-help educational and social organization," Ms. Thaler says. "A strong family feeling exists among group members, who frequently help each other out in times of sickness or other distress. The group sponsors many social events that may or may not include children. Recently the group has taken a bus trip with children to New York City to see the Nutcracker Ballet; sponsored a members' Sunday morning brunch; and organized a Christmas/Hanukkah party with everyone bringing a dish."

Each meeting is planned in advance, with speakers on subjects of interest invited once or twice a month. Recent speakers have included a woman attorney discussing wills, trust funds, and providing for children when the widowed remarry; a psychiatrist on the special emotional needs and the new identity of the widowed; and a travel agent on trips for the single.

In addition to these programs, one or two meetings a month are devoted to group "raps" led by Ms. Thaler. Subjects have included the impact of death on children; relationships with in-laws; starting again; and the special problems of widowed men.

The group has initiated a telephone service for widows and widowers who need practical information or an understanding ear. Persons calling "The Widowed Group Line" speak to someone who takes the caller's name and telephone number. A return call is made to the caller by a helpful widowed person as soon as possible. This service is provided with the cooperation of the Rockland Community Mental Health Center's Crisis Telephone Service.[4]

As noted, Alcoholics Anonymous (AA) is one of the oldest mutual-help organizations and has been a model for many of the groups that have followed. Alcoholics Anonymous was started in 1935 by two alcoholics as a way for *them* to stay sober. It has grown into a major approach to alcohol addiction but retains the mutual-help character of its early beginnings.

As a prototype, AA demonstrates that in order for the self-help or mutual-help process to work with the major problems of living, the person in need must make a major commitment, *with the support of others*, to changing the problem behavior. In AA in particular, the commitment includes a spiritual flavor, as illustrated in its "twelve steps." These twelve steps are the core of the AA program and describe the attitude and activities that AA members believe are important in helping them achieve sobriety (Alcoholics Anonymous, 1955).

1. We admitted we were powerless over alcohol—that our lives had become unmanageable.
2. Came to believe that a Power greater than ourselves could restore us to sanity.

3. Made a decision to turn our will and our lives over to the care of God as we understood Him.
4. Made a searching and fearless moral inventory of ourselves.
5. Admitted to God, to ourselves and to another human being the exact nature of our wrongs.
6. Were entirely ready to have God remove all these defects of character.
7. Humbly asked Him to remove our shortcomings.
8. Made a list of all persons we had harmed, and became willing to make amends to them all.
9. Made direct amends to such people wherever possible, except where to do so would injure them or others.
10. Continued to take personal inventory and when we were wrong promptly admitted it.
11. Sought through prayer and meditation to improve our conscious contact with God, as we understood Him, praying only for knowledge of His will for us and the power to carry that out.
12. Having had a spiritual awakening as the result of these steps, we tried to carry this message to alcoholics, and to practice these principles in all our affairs.

Home Dialysis Club for Patients, Families

■ ■ A "Home Dialysis Club" for patients and their families coping with the stresses of using an artificial kidney machine at home offers a way for families to get together and support each other, without feeling they are stigmatized as members of a psychotherapy group. "Patients had resisted the idea that they in any way needed psychiatric treatment, and had greatly feared being seen as emotionally sick. It was burdensome enough to cope with being physically sick," says author Helen Kress.

Kress began the club more than three years ago when she was with the VA hospital in New York City. It began as a club for wives of patients, where they could gain support and understanding for what they were experiencing. Now both the patient and spouse are included in the monthly three-hour meetings, and sometimes children are invited to attend also.

In addition to sharing problems and feelings, club members plan social events and act as "sponsors" for new people entering the home dialysis training program. Thus, new trainees have someone in addition to staff members to whom to turn for support, and they see club membership as the norm for home dialysis couples.

"The club approach (is) an unconventional but effective means of offering services to home dialysis patients and their families consonant with their needs for dignity, self-respect, and more control of the structure than is needed by some clients," concludes the author.[5]

Other mutual help groups that have gained a great deal of public awareness include Synanon, Gateway House, and Daytop Village. These programs have become models for approaches to dealing with people who are trying to escape from chemical addictions other than alcohol, and similar mutual-help programs for addicts have grown up all around the country. Such programs require great commitment on the part of their members in order to be successful, greater than in the case of most other mutual-aid groups.

What makes mutual-help systems successful

Although mutual-help groups have been in existence formally for more than forty years and informally for much longer than that, many questions remain as to why they function effectively. Systematic attempts to examine their processes and their effectiveness have only recently been started. Unfortunately, the little information that is available in regard to what makes them tick is speculative in nature. Some clues, however, are emerging (Hurley, 1987).

1. Self-help group members learn about common aspects of their problems from other group members. A predominant activity is information sharing.
2. Members may be enabled to reattribute the cause of their problem from a personal failure to an impersonal issue. For example, parents of a schizophrenic may learn that their child's faulty biochemistry is the problem, not the parents' child-rearing skills.
3. The member experiences strong group acceptance and shared understanding.
4. The member develops a sense of normalization: "There are many others just like me."

O. H. Mowrer (1971), a strong proponent of the mutual-help concept, has suggested that people become alienated (lose their sense of community) because of dishonesty, irresponsibility, and uninvolvement. The mutual-help group uses the opposite approach to become in effect a substitute for the extended family (Drakeford, 1967). The group attempts, in Mowrer's words, to help "lonely, frightened, alienated persons to be converted (turned-with), to 'join-up,' 'plug-in,' become socially integrated, reconciled, reconnected fully and truly."

In surveying mutual-help groups, it appears that the principles of honesty, responsibility, and involvement are common to all, even though the phraseology describing the concepts may differ from one group to another.

Honesty is defined as being straight with oneself and with others, not being self-protective or self-indulgent at the expense of others, disclosing one's being, not rationalizing, and not deceiving oneself or others. *Responsibility* means accepting the consequences of one's behavior and one's effect on others, making amends when necessary, keeping commitments, keeping one's word, not blaming others for what happens to oneself, and gaining control over one's behavior. *Involvement* is emotionally opening up to the group, in effect "buying in," not holding oneself aloof from the process or from one's *own* feelings, letting the group, its process, and its goals have meaning for oneself, and being available for the needs of others.

To what extent each of these factors contributes to the functioning of mutual-help groups is unclear. Certainly many other factors are likely to be involved. But with the increasing emphasis on the use of mutual-help groups in the human services sector, we can expect more interest in determining the critical factors in their use as a social policy option (Newsome and Newsome, 1983).

Mutual-help or self-help groups obviously provide significant assistance to many people in need. It appears that this approach can be expanded to many other people problems. However, this approach is not without problems and dangers. One obvious problem is that a group may be organized or structured in such a way that the group will fail in its purpose, perhaps leaving the group members in more dire straits than before the group was begun. Lemberg (1984) has identified a number of factors that may lead to ineffectiveness in a self-help group process:

Lack of external support

Few intact members

Lack of sharing of leadership and responsibility

Passive members

Communication only between leaders and members, not member to member

Superficial meetings, avoidance of "hot" or emotional issues

Noninvolved members

Leaders who do not admit the need for support

No risk taking or involvement

If these factors are avoided and the group becomes successful as an ongoing social support system, a number of other possible dangers may develop. Gartner and Riessman (1977) break down dangers into two sets, one set relating to the professional human services system, and one set relating to consequences to the client.

Dangers relating to the professional human service system:
1. The mutual-help system may be used to justify the reduction of other services.
2. It may be used to avoid responsibility by the appointed service providers.
3. The mutual-help approach may be taken over by the "establishment," which would negate a major focus of the current systems.[6]

Dangers relating to the mutual-help group client:

1. Emphasizing mutual-help approaches leads to the possibility of "victim blaming."
2. Participation rather than real help may be a resultant, and there are few controls over the delivery of the services.
3. Mutual help may interfere with persons obtaining needed *professional help* when it is appropriate and useful.
4. Mutual help may foster an unnecessary dependence on the part of the members.[7]

Even though such problems and dangers exist, it is very likely that judicious use of and emphasis on mutual-help systems can avoid many of the problems, and the existence of such dangers certainly does not justify the neglect of the possible benefits by human service workers.

Mutual-help groups and the human service worker

The human service worker can use the mutual-help concept in at least two ways. The first and most obvious is referral. If the mutual-help groups in the community are known, clients can be referred to such groups as an additional or sometimes primary support system. The best example here is Alcoholics Anonymous. If the human service worker identifies problem drinking as a major issue for a client, it makes sense to refer that person to AA. Even though most mutual-help systems do not use "professional" help, they are ordinarily receptive to referrals from formal human service systems and maintain good working relationships with them.

The second way in which the human service worker can utilize the mutual-help process is more complicated and difficult but perhaps more rewarding and meaningful in the long run. That is, the human service worker may be able to initiate and set up entirely new mutual-help systems. By no means is it being suggested that the human service worker attempt to replicate a national organization on the scale of Alcoholics Anonymous; rather, limited mutual-help groups on a local level should be the target. The widowed group and the dialysis club described earlier are prime examples of such projects; an identified problem at a local level was met through the creation of a limited mutual-help approach. The possibilities of types of mutual-help systems are limited only by the creativity of human service workers (Selig, 1977).

Summary

1. Two major human service strategies—peer therapy and mutual-help groups—have important potential for use with people in need. Both have the advantage of maximizing the slim resources available in the human services field.

2. Peer therapy has been demonstrated to be a technique that effectively uses the naturally significant persons in the client's life to stimulate and maintain significant adaptive behavior change.

3. Peer therapy seems to be effective for three reasons: (a) Naturally significant others are strongly motivated to help the person in need; (b) the significant other is already linked into the physical and psychosocial need system of the client; (c) significant others act as natural models or identification figures for the client.

4. When peers are used as change agents, they must be trained and have supervision available. Peers must have the opportunity to give feedback and receive support from a more experienced human service worker or another peer therapist.

5. A mutual-help or self-help group is composed of people who share the same concerns or problems and have banded together to give and receive help and support.

6. There are over 500,000 self-help or mutual-help groups nationwide. They can be grouped in four general types: groups for those with physical or mental illness, those for reforming addictive behavior, those for coping with a crisis in transition, and those for friends or relatives of the person with a problem.

7. Mutual-help or self-help groups share the principles of honesty, responsibility, and involvement.

8. The effective functioning of a mutual-help or self-help group may be compromised by a number of factors, such as lack of external support, a majority of disturbed or passive members, lack of shared leadership, lack of member involvement, or an absence of risk taking.

9. Even effective mutual-help or self-help groups may present dangers to the professional human service system, such as using the self-help movement to justify reducing funded services, and dangers for the client, such as victim blaming or fostering unnecessary dependence.

10. Human service workers can use the mutual-help or self-help approach in at least two ways: (a) referring clients to existing groups and (b) developing entirely new mutual-help or self-help groups for needy target populations.

Discussion Questions

1. What is the difference between peer therapy and mutual self-help?

2. Why is peer therapy effective?

3. What issues exist in using peer therapists?

4. What are the common elements of mutual-help systems?

5. What other factors may be operating in mutual-help groups?

Learning Experiences

1. Identify the self-help groups operating in your community by name and address. Keep the list for future reference. (A good starting point is the telephone directory.)

2. Ask a self-help group if you can observe meetings or participate.

3. Try to determine what new self-help groups your community needs.

4. Join a self-help group if you think you need to (for example, to stop smoking, to lose weight, and so on).

5. If your community has a peer therapy program, ask if you can observe it or perhaps join (for example, a campus hotline).

Endnotes

1. Reprinted by permission from *Innovations* (Vol. 2, No. 3, Fall, 1975), published by the American Institutes for Research, P.O. Box 1113, Palo Alto, CA 94302, under a collaborative grant from the National Institute of Mental Health.

2. Adapted from F. Hawkinshire. "Training Procedures for Offenders Working in Community Treatment Programs." Published in Guerney, Bernard G., Jr. (ED.), *Psychotherapeutic Agents: New Roles for Nonprofessionals, Parents, and Teachers*. New York: Holt, Rinehart and Winston, 1969. Reprinted by permission of the publisher.

3. A. Gartner and F. Riessman. *Self-Help in the Human Services*. San Francisco: Jossey-Bass, Inc., Publishers, 1977, p. 7. Reprinted by permission of the publisher.

4. Reprinted by permission from *Innovations* (Vol. 2, No. 2, Summer, 1975), pp. 32–33, published by the American Institutes for Research, P.O. Box 1113, Palo Alto, CA 94302, under a collaborative grant from the National Institute of Mental Health.

5. Reprinted by permission from *Innovations* (Vol. 3, No. 3, Fall, 1976), p. 40, published by the American Institutes for Research, P.O. Box 1113, Palo Alto, CA 94302, under a collaborative grant from the National Institute of Mental Health.

6. A. Gartner and F. Riessman. *Self-Help in the Human Services*. San Francisco: Jossey-Bass, Inc., Publishers, 1977, p. 20. Reprinted by permission of the publisher.

7. A. Gartner and F. Riessman. *Self-Help in the Human Services*. San Francisco: Jossey-Bass, Inc., Publishers, 1977, p. 21. Reprinted by permission of the publisher.

Recommended Readings

Gartner, A., and Riessman, F. (eds.). *The Self-Help Revolution*. New York: Human Services Press, 1983.

Powell, T. J. *Self-Help Organizations and Professional Practice*. Silver Spring, Md.: National Association of Social Workers, 1987.

Scheffler, L. W. *Help Thy Neighbor*. New York: Grove Press, 1984.

Silverman, P. *Mutual Help Groups: Organizations and Development*. Beverly Hills, Calif.: Sage Publications, 1980.

14

Social Intervention: Prevention Through Environmental Change

- How do personal and general environments contribute to the difficulties experienced by human service clients?
- What processes are involved in improving a person's immediate environment?
- What are some historical and current examples of attempts to change personal environments for the better?
- What can be done to change general social systems in order to reduce human service problems?
- What current trends are apparent in social change?

Many of the problems with which human service workers deal do not reside in the individual client as much as in the fabric of society. Some experts view a high incidence of problems such as poverty or crime as signs that society itself is "sick" (Naroll, 1969; Spivack, 1974). For example, there are over 25,000 homicides in the United States each year, most of which involve firearms. In England, with one-fourth as many people as the United States, there are only one twenty-fifth as many homicides involving firearms—about 1,000 each year. Is that difference due to there being more violent people in the United States who need help with their violent impulses, or is it due to differences in how the two societies deal with the availability and possession of firearms? Some experts suggest that the American culture has an "Old West gun-slinger" mentality, in contrast to European cultures, and that this social phenomenon results in both the high incidence of homicide and our reluctance to pass stringent gun control laws. Are we a people who have more difficulty controlling our aggressive urges because of individual weaknesses or because our culture is more accepting, perhaps even encouraging, of violent solutions to interpersonal problems? The answer to those questions may differ depending on one's viewpoint about the importance of individual as opposed to social factors in human problems.

Let us look at a less controversial example. When a client comes to us in need of financial aid, we may discover that this person has no high school degree, has held few jobs, has problems with drug use, is the only parent for several children, and lives in a cold-water walk-up in a deteriorating part of the city. Why? And what can we do about it?

> ■ ■ Carmen V. is the seventeen-year-old mother of three children between the ages of seven months and three years. During her first pregnancy she dropped out of high school, where she had been a failing student, and lived with her mother in order to care for Carmen's younger brothers and sisters while her mother worked. Carmen was shortly thereafter thrown out on the streets when her mother found her using drugs in the home. Carmen had been introduced to drugs by her boyfriend, the father of her first child.
>
> During the next few years Carmen held several short-lived jobs in fast-food restaurants. Because of Carmen's lack of punctuality and reliability, associated with her drug use and her successive pregnancies, none of the jobs lasted for more than a few weeks. Carmen's boyfriend began to "get on her case" about her use of drugs and the inadequate care he thought she was providing for the children. About a year ago, during Carmen's third pregnancy, her boyfriend (common-law husband) left the area and Carmen has not heard from him since.
>
> Although young and basically attractive and bright, Carmen projects a sense of helplessness and hopelessness. She sees little in her future that is more satisfying than her past and appears overwhelmed by the responsibilities of caring for three young children. The one thing that she experiences as positive in her life is her association with her "friends" who are deeply involved in drug use. The few times she has tried to quit using drugs, her lack of social support has led her back to that same group of associates.

If we see problems as residing in the individual, our approach will focus on changing that individual. In the example above, we might conclude that the person needs remedial education and job training at some point but that the immediate problem is lack of motivation (dropped out of high school), poor frustration tolerance (cannot hold a job), withdrawal (uses drugs to escape from the harsh realities of life), poor human relations (spouse was fed up and left), and sense of helplessness (does not have the strength to get out of the inner city). Since we perceive the problems as caused by the person's lack of inner capacities, we try to make drastic changes in the individual's psychological processes. If we are successful, the other problems can be solved by the individual: He or she can get an education and a good job and income, leave the inner city, and develop a loving relationship with a new spouse.

Another way of looking at the problems of an individual is to consider the impact of social factors on the person's life. Certainly the person described above needs individual help, and that help involves working on problems such as motivation, frustration, withdrawal, addiction, and feelings of helplessness. Of course, that person also may need more education and job training. But what about the social environment from which he or she comes? What can we do about the social factors that contribute to poor education, lack of jobs, drug abuse, unstable families, and substandard housing? Perhaps these are the most critical reasons why this person is in a needy state. If this person had been born and raised in different circumstances, would he or she be the same? If we could have provided good schools, jobs, and a safe environment, would we still see this person as needing helping services? These are questions that cannot be confidently answered. We do know, however, that broad social problems have profound effects on the people who must suffer with them.

Many human service workers are involved in activities designed to prevent the development of further damage to people in need. These activities involve changing the immediate environments of people who already need services and, on a broader scale, involve working toward major social changes that will reduce our society's production of psychosocial walking wounded. Human service workers may act as change agents through the process of social intervention (Seidman, 1983). When human service workers try to change the environment of a person or that of a small group of clients, the process can be called a *limited social intervention*. Some broad social factors, such as poverty, may cause a wide variety of human problems. When we try to change these broader aspects of society, the process is one of *comprehensive social intervention*. Whether social interventions are conducted on a limited scale or are more comprehensive, in essence the goal is *prevention* of human service problems.

Prevention in Human Services

Prevention in the human services has traditionally been conceptualized in a similar fashion to prevention in the field of medicine and public health. In this view there are three levels of prevention effort: primary prevention, secondary prevention, and tertiary prevention.

Primary prevention includes efforts intended to prevent a disorder from occurring to begin with. These efforts include two broad strategies: (1) system-directed approaches such as social policy development and modification of social environments designed to reduce sources of stress and to enhance life opportunities; and (2) person-centered strategies such as educational programs to impart adaptive skills and competencies as well as preventive interventions for specific risk groups (for example, for children of divorce). A core quality that links primary prevention efforts and sets them apart from other approaches is their intentional targeting to well people (Price, Cowen, Lorion and Ramos McKay, 1988).

Secondary prevention consists of the early detection of dysfunction and immediate intervention. With early detection and immediate treatment or intervention, disorders or dysfunctions are believed to be more easily and effectively treated. Some would argue that this is not really prevention, but is simply treatment. Others point out that what is being prevented is long term chronic disability.

Tertiary prevention includes those strategies we use to reduce the severity or level of disabilities once a disorder or dysfunction has become chronically impairing of an individual. Most of those activities that are called *rehabilitation* fall in this category.

The areas of secondary and tertiary prevention have received the lion's share of available resources in the human services. It has only been in relatively recent times, that more and more attention and resources are being directed towards primary prevention. However, in comparison to the resources directed towards secondary and tertiary prevention, primary prevention is only just beginning to be seen as important (Newton, 1988).

Limited Social Interventions

Limited social interventions attempt to make significant formal changes in the personal environments of needy people, and this can have a beneficial effect on those individuals' ability to adjust to life in the broader society. In this sense, one-to-one therapies, group therapies, peer therapy, and mutual-help groups, when first developed, would fit under this concept. However, in this chapter the focus will be on the modification of current environments or the development of new environments in such a manner that they become inherently positive or supportive of adequate functioning on the part of persons who experience them. The stimulus for changing the immediate environments of persons in need has grown out of the recognition by human service workers of two related major issues:

1. Most environments of people in need support, and in fact stimulate, *problem* behavior.
2. For many people in need, providing one hour of *treatment* contact per day or week is not sufficient to generate positive behavior change.

A prime example of the first issue is the negative effect of short- and long-term imprisonment on lawbreakers (Chaneles, 1987; Haney, Banks, and Zimbardo, 1973; Sommer, 1976). The penal setting has been found to be so negative to the process of rehabilitation that many sources have described prisons as schools for crime. Prisoners, particularly first offenders, learn little during their imprisonment other than how to do better at the type of *crime* they have committed or how to engage in new types of criminal activity. For the most part, for persons who have or will have contact with the corrections system, this problem also exists in the community. In the clearest example, lawbreakers or potential lawbreakers tend to relate mainly with other lawbreakers, and their problem behaviors are reinforced through social acceptance by their peers. In addition, once labeled as a delinquent or criminal, such people tend to be treated by society as if they must inevitably again behave criminally.

Gruenberg (1967, 1969) has described a concept called the *social breakdown syndrome*, which is considered to be an environmentally determined process often seen accompanying other difficulties in clients. It is particularly common in institutional environments such as nursing homes, prisons, and mental hospitals. The development of this syndrome occurs when people can no longer meet the demands of those around them. They become identified as *helpless*, accept that identity, and finally become unable to change. An extremely important aspect of this process is that such people are relieved of the need to maintain responsibility for their own behavior and existence.

Obviously, many personal environments have a negative effect on people and may well be a major factor in otherwise adequately functioning individuals' *becoming* persons in need. As possible examples of negative personal environments, one could consider the following:

- The friendless, resourceless life of many elderly citizens without families
- The stimulus-deprived environment of the ghetto infant or child
- Overcrowded, underfunded poverty-area schools
- The unstable environment of the migrant worker
- The delinquent gang peer-group culture
- The skid row environment of the chronic alcoholic

Certainly, such a list could go on and on, with examples from formal helping systems such as mental hospitals, prisons, and schools and from society at large. It is clear that many such negative environments exist, and there is virtually total agreement among human service professionals that such environments can have significantly negative effects on a person's behavior, even when the primary problem of the client is not considered to be a function of environmental causes. An excellent illustration of the effects of social environments on a nonenvironmentally caused problem can be taken from the fields of medicine and public health. The diagnosis and treatment of physical disorders such as syphilis, herpes, and AIDS are complicated by the attitudes and reactions of the public towards people who have these disorders. In the mid-1980s, for example, a small number of school-age children developed AIDS from receiving blood transfusions contaminated by the AIDS virus. (This is quite unlikely to occur in the future, since blood donor screening for AIDS is now routine.) These children suffered intense rejection by their communities because of the unrealistic fear of the lay public that the children would contaminate other children. They were shunned by friends and neighbors, and in many cases were not allowed to attend school. These unfortunate children were faced with the spectacle of otherwise rational, caring adults angrily marching in picket lines to protest the children's school attendance. The effects of rejection by friends and neighbors of these children, and of children in the future who develop AIDS, are not yet known, but are likely to be profound. The public tends to see disorders such as syphilis, herpes, AIDS, and even some other medical problems, such as disfiguring or disabling physical conditions, as shameful or upsetting, and is likely to stigmatize and reject those who suffer from them. The resulting embarrassment, shame, and need for concealment often leads these disease victims to avoid social situations, or even to avoid treatment, sometimes with disastrous results.

The second major factor that has stimulated social intervention approaches is the recognition that limited direct contacts, such as one hour of treatment per week, are often not sufficient for generating positive behavior change. This observation has been made for prisoners in penal systems, patients in mental hospitals, and students in mental retardation facilities. The failure of such systems is often attributed to this problem. Ex-convicts return to their criminal subculture, discharged mental patients return to their old problem-generating environments, and the mentally retarded return to their nonsupportive life situations, with the result that many of these people must return to the institutions they came from because they "can't make it on the outside."

A further complicating factor is the chronicity of the problem that the people in need experience. Very frequently, human service clients present with problems that have existed for many years, often since their childhood or adolescence. It is not uncommon to encounter clients who have manifested the same difficulties for five, ten, twenty, or thirty years. It seems highly unrealistic to expect such long-standing problems to be resolved by one-to-one or group counseling or by psychotherapy on a once-a-week basis in a relatively short period of time. Rather, what is needed is the creation of an *environment* in which the client can exist and in which all activities, occurrences, and events have a positive effect on the problem behavior.

Changing institutions versus changing persons

The major problem in human services today may be that the person in need is provided with only partial services. For the most part, our focus has been on changing people so that they can adjust to society's stresses, with the assumption that the problem most frequently lies within the client. Traditional human service approaches have focused their attention on one-to-one or small-group treatment approaches, which are labor intensive in the sense that one treatment provider can provide services to only a small number of clients. The traditional approaches by and large require intensive efforts directed at achieving significant change in how an individual client relates to an established social system. The recognition that labor-intensive intervention systems use costly resources in dealing with relatively small numbers of people has led us to a growing awareness of the need to intervene in social systems in order to provide alternative change strategies for people in need.

What appears to be required in the human service field is a major investment in discovering or developing natural growth experiences that will have a positive effect on the behavior and adjustment of clients. Obviously, no one such experience would be appropriate for all persons; rather, a range of experiences would have to be available.

As an example, the American primary-grade school system is a positive environment (experience) for a large number of children. For others, it obviously is not. Children who cannot benefit from the public school system as it is currently structured need an alternative experience to provide them with the same advantages. And some slight progress has been made in this direction. There has been, for example, the development of the Head Start program as well as other early childhood intervention systems (Zigler, 1985).

These types of limited social interventions are becoming more common and focus on changing the immediate social systems and organizations that impact on people in need, including social welfare agencies, institutions, facilities, and programs. The goal is to promote positive growth on the part of people in need by changing the systems with which they must interact, so that the social systems themselves do not produce or maintain problem behavior. Whatever problems are present in social systems, limited social intervention involves a similar process:

1. Identifying environments that have significantly negative effects on a client or clients
2. Identifying the aspects of the environment that can be changed
3. Determining how the negative aspects can be changed in a positive direction
4. Implementing the changes or creating entirely new environments that will have an ongoing positive effect

Historical examples

Several examples can be given of environmental changes that have had important impacts on human services. Such examples could be drawn from any of the subfields of human services: corrections, retardation, mental health, education, and child care. However, we shall focus on two of the larger systems: corrections and mental health.

As early as 1913, the corrections system of Wisconsin innovated a work release program (Clare and Kramer, 1976). In such programs, prisoners are allowed to seek and maintain gainful employment in the community while serving a sentence. The underlying premise of such programs is that they allow prison inmates to begin an appropriate transition to community life before the end of the sentence. The transition allows them to develop new social networks that will be supportive of the "straight" life after the sentence is complete.

In a similar vein, prerelease halfway houses for felons have been developed around the country. Their focus is to assist in the transition from prison life to life in the community. The emphasis in such settings is on employment, talking out one's problems, and sharing the difficulty of reentry into community life. Such settings have as major goals the breaking of old patterns of behavior and the development of new support systems.

In the mental health system, an environmental manipulation that has had both positive and negative results occurred in the early 1960s. At that time, it was considered that many people were inappropriately admitted and retained in mental hospitals. The criteria for admission to these very restrictive settings were not stringent and few community services were available. Since admission was easy and other resources were absent, mental hospitals became swollen with residents. Changes in treatment approaches, new legislation, and funding for increased community resources, combined with a changing viewpoint about the desirability of restrictive settings, led to the phenomenon we now call *deinstitutionalization:* the movement of patients and the responsibility for their care into community settings. This approach resulted in a steady reduction of inpatient population from a peak of 559,000 in 1955 to about 110,000 in 1989, where it remains today (see Figure 14-1). Fed-

Figure 14-1 *Patients in state and local public mental hospitals from 1955 to 1990, based on National Institute of Mental Health figures.*

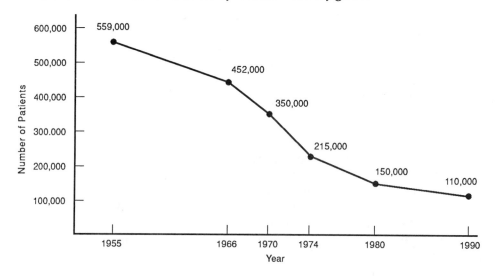

eral and state monies that were made available to support ex-mental patients in community settings led to the growth of a major new industry: nursing homes and sheltered-care facilities for discharged mental patients.

The process of deinstitutionalization was a success in part (Miller, 1985; Minkoff, 1987; Torrey, 1989). It resulted in many improvements in services in public mental hospitals. With lower census levels the institutions' funding could provide more services to the fewer remaining in-patients. In addition, many people who had been locked away were able to move into less restrictive community settings.

However, it is clear that many abuses occurred.[1] Many patients benefited tremendously from their placement in such community settings; unfortunately, many others found themselves in basically the same predicament, simply having exchanged the back ward of a mental hospital for the back ward of a private sheltered-care setting. Others have joined the ranks of the homeless street people. Today the issue of homeless street people, many of whom are discharged mental patients or other people who need treatment for mental illness, is gaining national attention as a major social problem (Roth and Bean, 1986). In this particular example of an environmental manipulation, it is clear that even though the negative aspects of the original settings (the back wards of state hospitals) were relatively obvious, the end results of the manipulation were not clearly thought out, and no one was able to foresee the problems that would occur.

Does limited social intervention really work?

The notion that changing an individual's environment for the better will prevent future problems is appealing. But does it work? Let us look at one example of what happened when such an approach was studied closely. The example involves an attempt to reduce the effects of a deprived environment on intellectual functioning in children.

A great deal of evidence indicates that mild mental retardation in children is much more prevalent in lower socioeconomic classes than can be accounted for by genetic or other organic reasons. We suspect that much of this mild retardation is due to psychosocial deprivation. If at least some of the children who are at risk for this type of mild retardation could be kept functioning at a higher intellectual potential, a major victory would be accomplished. Based on an early intervention program organized in Milwaukee in the 1970s, it appears that this may be possible.

The Milwaukee project focused on children in one geographic area of the city. That area contained only 2.5 percent of the children in the city but produced more than 30 percent of the mildly retarded children for the whole metropolitan area (Garber and Heber, 1977). The families at risk for producing these retarded children were those in which the mothers had IQs of 80 or below. The staff of the Milwaukee project decided to try to enrich the environment of these families to see if they could intervene in the retarding process. Since they were concerned about finding out if they had been successful, they wanted to compare the families with whom they worked with families who were similar but for whom they could not provide services.

Forty children of mothers with IQs of 75 or lower were identified, and half the children and their mothers were worked with. The other half were periodically evaluated but did not receive environmental intervention. The environmental change that was implemented for the families that received services was quite comprehensive. Indigenous human service workers entered each child's life and spent five days a week, most of the waking day, with the child, enriching the environment. This "teacher" was responsible for feeding, bathing, and cuddling the child and for providing exciting, interesting activities. The staff organized group activity programs for the children to provide intellectual and social stimulation. They taught the mothers these child care skills and instructed them in job skills, reading, and homemaking. At the end of this program, the mothers of the intervention groups were more positive in their self-concept and more verbal and responsive to their children than the mothers who had not received the social intervention, and more were employed.

The differences in the two groups of children were even more noticeable. The program began when the children were three months old, and direct involvement ended when they were about eighteen months old. The mothers continued in their training until the children were six. At the beginning, the children who received the intervention and those who did not were very similar in intellectual performance. The children were followed up until they were nine years old. At that age, children who had received the intervention had maintained their level of intellectual functioning, whereas children who had received no intervention had declined in intellectual functioning. The environmental changes that were provided to the intervention groups led to an average 20-point difference in IQ between children who had received services and those who had not. Although the supporting data for this study have been questioned, it appears that the program of limited social intervention did have important effects on these children (Sommer and Sommer, 1983; Garber, 1984).

Will the effects last? We do not know. Children in the intervention group began to score more poorly as time went by, after the program ended because of a lack of funding. These data, however, also demonstrate the positive impact of environmental enrichment as an early intervention for deprived children.

Current examples of limited social intervention

The following examples of limited social intervention provide some sense of the range of environmental changes that have been tried and can be attempted today. The changes in a client's environment made by human service workers can vary from changing one simple element to a complete overhaul of the client's life space.

For Ex-Offenders

■ ■ After its first two years in operation, DESEO, a program for convicted public offenders in Albuquerque, New Mexico, can point to a recidivism rate of less than 10 percent among its active participants. National statistics, on the other hand, show that approximately 75 percent of all parolees commit new crimes during the first two years of parole.

DESEO ("I desire," in Spanish) got its start when ex-offenders involved in a weekly therapy group at the Bernalillo County Mental Health-Mental Retardation Center developed the concepts for the program, and obtained the support of the center and funding from the Law Enforcement Assistance Administration, the state of New Mexico, and the city of Albuquerque.

Joanne Sterling, Ph.D., the center's assistant director of special programs, and Robert W. Harty, a former offender who is the program's coordinator, attribute much of the success of DESEO to the fact that offenders have been involved from the beginning in its design. In addition, two of the three field office staff are ex-convicts themselves.

DESEO is housed in a community-based facility as accessible as possible to the client population and the judicial and correctional components of the city, county, and state. Harty says the site has an added advantage because individuals who are hesitant to seek services at the main center are considerably less hesitant to visit the satellite center.

DESEO has active programs in a number of areas, with emphasis on strengthening the family support structure, both while the offender is incarcerated and during the crucial three to six months after his reentry into the community.

Essential components of the DESEO program include prerelease groups; counseling-treatment groups; a women's group for wives, girl friends, and mothers of offenders; bus service to the penitentiary; employment and training; and public education.

DESEO works hard to establish relationships with prisoners before they are paroled in Bernalillo County. One prerelease group meets weekly at Los Lunas Correctional Center, and another meets monthly at the New Mexico State Penitentiary. "At the same time, we are involved with his family, so both the inmate and his family are becoming more realistic about what to expect of each other, and themselves, before release," Harty says. The State Parole Board has begun requesting recommendations from DESEO staff about parole status and planning.

DESEO works to strengthen the ex-offender's social support system by holding weekly women's group meetings to provide socializing and discussion of mutual problems, and by providing weekly transportation for family members to the penitentiary.

Other ways in which DESEO helps its clients' families:

- It acts as advocate to helping agencies the family may know nothing about or is reluctant to approach.
- It sponsors, with local churches and civic clubs, recreational programs for clients' children, such as Little League Baseball and Big Brother type of activities.
- It intervenes in crises, whether they are emotional or practical needs for assistance with housing, welfare benefits, utility bills, or transportation.
- It utilizes the specialized treatment resources available through the mental health center.

Another area in which DESEO has a deep commitment is employment and training. "Research completed elsewhere has shown that a key factor in reducing recidivism is placement in a satisfactory job setting," Harty says. "Thus the program's staff has established links with all available resources within the community in this area, including the Division of Vocational Rehabilitation, the Employment Security Commission, and so on. In addition, a high percentage of the 2,400 hours provided to individual client services in the first year were devoted to this area."

Harty has these suggestions to anyone thinking of starting a similar program:

- Don't negate input from clients. The ex-offender must know that it is his program and he can get out of it whatever he puts in.
- The program must actively seek public exposure and gain public support through all forms of media.
- A close liaison must be maintained with agencies that might perceive the program as "radical" or a threat to them.
- For maximum delivery of services, a team approach is by far more effective than a hierarchical one.
- It is essential, unless the program is a nonprofit corporation, that it receive strong administrative support from the sponsoring agency, and that this agency also have strong community support. This is especially true in the area of devising funding methods for the program's continuation.
- Continuing efforts for minimal staff expansion must be made or a steadily increasing client load will eventually erode the energy, enthusiasm, and productivity of staff personnel.
- Probably most important is that the program not become an "institution" that drifts in the direction of meeting needs as they are perceived by professionals and administrators, rather than as they in fact are, and as they are perceived by the clients they serve.[2]

The environmental changes that have been made by DESEO and similar programs include maximizing social support networks for ex-offenders, employment, community involvement, crisis intervention, and residential services (Davis, 1984). In systems where such programs are unavailable, the ex-offender is likely to return to an environment in which the most supported response is renewed criminal activity. Programs like DESEO are likely to become much more important in the years to come, since there has been a tremendous increase in the numbers of prisoners in correctional facilities in the past fifteen years (see Figure 14-2). In fact by 1990, the number of prisoners in federal, state, and county correctional facilities had soared to over 700,000 (Chaneles, 1987).

Another example of a group in need of social intervention is the mentally retarded. The deinstitutionalization that occurred in mental hospitals (described previously) was followed fifteen years later by a similar though less dramatic reduction in the population of institutions for the mentally retarded (see Figure 14-3). The deinstitutionalization of the mentally retarded was assisted by the development of small residential facilities in the community in which the retarded who needed some support could live. In 1960,

Figure 14-2 *Adult prisoners in state and federal institutions, 1955 to 1990.*

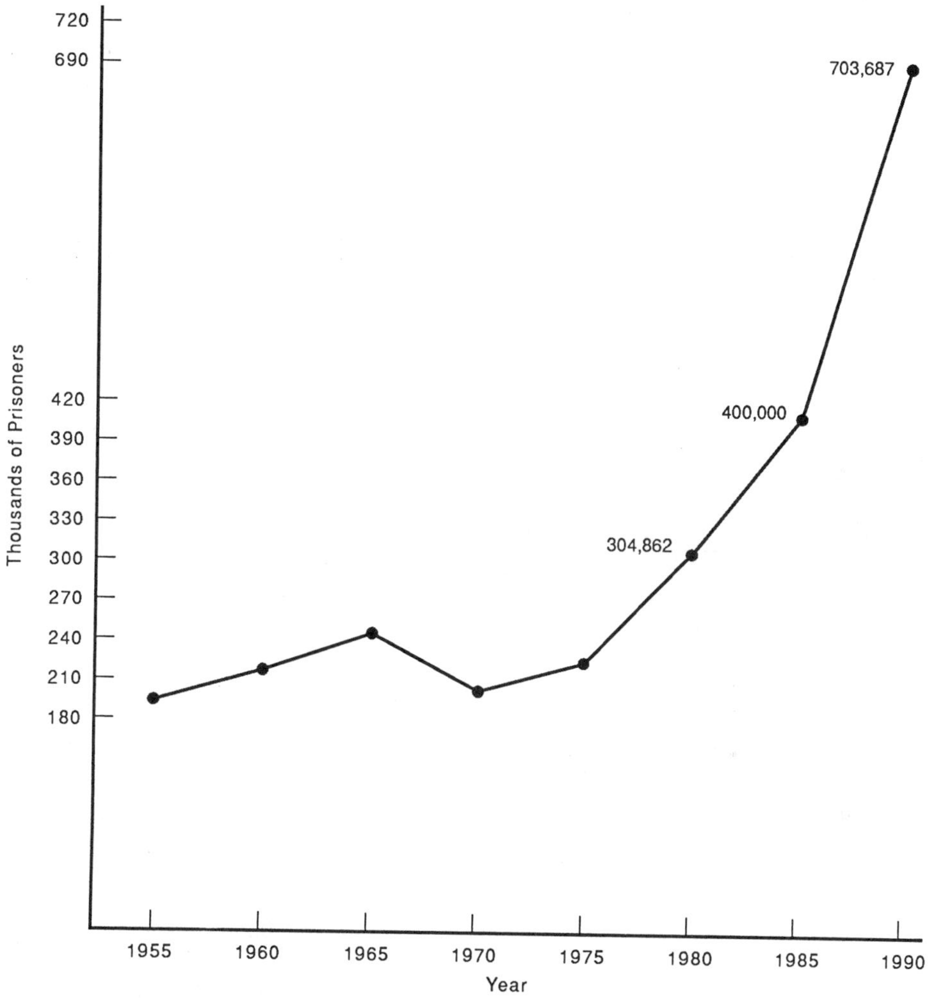

Source: Adapted from *Directory, Juvenile and Adult Correctional Departments, Institutions, Agencies and Paroling Authorities, United States and Canada*, 1982 ed., p. xxii. Used by permission of American Correctional Association, College Park, Md. Census total for 1985 based on Bureau of Justice Statistics, 1985. 1990 statistics from Church, 1990.

there were about 200 such community facilities. By 1983, there were more than 6,000 (Janicki, Mayeda, and Epple, 1983). Most of the individuals placed in these facilities were mildly or moderately retarded. For them and for other mentally retarded individuals in the community, some social changes are necessary in order to promote a more favorable living climate. A program in

Figure 14-3 *Resident census of persons in public institutions for the mentally retarded.*

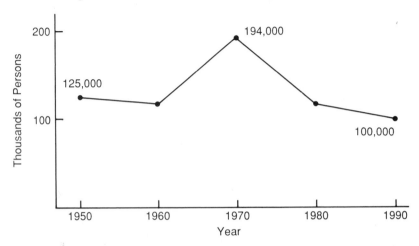

Source: Data based on Lakin, K. Demographic Studies of Residential Facilities for the Mentally Retarded, Developmental Disabilities Project on Residential Services and Community Adjustment, Department of Psychoeducational Studies. University of Minnesota, Minneapolis, 1980; 1990 projection based on Braddock (1981).

Minnesota approached this problem of developing life skills for this population in a rather innovative attempt at social change. The program involved providing an environment that encouraged self-reliance: wilderness camping.

Who Can't Canoe?

■ ■ A five-day, twenty-five-mile canoe trip into the Boundary Waters Canoe Area in Northwestern Minnesota has been a summer highlight for mildly and moderately retarded citizens from the northwestern region of the state for the past two summers. The voyagers traveled in the wilderness area with all of their camping equipment, portaging their canoes, cooking over campfires, and in general living the quality and type of life of the early fur traders.

The program was initiated because many persons, especially staff and participants of the area's sheltered workshops, were concerned with the lack of an appropriate summer recreational experience for educable retarded citizens.

"The Northwestern Region of Minnesota had, for a number of years, provided a relatively structured camping experience for trainable mentally retarded," says Dan Wilson, developmental disability specialist at the Northwestern Mental Health Center in Crookston. "Initially, educable mentally retarded were also included in that camping experience. However, in many cases, mildly retarded adult citizens found themselves being counseled by high school age and young college people at this camp in areas of arts and crafts or beginning waterfront activities. These retarded persons felt that this particular camping experience was beneath them. As a result, they lost interest and few continued in subsequent years."

A representative of the local National Association for Retarded Citizens, together with a representative of the sheltered workshop and the Northwestern Mental Health Center, worked out a camping package that would meet the levels and the challenges necessary to stimulate these higher functioning mentally retarded persons as well as to help them on the road to independent living, Wilson says.

"After consulting with the many agencies involved, we were able to develop a program on agency time borrowed from the local welfare departments, from the state hospital, from the sheltered workshops, as well as from the area community mental health center.

"The local welfare departments agreed the first year to finance the program (which costs $50 per participant)," Wilson explains. "The second year, case planning was begun six months in advance so that the families and the individuals involved were able to pay for their own expenses. (In late 1973, the state changed its policy that had allowed use of Title IV-A [Social Security Act] funds for camping fees.) Since most of the program was put together on borrowed agency time, we decided to use a private outfitter rather than try to assemble all the equipment necessary to make a camping trip successful. Responsibilities of the mental health center staff included selection of the staff, screening of the participants, organizing the transportation, and arranging finances. One person was excluded in the screening process due to a number of phobic responses which could not be dealt with through behavior modification in the limited time available."

"The screening process," according to Wilson, "involved a simple sampling of the kinds of behaviors that each of the participants would be expected to demonstrate once in the Boundary Waters Area. During the screening process, the participants were trained to get in and out of a canoe, to paddle a canoe, to select a paddle, to load and unload a pack sack, to roll and unroll a sleeping bag, to carry or help carry a canoe, to load and unload the canoe, to roll and unroll a tent, and to help set up a tent.

"As was previously suspected, the screening process revealed that it would be difficult to train mentally retarded persons to function as a sternsman in a canoe. The skill required to adequately steer a canoe was more than could be acquired in a relatively short period of time. For this reason, the staff ratio was predetermined at one staff person to two participants. In other words, one counselor would steer the canoe from the stern and the mentally retarded participants would paddle from the bow and the middle of the canoe.

"One of the keys to the success of this project was the staffing pattern. Throughout the camping trip, everything was done in threes by canoe: the counselor stayed with the two occupants of his canoe while traveling across the water, cooking, dishwashing, woodcutting, or setting up the tent. Each counselor was responsible for the supervision of only two other persons. In this way, no single person carried a greater supervisory responsibility than any other; and as a result, the trip was a vacation for all. Camping chores were broken down into modules and rotated three times a day. Each of the participants was trained in each of the modules and took equal responsibility for such tasks as woodcutting, dishwashing, cooking, etc."

These goals were achieved on the trip, Wilson says:

- Participants from both the sheltered workshop and the day activity center were provided with a five-day independent camping experience, totally apart from "civilization."
- A number of workers from both the state hospital and the county welfare departments were trained in the special needs of retarded persons, as well as made aware of their heretofore untapped potential.
- Workers from many agencies were able to work together on an immediate goal from a team approach; this has since helped in planning for larger and more difficult goals.
- The mentally retarded persons who participated in the camping experience did, in fact, become more independent. Seven of the ten participants on the first canoe trip were later placed in community employment and have continued to maintain themselves independently.
- The participants have learned to save money for their own interests as a result of this trip.
- The governing board of the regional camp for retarded has incorporated the EMR camping program as a part of the regular summer camping experience.

"A wilderness canoe trip is only one of the many ways that alternative camping experiences can be provided to higher functioning mentally retarded persons," Wilson says. He concludes: "Too often in the past we've encouraged dependence by providing camping experiences too structured and not very challenging to the potential of these persons. Very often we have been concerned about the safety of mentally retarded persons and have not allowed them to take the same risks that we would take ourselves in a camping experience. Our experience here has demonstrated that these handicapped persons showed the wisdom to recognize their own limitations, and as a result, we had no accidents of any sort either year. The assumptions that we have held, that any skill which we as 'normal' persons find difficult at first, is impossible for the retarded, is quite untrue. I believe that if we tried we would find that most of the experiences that we find gratifying to ourselves and by which we grow intellectually and emotionally, would also be growing and gratifying experiences for the developmentally disabled.

"Our challenge is to dare to help these people to not need us anymore."[3]

Mentally retarded citizens often experience an environment that does not allow them to develop fully. The environmental change just described is a small step toward providing an environment that supports retarded citizens in discovering their fuller potential.

In the examples of DESEO and wilderness camping, the change of the environment was relatively minor although still important. In the example that follows, a major reconstruction of the environment of a group of clients was attempted. This microenvironmental change is fully described in two texts: *Community Life for the Mentally Ill: An Alternative to Institutional Care*, by Fairweather, Sanders, Cressler, and Maynard (1969), and *Creating Change in Mental Health Organizations*, by Fairweather, Sanders, and Tornatzky (1974).

The community lodge program

In the mid-1960s, a group of researchers led by George Fairweather (then at the Veterans Administration Hospital in Palo Alto, California) became determined to attack the problem of the lack of appropriate environments into which chronic mental patients could be discharged. At this time, it had become clear that many people were hospitalized mainly because there was no place for them to go, rather than because their behavior was so extremely deviant that they required protection and treatment. Such patients did express strange behaviors, including delusions, hallucinations, extreme mannerisms, and other eccentricities. It was the premise of Fairweather's group

A good example of deinstitutionalization is the sheltered workshop, which allows mentally retarded individuals to lead more active, self-sufficient lives.

that such persons could live fairly productively if the appropriate circumstances were arranged.

Fairweather and his group embarked on a very ambitious project—in essence, they decided to create a new environment in the community in which these chronic patients could live a self-determined life. Funding was obtained to provide for the leasing of an entire motel, in which the patients would live, and a business was set up that was to be completely operated by them. The patients were trained and supervised by several staff supervisors who slowly withdrew their support and control over the course of about one year.

The patients (all men) were discharged from the hospital and had responsibility for their own self-care, personal hygiene, medication, food, and government (making and keeping rules) and for the operation of their grounds-keeping and janitorial business. In addition, each took responsibility on himself for his own behavior and the behavior of his fellows, since they knew the community would not tolerate them if they became too "disturbed."

In many ways, this communelike living experience for ex–mental patients was a remarkable success. Although not all the members were able to remain out of the hospital, many did. They became relatively self-supporting and self-directing and were able to operate a functional business venture for several years. The results of the project have been considered so significant that similar community lodge programs have been started around the country.

Changing personal environments

The simplest aspect of the process of changing personal environments is identifying environments that one considers bad, or in need of change. One need only examine the human service literature to find many situations that are considered to be detrimental to the adjustment or growth of persons in need. Once an environment is selected to be changed, the real difficulty begins (Reppucci and Saunders, 1983).

Fairweather, Sanders, and Tornatzky (1974) have made an extensive study of the process of changing environments that have detrimental effects on people. Many of these environments are part of human service systems. For example, the mental hospital has often been criticized as having detrimental effects on patients in spite of providing treatment. Fairweather and his colleagues suggest that a number of principles should be followed if one wants to be successful in changing some aspect of an organized service system. Implementing change is not an easy task.

Guidelines for change include these hints:

1. *Have perseverance.* Change is never easy, and it will not occur overnight. The human service worker must persevere in order to obtain change.

2. *Change is independent of resources.* Even resource-poor systems can change. Change is more a function of the involvement of people than of the availability of resources.
3. *Outside intervention is best.* People who are external to an agency are more likely to have success as change agents.
4. *Change requires action.* Doing is better than planning, since planning can be a way of avoiding taking action.
5. *Start small.* Early changes should be nonthreatening.
6. *Use a grass roots approach.* Change is likely to be resisted by those in power.
7. *Obtain wide involvement.* The greater the number of people who feel that the change is "their" project, the more likely success will be.
8. *Act as part of a group.* Partners can provide each other with mutual support.
9. *Plan on continuous effort.* Once change has occurred, it has to be monitored. If it is not working, other changes may be necessary.

Even if one successfully follows these guidelines, this does not guarantee success. If the guidelines are not followed, however, success is very unlikely.

Comprehensive Social Intervention

The concept of comprehensive social intervention can be defined as (1) the process of identifying broad social problems that contribute to or possibly cause maladaptive behaviors and (2) the subsequent modification of the social systems or policies that contribute to the problems, in a planned attempt to eradicate those problems. A prime example of a broad social problem that is currently of great concern is the issue of poverty. What can be done to ease the plight of the nation's poor? It is clear that poverty in and of itself is a major contributor to human service problems. Crime rates are high among the urban poor, there is a higher incidence of drug abuse, infant death rates are higher, and most other types of major behavioral problems tend to have a higher incidence in poverty-stricken individuals. Using the concept of comprehensive social intervention, the approach to the problems exhibited by the nation's poor would be to discover a solution to *poverty* rather than attempt to help *individual* clients by means of direct assistance to them or through the modification of *their* immediate environments.

In previous works, it has been pointed out that most of the major behavioral changes in humanity have been a function of broad socioenvironmental restructurings, including changes in economy, political systems, social systems, and religious systems (Fisher, Mehr, and Truckenbrod, 1974). The philosopher-historian Bertrand Russell (1960) has suggested that major changes in social systems have influenced the level of deviance in various societies. For example, he indicates that in Renaissance Italy, traditional moral restraints and controls became weak because they were felt to be a result of superstition. As a result, the liberation from such controls fostered the genius of energetic and creative individuals (such as Leonardo da Vinci) while at the same time leading to an era of anarchy and treachery, with little regard for human life.

Fried (1964) has developed a working definition of social change:

> For a working definition of social change, we can speak of gross alterations in the institutions of a society such as the structure of the family, the organization of occupational activities, the patterns of economic exchange or the political system. However, the specific effects of social change on the individual derive more directly from changes in the criteria for social role performance or fulfillment and in the expectations people have of one another with respect to any form of interaction.

It should be pointed out that Fried and many others speak of social-environmental change in regard to its negative effects. That is, they describe its disruptive effects on individuals, which include anxiety, fear, confusion, and disturbed behavior. These effects on individuals do often occur, especially when the change is rapid and unexpected. However, when one takes the broader view, it is clear that major social changes also have positive effects.

Riessman and Miller (1964), writing at about the same time as Fried, pointed out that the concept of social change has been largely neglected since the 1930s in favor of dealing with people problems on an individual basis. However, they provide examples of socioenvironmental changes that have had a major impact on the behavior patterns of large groups of people—racial integration and the desegregation of schools. It is difficult to predict the totality of effects of large-scale changes in society and the environment, and often the results are both positive and negative, depending on one's viewpoint. In fact, frequently the effects of major changes are totally unforeseen and perhaps impossible to expect. However, if major changes are to occur in the level of problems such as poverty, crime, delinquency, drug usage, unemployment, and a host of other issues, major environmental changes are probably needed.

Examples of early comprehensive social intervention

The Emancipation Proclamation

It is extremely unlikely that today anyone would seriously suggest that slavery is an acceptable condition of life for any human being. But certainly, before the Civil War, that was a widely held belief. What is of interest here regarding that period are the attitudes and expectations that the slaveholder held toward slaves. Slaves were seen as just slightly more human than animals. There was a common belief that slaves were of low intelligence and were amoral in behavior. These characteristics were viewed as innate biological factors even by many well-educated whites. For example, Benjamin Rush, a signer of the Declaration of Independence and revered as the "father of American psychiatry," in the late 1700s and early 1800s wrote articles in which he suggested that black skin was in fact a symptom of a racial disease. The disease was supposedly associated with lack of energy and motivation, lack of intelligence, and a need for structure, direction, and control by others (whites). Even today there are a small number of researchers who believe that there is evidence for an innately lower average level of intellectual ability among blacks (Jensen, 1973). In today's culture, however, this is an extremely unpopular view and is the subject of great controversy. By far the majority of researchers do not accept this notion and are very skeptical of the validity of any data invoked to support it. The more prevailing opinion is that the higher representation of black Americans in special education classes, prisons, and other service settings is the result of negative social factors rather than the result of innate differences between blacks and whites.

During the time of slavery in the South the dominant white culture created an environment that elicited the role behaviors that slaveholders expected of slaves. That environment sometimes involved the use of forceful punishment of slaves who violated the expected behaviors, but often consisted of the application of subtle or not-so-subtle social pressure. For example, since slaves did not learn to read, the view was that they were incapable of reading because of a lack of intelligence. Since it was believed that slaves were incapable of reading, no attempt was made to teach them. Thus a belief led to the creation of a behavior (or lack of behavior) and the lack of reading behavior was used as data to support the belief. In time, of course, some slaves did learn to read, and behaved in other ways which refuted the prevailing slaveholder beliefs, leading to controversy about those very beliefs.

The "problem" behaviors of slaves (supposed lack of intelligence, morals, independence, energy, motivation, and so on) were not solved by finding out what was "wrong" with individual slaves and "treating" them, but rather were dealt with by determining that the social institution of slavery was wrong. In 1863, President Lincoln made it official: He issued the Emancipation Proclamation, freeing all the slaves. But by then the Civil War was well under way. It took a major war and a federal political action to correct the situation, and even then the negative effects of slavery remain with us today in the aftereffects of prejudice and discrimination.

Prohibition
Shortly after World War I, the United States government prohibited the manufacture and marketing of alcoholic beverages. The impetus for this legislation came from concern over the negative effects of alcohol consumption, in-

cluding alcoholism. Unfortunately, in this comprehensive social intervention, the "solution" was ineffective and in fact created other problems. Not only did the laws not have the desired effect (most people still drank), but in addition an unexpected side effect was to provide a major source of revenue and growth for organized crime through the creation of an environment conducive to bootlegging. The legislation was so ineffective that within a few years it was repealed. Alcohol use continues to create problems for our society. Each year 25,000 people die in alcohol-related automobile accidents and hundreds of thousands of people are injured; about 18 million people in the United States are alcoholics.

Social Security
A comprehensive social intervention that has been moderately successful has been federal involvement in welfare services, dating from the Social Security Act of 1935. Before that time, national social policy fell far short of recognizing any broad responsibility to assist the needy members of society. Since then, major strides have been made in assisting these populations, to the extent that the number of people estimated to be living in poverty was reduced from 40 million in 1960 to 22 million in 1968 (Cohen, 1968). Far too many of our citizens remain in financial need for the social welfare system to be considered a major success; further changes are clearly necessary (Whitman, 1988).

A major current problem is the danger of bankruptcy of the Social Security Administration. By the year 2000, there may not be adequate funding to support even the current level of benefits for people over the age of sixty-five and those below age sixty-five who are disabled.

Trends in comprehensive social intervention

It is difficult if not impossible to transcend one's environment and accurately predict major social change events that will occur in the future. One can, however, note recent changes that may have an important impact on our society and therefore on the field of human services. The analysis of the impact of social change is unfortunately limited by our lack of understanding of its processes. Coelho and Rubinstein (1972) have identified several areas in which we must expand our knowledge in order to monitor the effects of such change:

1. The institutional and cultural factors in the social system that produce the change
2. The means by which that change is propagated, diversified, and incorporated in the system
3. The direction and extent of change
4. Its differential impacts on different generations through the life cycle

Although we do not fully understand the process and resultants of major social change, we can identify recent changes that seem to have had and are having major impacts on society. The four examples that follow illustrate the types of occurrences that currently fall in this category.

Civil rights legislation

Since the 1950s, major changes have occurred in our society as a result of a strong governmental concern over the issue of equal rights for all people regardless of race, color, religion, or sex. Obviously, discrimination and prejudices continue to exist in spite of the changes; however, most people would agree that progress has been made—more school systems are desegregated, and more members of minority groups are entering the middle class. As larger numbers of the disadvantaged minorities gain access to the mainstream, we can expect some reduction in the problems that are a function of membership in disadvantaged classes.

Women's liberation

An extremely interesting social change in recent years has been the evolution of the women's liberation movement. This movement, which is reflective of changing attitudes and also is a prime force in the *changing* of attitudes, has had important effects on society. Even though only a small percentage of women actively belong to groups such as the National Organization for Women (NOW), the basic concepts and attitudes of the movement have almost imperceptibly become part of the thinking of large numbers of American women and men. The consciousness-raising aspect of these attitudes has affected the style of life of many members of our society. The effects of the movement are beginning to appear in styles of family life, occupational patterns, leisure activities, and so on. The movement has to some extent affected the human services field directly, in that some have suggested that male human service workers, when dealing with female clients, tend to perpetuate the male dominance role in the relationship, to the client's detriment. Even though such assertions are speculative, they provide food for thought.

Gay liberation

Is homosexuality a disease? Is it a human service problem? Members of the gay liberation movement would undoubtedly answer these questions with a resounding no. The prevailing attitude among "straight" society has been that homosexuality is a psychological problem and that if one is "normal" psychologically, one will not be a homosexual. The basically negative attitude of society toward homosexuals has been challenged by the homosexual liberation movement. The major message of the movement is that homosexuals are the same as anyone else (with the exception of their sexual preference) and should be accepted as they are. The consciousness-raising efforts of the movement have led many closet homosexuals openly to declare their sexual preferences. It also seems to have made some inroads in changing popular attitudes.

It should be pointed out, however, that the sociopolitical aspects of the gay liberation movement may in the long run tend to polarize attitudes about homosexuality. This already seems to be occurring in some parts of the country. Those whose attitudes toward homosexuality are negative may end up mobilizing against the movement. In several areas of the United States, legislation against discrimination toward homosexuals has been defeated by a wide margin. The issue of polarization of attitudes may be an important one in social change events, no matter what the area of concern.

Medicare-Medicaid and national health insurance

The Social Security Act was changed in 1968 to provide increased benefits through the programs called Medicare and Medicaid, which fund health care services for aged persons and the medically disabled. Before this change, most aged and disabled people were in extremely dire straits because of their inability to afford health care. As an outgrowth of the change in attitude from the belief that acceptable-quality health care is a privilege of the rich to the belief that such care is a *right* of all citizens regardless of economic status, we have seen major emphasis recently placed on the issue of national health insurance (health care insurance funded by tax dollars that would provide funding for basic health care for *all citizens* regardless of economic standing). The effects of such a program are not totally predictable, but it is clear that its implementation would result in major changes in health care delivery, including in the human services. At a minimum, more services would be available to more people. New tax-supported programs such as this, however, depend on the availability of public funding. The public mood in the 1990s may not support expensive additions to federal welfare programs.

Speculative examples of comprehensive social interventions

As examples of the possibilities that may result from intentioned (rather than unplanned and unexpected) social change, one can consider the areas of poverty and certain criminal behaviors. Crime and poverty have been identified as two major human service problems. Numerous solutions have been proposed for both problems, but to date little real gain has been made in dealing with them. In the material that follows, the comprehensive social change approach will be illustrated through speculations on what *might* occur through the application of this approach to these two problems.

Poverty

The application of comprehensive social interventions to the problem of poverty is quite simple in its broad design. It consists basically of a plan for the implementation of a federal *guaranteed income*. That is, the establishment of an economic survival level for families, based on their size, would ensure the families' minimum economic need. If a family were without resources to maintain this level, it would be aided by the federal government. An alternative system would be to provide every family with this income and then collect a proportionate amount in return from families who earn monies above that level.

The implementation of such a program is hindered by a number of problems (Reischauer, 1986; Wittman, 1972), including the following:

1. Change in public attitudes
2. Cost requirements and the inevitable increase in taxation
3. Development of adequate delivery systems

Even though the solution to poverty in this framework appears simplistic, that is because it is a *simple problem:* lack of money. Such a program could come very close to wiping out poverty; however, many ancillary problems would remain, and additional solutions would have to be sought to deal with them. The most complex part of the solution, of course, is finding the tax money to support it.

Criminal behavior

It has been proposed that for many kinds of criminal behavior (almost always in regard to victimless crime), the way to deal with the problem is decriminalization. In brief, this means to revoke the law prohibiting the behavior and often to implement a process for controlling the previously illegal behavior in a manner that safeguards society but does not invoke criminal legal sanctions. Crimes that are often considered in this light include public drunkenness, illegal possession of drugs, and prostitution.

The prime candidate for such an approach appears to be the problem of illegal possession and sale of addictive drugs. Interestingly enough, for many years England has had a program that has often been proposed for the United States (Schur, 1962). In England, addicts are able to purchase drugs by prescription for the maintenance of a habit, and even though the addiction problem exists, it is nowhere near the scale it is in this country. In fact, there are fewer than several thousand opiate (heroin) addicts in England, compared with more than 500,000 in the United States, even though England has one-fourth the population of the United States. More pertinently, the problem of black market and illegal drug activity is minor compared with the United States. In effect, our current approach to drug usage in the United States is very similar to the situation that occurred during the prohibition of alcohol in the 1920s. With legalization, one would expect a significant decrease in the need for intervention by the criminal justice system since there would be a decrease in addict-related crimes and illegal drug traffic, and possibly a reorienting of efforts toward the psychosocial problem of *addiction* per se.

These two brief examples provide a glimpse of the possible results of two major social change endeavors. In both cases, the proposed approaches require federal and state legislative changes that are complex and to which there would undoubtedly be strong resistance. Unfortunately, we cannot predict with great accuracy the long-term benefits and disadvantages of such changes.

Human Services and Social Advocacy

A significant role for human service workers has been and will be that of an advocate: one who pleads and fights for services, policies, rules, regulations, and laws for the clients' benefit. A human service worker in the role of an advocate generally can exert more influence on the powers that be than can individual disadvantaged people. The changes in services, policies, laws, and rules that advocacy can achieve may have a positive impact on large numbers of people in need. It is within this advocacy role that individuals or small groups of human service workers have engineered the types of limited social interventions described in the first part of this chapter (Paster, 1986). Yet even in that context, the efforts of one or a few human service workers are limited in their effect (Crossman, 1985).

A more powerful approach appears to be the mobilization of the disadvantaged themselves into groups as advocates or activists on their own behalf (Schensul and Schensul, 1982). This mobilization of the disadvantaged as their own advocates not only maximizes the numbers of people agitating for social change but also has an impact on the self-perception of the needy. This process of social mobilization is an empowerment activity. That is, the power to work for change is shared with (given to) those whom the change can benefit. The human service worker in effect says, "I will not decide for you and do for you, but rather I will help *you* decide what you need and want, and help you find ways to achieve it." When the needy or disadvantaged discover that they can be involved in changing not only their own lives but the very society in which they live, discover that they have more control over their destiny than they believed, they develop a sense of empowerment and worth not present before (Egan, 1985; Kahn and Bender, 1985; Rose and Black, 1985). Thus, like the mutual-help groups that focus on dealing with personal problems, social advocacy groups can have an impact on the individual functioning of their members. Social advocacy groups' primary goal, however, is social change.

The development of social advocacy groups is based upon a specific viewpoint about the development of social problems and the behavior of individuals, which can be called the social structuralist viewpoint. Social structuralists seek to account for individual behavior in terms of the organization and distribution of resources within the societal framework. Structuralists blame oppressive institutions, inequitable systems of distribution, and systematic discrimination for negative social and economic conditions among members of subgroups within a society. They believe that aspects of the existing social order must change to facilitate more effective individual adaptations. Thus, the action-oriented structuralist will seek to change the institutions that seem to have an impact upon and that shape the lives of individuals.

The widely accepted competing view, as we have discussed, sees behavior primarily as a product of individual biopsychological development. The individual must change in order to adapt more effectively to the existing social order. The action-oriented individualist seeks to identify and provide services and support that will change personal or individual inadequacies believed to account for negative behavior. While support may come from individual or group-oriented services, the focus is on the individual's need for changing behavior. As noted earlier in this text, these views are not necessarily mutually exclusive, and individual behavior is a product of interactive factors, both personal and environmental.

However, a focus on one or another of these general viewpoints in the organization of an intervention group will play a role in determining the group's actions and objectives. For example, the interpretation of the condition of blacks in American society as a product of white racist institutions and inequitable distribution of resources resulted in the Black Power movement of the late 1960s—an attempt to change institutions to promote more access for blacks. But a view of that condition as a result of the intrinsic inadequacies of individual members of the black American population generates a much different set of activities aimed at affecting the individual behavior—economic, social, educational—of black people in a white-oriented and -dominated society.

It is the thesis of this book that it makes much more sense to approach social and economic problems from a social advocacy approach. Social advocacy groups must address attention to creating changes in access and distribution of resources in relation to economically and socially oppressed peoples. Social advocacy groups already include organizations linked to the nationally known black, brown, and gray power movements, as well as neighborhood collectives focused on more immediate and local concerns. They use the tools of mobilization and collective action to communicate in the sociopolitical arena. Their abilities to reflect accurately the needs of their constituency and to mobilize members of that constituency for collective action are frequently their only resources.

A wide range of social advocacy groups exist; they may differ significantly, depending upon the perceived needs of their respective constituencies. Despite their differences, social advocacy groups do share certain basic commonalities.

1. The primary goal of each is to represent the service needs of a larger constituency in the public/social sector. Participants believe that because they either are deeply involved in or are residents in their community constituen-

cies, they have the right to speak for them. Social advocacy groups recognize that they do not have access to sufficient information about their constituencies fully to defend the need for services or to argue for appropriate services. This often leads the group to sponsor research on their constituency, which shapes and confirms the beliefs of the group concerning inadequacy of service provision in their communities.

2. Their objective is to change the current pattern of distribution of resources. Members of advocacy groups believe that sufficient access to service resources is selectively denied to their constituencies. Their strategies, therefore, revolve around identifying these resources in the public sector on the one hand, and establishing and developing the strength of the social advocacy/citizens' group on the other.

3. The groups organize in the belief that united action will be effective in the demand for resources. They believe that no single individual has the right to speak for his or her constituency, but that collective groups with open membership can take such responsibility. They also believe that community or constituency-based groups, when clear about their objectives, can impact significantly on the wider system of health or other service delivery. Groups meet regularly, spend much of their time working out differences of opinion within the group itself, and consistently present a united front when arguing in public in support of financial or service resources.

4. Social advocacy groups often use the outside expertise of human service workers and others to assist in the achievement of their objectives. At the same time they maintain basic control of direction and decision making.

This chapter has given numerous examples of successful and not-so-successful attempts at both limited and comprehensive social interventions. The manner in which a human service worker may be able to have impact as a change agent on the personal environment of his or her immediate clients is clear (though definitely not simple).

In contrast, the individual human service worker is unlikely to be able to make a significant impact on changing the major social and economic systems through his or her individual efforts. What then can human service workers do about these broader issues? At the least, human service workers can become vocal advocates of the social changes in which they believe. Individually, one can, of course, engage in written correspondence with legislators on the local, state, and national levels and join organizations that can exert political leverage to create social change.

On a more immediate level, human service workers can join local or national social advocacy groups that are trying to generate social change in which the worker believes. Some human service workers who have the necessary leadership qualities, expertise, and energy may focus their careers on developing and nurturing new social advocacy groups in order to address current and future social problems.

Summary

1. Many of the problems of people in need are due to or complicated by societal factors such as poverty. The immediate environment of the individual may contribute substantially to the development and maintenance of problem behaviors such as apathy, joblessness, drug use, and criminal activities.

2. Major social ills also may lead to problem behavior among people who suffer the brunt of social problems such as discrimination, poor health care, or poor housing. Changing the person is unlikely to help much unless the individual's environment, the relevant social systems, and the social ills are modified. Thus, for the human service worker, social interventions are an important facet of helping services.

3. The phrase *limited social intervention* describes the attempt to make significant formal changes in the immediate environment of a client or group of clients that will have a remedial effect on the problems of that client or group.

4. The concept of limited social intervention has grown out of the virtually universally recognized fact that the environment of people in need often supports or stimulates problem behaviors and that single treatment contacts, whether in an institution or in the community, tend not to be sufficient in generating lasting major changes in a person's behavior.

5. Limited social interventions involve a four-step process: (a) identifying negative environments, (b) identifying environmental factors that can be changed, (c) determining how negative aspects can be changed in a positive direction, and (d) implementing the changes or creating entirely new positive environments.

6. The effectiveness of limited social intervention is demonstrated in the description of a community intervention program that focused on the intellectual enhancement of children at risk for psychosocial mental retardation. Children who received services were better off after the intervention compared with similar children who received no services.

7. Examples of limited social change include the areas of community corrections, deinstitutionalization of the mentally ill and the retarded, community programs for the retarded, and a community program for ex–mental patients.

8. A number of principles of social change have general applicability to the concept of limited social interventions. Even though the principles do not constitute how-to instructions, they illustrate important issues that must be considered by human service workers who contemplate environmental change strategies.

9. The concept of comprehensive social intervention has been defined as (a) the process of identifying broad social problems that contribute to or cause maladaptive behavior and (b) the subsequent modification of social systems or policies that contribute to the problems, in an attempt to eradicate them.

10. Many experts have focused on the negative effects of social change. However, it is clear that social change can be a positive factor in the reduction of social problems.

11. Examples of major social system and social policy change events demonstrate both effective and ineffective attempts to deal with social problems. Examples include the Emancipation Proclamation, the prohibition of alcohol, and the Social Security Act.

12. If comprehensive social interventions are to be effective, knowledge must be expanded in the areas of (a) institutional and cultural factors that produce change, (b) the means whereby change is propagated, diversified, and incorporated into the system, (c) the direction and extent of change, and (d) the differential impacts of change.

13. Four examples of currently ongoing social change are civil rights legislation, the women's liberation movement, gay liberation, and Medicare-Medicaid and national health insurance.

14. Speculative comprehensive social interventions have been described for the social welfare/social policy problems of poverty and criminal behavior.

15. The individual human service worker is unlikely to be able to engage in comprehensive social interventions because of personal social and political powerlessness. However, membership in and support of social advocacy groups appears to be a powerful strategy for the implementation of comprehensive social change.

Discussion Questions

1. What are limited social interventions?

2. What advantages are there for limited social interventions over direct interpersonal intervention if a choice must be made between them, and vice versa?

3. What processes does limited social intervention include?

4. Which of the guidelines for creating change seem most important? Are any more important than others?

5. What are the positive and negative effects of social change?

6. Why do you think prohibition failed?

7. What are the current trends in social change that seem important? Why do these trends seem important? What will their effects be?

8. How can human service workers become involved in comprehensive social interventions? Should they?

Learning Experiences

1. Have any limited social interventions been developed in your community? If so, visit the setting and try to find out why the intervention was developed, how it was developed, and whether it is working.

2. Determine if any new limited social interventions need to be created. How would you go about doing it? What resources would you need? Whom would you have to convince?

3. Contact your federal legislators to find out what they think about a guaranteed annual income or national health insurance.

4. Contact a doctor to find out what he or she thinks of national health insurance.

5. Survey your acquaintances about what they think are the major social problems facing our country and what should be done about them.

6. Decide what *you* think is the major social problem facing us and what *should* be done about it. What can *you* do about it?

Endnotes

1. *Returning the Mentally Disabled to the Community: The Government Needs To Do More.* Reports to the Congress by the Comptroller General of the United States, January, 1977.

2. Reprinted by permission from *Innovations* (Vol. 2, No. 3, Fall, 1975), pp. 5–7, published by the American Institutes for Research, P.O. Box 1113, Palo Alto, Calif. 94302, under a collaborative grant from the National Institute of Mental Health.

3. Reprinted by permission from *Innovations* (Vol. 2, No. 2, Summer, 1975), pp. 32–33, published by the American Institutes for Research, P.O. Box 1113, Palo Alto, Calif. 94302, under a collaborative grant from the National Institute of Mental Health.

Recommended Readings

Alinsky, S. *Rules for Radicals: A Primer for Realistic Radicals.* New York: Random House, 1971.

Illich, I. *Deschooling Society.* New York: Harper and Row, 1970.

Newton, J. *Preventing Mental Illness.* London: Routledge and Kegan Paul, 1988.

Price, R. H.; Cowen, E. L.; Lorion, R. P.; and Ramos-McKay, J. *Fourteen Ounces of Prevention: A Casebook for Practitioners.* Washington, D.C.: American Psychological Association, 1988.

Reppucci, N. D., and Saunders, J. T. "Focal Issues for Institutional Change." *Professional Psychology: Research and Practice* 14 (1983).

Seidman, E. (ed.). *Handbook of Social Intervention.* Beverly Hills, Calif.: Sage Publications, 1983.

15

Social Control, Human Rights, Ethics, and Social Policy

- What impact does the law have on human behavior?
- How have psychological, social, and medical viewpoints influenced the application of law to human behavior?
- What are the legal rights of human service clients?
- What are the ethical standards followed by human service workers?
- How is social policy developed?

The law of the land has both a direct and an indirect impact on human behavior and human services. In a direct sense, the law tells us what it is legal to do, what behavior is illegal, and what the consequences are for illegal behaviors. Thus the law codifies many of society's rules of conduct. Indirectly, the existence of laws that proscribe certain individual behaviors influence some people to behave prosocially, that is, for the common good. The law also influences the behavior or functioning of groups or of society as a whole in regard to its individual members. It defines individual rights and society's obligations. In an abstract sense, laws provide for human survival.

Law serves at least three specific functions. First, of course, it defines certain behaviors as wrong or unacceptable and subject to social sanction. These behaviors include theft, murder, exceeding the speed limit, and driving while intoxicated. The second function is to protect the individual's *rights* in a free and democratic society. For example, law not only defines certain behaviors as criminal but also protects those who are accused of those behaviors. Thirdly, law is used to codify local, state, and federal government positions on *social policy*. One example of this social policy function of law was the Economic Opportunity Act of 1964, which was a set of laws establishing a federal department with the goal of providing training and employment programs for the disadvantaged. In all three of these functions, the law and the legal system overlaps with the human service sector in dealing with human behavior.

We have seen in recent years an increase in the interaction between the legal system and the human services system. This increased interaction has developed as a result of a number of factors. Slovenko (1973) has identified eight factors that he considers significant. These can be paraphrased as follows:

1. Increased population concentration in urban areas makes relationships between people, as formalized in law, more important. As urban interactions become more intense, there is a greater probability that individuals will violate the rights of others.
2. Human services has taken over the role of religion in many instances, explaining the causality of behavior that is often considered to be of a lawbreaking nature. Behaviors that once were considered sinful or unlawful are now defined as being due to psychological, emotional, or social causes for which an individual has no personal responsibility.

The availability of law libraries in prison settings has allowed many inmates to engage in a self-help process.

3. A greater emphasis is being placed on the rehabilitation of offenders rather than on revenge and retribution. If misbehavior is to be rehabilitated, it should be treated; the person should be helped, not punished by legal sanctions.
4. Under the *parens patriae doctrine* (the doctrine of society acting as a responsible parent for its citizens), the state is seen as having the obligation to intervene in the lives of minors (or in the lives of those who are considered unable to make decisions that are in their own best interest) who might become community problems.
5. Lawyers have become more interested in dealing with a variety of human service system problems for a number of reasons, not the least of which is that there is increasing financial support for such activities from public, private, and charitable organizations.
6. Legal issues in human services have become popularized through the writings of individuals such as Chief Judge David L. Bazelon of the District of Columbia Circuit Court of Appeals and the psychiatrists Dr. Karl A. Menninger and Dr. Thomas S. Szasz.
7. In recent years, there have been major studies and much research into the relationship between human service systems and the judicial process, and a number of professional organizations for people with combined interests in law and the behavioral sciences have developed.
8. There has been an increased familiarity among judges and lawyers with the subfields of human services and a corresponding increase in their interactions with those systems.

To Slovenko's eight factors, we can add a ninth that is perhaps important in a broad sense:

9. Recent years have seen an increased concern with the constitutional rights of our citizens, particularly in the human services sector, in regard to the concepts of involuntary treatment or incarceration, paralleling the concern over civil rights issues such as racial discrimination.

The Therapeutic State

Much of the concern of the judiciary system regarding human services has focused on the development of the phenomenon called the *therapeutic state* (Kittrie, 1971; Szasz, 1965). This term refers to a legal system based on the notion that socially proscribed behavior (including illegal acts) is often not a function of free will but rather is determined by psychological, social, or medical causes, so that it should not be punished but *treated*. Although such a notion seems enlightened, its critics have pointed out that it results in a number of abuses of personal liberty of the people to whom it is applied.

A major problem with the therapeutic state approach is that it has led to a situation in which indeterminate "sentences" of incarceration in restrictive human services settings have supplanted determinate sentences in jails or prisons. To illustrate, we use the following example (Arens, 1964):

> In the District of Columbia, Frederick C. Lynch was charged with passing bad checks. Although Lynch maintained that his behavior was an act of free will, psychiatrists testified that he was mentally ill at the time of the crimes. The court found him not guilty by reason of insanity and confined him to a mental hospital. If he had been found guilty, he would have received a maximum sentence of twelve months in jail. Lynch, facing a lengthy period of hospitalization against his will, committed suicide.

The Lynch case is not unique. Thousands of individuals around the country are incarcerated in mental hospitals, juvenile detention homes, and mental retardation facilities for an indeterminate period until they are "cured" of whatever problem supposedly led them to engage in criminal behavior. In addition, many people are locked up because there is a *threat* that *in the future* they will engage in behavior that *may* be dangerous to themselves or others. The reality of this threat has been criticized by many who have been involved in such cases.

One major study (Steadman and Cocozza, 1974) has demonstrated that most people locked in mental hospitals who are labeled as "dangerous" and who are being kept hospitalized because of that label are for the most part no more dangerous than anyone else. In their study, they found that of 967 patients who were labeled "dangerous" in a maximum security hospital and who were transferred *administratively* to civil hospitals (owing to a court order) and then subsequently discharged, only 5 percent were later involved in a felony arrest. For these 967 people, involuntary imprisonment in mental hospitals *exceeded* the *maximum* sentence to *prison* (which they might have received if they had been convicted) by an average of eight years. In total, only 15 percent of the group exhibited dangerous behavior (assault) during a four-year follow-up. More than 800 people had been improperly locked up for many years on the basis of a false prediction of dangerousness.

The issue of involuntary treatment is an important one, since each state government has a body of legislation that sets up the requirements for involuntary admission to human service facilities such as mental hospitals, juvenile detention facilities, and mental retardation facilities. In all cases, these statutes are much less well defined than the criminal codes and therefore much more subject to abuse.

Human Rights Issues and Human Services

Experience with the current human services systems has demonstrated that a series of issues in regard to the rights of the clients must be considered by all human service workers:

1. Voluntary versus involuntary services
2. Due process and equal protection
3. The right to services
4. The right to refuse services
5. The issue of the least drastic or restrictive alternative
6. The privilege of confidentiality.

Since most issues that have arisen are particularly critical concerning the involuntarily confined, that issue must be examined before others can be dealt with.

Voluntary versus involuntary services

There are clear differences between voluntary and involuntary services. The concept of voluntary service implies the following:

1. Clients make an informed decision that help is needed and that they want to change.
2. Clients set their own goals and objectives for the helping service.
3. Clients enter into a clear "contract" with the service provider on what will happen.
4. Clients can *terminate* the relationship at *will*.

Service is involuntary if:

1. Persons *other* than the clients decide that they will receive service.
2. Others (relatives, therapists, prosecuting attorneys, the courts) *require* that the clients have service and set the goals and objectives.
3. The clients are relatively powerless in deciding what kind of service they will receive.
4. The clients are not allowed to terminate at will; rather, some authority figure makes the decision for them.

Opinions on involuntary service run the gamut from the "abolitionists" who believe that it should be abolished to those who recognize that it can be abused but feel it is not only necessary but beneficial (Hoaken, 1986). Chodoff (1976) is representative of the latter group. He takes the position that with constructive legal safeguards, involuntary service can be a valuable social tool. He cites the following cases to illustrate the need for such an alternative:

■ ■ Passersby and station personnel observe that a young woman has been spending several days at Union Station in Washington, D.C. Her behavior appears strange to others. She is finally befriended by a newspaper reporter who becomes aware that her perception of her situation is profoundly unrealistic and that she is, in fact, delusional. He persuades her to accompany him to St.

Elizabeth's Hospital where she is examined by a psychiatrist who recommends admission. She refuses hospitalization and the psychiatrist allows her to leave. [According to the law, the psychiatrist had no legal right to keep her against her will.] She returns to Union Station. A few days later she is found dead, murdered, on one of the surrounding streets.

■ ■ Passersby in a campus area observe two young women standing together, staring at each other, for over an hour. Their behavior attracts attention, and eventually the police take the pair to a nearby precinct station for questioning. They refuse to answer questions and sit mutely, staring into space. The police request some type of psychiatric examination but are informed by the city attorney's office that state law (Michigan) allows persons to be held for observation only if they appear obviously dangerous to themselves or others. In this case, since the women do not seem homicidal or suicidal, they do not qualify for observation and are released.

Less than thirty hours later the two women are found on the floor of their campus apartment, screaming and writhing in pain with their clothes ablaze from a self-made pyre. One woman recovers; the other dies.[1]

In contrast to the Frederick Lynch case cited earlier in this chapter, situations such as these seem to require involuntary systems of treatment if disastrous results are to be avoided.

Martin (1975) suggests that unless behavior is "intolerable," one should not try to *make* people change against their will. He points out, however, that a major problem exists in defining intolerable, and he raises the question, Intolerable to whom? Human service workers (and society in general) have been left with the very real problem of balancing individual human rights against the need to protect society against harm from its members.

Due process and equal protection

Even though involuntary service is a major issue of contention, it *is* currently a fact of life, and a number of issues revolve around its use. Among these are due process and equal protection. The due process clause of the Constitution provides that if government activities affect a citizen in a way that would deprive him or her of liberty or property, this must be done with due process of law. The courts have ruled that due process requires a hearing before an impartial entity, with the opportunity for witnesses to testify, with representation of the client by an attorney (or other counsel), and with the opportunity for the client to appeal. In order to provide this due process, state statutes provide for a hearing before the court before a client can be committed for involuntary service for an unspecified period of time.

The due process clause has impacts on all human service systems. For example, recent interpretations of the due process clause require school administrators to specify in writing those offenses for which children can be disciplined (Guttesman, 1982). They must notify the children that the rule is going to be applied and must conduct a hearing at which the children and their parents can be present when an action such as expulsion is considered. Similar requirements pertain to the use of punitive action such as isolation in prisons.

The Constitution's equal protection clause provides that citizens cannot be denied the equal protection of the law. In this sense, a state agency cannot treat one group differently from another when both are entitled to the same treatment. This clause is quite important in the right-to-services issue, as we shall see, but it also prevents certain groups from being dealt with in a *harsher* manner than others; for example, psychosurgery cannot be applied only to blacks in a prison setting. However, these laws (and others) do not prevent abuses in and of themselves; they provide the means of protection only if they are enforced.

The right to services

It is now an accepted assumption of litigation in the United States that individuals who are involuntarily deprived of freedom because they have engaged in some activity that demonstrates that they are unable to care for themselves or are dangerous to others have the *right* to helping services (Stone, 1975). The right to service has become an issue due to the problem of persons' being confined in restrictive settings and languishing there with little but food, lodging, and tranquilizing medication; in effect, this is a situation that amounts to little more than imprisonment. It has now become clear that facilities must demonstrate that they really are providing the service for which the client was committed, or the commitment itself becomes ludicrous.

In recent years the right to receive services has been extended to community settings. Even when people are not involuntarily deprived of their right to freedom, their membership in a disadvantaged class may entitle them to demand services from society in the form of civil government (Herr, 1983).

The right to refuse services

For many years, it was a common assumption that helping professionals could administer services even when the patients or clients resisted. It was assumed that the services were in the clients' best interest and that their objections were a function of a disordered mind. Recent case law has confirmed, however, that clients *do* have the right to refuse service. If, for example, patients in a mental hospital refuse to take a prescribed medication, it is illegal to force them to do so unless a court of law judges the patients to be incompetent to make such a decision. Unfortunately, this patient right is routinely violated in most current systems, and the problem is compounded by the fact that many courts seem to be overly willing to declare persons incompetent. The extent to which an individual has the right to refuse services that will change behaviors depends on the behaviors in question and continues to be a controversial issue (Michels, 1981).

The least drastic or restrictive alternative

Patients or clients have the right to be helped in an effective manner that is the least restrictive. For example, a client who can manage in the community while receiving outpatient services should not be hospitalized since hospitalization is more restrictive of personal liberty and freedom. Few would argue this point, but until community alternatives are available, this may simply mean that the least restrictive alternative results in no service at all. This right is particularly applicable to the many people who are in correctional settings, mental retardation facilities, mental hospitals, residential nursing homes or sheltered-care settings, and educational institutions simply because there are no less restrictive alternatives in the community.

The privilege of confidential communication

Trust between client and service provider is of prime importance in most helping relationships, and a major ingredient of such trust is confidentiality. The principle of confidentiality requires that human service workers maintain a confidential relationship with their clients; that is, that the clients' identity be protected *unless* they agree (in writing) that their identity and personal information may be shared with other professionals or agencies. Client confidentiality is respected even in court settings such as criminal or civil trials *unless* this information bears directly on the issues being tried. Thus, confidentiality is not a right; it is a privilege. Some human service workers (Dubey, 1974) feel that confidentiality should be an absolute privilege (that is, under no circumstances should helping professionals have to testify in court about their clients); others believe that in some situations confidentiality *must* be breached. Under some circumstances, in fact, there appears to be a legal duty to breach confidentiality, such as the duty to warn others of a dangerous threat made by a client.

The duty to warn

Tancredi, Lieb, and Slaby (1975) raise the issue of the *duty to warn*, which is based on the notion that if the helping service providers have good evidence that their client intends to harm someone, the service providers must warn the person in danger. A number of court cases have established that a human service worker does have a legal duty to warn others of a client's threats if the human service worker in good conscience believes the threats may be acted upon (Kermani and Drob, 1987). If the worker does *not* warn a potential victim of physical danger, and the client acts on the threat, the human service worker may be sued for negligence. Some professionals object that the requirement to warn is fraught with problems, particularly the difficulty of being *sure* that the client really means the threats. Another problem area is that the duty to warn may compromise the trust relationship with patients who make threats (many do) but who actually would not act upon them, since therapists will warn more often than necessary out of fear of being sued if they make a mistake. In spite of these issues, the duty to warn remains a legal requirement.

A human services bill of rights

The redefinition of the rights of human service clients and the legal responsibilities of human service workers and systems has not grown out of a vacuum. It is clearly responsive to problems and injustices that have existed for many years but that in some cases are only recently being recognized. The concern over these issues has led to the development of a number of model *human services bills of rights* for clients. Nicholas Kittrie (1971), a proponent of expanded rights for human service clients, has proposed one such bill of rights that is the model for the following.

1. No person shall be *compelled* to receive services except for the defense of society.
2. One's innate right to remain free of excessive forms of human modification shall be inviolable.
3. No social sanctions may be invoked unless the person receiving human services has demonstrated a clear and present danger through truly harmful behavior that is immediately forthcoming or has already occurred.
4. No person shall be subjected to involuntary incarceration or human services on the basis of a finding of a general condition or status alone. Nor shall the mere conviction of a crime or a finding of not guilty by reason of insanity suffice to have a person automatically committed or treated.
5. No social sanctions, whether designated criminal, civil, or therapeutic, may be invoked in the absence of the previous right to a judicial or other independent hearing, appointed counsel, and an opportunity to confront those testifying about one's past conduct or therapeutic needs.
6. Dual interference by both the criminal and the human services process is prohibited.
7. An involuntary client shall have the right to receive helping services.
8. Any compulsory service must be the least required reasonably to protect society.
9. All committed persons should have direct access to appointed counsel and the right, without any interference, to petition the courts for relief.
10. Those submitting to voluntary service should be guaranteed that they will not be subsequently transferred to a compulsory program through administrative action.[2]

Such bills of rights are clearly reflective of the growing concern for the rights of individuals of whom society *requires* behavior change if they are to return to ordinary community life. The fact that such bills of rights have been proposed and that there is a major concern for the rights of human service clients provides evidence that such rights have been violated significantly in the past. If they are to be effective advocates of the client, human service workers must retain a healthy respect for the rights of the client in order to prevent the possible abuse that can occur (Rubenstein, 1986).

Ethical Standards for Human Service Workers

Any profession, regardless of its other characteristics, maintains standards that guide its members' functioning. In the helping professions, certain ethical standards have grown over the years from the experience of people engaged in those activities. The standards that human service providers follow, while recognizing the basic minimal rights of clients as set down in law, go beyond these rights to suggest broader guidelines in regards to human service worker-client relationships. To date, since there is no nationally recognized single professional standards group for human service workers, there is no single set of ethical standards. However, the following ethical standards are representative of the standards of most professional groups in the helping professions.

1. Treat clients with dignity and respect. Do not treat them like second-class citizens because they cannot cope as well as you. Avoid using demeaning words and labels like *junky, nut case, hillbilly,* or *ex-con.*
2. Help *every* client to the best of your ability. Do not avoid clients or give less than your best effort because the client is unattractive, dirty, or hostile or has done something you find abhorrent.
3. Respect the client's privacy. Learn only what you need to know; never indulge your idle curiosity. For example, if the client's sexual relationships are irrelevant to the problem, you have no right to find out about them.
4. Maintain confidential relationships. Do not tell stories about clients to your friends or relatives.
5. Engage only in activities in which you are competent. If clients require services you are not trained to provide, refer them to appropriate agencies. Do not try to go it alone. If there are services you wish to offer but have not been trained for, obtain adequate training and experienced supervision.
6. Maintain a professional helping relationship. Do not use your client to satisfy the needs that should be satisfied by your friends, spouses, and relatives. A warm, caring relationship with a client does not involve romantic love or sexual involvement.

7. Continue to upgrade your skills. Developing human service skills is a career-long process. Continuing education and training is important for human service workers.
8. Protect your community against the unethical practices of others. Ethical behavior requires that you report those who abuse the client-worker relationship.
9. Respect your colleagues and relate to them in a professional manner. Each of the professions has something to contribute, and *unjustified* criticism should be avoided. In particular, it is unethical to impose your prejudices about other professional groups on clients.

The Law and Social Policy

As the field of human services has been described and discused throughout this text, it may not have been apparent that human services would not exist but for significant changes in social policy over the past fifty years. Yet that *is* the case, and each human service worker owes his or her occupation to current social policies as those policies are codified in the law and governmental rules and regulations.

Social policy refers to principles, guidelines, and concepts which guide a society's actions towards its members, usually formalized as governmental laws, regulations, and rules. In the realm of human services, the most important social policies are usually referred to as "Social Welfare Policies." Time after time in this text, issues have been raised and social responses have been described that are reflections of current or changing social welfare policies.

Social policies do change. Policies are modified, rejected, or created to meet the perceived needs of society at a particular moment in time, and the perception of what constitutes a need does as we have seen, change from time to time. The formulation of social policy first requires that social needs be identified. As has been documented in previous sections of this text, that is not a simple clear cut task! Once needs *have* been identified a process then occurs in which the needs are evaluated for priority. The prioritization of social needs is a complex and difficult task, but clearly necessary when resources are not available to adequately deal with all social needs. That has always been, and will always be the case.

There is no absolute scale on which social needs can be ranked. The setting of priorities often depends on citizen advocacy, advocacy by professionals, by researchers, and by lobbying efforts brought to bear on local, state, and federal elected officials. At any point in time the priority of competing needs will be advocated by different groups, some of whom will succeed and some of whom will fail.

As some needs are successfully identified as deserving action, policies will be formulated through negotiation by those need's advocates, the government, and at times through voter referendum. The resulting social policy must then be turned into action.

The action phase of social policy implementation requires the development of specific plans and programs. At this stage, law makers, the courts, and governmental bodies begin to interpret what the policy requires. Programs are designed to meet the social need based on interpretation of the more general social policy. Of extremely critical significance at this and later stages of social policy implementation is the availability of local, state, and federal funding. Lack of adequate funding has frequently prevented the effective implementation of sound social policy.

Once social policies are codified through law, rule, and governmental regulation, and programs are developed, funded, and implemented, the tale still continues. Policies and programs are not static, they are continually changing and undergoing modification, not only because we may find new ways of doing things, but because society is ever changing, ever redefining its priorities.

The human service worker must also be prepared to change, as social needs change, social policies change, laws change, interventions change, and the human service workers themselves change.

Summary

1. The law has both direct and indirect impacts on human behavior. It proscribes certain behaviors and assign consequences in order to maintain social order. It also protects the rights of individuals against unjust actions by the social group.

2. The judicial system has become more involved in considering the rights of human service clients and the obligations of the human service system.

3. The therapeutic state sees misbehavior as a problem that is due to psychological, social, or medical causes. It sometimes can result in abuses of liberty in the name of helping services.

4. A number of issues have been raised regarding the delivery of human services from the viewpoint of the therapeutic state:
   a. The issue of voluntary versus involuntary helping services
   b. Due process and equal protection
   c. The right to services
   d. The right to refuse services
   e. The issue of the least drastic or restrictive alternative
   f. The privilege of confidentiality

5. A human services bill of rights has been presented that specifies the proposed obligations and limits of society in the rendering of services.

6. Human service workers have certain obligations and limits in the delivery of helping services that go beyond the written laws. Guidelines for ethical standards have been developed for human service workers.

7. Social policy consists of principles, guidelines, and concepts that guide social action. It is developed through a complicated process of advocacy and legislative action, and is constantly changing in interpretation.

Discussion Questions

1. How does the law affect people's behavior?

2. Why has there been an increase in the interaction between the legal system and human services?

3. What is the therapeutic state?

4. What are the important differences between voluntary and involuntary services?

5. What should happen in regard to the issue of involuntary services?

6. How do the concepts of due process, equal protection, right to services, right to refuse services, least drastic alternative, and confidentiality relate to the various subfields of human services?

7. Is a human services bill of rights really necessary?

8. Why are ethical standards for human service workers necessary?

9. What is the dilemma of human service workers in regard to these issues?

Learning Experiences

1. Interview someone who has been arrested, tried, or convicted. How does he or she feel about it?

2. Visit a juvenile court. Note how the juvenile is treated. Visit an adult court. Note the difference as it relates to this chapter.

3. If the opportunity is available, visit and observe a mental health court and record your reaction.

4. Interview a committed (involuntary) client. How does he or she feel about it?

5. Interview a lawyer or judge about the issues presented. What is his or her opinion?

6. What is your reaction to being *forced* to do something? Considering your reaction, how would *you* feel if you were forced to have *services* or *treatment* that would change you "for your own good"?

7. Reflect on how you felt when someone you confided in told others what you said. How did you feel? Did you still trust that person? Will you ever confide in him or her again?

Endnotes

1. Chodoff, P. "The Case for Involuntary Hospitalization of the Mentally Ill." *American Journal of Psychiatry*, vol. 133:5, pp., 496–497, 1976. Copyright, 1976, the American Psychiatric Association.

2. Kittrie, Nicholas N. *The Right to be Different: Deviance and Enforced Therapy*. Baltimore: The Johns Hopkins University Press, 1971. List of therapeutic bill of rights, items 1–10, pp. 402–404. Reprinted by permission of the publisher.

Recommended Readings

Hannah, G. T.; Christian, W. P.; and Clark, H. B. *Preservation of Client Rights: A Handbook for Practitioners Providing Therapeutic, Educational, and Rehabilitative Services*. New York: The Free Press, 1981.

Kittrie, N. N. *The Right to be Different: Deviance and Enforced Therapy*. Baltimore: The Johns Hopkins Press, 1971.

Martin, R. *Legal Challenges to Behavior Modification: Trends in Schools, Corrections, and Mental Health*. Champaign, Ill.: Research Press, 1975.

Woody, R. H., and Associates. *The Law and the Practice of Human Services*. San Francisco, Calif.: Jossey-Bass, 1984.

GLOSSARY

Achieved role A social role that an individual is able to obtain through his or her efforts, such as the role of doctor, police officer, etc.

Acting out Expressing problems through behavior rather than holding problems within.

Actualization The process of achieving one's full potential.

Addiction Strong dependence, usually both physical and psychological, on a drug or chemical.

Advocacy The process of being for and supporting some person, object, or idea.

Alienation A feeling of being separate from something, of not belonging.

Altered state of consciousness The experience of perceiving things from an unusual perspective, such as when under the influence of drugs or in a psychotic state.

Altruism The unselfish giving of oneself to help others.

Amnesia The inability to recall past experiences.

Ancillary variable A factor that accompanies an event and has an impact on it.

Antabuse A drug used in the treatment of alcoholism that causes a very unpleasant physical reaction when alcohol is ingested.

Antihistamine A drug used in the treatment of allergic responses.

Arteriosclerosis A gradual narrowing of the inner diameter of the body's arteries caused by the deposit of fatty tissue, which decreases blood flow to various parts of the body, including the brain.

Ascribed role A social role that is given to the individual as a result of natural circumstance such as birth or genetics. *Ascribed roles* include man, woman, husband, child, and parent.

Atavistic Reappearing after an absence of several generations.

Back ward A hospital ward that has no treatment programs and provides only custodial care.

Battle fatigue A psychological disorder presumed to be a function of the stress of combat experience.

Behavior modification The systematic attempt to change behavior, usually using principles of learning theory.

Behavior therapy See *Behavior modification.*

Behavioral dysfunction The lack of functioning of appropriate behavior.

Behavioral sciences Those sciences concerned with the study of human functioning.

Behavioral technologies The techniques related to the changing of human behavior.

Behavioral treatment program A treatment program that applies the theories of learning to a systematic attempt to change human behavior.

Behaviorists People trained as behavior changers using learning theory.

Black Death A highly contagious infectious disease (bubonic plague) that caused massive epidemics during the late Middle Ages.

Bleeding A medical treatment of hundreds of years ago in which the person was bled to cure his or her illness.

Bromide An early sedative.

Catharsis The expression of intense feeling leading to a sense of relief.

Cautery Destruction of tissue through the application of a very hot or very cold instrument.

Change agent One who attempts to change ongoing situations.

Change-of-life period Late middle age, when women lose the ability to bear children and both men and women sense the ending of their youth.

Chemotherapy The use of chemicals to treat physical or emotional disorders.

Cherishable self That part of one's self-concept that one can value and accept.

Clientele A group of persons who receive a set of services.

Closet homosexual A homosexual who hides his or her sexual preferences from most friends, relatives, and the general public.

Combat neurosis See *Battle fatigue*.

Commitment A legal process in which individuals are placed in mental institutions, often against their will.

Compulsion An irresistible impulse to act regardless of the rationality of the motive.

Concordance A statement of agreement.

Conditioning The linking of stimulus with response.

Correctional institution An institution that attempts to correct the behavior of those who reside in it.

Credentialed Having credentials (evidence) that indicate that one is specially educated or trained.

Crisis-prone Particularly sensitive to stress that results in a crisis state.

Cultural expectations The expectations of one's culture, for example, the expectation that one will dress within certain bounds of modesty.

Custodial approach An approach to service delivery in the mental health system. Little treatment is given; the focus is primarily on providing food and shelter.

Debilitation The process of becoming weakened or feeble.

Decompensation A process in which a system operates less effectively than in the past.

Deinstitutionalization The process of removing or assisting the removal of persons from institutional settings, such as mental hospitals, and placing them in the community.

Delinquency Failure to do what is required; often used to label the law-violating behaviors of youth.

Delusion A strong belief held in spite of adequate evidence to the contrary.

Denigration The process of impugning a person's character or reputation.

Deviance Behavior that differs from an acceptable standard.

Diagnosis The act of identifying the nature of a disease through examination, or the label applied to a disease process.

Diminished responsibility A concept that implies that an individual cannot be held accountable for behavior that results from psychological disturbance.

Discordancies Things that are not in agreement with others.

Disenfranchise To deprive an individual of a privilege of citizenship previously granted by a government or state or of a statutory or constitutional right, such as the right to vote.

Due process The formal legal proceedings required by the Constitution before an individual may be deprived of any rights or liberties.

Dysfunctional Not functioning as it should.

Ego defense   A psychological mechanism that protects the self from experiencing anxiety.

Empathic understanding   Understanding accurately the feelings, thoughts, and motives of another.

Enuresis   Involuntary urination.

Epilepsy   A nervous disorder characterized by recurring attacks of motor or sensory malfunction, often accompanied by convulsive movements.

Erogenous zones   The areas of the body that provide pleasurable sexual stimulation.

Extended family   The members of the family beyond parents and siblings, such as uncles, aunts, and in-laws.

Facilitator   One who assists the occurrence of something.

Feces   Solid waste products of an animal or human body.

Feedback   Data relating to output that are put back into the system as a control process.

Fixation   A strong attachment to a person, thing, or event in one's past history that influences current behavior.

Foster care   Organized formal care given to children by persons unrelated to the children, especially when controlled and organized by a governmental agency.

Frontal lobes   The forepart of the brain that is considered to be the seat of judgment.

Gay liberation   An organized movement of homosexuals that attempts to change attitudes expressed toward them and to obtain full legal rights.

Genetic   Affecting or affected by genes (the mechanism of biological inheritance).

Genocide   The systematic, planned annihilation of a racial, cultural, or political group.

Ghetto   A city section occupied primarily by minority group members who live there as a result of social or economic pressure.

Grandiose   Characterized by greatness of scope; usually used to describe one who presents an unrealistically grand self-impression.

Grass roots level   Society's basic local level.

Gray Panthers   A social-political organization of elderly citizens who work actively for their rights.

Habilitation program   A program that attempts to supply people with the resources they need, including personal skills.

Hallucination   A perception for which there is no external stimulus.

Heredity   The totality of characteristics transmitted from parents to offspring by genes.

HEW   The federal Department of Health, Education and Welfare, now separated into two separate agencies; one for health and welfare, one for education.

Homosexuality   Sexual behavior involving members of the same sex.

Human services   All those services designed or available to help people who are having difficulty with life and its stress.

Huntington's chorea   A degenerative brain disease that is irreversible.

Hyperactive   Excessively or abnormally active.

Hypertension   Abnormally high arterial blood pressure.

Hypnotism   The practice of inducing an artificial condition in which an individual is extremely responsive to suggestions.

Identification figure   A person with whom one identifies, that is, to whom one desires and tries to be similar.

Incestuous   Relating to sexual union between persons who are so closely related that the union is forbidden by law or custom.

Incontinent   Incapable of holding back; often used to describe persons who cannot control the bowel or bladder.

Indigenous worker A worker native to an area or group.

Inner person Those aspects of a person that occur within the personality and influence the person's behavior.

Inpatient One who receives treatment while living in the treatment facility.

Insanity A legal term describing a state in which persons are not legally responsible for their actions.

Insight A state of self-awareness of one's motives and the causes of one's behavior.

Instinctual Arising from inborn characteristics that are unlearned.

Insulin shock therapy A psychiatric treatment that consists of administering insulin to persons until they enter an insulin coma.

Interloper One who interferes in the affairs of others.

Intrapsychic Within the mind.

Introject Take into one's personality the characteristics of another person.

Introspection The state of turning one's thoughts inward and examining one's feelings.

Irresistible impulse An impulse toward behavior that one does not have the ability to resist.

Jargon The specialized or technical language of a trade, profession, or other group; it often is obscure to nonmembers.

Journeyman An experienced, competent worker, often one who has finished an apprenticeship.

Layperson One who does not have specialized training in a field.

Learning theory The body of theory or theories that proposes how the process of learning takes place.

Libido Psychic and emotional energy associated with instinctual biological drives.

Life matrix The combination of factors that influence how one leads one's life.

Logico-empirical thinking A thinking process that is characterized by following the laws of logic and is based on empirical evidence.

Major tranquilizer A chemical that quiets major emotional upsets.

Malaise A feeling of illness or depression.

Manic-depressive syndrome A psychological disorder characterized by extreme mood swings of elation and depression, sometimes accompanied by disorders of perception and belief.

Mediator One who resolves or settles differences by acting as an intermediary between two conflicting parties.

Medical/psychiatric model An approach to behavior disorder that conceptualizes problems as diseases with medical causes and treatments.

Mental deficiency Below normal intellectual development.

Mental disorder A broad term used to refer to any disorder of intellect, emotion, or behavior.

Mental measurement movement A movement in the early 1900s that focused on the development of accurate psychological testing techniques.

Mentally ill Having an intellectual, emotional, or behavioral problem caused by an illness of physical or psychological origin.

Mentally retarded Having subnormal intellectual functioning.

Metabolism The complex physical and chemical processes involved in the maintenance of life.

Methadone A drug used as a substitute for heroin in the treatment of heroin addicts.

Metrazol shock A treatment comprised of the induction of a convulsive seizure through the injection of a camphor derivative.

Minor tranquilizer A chemical that quiets or tranquilizes mild to moderate emotional states, primarily anxiety.

Molar Pertaining to a body of matter as a whole.

Mood elevator A chemical that causes one's mood to rise or be more positive.

Motivational state A state of an individual that acts as a motivator toward action.

Motoric act A behavior that is primarily expressed in motor behavior.

Mutism A state of not speaking, either voluntarily or involuntarily, for long periods of time.

Naturalistic observation Observing the world (nature) as it is in order to find out facts.

Neurological Pertaining to the nervous system.

Neurosis A functional disorder of the mind or emotions without organic lesion, which is characterized primarily by anxiety.

NIMH National Institute of Mental Health.

Norm A standard of behavior regarded as typical of a specific group.

Normal curve A statistical model of the probability of frequency distributions. Also known as a *bell-shaped curve*.

Operant Characterizing a response elicited or changed by an environment rather than a specific stimulus. The environment "operates" on the behavior and the behavior operates on the environment.

Operant conditioning The establishment of a behavior, or its modification, by manipulating the environmental effects of that behavior.

Opiate addict One who is addicted to the opiates, such as heroin.

Organic brain syndrome A disorder that is a function of damage to the brain tissue.

Organismic energy The energy of the living organism.

Outpatient An individual who is being treated for a disorder while not a resident of the treatment facility.

Parahelper An individual who provides helping services although not employed specifically for that service.

Paranoid schizophrenic One who exhibits the symptoms of extreme suspiciousness, deluded beliefs, and, frequently, hallucinations.

Paraprofessional A worker trained to engage in helping services who has not reached a professional level of education or function.

Passivity The condition of not taking action, of being submissive and compliant.

Pathology The anatomic or functional manifestation of disease.

Patient government A system in which residential patients are given the opportunity to make large numbers of decisions in regard to things that affect them through a democratic process.

Phenylketonuria An inherited disorder of metabolism that, if uncorrected, can cause mental retardation.

Phobia An unreasonable fear of an object or situation.

Placebo A substance or treatment having no medical or remedial value.

Professional myopia The shortsightedness of professionals who insist that they are the primary service deliverers of importance.

Protoplasmic Pertaining to the primary substance that constitutes the living matter of animal and plant cells.

Psychiatric nurse A nurse with special training and education in psychiatry.

Psychiatrist A medical doctor with special training in psychiatry.

Psychoactive chemical A chemical that affects the mind or emotions.

Psychodynamics The psychological processes that govern behavior, especially those proposed by Freudian theorists.

Psychological dynamics The psychological processes that govern behavior.

Psychologist An individual with advanced training and education in psychology, usually having a Ph.D. degree.

Psychopathy A condition in which an individual acts as if he or she had no conscience, that is, feels no guilt or anxiety.

Psychosexual stages Stages of development as defined by Freudian theorists in which sexual energy is centered in various zones of the body, depending on the person's maturation and growth.

Psychosomatic Pertaining to phenomena that are both physical and psychological in origin, such as ulcers and hypertension.

Psychosurgery Surgery on the brain for the purpose of changing behavior.

Psychotherapy Treatment of disorders of thinking, emotion, and behavior, which is usually verbal (the talking cure).

Psychotic Manifesting psychosis, a severe disorder that is characterized by extreme withdrawal from reality.

Psychotropic medication Medication that affects the thinking and emotional processes.

Radical student movement A political movement of students who advocate extreme measures to change what they consider to be the ills of society.

Rationalizing Developing self-satisfying but inaccurate reasons for behavior.

Reality contact The process of accurately perceiving and relating to one's environment.

Recalcitrant Stubbornly resistive to authority or guidance.

Referent group A group that contributes to one's sense of-identity.

Reinforcement program A program that provides positive reinforcement for behaviors defined as appropriate and withholds positive reinforcement or applies negative reinforcement for behaviors defined as inappropriate.

Repression The exclusion of painful thoughts and memories into the unconscious.

Ritalin A drug given to quiet hyperactive children.

Schizophrenia A severe mental disorder characterized by lack of contact with reality, withdrawal, and bizarre behavior.

Self-mutilating behavior The act of causing physical damage to one's own body, usually short of causing death.

Seminal fluid The fluid in which sperm cells are carried.

Senility The mental deterioration of old age, which includes forgetfulness.

Shaping A process of sequential modifications of behavior, each step of which more closely approximates the desired result.

Sheltered living facility A facility that provides supervised living situations for individuals who are unable to be independent.

Significant others Persons who have special important meaning to an individual.

Skinnerian One who follows the teachings of the behaviorist B. F. Skinner.

Slip of the tongue A verbal error that supposedly gives insight into what a person really means.

Social breakdown syndrome A state in which individuals lose many of their previously learned skills and become dependent on others.

Social support network Social systems that support independent living: friends, employers, union, religious congregations, and so on.

Social worker A trained worker who usually has a master's degree in social work and who focuses on the social systems of clients.

Sociocultural Pertaining to society and culture.

Socioeconomic class The social and economic level to which a person belongs.

Socioeconomic strata See *Socioeconomic class*.

Socioenvironmental Pertaining to social and environmental factors.

Somatic Pertaining to the body.

Spastic Characterized by random muscle spasms.

Stages of development Psychological, social, and physical states that are characteristics of the individual from birth to maturity.

Stigmatize To characterize as disgraceful or unacceptable.

Substance abuse The excessive use of a substance to cause psychological or physiological change, such as alcohol, heroin, cannabis, LSD, and so on.

Suicide center A program whose prime goal is to prevent suicide or to reduce its incidence through providing counseling and other assistance to persons who are suicidal risks.

Symptom A phenomenon usually regarded as a characteristic of a condition or event.

Syphilitic spirochete The organism that invades the human body and causes syphilis, a venereal disease.

Tertiary syphilis The third stage of syphilis, which often results in severe brain damage.

Thalamus A part of the lower portion of the brain that functions as an integrator through which sensory information is relayed.

Therapy A treatment of illness or disability.

Total institution An institution in which the great majority of decisions are made *for* the members without their input, such as hospitals, prisons, and the military service.

Trephining A treatment from early history in which a hole was cut or chipped in the skull to expose the brain.

Triage From the French language, meaning "to sort." A process of identifying problems, determining their severity, and making a decision as to whether resources should be provided to deal with the problems.

Unconscious motivation Motivations that lead people to act but that are not in their conscious awareness.

Vagrant One who wanders, not having a fixed residence or employment; one who lives by begging, theft, or temporary employment but is usually without funds.

Vicarious learning Learning that occurs when one is not the focus of the instruction, for example, when one is a bystander or onlooker.

Victimless crime A crime in which no identifiable victim is clearly injured, as in prostitution or gambling.

Visceral Pertaining to the internal organs of the body, for example, a "gut feeling."

Vocational rehabilitation The training or retraining of job skills in individuals who have been unemployed because of illness or disability.

Vulnerable The state of having lowered defenses so that one is more open to injury; also more open to intimacy.

__ANNOTATED BIBLIOGRAPHY_____

Alley, S.; Blanton, J.; Feldman, R. E.; Hunter, G. D.; and Rolfson, M. *Case Studies of Mental Health Paraprofessionals: Twelve Effective Programs*. New York: Human Sciences Press, 1979.
Extensive study of twelve mental health systems that effectively use human service workers. Each program represents a different subarea of human services, including aging, drug abuse, children, inpatient, and outpatient.

Austin, M. *The Florida Human Services Task Bank*. Florida Board of Regents, 1975.
A major job analysis of a large sample of human service workers in Florida. Provides empirical data regarding those activities in which human service workers engage.

Banks, W., and Martens, K. "Counseling: The Reactionary Profession." *Personnel and Guidance Journal* 51 (1973).
The authors view the traditional counseling and psychotherapy approaches as supporters of the societal status quo, as agents of social control. They contend that counselors and psychotherapists must begin to work for social change if they are to be more responsive to their clients' needs. Suggests possible approaches.

Bay, J., and Bay, C. "Professionalism and the Erosion of Rationality in the Health Care Field." *American Journal of Orthopsychiatry* 43 (1973).
Highlights the self-serving character of the professions. Demonstrates how professionals have a vested interest in maintaining the exclusiveness of the ranks of helpers.

Bellack, A. S., and Hersen, M. (eds.). *Dictionary of Behavior Therapy Techniques*. Elmsford, N.Y.: Pergamon Press, 1985.
Defines and describes 158 terms and techniques important in behavior therapy. More than a dictionary, this text verges on being a "cookbook" for behavior therapy. It is an easy reference source for the instructor, student, or human service professional who wishes or needs to have concise information on a range of behavioral terms and technique.

Biegel, D. E.; Shore, B. K.; and Gordon, E. *Building Support Networks for the Elderly: Theory and Applications*. Beverly Hills, Calif.: Sage, 1984.
Provides examples of programs using informal support networks (family, friends, neighbors, volunteers, and other community members) to meet the needs of older adults. Examines primary, secondary, and tertiary prevention programs. Targets include frail aged at risk for institutionalization, adult children of aging parents facing the stress of caregiving, and well elderly who volunteer to help others.

Browning, P.; Thorin, E.; and Rhoades, C. "A National Profile of Self-Help/Self-Advocacy Groups of People with Mental Retardation." *Mental Retardation* 22 (1984).
The authors identify 152 self-help/self-advocacy groups for the mentally retarded. Ninety percent of the groups meet monthly. Average membership is twenty-three. The groups engage in a variety of activities: socializing, recruiting, fund raising, and political work. Groups are usually organized with elected member leaders and human service worker advisers. Human service advisers emphasized the importance of the groups for self-advocacy, self-help, group advocacy, and leisuretime involvement of their members.

Butler, S., and Kondratas, A. *Out of the Poverty Trap: A Conservative Strategy for Welfare Reform.* New York: The Free Press, 1987.
Welfare dependency and the creation of poverty: these are the results of a failed welfare system. The authors offer a way to get the poor onto real payrolls. Their point-by-point program includes block grants to states, enforcement of parental responsibility, a redirected public education and health care system, and the use of family and community strength as a ladder out of the poverty trap.

Caputo, R. *Management and Information Systems in Human Services.* New York: The Haworth Press, Inc., 1988.
Provides an understanding of how information systems can impact organizational structure and decision making. Useful for students of management and administration, as well as for professionals who need to know the important relationship between information systems and the programmatic responsibilities of the professional.

Carkhuff, R., and Berenson, B. *Teaching as Treatment: An Introduction to Counseling and Psychotherapy.* Amherst, Mass.: Human Resource Developments Press, Inc., 1976.
The authors present the concept of therapy as teaching. Effective helping requires empathy, commitment, and organization. The text provides a basic orientation to the approach developed by Carkhuff over the past few years. Highly relevant to human service workers.

Collins, A. H. *The Human Services: An Introduction.* Indianapolis: The Odyssey Press, a Division of Bobbs-Merrill Company, 1973.
Generally reviews the tasks of human service workers and gives examples of their functions in working with children, with families, in the community, and in institutions. Provides a feeling for the types of jobs human service workers may find.

Corsini, R. (ed.). *Current Psychotherapies.* Itasca, Ill.: F. E. Peacock, 1973.
Provides a comprehensive overview of the major psychotherapeutic approaches. A good reference text for the advanced human services student.

Dangel, R. F., and Polster, R. A. *Teaching Child Management Skills.* New York: Pergamon Press, 1988.
Detailed, step-by-step child management skills to help parents work effectively with three- to twelve-year olds who display common behavior disorders. The authors cover disorders such as noncompliance, aggression, annoying habits, tantrums, opposition, poor school performance, and bedtime or mealtime conflicts. Offers useful approaches for human service workers.

Denham, W., and Schatz, E. "Impact of the Indigenous Nonprofessional on the Professional's Role." In *Human Services and Social Work Responsibilities,* edited by W. C. Richan. New York: National Association of Social Workers, 1969.
Examines the reaction of professionals to the indigenous nonprofessionals working in metropolitan human services agencies. Defines issues and questions arising from these settings in terms of implications for the future.

Duehn, W. D., and Mayadas, N. S. "Starting Where the Client Is: An Empirical Investigation." *Social Casework: The Journal of Contemporary Social Work* 60 (1979).
Studies the degree to which therapists really hear what clients are saying. Finds that the greater the diversity between helper and helpee, the less likely the helper is to understand clients' problems. Emphasizes that active listening is difficult and cannot be approached casually.

Dugger, J. G. *The New Professional: Introduction for the Human Services/Mental Health Worker.* Monterey, Calif.: Brooks/Cole Publishing Co., 1975.
A short text that introduces the concept of the human services/mental health worker. Briefly covers career development, attitudes, abnormal behavior, cultural differences, interviewing, crisis, group work, community resources, and research.

Evans, D. P. *The Lives of Mentally Retarded People.* Boulder, Colo.: Westview Press, 1983.

An account of the services currently provided to mentally retarded children and adults. Focuses on formal and informal service systems, including familial, educational, psychotherapeutic, legal, occupational, and residential support systems. Includes survey of rewards and problems for staff members working with this population. A good introductory text.

Fisher, R. G. "The Legacy of Freud—a Dilemma for Handling Offenders in General and Sex Offenders in Particular." *University of Colorado Law Review* 40 (1968).

Identifies the problems that the concept of psychological processes (particularly the idea of unconscious motivation) creates for the judiciary system. Illustrates the pervasive character of the medical model.

Flores, P. J. *Group Psychotherapy with Addicted Populations.* New York: The Haworth Press, 1988.

Outlines useful recommendations for the treatment of addiction by group psychotherapy. This book examines the skills needed by practitioners and stresses recovery as a time-dependent process. It examines the ways in which a therapy group can deal with the array of emotions in the first few months of abstinence and the special problems faced by group leaders.

Gartner, A.; Jackson, V. C.; and Riessman, F. *Paraprofessionals in Education Today.* New York: Human Sciences Press, 1977.

A collection of articles that describe the many facets of roles that human service workers play in the subfield of education.

Gartner, A., and Riessman, F. (eds.). *The Self-Help Revolution.* New York: Human Sciences Press, 1983.

Nineteen original chapters describing and assessing the self-help movement. The advantages and problems of human service workers in self-help groups are identified and described. A wide range of these groups are discussed, including those for women, cancer patients, drug users, criminal offenders, mentally ill people, overeaters, and homosexuals. Examines self-help group functions, participant roles, and ways for human service workers to sponsor new groups or collaborate with existing groups.

Gartner, A., and Riessman, F. *The Service Society and the Consumer Vanguard.* New York: Harper and Row, 1974.

The authors provide an analysis of an interesting concept: We are becoming a service-oriented society rather than a product-oriented society. They explore the implications of this change for the human services and suggest that the consumer of services must become and is becoming a producer.

Getz, W.; Wiessen, A.; Sue, S.; and Ayers, A. *Fundamentals of Crisis Counseling.* Lexington, Mass.: Lexington Books, 1974.

A basic introductory text on the principles and techniques of crisis counseling. Good additional reading for those who are considering employment in activities such as a crisis center, hotline, etc.

Greenblatt, F. S. *Therapeutic Recreation for Long-Term Care Facilities.* New York: Human Sciences Press, 1987.

In a developmental framework, this volume identifies and analyzes the issues and concerns affecting the recreation needs of the long-term care client and nursing home patient. Explains the principles and procedures of therapeutic recreation services and a methodology for applying them to a successful recreation program within the long-term care facility.

Grier, W. H., and Cobbs, P. M. *Black Rage.* New York: Basic Books, 1968.

An interesting psychiatric assessment of the personality development of blacks and how they are affected by the U.S. culture. Written by two black psychiatrists who suggest that blacks must be suspicious to survive in the dominant white culture.

Hasenfeld, Y. *Human Service Organizations.* Englewood Cliffs, N.J.: Prentice-Hall, 1983.

Examines the bureaucratic character of human service organizations from a variety of perspectives. Presents salient features of organization-environment relations, organizational goals and technologies, and the use of and abuse of power. Describes the problems of creating dependence in clients and describes staff-client relationships. Discusses organizational effectiveness and how to measure it. Examines procedures for changing organizations. A complex and sophisticated analysis of the human service system.

Helgeson, E., and Willis, S. C. *Handbook of Group Activities for Impaired Older Adults.* New York: The Haworth Press, 1987.

A practical and effective handbook that provides the foundation for a daily activities program with severely impaired elders. The activities (over seventy of them) are creatively designed and well organized to help enable these clients to achieve a sense of self-worth and obtain as much human interaction as is possible.

Hershenson, D. B., and Power, P. W. *Mental Health Counseling: Theory and Practice.* New York: Pergamon Press, 1987.

Introduces the roles and functions of the mental health counselor and the characteristics of mental health counseling. The authors take a developmental, growth-oriented approach. They emphasize the role of the environment and focus on empirically validated techniques for assisting clients to cope with their problems by identifying, mobilizing, and developing personal assets and skills and by making their environment more facilitative.

Hussain, R. A., and Davis, R. L. D. *Responsive Care: Behavioral Interventions with Elderly Persons.* Champaign, Ill.: Research Press, 1985.

A guide for the use of behavioral analysis and treatment with impaired elderly patients under home care or in residential settings. The approach is presented at a basic level so that the book can be used effectively by paraprofessional health care workers and family members. Appendices cover general behavior management, patient drug education, control of wandering, reduction of agitation and combativeness, and treatment of inappropriate sexual behavior.

Kaslow, F. W., and Associates (eds.). *Issues in Human Services.* San Francisco: Jossey-Bass Publishers, 1972.

A series of articles that deal with the effective delivery of human services. Provides history and philosophy of human services and analyzes theory and practice.

Kozol, J. *Rachel and Her Children: Homeless Families in America.* New York: Crown Books, 1987.

Jonathan Kozol describes the plight of the homeless in America, focusing on the day-to-day life of a woman named Rachel and her three children. He exposes the shortsightedness of the welfare bureaucracy that is creating a "diseased, distorted, undereducated and malnourished generation of children." Kozol concludes that Americans today place a high value on economic conservatism, which makes them willing and ready to cut back on programs that help the poor. Highly recommended reading for human service workers.

Lamb, H. R. *The Homeless Mentally Ill.* Washington, D.C.: American Psychiatric Association, 1984.

A large proportion of homeless street people are ex–mental patients or young mentally ill people who have not yet been hospitalized. An up-to-date summary of the mental health problems of the homeless. Describes necessary support systems, service programs, and requirements for shelter and housing of this multiproblem group.

Lamb, H. R. "Therapist-case Managers: More than Brokers of Services." *Hospital and Community Psychiatry* 31 (1980).

Points out that brokering of services is incomplete or ineffective if the helper does not become involved in helping relationship therapy with the client. Brokering alone is too impersonal an approach.

Landon, J. W. *The Development of Social Welfare.* New York: Human Sciences Press, 1986.
Traces the development of the institution of social welfare from earliest times to the present. Discusses the origins of people's concern for their fellows, the emergence of the Judeo-Christian tradition and its gradual secularization, and the European and American experiences. Provides a perspective on current developments in human services.

Lederman, E. F. *Occupational Therapy in Mental Retardation.* Springfield, Ill.: Charles C. Thomas, 1984.
A clinical discussion of occupational therapy for mentally retarded clients. Presents a good balance of tried-and-true interventions and new assessment/intervention techniques. The text also lists assessment/intervention tools and provides references for specific techniques. Uses the unfortunate term "retardate" throughout, however.

Leiter, M. P., and Webb, M. *Developing Human Service Networks.* New York: Irvington Press, 1983.
Describes human service networks in terms of systems theory. Examines not only organizations' internal processes or functions but also their environment. Accounts for the growth, evolution, and maintenance of these networks over time. The authors also address the many thorny issues related to network stability, not the least of which is securing adequate financial support, and suggest marketing and sales techniques.

Lynton, E. F. "The Non-Professional Scene." *American Child* 49 (1967).
Covers the problems and issues of new careerists in the child care field. Examines career ladders, credentials, job analysis, recruitment, and relationships with professionals.

Maier, H. W. *Developmental Group Care of Children and Youth: Concepts and Practice.* New York: The Haworth Press, 1987.
This insightful and inspiring volume focuses on group care of children and presents Dr. Maier's thoughts on human development, the role of human service workers, the environment in which they work, the preparation of child and youth workers, the meaning of care, and the nuts and bolts of how to do it well. A useful handbook for child and youth care workers.

McGee, J. J.; Menolascino, F. J.; Hobbs, D. C.; and Menousek, P. E. *Gentle Teaching: A Non-Aversive Approach to Helping Persons with Mental Retardation.* New York: Human Sciences Press, 1987.
This work rejects current punishment-based practices and presents nonpunitive strategies to serve persons with aggressive, self-injurious, and self-stimulatory behaviors. It describes methods to teach persons with mental retardation and severe behavioral problems the value inherent in human presence, human interaction, and human reward. It examines these methods from the perspectives of family settings, schools, group homes, institutions, and work. Case studies illustrate how the caregiver's beliefs deeply influence the treatment and teaching process.

Mowrer, O. H. "Peer Groups and Medication: The Best Therapy for Professionals and Laymen Alike." *Psychotherapy: Theory, Research and Practice* 8 (1971).
Mowrer proposes that traditional psychotherapy is relatively ineffective compared with the use of peer groups and medication. He focuses on the types of peer groups in which he has been involved, discusses why he thinks they work, gives examples of the process, and considers their future.

Offer, D., and Sabshin, M. *Normality.* New York: Basic Books, 1974.
The authors describe four current approaches to defining normality: the psychoanalytic, the normative, the cross-cultural, and the biological. They attempt to bring these views together into a comprehensive definition of normality.

Okun, B. F. *Effective Helping, Interviewing and Counseling Techniques.* (3d Ed.) Monterey, Calif.: Brooks/Cole, 1987.

Presents a human relations counseling model emphasizing the helping relationship and fo-cusing on the theory and practice of communications skills and relationship building. New or expanded in this edition are the theory chapter and sections on contemporary psychoan-alytic theory, control theory, and cognitive behavior therapy, multimodel therapy, feminist therapies, short-term psychotherapy, and terminating counseling.

Orlans, H. *Human Services Coordination.* New York: Pica Press, 1982.

Edited report and invited papers of a series of four regional meetings sponsored by the Council of State Governments and the National Academy of Public Administration in 1980. Presents issues involved in improving the coordination and delivery of human ser-vices. Focuses on the special problem areas of children and the elderly and describes the experience of program or service coordination in the South, the state of Washington, New York, and generally across the country. Identifies examples of successes and of problems hindering effective coordination.

"Paraprofessionals Speak Out: What It's All About." *Personnel and Guidance Journal* 53 (1974).

Ten paraprofessionals describe their work, training, and lives. Provides interesting insight into what they do and what they think about it.

Pearl, A., and Riessman, F. *New Careers for the Poor: The Nonprofessional in Human Service.* New York: Free Press, 1965.

This early work is an interesting account of one of the first paraprofessional programs in the country. It sets down the principles and issues that are still important in the devel-opment, implementation, and effective use of such workers.

Powell, T. J. *Self-help Organizations in Professional Practice.* Silver Spring, Md.: National Association of Social Work, 1987.

Deals with such topics as the effectiveness of self-help organizations, social science concep-tualizations of the organizations, and professionals' relationships with the self-help system. Separate chapters analyze what the author describes as habit-disturbance, general-purpose, life-style, significant-other, and physical-handicap organizations.

Riessman, F. "The Helper-Therapy Principle." *Social Work* 10 (1965).

The author spells out the concept of the helper-therapy principle: the principle that the one who helps others also experiences growth as a function of that activity. The principle is important for self-help or mutual aid programs in particular and more generally for all of those who are helpers.

Roberts, A. (ed.). *Social Work in Juvenile and Criminal Justice Settings.* Springfield, Ill.: Charles C. Thomas, 1983.

An edited collection of articles describing the current state of the art of human services in juvenile and criminal justice settings. Discusses roles and activities primarily from a social service perspective. Identifies problems, challenges, and ethical implications of working with these populations.

Ropers, R. H. *The Invisible Homeless: A New Urban Ecology.* New York: Human Sci-ences Press, 1988.

This important study of the contemporary homeless, bringing together the insights of his-tory, sociology, psychology, political science, and epidemiology, shows that at least 250,000 and perhaps as many as 3 million people nationwide are homeless on any given night. These findings are based on three empirical research studies of the homeless problem in Los Angeles County (designated by H.U.D. to be the homeless capital of America), le-gal declarations of homeless people, and research findings conducted in major cities by various government agencies. The reader is provided with a historical account of homeless-ness since the end of the American Civil War and an examination of historical and social structural factors which are believed to have given rise to the new urban homeless of the 1980s.

Sarason, S. B.; Carroll, C. F.; Maton, K.; Cohen, S.; and Lorentz, E. *Human Services and Resource Networks*. San Francisco: Jossey-Bass Publishers, 1977.
The text describes the deliberate development of a network of human service providers including teachers, professors, private agencies, and public agencies for the exchange of services and a sense of community. The current emphasis on networking makes this book important for human service workers.

Sauber, S. R. *The Human Services Delivery System*. New York: Columbia University Press, 1983.
Presents a systems approach to human services delivery system integration. Advocates integration of services, comprehensiveness and accessibility, emphasis on client problems, and accountability. Criticizes current system as competitive, distrustful, and prejudicial. Good review of criminal justice, social welfare, education, and health services systems.

Schulberg, H.; Baker, F.; and Roen, S. (eds.). *Developments in Human Services*. Vol. 1. New York: Behavioral Publications, 1973.
The ten contributors survey a wide variety of concepts and issues in the human services. They cover the general concept of human services, administration, planning, strategies, education, and manpower. Particularly worthwhile for the broad perspective on human services.

Schulman, E. *Intervention in Human Services*. St. Louis: C. V. Mosby, 1974.
The author focuses primarily on the interview as an intervention technique. Excellent presentation of concepts and issues of interviewing; however, neglects other intervention techniques. A good text for learning interviewing.

Seidman, E. (ed.). *Handbook of Social Intervention*. Beverly Hills, Calif.: Sage Publications, 1983.
Twenty-eight chapters written by authorities from a wide range of fields including economics, sociology, psychology, program evaluation, education, social policy, criminal justice, and management. It presents philosophical, theoretical, and practical information on the impact of social interventions.

Shulman, L. *The Skills of Helping: Individuals and Groups*. (2d Ed.) Itasca, Ill.: F. E. Peacock, 1984.
This book intends to identify, illustrate, and transmit the skills that contribute to helping. The author clearly describes the generic aspects of helping skills. The text begins with issues related to individuals and proceeds to family and group interventions. It deals effectively with issues arising throughout the helping process. Amply illustrated with case materials, which are particularly helpful in illuminating the skills discussed. It concentrates not only on psychological or intrapsychic issues but also on the environment.

Sobey, F. *The Nonprofessional Revolution in Mental Health*. New York: Columbia University Press, 1970.
The author reports on a major survey of 10,000 nonprofessionals working in 185 mental health programs. Provides a comprehensive picture of use patterns of such workers in the mental health field and discusses implications for the future.

Sommer, R. *The End of Imprisonment*. New York: Oxford University Press, 1976.
An interesting work that discusses the history of American prisons, the logic behind punishment, and the failure of imprisonment. Proposes a gradual phasing out of prisons. An alternative system is proposed.

SREB. "Staff Roles for Mental Health Personnel: A History and Rationale for Paraprofessionals." Southern Regional Education Board, Atlanta, 1978.
In spite of its title focusing on mental health personnel, discusses the roles of paraprofessionals in both mental health and the broader human services context. Discusses trends, rationales, background, work objectives, patterns of utilization, and levels; makes recommendations for the future.

SREB. "Mental Health/Human Service Worker Activities: The Process and the Products." Southern Regional Education Board, Atlanta, 1979.
This report details a task analysis survey conducted by SREB and cluster analyzes the results and considers the issues of competency and credentialing.

Stone, A. A. "The Myth of Advocacy." *Hospital and Community Psychiatry* 30 (1979).
The president of the American Psychiatric Association presents his negative view of patient rights advocacy as it is now conducted. He feels that the current adversary relationship between rights advocates and human service workers in the mental health field works to the ultimate detriment of the client.

Sundel, M., and Sundel, S. *Behavior Modification in the Human Services.* New York: John Wiley and Sons, 1975.
A programmed text on behavioral concepts and techniques. Assumes little or no prior formal exposure to such concepts. Uses case examples, pretests, and posttests. Excellent for self-paced learning. Highly relevant to the human service worker.

Sunley, R. *Advocating Today: A Human Service Practitioner's Handbook.* New York: Family Service America, 1983.
Describes how human service workers can advocate planned change of institutional systems, conditions, and administrative practices. In this text, advocacy refers to the broad range of activities oriented toward planned and purposive change. Addresses the purposes of advocacy in promoting equality, equity, and client participation and self-determination. Describes how human service workers must seek empowerment of clients through the benefits of participation.

Talbott, J. A. (ed.). *State Mental Hospitals: Problems and Potentials.* New York: Human Science Press, 1980.
Twelve authors consider the problems and potentials of state-operated mental hospitals. Discusses the future role of such institutions in the human services.

Taylor, J. B., and Randolph, J. *Community Worker.* New York: Jason Aronson, 1975.
Outlines the issues and problems facing the newcomer to community work in human services. Amusingly written how-to book based on the authors' experience in starting, running, and evaluating a new community agency. Presents a down-to-earth picture of the frustrations and satisfactions awaiting the human service worker in the community.

Thyer, B. A. (ed.). *Progress in Behavioral Social Work.* New York: The Haworth Press, 1988.
This collection presents empirically based practice and qualitative research findings that illustrate the validity of behavioral approaches to social work. Chapters report findings that employ either conventional group research methods or single-subject approaches; report on the state of the art behavioral social work; and describe a number of treatment modalities, among them individual, marital and family, and group work.

Trattner, W. I. *From Poor Law to Welfare State: A History of Social Welfare in America.* (3d Ed.) New York: Free Press, 1986.
A comprehensive history of the development of social welfare policy from the time of the colonies to the present. Interestingly written book that helps place current human service systems in a historical perspective.

Tyor, P. L., and Bell, L. V. *Caring for the Retarded in America: A History.* Westport, Conn.: Greenwood Press, 1984.
A comprehensive history of the development and decline of state institutions for the mentally retarded. Traces the important movements in the social and behavioral sciences as they influenced change in the institution as an agency. Documents the impact of the eugenics and mental measurement movements. Relates the deinstitutionalization of the mentally retarded to changed social perceptions of the mentally retarded and increased knowledge in the behavioral and biologic sciences.

Walker, C. E.; Bonner, B. L.; and Kaufman, K. L. *The Physically and Sexually Abused Child: Evaluation and Treatment.* New York: Pergamon Press, 1987.

The assessment and treatment of both physically and sexually abused children and their families. Covers case management issues such as the importance of recording sessions so that the child does not have to repeat the story over and over again. Describes various combinations of human service approaches and provides a framework for helping child protection workers and the courts decide when families can be kept intact and when this is not possible for the safety of the child.

Youngblood, G. S., and Bensberg, G. J. *Planning and Operating Group Homes for the Handicapped.* Lubbock, Tex.: Research and Training Center in Mental Retardation, 1983.

Covers important issues involved in developing or operating group homes for the handicapped. Topics covered include staffing models, key sources of funding, strategies for locating facilities and overcoming restrictive zoning, meeting accreditation standards, developing quality programming, and training staff. Based on the authors' personal experiences. A valuable resource for human service workers involved with the development or operation of group homes.

Zarit, S. H. *Aging and Mental Disorders.* New York: Free Press, 1980.

Although the title implies a focus on mental health disorders, this text emphasizes problems and services relevant to most aged persons. One section deals with "accommodation services" such as Meals on Wheels and telephone links that help maintain the elderly in their homes. An excellent introduction to the field of aging for human service workers.

__REFERENCES_____

Aiken, L. S.; Lo Sciuto, L. A.; and Ausetts, M. A. "Paraprofessional versus Professional Drug Counselors: The Progress of Clients in Treatment." *International Journal of the Addictions* 19 (1984).

Albee, G. W. *Mental Health Manpower Trends.* New York: Basic Books, 1961.

Alcoholics Anonymous. New York: Alcoholics Anonymous World Services, Inc., 1955.

Allderidge, P. "Hospitals, Madhouses and Asylums: Cycles in the Care of the Insane." *British Journal of Psychiatry* 134 (1979).

Alley, S.; Blanton, J.; and Feldman, R. E. (eds.). *Paraprofessionals in Mental Health: Theory and Practice.* New York: Human Sciences Press, 1979. (a)

Alley, S.; Blanton, J.; Feldman, R. E.; Hunter, G. D.; and Rolfson, M. *Case Studies of Mental Health Paraprofessionals: Twelve Effective Programs.* New York: Human Sciences Press, 1979. (b)

American Psychological Association Monitor. "Turnaround Slated for Mental Health Training: Providers Wonder, Bombshell or Shellgame." American Psychological Association 7 (1976).

Amidei, N. "How to Be an Advocate in Bad Times." *Public Welfare* 40 (1982).

Andreasen, N. *The Broken Brain: The Biological Revolution in Psychiatry.* New York: Harper and Row, 1984.

Arens, R. "Due Process and the Rights of the Mentally Ill: The Strange Case of Frederick Lynch." *Catholic University Law Review* 13 (1964).

Atkinson, E. "Four Hours on the Suicide Phones." *Bulletin of Suicidology* 7 (1970).

Atwood, J. D. "Self-Awareness in Supervision." *Clinical Supervisor* 4 (1986).

Austin, M. *The Florida Human Services Task Bank.* Florida Board of Regents, 1975.

——. *Professionals and Paraprofessionals.* New York: Human Sciences Press, 1978.

Ayllon, T., and Azrin, N. *The Token Economy: A Motivational System for Therapy and Rehabilitation.* New York: Appleton-Century-Crofts, 1968.

Azrin, N. H., and Powers, M. A. "Eliminating Classroom Disturbances of Emotionally Disturbed Children by Positive Practice Procedures." *Behavior Therapy* 6 (1975).

Bachrach, A.; Erwin, W.; and Mohr, J. "The Control of Eating Behavior in an Anorexic by Operant Conditioning Techniques." In *Case Studies in Behavior Modification,* edited by L. Ullman and L. Krasner. New York: Holt, Rinehart and Winston, 1965.

Bale, R. N., et al. "Therapeutic Communities vs. Methadone Maintenance." *Archives of General Psychiatry* 37 (1980).

Bandura, A. "Self-Efficiency Mechanisms in Human Agency." *American Psychologist* 37 (1982).

——. "The Self-System in Reciprocal Determinism." *American Psychologist* 33 (1978).

——. *Social Learning Theories.* Englewood Cliffs, N.J.: Prentice-Hall, 1977.

Bassuk, E., and Gerson, S. "Chronic Crises Patients: A Discrete Clinical Group." *American Journal of Psychiatry* 137 (1980).

Bassuk, E., and Rubin, L. "Homeless Children: A Neglected Population." *American Journal of Orthopsychiatry* 52 (1987).

Bassuk, E.; Rubin, L.; and Lauriat, A. "Is Homelessness a Mental Health Problem?" *American Journal of Psychiatry* 141 (1984).

Bateson, P. "Biological Approaches to the Study of Behavioral Development." *International Journal of Behavioral Development* 10 (1987).

Bay, J., and Bay, C. "Professionalism and the Erosion of Rationality in the Health Care Field." *American Journal of Orthopsychiatry* 43 (1973).

"Beauticians/Barbers Learn Mental Health Helper Role." *Innovations: Highlights of Evolving Mental Health Services.* American Institutes for Research 2 (Summer, 1975).

Becker, R. E.; Heimberg, R. G.; and Bellack, A. S. *Social Skills Training Treatment for Depression.* New York: Pergamon Press, 1987.

Beitman, B. D. "Pastoral Counseling Centers: A Challenge to Community Mental Health Centers." *Hospital and Community Psychiatry* 33 (1982).

Bellack, A. S., and Hersen, M. (eds.). *Dictionary of Behavior Therapy Techniques.* Elmsford, N.Y.: Pergamon Press, 1985.

Bellack, A. S.; Hersen, M.; and Kazdin, A. E. (eds.). *International Handbook of Behavior Modification and Therapy.* New York: Plenum, 1982.

Bergantino, L. *Psychotherapy, Insight, and Style: The Existential Moment.* Boston: Allyn and Bacon, 1981.

Berne, E. "Ego States in Psychotherapy." *American Journal of Psychotherapy* 11 (1957).

———. *Principles of Group Treatment.* New York: Oxford University Press, 1966.

Black, J. L., and Bruce, B. K. "Behavior Therapy: A Clinical Update." *Hospital and Community Psychiatry* 40 (1989).

Blake, R. "Normalization and Boarding Homes: An Examination of Paradoxes." *Social Work in Health Care* 11 (1985/86).

Bloom, G. L. "The 'Medical Model,' Miasma Theory and Community Mental Health." *Community Mental Health Journal* 1 (1965).

Blum, A. "Differential Use of Manpower in Public Welfare." *Social Work* 11 (1966).

Bogdan, R., and Taylor, S. "The Judged, Not the Judges: An Insider's View of Mental Retardation." *American Psychologist* 31 (1976).

Bokan, J. A., and Campbell, W. "Indigenous Psychotherapy in the Treatment of a Laotian Refugee." *Hospital and Community Psychiatry* 35 (1984).

Bowman, G., and Klopf, G. *Auxiliary School Personnel: Their Roles, Training and Institutionalization.* New York: Bank Street College of Education, 1968.

Braddock, D. "Deinstitutionalization of the Retarded: Trends in Public Policy." *Hospital and Community Psychiatry* 32 (1981).

———. "Interview." *Equalizer* 4 (1990).

Braginsky, B. M.; Braginsky, D.; and Ring, K. *Methods of Madness: The Mental Hospital as a Last Resort.* New York: Holt, Rinehart and Winston, 1969.

Brawley, E. A. "Bachelor's Degree Programs in the Human Services: Results of a National Survey." *Journal of the National Organization of Human Service Educators* 4 (1982).

———. "Paraprofessional Social Welfare Personnel in International Perspective: Results of a World-Wide Survey." *International Social Work* 29 (1986).

Breggin, R. "The Second Wave." *Mental Hygiene* 3 (1973).

Brown, W. F. "Effectiveness of Paraprofessionals: The Evidence." *The Personnel and Guidance Journal* 53 (1974).

Browning, P.; Thorin, E.; and Rhoades, C. "A National Profile of Self-Help/Self-Advocacy Groups of People with Mental Retardation." *Mental Retardation* 22 (1984).

Bruck, C. "Battle Lines in the Ritalin War." *Human Behavior* 5 (1976).

Buckley, S. "Parent Aides Provide Support to High-Risk Families." *Children Today* 14 (1985).

Burt, M. R., and Cohen, B. E. *America's Homeless: Numbers, Characteristics, and Programs that Serve Them.* Washington, D.C.: Urban Institute Press. 1989.

Buss, A. H. *Psychopathology.* New York: Wiley, 1966.

Byers-Lang, R. E. "Peer Counselors, Network Builders for Elderly Blind." *Journal of Visual Impairment and Blindness* 78 (1984).

Bynum, W. F.; Porter, R.; and Shepherd, M. (eds.). *The Anatomy of Madness: Essays in the History of Psychiatry* (Vol. 2). New York: Tavistock Press, 1985.

"Calming Family Crises." *Innovations: Highlights of Evolving Mental Health Services.* American Institutes for Research 2 (Winter, 1975).

Caplan, G. *Principles of Preventative Psychiatry.* New York: Basic Books, 1964.

Chaneles, S. "Growing Old behind Bars." *Psychology Today* 21 (1987).

Chasnoff, I. J., and Schnoll, S. H. "Consequences of Cocaine and Other Drug Use In Pregnancy." In *Cocaine: A Clinicians Handbook,* edited by A. M. Washton and M. S. Gold. New York: The Guilford Press, 1987.

Chodoff, P. "The Case for Involuntary Hospitalization of the Mentally Ill." *American Journal of Psychiatry* 133 (1976).

Chutis, L. "Special Roles of Mental Health Professionals in Self-Help Group Development." *Prevention in Human Services* 2 (1983).

Church, G. J. "The View From Behind Bars." *Time* 136 (1990).

Christmas, J. J.; Wallace, H.; and Edwards, J. "New Careers and Mental Health Services: Fantasy or Future?" *American Journal of Psychiatry* 126 (1970).

Clare, P. K., and Kramer, J. H. *Introduction to American Corrections.* Boston: Holbrook Press, 1976.

"Clergy-Youth Counseling Works." *Innovations: Highlights of Evolving Mental Health Services.* American Institutes for Research 2 (Fall, 1975).

Clubok, M. "Four-Year Human Service Programs." *Journal of the National Organization of Human Service Educators* 6 (1984).

Coelho, G. V., and Rubinstein, E. A. *Social Change and Human Behavior: Mental Health Challenges of the Seventies.* National Institute of Mental Health, D.H.E.W. Publication Number (HSM) 72-9122, 1972.

Cohen, B. "A Cognitive Approach to the Treatment of Offenders." *British Journal of Social Work* 15 (1985).

Cohen, R. E. "The Armero Tragedy: Lessons for Mental Health Professionals." *Hospital and Community Psychiatry* 38 (1987).

Cohen, W. J. "A Ten Point Program to Abolish Poverty." *Social Security Bulletin* 31 (1968).

Cohn, V. "Panel Upholds Surgery to Change Behavior." *Chicago Sun Times,* September 12, 1976.

Coleman, J. *Abnormal Psychology and Modern Life.* Chicago: Scott, Foresman and Co., 1956.

Collins, A. H. *The Human Services: An Introduction.* Indianapolis: The Odyssey Press, a Division of Bobbs-Merrill Company, 1973. (a)

——. "Natural Delivery System: Accessible Sources of Power for Mental Health." *American Journal of Orthopsychiatry* 43 (1973). (b)

Cordes, C. "The Plight of the Homeless Mentally Ill." *APA Monitor* 15 (1984).

Cormier, W. H., and Cormier, L. S. *Interviewing Strategies for Helpers: Fundamental Skills and Cognitive-Behavioral Intervention.* (2d Ed.) Monterey: Brooks/Cole, 1985.

Corsini, R. (ed.). *Current Psychotherapies.* Itasca, Ill.: F. E. Peacock, 1973.

Costa, C. *A Comparative Study of Career Opportunities of Anti-poverty Program Graduates as First Year Teachers.* New York: New Careers Training Laboratory, Queens College, 1975.

Craighead, W. E., and Mercatoris, M. "Mentally Retarded Residents as Paraprofessionals: A Review." *American Journal of Mental Deficiency* 78 (1983).

Crossman, L. "I Am Sure that Change Will Come." *Generations* 10 (1985).

Dangel, R. F., and Polster, R. A. *Teaching Child Management Skills.* New York: Pergamon Press, 1988.

Danish, S. J., and Hauer, A. L. *Helping Skills: A Basic Training Program.* New York: Behavioral Publications, 1973.

Davis, D.; Jemison, E.; Rowe, M.; and Sprague, D. "Cluster Homes: An Alternative for Troubled Youths." *Children Today* 13 (1984).

Davison, G., and Stuart, R. "Behavior Therapy and Civil Liberties." *American Psychologist* 30 (1975).

DeAngelis, T. "Armenian Earthquake Survivors Still Suffer Mental, Physical Pain." *APA Monitor* 21 (1990).

DeLeon, G., and Schwartz, S. "Therapeutic Communities: What Are the Retention Rates?" *American Journal of Drug and Alcohol Abuse* 22 (1986).

DeLeon, G., and Ziegenfuss, J. T. (eds.). *Therapeutic Communities for Addictions: Readings in Theory, Research and Practice.* Springfield, Ill.: Charles C. Thomas, 1986.

Demone, H., and Harshbarger, D. (eds.). *A Handbook of Human Service Organizations.* New York: Behavioral Publications, 1974.

Deutsch, A. *The Mentally Ill in America.* Garden City, N.Y.: Doubleday, Doran & Co., 1937.

Dewey, R., and Humber, W. *The Development of Human Behavior.* New York: Macmillan, 1951.

Drakeford, J. W. *Integrity Therapy—A Christian Evaluation of a New Approach to Mental Health.* Nashville: Broadman Press, 1967.

Dubey, J. "Confidentiality as a Requirement of the Therapist: Technical Necessities for Absolute Privilege in Psychotherapy." *American Journal of Psychiatry* 131 (1974).

Duggan, H. A. *Crisis Intervention: Helping Individuals at Risk.* Lexington, Mass.: Lexington Books, 1984.

Dugger, J. G. *The New Professional: Introduction for the Human Services/Mental Health Worker.* Monterey: Brooks/Cole Publishing Co., 1975.

Durlak, J. A. "Comparative Effectiveness of Paraprofessional and Professional Helpers." *Psychological Bulletin* 36 (1979).

D'Zurilla, T. J. "Current Status of Rational-Emotive Therapy." *Contemporary Psychology* 35 (1990).

Eaton, W. W. *The Sociology of Mental Disorders.* (2d Ed.) New York: Praeger, 1986.

Edelstein, B. A., and Michelson, L. *Handbook of Prevention.* New York: Plenum Press, 1986.

Egan, G. *Change Agent Skills in Helping and Human Service Settings.* Monterey: Brooks/Cole, 1985.

Ellis, A. *A Humanistic Psychotherapy: The Rational-Emotive Approach.* New York: Julian Press, 1973.

Emrick, R. E. "Self-Help Groups for Former Patients: Relations with Mental Health Professionals." *Hospital and Community Psychiatry* 41 (1990).

Evans, D. P. *The Lives of Mentally Retarded People.* Boulder, Colo.: Westview Press, 1983.

Eysenck, H. "Biological Basis of Personality." *Nature* (1963).

———. *The Effects of Psychotherapy.* New York: International Science Press, 1966.

Eysenck, H., and Eysenck, M. *Personality and Individual Differences: A Natural Science Approach*. New York: Plenum Press, 1985.

Fairweather, G. W.; Sanders, D. H.; Cressler, D. L.; and Maynard, H. *Community Life for the Mentally Ill: An Alternative to Institutional Care*. Chicago: Aldine Publishing Company, 1969.

Fairweather, G. W.; Sanders, D. H.; and Tornatzky, L. G. *Creating Change in Mental Health Organizations*. Elmsford, N.Y.: Pergamon Press, 1974.

Farberow, N. "Mental Health Response in Major Disasters." *The Psychotherapy Bulletin* 10 (1977).

Farrington, D. P. "Environmental Stress, Delinquent Behavior, and Convictions." In *Stress and Anxiety* (Vol. 6), edited by I. G. Sarason and C. D. Speilberger. Washington, D.C.: Hemisphere Press, 1979.

Feringer, R., and Jacobs, E. "Human Services: Is It a Profession." *The Link* 9 (1987).

Ferrero, G. *Criminal Man According to the Classification of Cesare Lombroso*. New York: G. P. Putnam, 1911.

Fields, S. "The Children's Hour: 1. Parents as Therapists." *Innovations: Highlights of Evolving Mental Health Services*. American Institutes for Research 2 (Fall, 1975).

——. "The Greening of Old Age." *Innovations: Highlights of Evolving Mental Health Services*. American Institutes for Research 2 (1977)

Fine, R. "Psychoanalysis." In *Current Psychotherapies*, edited by R. Corsini. Itasca, Ill.: F. E. Peacock, 1973.

Fisher, R. G. "The Legacy of Freud—a Dilemma for Handling Offenders in General and Sex Offenders in Particular." *University of Colorado Law Review* 40 (1968).

Fisher, W.; Mehr, J.; and Truckenbrod, P. *Human Services: The Third Revolution in Mental Health*. Port Washington, N.Y.: Alfred Publishing Co., 1974.

Frank, J. D. "The Present Status of Outcome Studies." *Journal of Consulting and Clinical Psychology* 47 (1979).

Franklin, D. "Hooked, Not Hooked: Why Not Everyone Is an Addict." *Health* 4 (1990)

Franks, C. *Behavior Therapy, Appraisal and Status*. New York: McGraw-Hill, 1969.

Fraser, J. S. "The Crisis Interview: Strategic Rapid Intervention." *Journal of Strategic and Systematic Therapies* 5 (1986).

Freud, S. *The Standard Edition of the Complete Psychological Works of Sigmund Freud*. 24 Vols. London: The Hogarth Press, 1953–1964.

Fried, M. "Effect of Social Change on Mental Health." *American Journal of Orthopsychiatry* 34 (1964).

Frumkin, M.; Imershein, A.; Chackerian, R.; and Martin, P. "Evaluating State Level Integration of Human Services." *Administration in Social Work* 7 (1983).

Fuoco, F. J.; Naster, B. J.; Morely, R. T.; and Middleton, J. F. *Behavioral Procedures for a Psychiatric Unit and Halfway House*. New York: Van Nostrand Reinhold, 1985.

Gage, R. W. "Integration of Human Service Delivery Systems." *Public Welfare* 34 (1976).

Garber, H. "Comment: On Sommer and Sommer." *American Psychologist* 39 (1984).

Garber, H., and Heber, F. R. "The Milwaukee Project: Indications of the Effectiveness of Early Interventions in Preventing Mental Retardation." In *Research to Practice in Mental Retardation* (Vol. 1), edited by P. Mittler. Baltimore: University Park Press, 1977.

Gardner, S. L. "The Future of Human Services: Building New Constituents." *Public Welfare* 42 (1984).

Garland, D. R. "Residential Child Care Workers as Primary Agents of Family Interventions." *Child and Youth Care Quarterly* 16 (1987).

Gartner, A. "The Effectiveness of Paraprofessionals in Service Delivery." In *Parapro-fessionals in Mental Health,* edited by S. Alley, J. Blanton, and R. E. Feldman. New York: Human Sciences Press, 1979.

———. *Paraprofessionals and Their Performance.* New York: Praeger Publishers, 1971.

Gartner, A., and Riessman, F. *Self-Help in the Human Services.* San Francisco: Jossey-Bass Publishers, 1977.

———. "Self-Help and Mental Health." *Hospital and Community Psychiatry* 33 (1982).

———. (eds.). *The Self-Help Revolution.* New York: Human Sciences Press, 1983.

Gavzer, B. "What We Can Learn From Those Who Survive AIDS." *Parade Magazine,* June 10, 1990.

Gaylord, M. S., and Galliher, J. F. *The Criminology of Edwin Sutherland.* New Brunswick, N.J.: Transaction Books, 1988.

Geller, M. I.; Wildman, H. E.; Kelly, J. A.; and Laughlin, G. "Teaching Assertive and Commendatory Social Skills to an Interpersonally Deficient Retarded Adoles-cent." *Journal of Clinical Child Psychiatry* 9 (1980).

Gendlin, E. T. "Forecast and Summary." In *New Directions in Client Centered Therapy,* edited by J. Hart and T. Tomlinson. Boston: Houghton Mifflin Co., 1970.

Getz, W.; Wiessen, A.; Sue, S.; and Ayers, A. *Fundamentals of Crisis Counseling.* Lex-ington, Mass.: Lexington Books, 1974.

Gilson, S. F., and Levitas, A. "Psychosocial Crisis in the Lives of Mentally Retarded People." *Psychiatric Aspects of Mental Retardation Reviews* 6 (1987).

Glasser, W. *Reality Therapy.* New York: Harper and Row, 1965.

Goffman, E. *Asylums: Essays on the Social Situation of Mental Patients and Other In-mates.* Garden City, N.Y.: Doubleday Anchor, 1961.

Goldfried, M., and Davison, G. *Clinical Behavior Therapy.* New York: Holt, Rinehart and Winston, 1976.

Gordon, J. "Project Cause: The Federal Anti-poverty Program and Some Implications of Sub-professional Training." *American Psychologist* 20 (1965).

Gottesman, I. *Schizophrenia Genesis: The Origins of Madness.* New York: W. H. Free-man and Company, 1990.

Grier, W. H., and Cobbs, P. M. *Black Rage.* New York: Basic Books, 1968.

Grimes, P. "Youth Suicide." *The Link* 8 (1986).

Grossinger, K. "Organizing in the Human Service Community." *Catalyst: A Socialist Journal of the Social Sciences* 5 (1985).

Gruenberg, E. M. "From Practice to Theory: Community Mental Health Services and the Nature of Psychosis." *Lancet* (April, 1969).

———. "The Social Breakdown Syndrome—Some Origins." *American Journal of Psy-chiatry* 123 (June, 1967).

Guerney, B. (ed.). *Psychotherapeutic Agents: New Roles for Nonprofessionals, Parents, and Teachers.* New York: Holt, Rinehart, and Winston, 1969.

Guerney, L., and Moore, L. "Phone Friend: A Prevention-Oriented Service for Latchkey Children." *Children Today* 12 (1983).

Gutheil, I. A. "Sensitizing Nursing Home Staff to Residents' Psychosocial Needs." *Clinical Social Work Journal* 13 (1985).

Guttesman, R. "Due Process and Students' Rights." *Social Work in Education* 4 (1982).

Haney, C.; Banks, C.; and Zimbardo, P. "Interpersonal Dynamics in a Simulated Prison." *International Journal of Criminology and Penology* 1 (1973).

Hansell, N. *The Person-In-Distress: On the Biosocial Dynamics of Adaptation.* New York: Human Services Press, 1976.

Hansell, N.; Wodarczyk, M.; and Handlon-Lathrop, B. "Decision Counseling Method: Expanding Coping at Crisis in Transit." *Archives of General Psychiatry* 21 (Spring, 1970).

Harper, R. *Psychoanalysis and Psychotherapy: 36 Systems.* Englewood Cliffs, NJ.: Prentice-Hall, 1960.

Harrington, M. *The Other America.* New York: Macmillan, 1962.

Hasenfeld, Y. *Human Service Organizations.* Englewood Cliffs, NJ.: Prentice-Hall, 1983.

Hattie, J. A.; Sharpley, C. R.; and Rogers, H. "Comparative Effectiveness of Professional and Paraprofessional Helpers." *Psychological Bulletin* 95 (1984).

Haveliwala, Y. A.; Scheflen, A. E.; and Ashcraft, N. *Common Sense in Therapy: A Handbook for the Mental Health Worker.* New York: Brunner-Mazel, 1979.

Hawkinshire, F. "Training Procedures for Offenders Working in Community Treatment Programs." In *Psychotherapeutic Agents: New Roles for Nonprofessionals, Parents, and Teachers,* edited by B. Guerney. New York: Holt, Rinehart and Winston, 1969.

Hergenhahn, B. R. *An Introduction to Theories of Personality.* Englewood Cliffs, N.J.: Prentice-Hall, 1984.

Herr, S. *Rights and Advocacy for Retarded People.* Lexington, Mass.: Lexington Books, 1983.

Hersch, P. "Coming of Age on City Streets." *Psychology Today* 22 (1988).

Hersen, M., and Bellack, A. S. (eds.). *Behavioral Assessment: A Practical Handbook.* New York: Pergamon Press, 1976.

Hines, L. "A Nonprofessional Discusses Her Role in Mental Health." *American Journal of Psychiatry* 126 (April, 1970).

Hoaken, P. C. "Psychiatry, Civil Liberty and Involuntary Treatment." *Canadian Journal of Psychiatry* 31 (1986).

Hoff, L. A. *People in Crisis: Understanding and Helping.* (2d Ed.) Menlo Park, Calif.: Addison-Wesley, 1984.

Hogan, R. "Gaining Community Support for Group Homes." *Community Mental Health Journal* 22 (1986).

Hollingshead, A. V., and Redlich, F. C. "Social Stratification and Psychiatric Disorders." In *Behavior Disorders, Perspectives, and Trends,* edited by O. Milton. New York: Lippincott, 1965.

"Home Dialysis Club for Patients, Families." *Innovations: Highlights of Evolving Mental Health Services.* American Institutes for Research 3 (Fall, 1973).

Hurley, D. "Getting Help from Helping." *Psychology Today* 22 (1988).

Hurvitz, N. "Peer Self-Help Psychotherapy Groups and the Implications for Psychotherapy." *Psychotherapy: Theory, Research, and Practice* 7 (1975).

Hussain, R. A., and Davis, R. L. D. *Responsive Care: Behavioral Interventions with Elderly Persons.* Champaign, Ill.: Research Press, 1985.

Jackson, D. "The Question of Family Homeostasis." *Psychiatric Quarterly Supplement* 31 (1957).

James, V. "Paraprofessionals in Mental Health: A Framework for the Facts." In *Mental Health: Theory and Practice,* edited by S. Alley, J. Blanton, and R. E. Feldman. New York: Human Sciences Press, 1979.

Janicki, M. P.; Mayeda, T.; and Epple, W. A. "Availability of Group Homes for Persons with Mental Retardation in the United States." *Mental Retardation* 21 (1983).

Jensen, A. "The Differences Are Real." *Psychology Today* 7 (1973).

Johnson, L. C. "Networking: A Means of Maximizing Resources." *Human Services in the Rural Environment* 8 (1983).

Johnson, R. *Hard Times: Understanding and Reforming the Prison.* Monterey: Brooks/Cole, 1987.

Jones, M. C. "Albert, Peter and J. B. Watson." *American Psychologist* 29 (1974).

Kahn, A., and Bender, E. I. "Self-Help Groups as a Crucible for People Empowerment in the Context of Social Development." *Social Development Issues* 9 (1985).

Kaplan, G. *From Aide to Teacher: The Story of the Career Opportunities Program.* Washington, D.C.: U.S. Government Printing Office, 1977.

Katz, A. H. "Self-Help and Mutual Aid: An Emerging Social Movement?" *Annual Review of Sociology* 7 (1981).

Kazdin, A. E. "The Token Economy: A Decade Later." *Journal of Applied Behavior Analysis* 15 (1982).

Kempler, W. "Gestalt Therapy." In *Current Psychotherapies,* edited by R. Corsini. Itasca, Ill.: F. E. Peacock, 1973.

Kermani, E. J., and Drob, S. L. "Tarasoff Decision: A Decade Later Dilemma Still Faces Psychotherapists." *American Journal of Psychotherapy* 41 (1987).

Kestenbaum, S. E., and Bar-On, Y. "Case Aides: An Answer for Israel." *Public Welfare* 40 (1982).

Kittrie, N. N. *The Right to Be Different: Deviance and Enforced Therapy.* Baltimore: The Johns Hopkins Press, 1971.

Koop, C. E. *Acquired Immune Deficiency Syndrome.* Surgeon General's Report. Washington, D.C.: U.S. Dept. of Health and Human Services, 1986.

Kornetsky, C. *Pharmacology: Drugs Affecting Behavior.* New York: John Wiley and Sons, 1976.

Kozol, J. *Rachel and Her Children: Homeless Families in America.* New York: Crown, 1987.

Krassner, M. "Effective Features of Therapy from the Healer's Perspective: A Study of Curanderismo." *Smith College Studies in Social Work* 56 (1986).

Krause, N. "Chronic Financial Strain, Social Support and Depressive Symptoms among Older Adults." *Psychology and Aging* 2 (1987).

Kronick, R. "Professional Development in Human Services." *The Link* 9 (1987).

———. "What Is Human Services: It Is Multidisciplinary and Professional." *The Link* 8 (1986).

Lamb, H. R. *The Homeless Mentally Ill.* Washington, D.C.: American Psychiatric Association, 1984.

Landon, J. W. *The Development of Social Welfare.* New York: Human Sciences Press, 1986.

Lapolla, A., and Jones, H. "Placebo-Control Evaluation of Desipramine in Depression." *American Journal of Psychiatry* 127 (1970).

Lemberg, R. "Ten Ways for a Self-Help Group to Fail." *American Journal of Orthopsychiatry* 54 (1984).

Leukefeld, C. G. "Psychosocial Issues in Dealing With AIDS." *Hospital and Community Psychiatry* 40 (1989).

Levine, I. S., and Rog, D. J. "Mental Health Services for Homeless Mentally Ill Persons." *American Psychologist* 45 (1990).

Lieb, J.; Lipstich, I.; and Slaby, A. E. *The Crisis Team.* New York: Harper and Row, 1973.

Lindemann, E. "Symptomatology and Management of Acute Grief." *American Journal of Psychiatry* 101 (1944).

Lindner, R. *The Fifty-Minute Hour.* New York: Rinehart and Co., 1955.

Lindsey, J. D. "Paraprofessionals in Learning Disabilities." *Journal of Learning Disabilities* 16 (1983).

Lopez, D., and Getzel, G. S. "Strategies for Volunteers Caring for Persons with AIDS." *Social Casework* 65 (1987).

Macht, J. "News from CSHSE." *The Link* 7 (1985).

———. "What is human services? It is dynamic." *The Link* 8 (1986).

MacLeod, C. *Horatio Alger, Farewell*. New York: Seaview Books, 1980.

Maher, B. *Principles of Psychopathology: An Experimental Approach*. New York: McGraw-Hill, 1966.

Maier, H. W. *Developmental Group Care of Children and Youth: Concepts and Practices*. New York: The Haworth Press, 1987.

Mandell, B. R. "Blurring Definitions of Social Services: Human Services vs. Social Work." *Catalyst* 4 (1983).

Mandell, B. R., and Schram, B. *Human Services: An Introduction*. New York: John Wiley and Sons, 1983.

March, M. "The Neighborhood Center Concept." *Public Welfare* 26 (1968).

Marcia, J. "Empathy and Psychotherapy." In *Empathy and Its Development*, edited by N. Eisenberg and J. Strayer. Cambridge, England: Cambridge University Press, 1987.

Martin, R. *Legal Challenges to Behavior Modification: Trends in Schools, Corrections, and Mental Health*. Champaign, Ill.: Research Press, 1975.

Maslow, A., and Mittelman, B. *Principles of Abnormal Psychology*. New York: Harper and Bros., 1951.

Matson, J. L., and Zeiss, R. A. "Group Training of Social Skills in Chronically Explosive, Severely Disturbed Psychiatric Patients." *Behavioral Engineering* 5 (1978).

McAuliffe, W. E., and Ch'ien, J. M. "Recovery Training and Self-Help: A Relapse Prevention Program for Treated Opiate Addicts." *Journal of Substance Abuse Treatment* 3 (1986).

McClam, T., and Woodside, M. R. "A Conversation with Dr. Harold McPheeters." *Human Service Education* 9 (1989).

McGee, J. J.; Menolascino, F. J.; Hobbs, D. C.; and Menousek, P. E. *Gentle Teaching: A Non-Aversive Approach to Helping Persons with Mental Retardation*. New York: Human Sciences Press, 1987.

McLeod, B. "Real Work for Real Pay." *Psychology Today* 14 (1985).

McQuaide, S. "Human Service Cutbacks and the Mental Health of the Poor." *Social Casework* 64 (1983).

Mehr, J. *Abnormal Psychology*. New York: Holt, Rinehart and Winston, 1983.

———. "Aggression and Violence: A Clinician Administrator's Odyssey Towards a Treatment Perspective." *The Ohio Forensic Reporter* 1 (1980).

———. "The Extended Degree: A New Payoff for Inservice Training in Community Mental Health Centers." Proceedings of the Annual Conference of the National Council of Community Mental Health Centers, Washington, D.C., 1975.

———. "Helping versus Healing: A Concept in Treatment through Institutional Change." Presented at the Illinois Psychological Association, Chicago, 1973.

———. "What Is Human Services: It Is Whole-Person Focused." *The Link* 8 (1986).

Meichenbaum, D. *Cognitive-Behavior Modification: An Integrated Approach*. New York: Plenum, 1977.

Meltzoff, J., and Kornreich, M. *Research in Psychotherapy*. New York: Atherton Press, 1970.

Meyer, H. "Sociological Comments." In *Nonprofessionals in the Human Services*, edited by C. Grosser, W. C. Henry, and J. G. Kelly. San Francisco: Jossey-Bass Publishers, 1969.

Michels, R. "The Right to Refuse Treatment: Ethical Issues." *Hospital and Community Psychiatry* 32 (1981).

Mikulecky, T. (ed.). *Human Services Integration*. Washington, D.C.: American Society for Public Administration, 1974.

Miller, A. D. "Reinstitutionalization in Retrospect." In Katz, S. E. (ed.), "The Renaissance of the State Psychiatric System." *Psychiatric Quarterly* 52 (Special Issue) (1985).

Miller, K.; Fein, E.; Howe, G. W.; Gaudio, C. P.; and Bishop, G. V. "Time-Limited, Goal Focused Parent Aide Services." *Social Casework* 65 (1984).

Minkoff, K. "Beyond Deinstitutionalization: A New Ideology for the Postinstitutional Era." *Hospital and Community Psychiatry* 38 (1987).

Morris, R. "Overcoming Cultural and Professional Myopia in Education for Human Service." In *A Handbook of Human Service Organizations*, edited by H. Demone and D. Harshbarger. New York: Behavioral Publications, 1974.

Moustakas, C. "Being In, Being For, and Being With." *Humanistic Psychologist* 14 (1986).

Mowrer, O. H. "Peer Groups and Medication: The Best Therapy for Professionals and Laymen Alike." *Psychotherapy: Theory, Research, and Practice* 8 (1971).

Murphy, S. "Expanding Horizons for MR's: Who Can't Canoe?" *Innovations: Highlights of Evolving Mental Health Services.* American Institutes for Research 2 (Summer, 1975).

Myrdal, G. *An American Dilemma.* (2d Ed.) New York: McGraw-Hill, 1964.

Nadi, S.; Nurnberger, J.; and Gershon, E. "Inherited Trait Marks Depression." *Science 84* 5 (1984).

Nardone, M. J.; Tryon, W. W.; and O'Connor, K. "The Effectiveness and Generalization of a Cognitive-Behavioral Group Treatment to Reduce Impulsive/Aggressive Behavior for Boys in a Residential Setting." *Behavioral and Residential Treatment* 1 (1986).

NARF. "Rehabilitation Review." National Association of Rehabilitation Facilities 4 (1983).

Naroll, R. "Cultural Determinants and the Concept of the Sick Society." In *Changing Perspectives in Mental Illness*, edited by S. Plog and R. Edgerton. New York: Holt, Rinehart and Winston, 1969.

Nash, K. B.; Lifton, N.; and Smith, S. E. *The Paraprofessional: Selected Readings.* New Haven, Conn.: Advocate Press, 1978.

National Institute of Mental Health. *Research in the Service of Mental Health.* D.H.E.W. Publication No. (ADM) 75–236. Washington, D.C.: Superintendent of Documents, 1975.

Nebelkopf, E. "The Therapeutic Community and Human Services in the 1980's." *Journal of Psychoactive Drugs* 18 (1986).

Neugebauer, R. "Medieval and Early Modern Theories of Mental Illness." *Archives of General Psychiatry* 36 (1979).

New Human Services Institute. *College Programs for Paraprofessionals.* New York: Human Sciences Press, 1975.

"New Law Bolsters Mental Health Care for Homeless People." *Hospital and Community Psychiatry* 38 (1987).

News and Notes. NIMH report presents latest data on inpatient psychiatric services for patients 65 and over. *Hospital and Community Psychiatry* 38 (1987).

Newsome, B. L., and Newsome, M., Jr. "Self Help in the United States: Social Policy Options." *Urban and Social Change Review* 16 (1983).

Newton, J. *Preventing Mental Illness.* London: Routledge and Kegan Paul, 1988.

Nicks, T. L. "Inequities in the Delivery and Financing of Mental Health Services for Ethnic Minority Americans." *Psychotherapy: Theory/Research/Practice/Training* 22 (1985).

Offer, D., and Sabshin, M. *Normality*. New York: Basic Books, 1974.

O'Hara, J. J., and Stangler, G. J. "AIDS and the Human Services." *Public Welfare* 44 (1986).

Opler, M. *Culture, Psychiatry and Human Values*. Springfield, Ill.: Charles C. Thomas, 1956.

Orlans, H. *Human Services Coordination*. New York: Pica Press, 1982.

Parad, H. J., and Resnik, H. L. P. "The Practice of Crisis Intervention in Emergency Care." In *Emergency Psychiatric Care: The Management of Mental Health Crises*, edited by H. L. P. Resnik and H. Ruben. Bowie, Md.: Charles Press, 1975.

Parham, I. "Constraints in Implementing Services Integration Goals—The Georgia Experience." In *Human Services Integration*, edited by T. Mikulecky. American Society for Public Administration, March, 1974.

Paster, V. S. "A Social Action Model of Intervention for Difficult to Reach Populations." *American Journal of Orthopsychiatry* 56 (1986).

Patterson, G. "Behavioral Intervention Procedures in the Classroom and in the Home." In *Handbook of Psychotherapy and Behavior Change: An Empirical Analysis*, edited by A. Bergin and S. Garfield. New York: Wiley, 1971.

Paul, G. "Insight versus Desensitization in Psychotherapy, Two Years after Termination." *Journal of Consulting Psychology* 31 (1967).

Pearl, A., and Riessman, F. *New Careers for the Poor: The Nonprofessional in Human Service*. New York: Free Press, 1965.

Pearlman, M. H., and Edwards, M. G. "Enabling in the Eighties: The Client Advocacy Group." *Social Casework* 63 (1982).

Perls, S. "A Follow-up Study of Graduates of an Associate-Degree Program for Mental Health Workers." *Hospital and Community Psychiatry* 30 (1979).

———. "Paraprofessionals a Decade Later: What's in a Name?" *Hospital and Community Psychiatry* 29 (1978).

Petrie, R. D. "Competence and Curriculum." *Journal of the National Organization of Human Service Educators* 6 (1984).

———. "Facilitating a Working Knowledge of Community Human Service Resources." *Journal of Humanistic Education and Development* 24 (1986).

Pinderhughes, E. B. "Empowerment for Our Clients and for Ourselves." *Social Casework* 64 (1983).

Powell, T. J. *Self-Help Organizations in Professional Practice*. Silver Spring, Md.: National Association of Social Work, 1987.

Price, R. H.; Cowen, E. L.; Lorion, R. P.; and Ramos-McKay, J. *Fourteen Ounces of Prevention: A Casebook for Practitioners*. Washington, D.C.: American Psychological Association, 1988.

Program on Chronic Mental Illness. National Survey on "Public Attitudes Toward People with Chronic Mental Illness." The Robert Wood Johnson Foundation, Boston Mass. April, 1990.

Rapoport, L. "The State of Crisis: Some Theoretical Considerations." *The Social Service Review* 36 (1962).

Redlich, F. C.; Hollingshead, A. B.; Roberts, B. A.; Robinson, H. A.; Freedman, L. Z.; and Myers, J. K. "Social Structure and Psychiatric Disorders." *American Journal of Psychiatry* 109 (1953).

Reid, A. H. "Psychiatric Disorders in Mentally Handicapped Children: A Clinical and Follow-Up Study." *Journal of Mental Deficiency Research* 24 (1980).

Reid, W. J., and Epstein, L. *Task-Centered Casework*. New York: Columbia University Press, 1972.

Reischauer, R. D. "The Prospects for Welfare Reform." *Public Welfare* 44 (1986).

Reppucci, N. D., and Saunders, J. T. "Focal Issues for Institutional Change." *Professional Psychology: Research and Practice* 14 (1983).

Rickard, H. C. (ed.). *Behavioral Intervention in Human Problems*. New York: Pergamon Press, 1971.

Riessman, F. "The Helper-Therapy Principle." *Social Work* 10 (1965).

———. "Self-Help." In *Paraprofessionals in Mental Health*, edited by S. Alley, J. Blanton, and R. E. Feldman. New York: Human Sciences Press, 1979.

Riessman, F., and Miller, S. M. "Social Change versus the 'Psychiatric World View.'" *American Journal of Orthopsychiatry* 34 (1964).

Riessman, F., and Popper, H. *Up from Poverty: New Career Ladders for Non-Professionals*. New York: Harper and Row, 1968.

Rimland, B. "Psychogenesis versus Biogenesis: The Issues and the Evidence." In *Changing Perspectives in Mental Illness*, edited by S. Plog and R. Edgerton. New York: Holt, Rinehart and Winston, 1969.

Rioch, M. "Changing Concepts in the Training of Therapists." *Journal of Counseling Psychology* 30 (1966).

Rioch, M.; Elker, C.; Flint, A.; Usdansky, B.; Newman, R.; and Silber, E. "National Institute of Mental Health Pilot Study in Training Mental Health Counselors." *American Journal of Orthopsychiatry* 33 (1963).

Roberts, A. (ed.). *Social Work in Juvenile and Criminal Justice Settings*. Springfield, Ill.: Charles C. Thomas, 1983.

Rogers, C. *Client-Centered Therapy: Its Current Practice, Implications and Theory*. Boston: Houghton Mifflin, 1951.

———. *Counseling and Psychotherapy*. Boston: Houghton, 1942.

———. "The Necessary and Sufficient Conditions of Therapeutic Personality Change." *Journal of Consulting Psychology* 21 (1957)

Rogers, C.; Gendlin, E.; Kiesler, D.; and Louax, C. *The Therapeutic Relationship and Its Impact: A Study of Psychotherapy with Schizophrenics*. Madison: University of Wisconsin Press, 1967.

Romanyshyn, J. M. *Social Welfare: Charity to Justice*. New York: Random House, 1971.

Ropers, R. H. *The Invisible Homeless: A New Urban Ecology*. New York: Human Sciences Press, 1988.

Rose, S. M., and Black, B. L. *Advocacy and Empowerment: Mental Health Care in the Community*. London: Routledge and Kegan Paul, 1985.

Rosel, N. "The Hub of a Wheel: A Neighborhood Support Network." *International Journal of Aging and Human Development* 16 (1983).

Rossi, P. H. "The Old Homeless and The New Homelessness In Historical Perspective." *American Psychologist* 24 (1990).

Roth, D., and Bean, G. J. "New Perspectives on Homelessness: Findings from a Statewide Epidemiological Study." *Hospital and Community Psychiatry* 37 (1986).

Roy, P. F., and Sumpter, H. "Group Support for the Recently Bereaved." *Health and Social Work* 8 (1983).

Rubenstein, L. S. "Treatment of the Mentally Ill: Legal Advocacy Enters the Second Generation." *American Journal of Psychiatry* 143 (1986).

Russell, B. *A History of Western Philosophy*. New York: Simon and Schuster, 1960.

Russo, J. R. *Serving and Surviving as a Human Service Worker*. Monterey: Brooks/Cole, 1980.

Rynearson, E. K. "Psychological Effects of Unnatural Dying on Bereavement." *Psychiatric Annals* 16 (1986).

Sabshin, M. "Normality and The Boundaries of Psychopathology." *Journal of Personality Disorders* 3 (1989).

Sackeim, H. A. "The Case for ECT." *Psychology Today* 19 (1985).

Sakauye, K. M. "A Model for Administration of Electroconvulsive Therapy." *Hospital and Community Psychiatry* 37 (1986).

Sancilio, M. F. "Peer Interaction as a Method of Therapeutic Intervention with Children." *Clinical Psychology* 7 (1987).

Sarason, I., and Ganzer, V. "Concerning the Medical Model." *American Psychologist* 23 (1968).

Sarason, S. B.; Carroll, C. F.; Maton, K.; Cohen, S.; and Lorentz, E. *Human Services and Resource Networks.* San Francisco: Jossey-Bass Publishers, 1977.

Sarbin, T. "Notes on the Transformation of Social Identity." In *Comprehensive Mental Health: The Challenge of Evaluation,* edited by L. M. Roberts, N. Greenfield, and M. Miller. Madison: University of Wisconsin Press, 1968.

Satir, V. *Conjoint Family Therapy.* Palo Alto, Calif.: Science and Behavioral Books, 1964.

Sauber, S. R. *The Human Services Delivery System.* New York: Columbia University Press, 1983.

Scarr, S. "Genetics and the Development of Intelligence." In *Child Development Research* (Vol. 4), edited by F. D. Horowitz. Chicago: University of Chicago Press, 1975.

Scheerenberger, R. C. *A History of Mental Retardation.* Baltimore: Paul H. Brooks, 1983.

Scheff, T. *Being Mentally Ill: A Sociological Theory.* (2d Ed.) Chicago: Aldine, 1984.

Scheffler, L. W. *Help Thy Neighbor.* New York: Grove Press, 1984.

Schensul, S. L., and Schensul, J. J. "Self-Help Groups and Advocacy: A Contrast in Beliefs and Strategies." In *Beliefs and Self-Help: Cross Cultural Perspectives and Approaches,* edited by G. H. Weber and L. M. Cohen. New York: Human Sciences Press, 1982.

Schneider-Corey, M., and Corey, G. *Becoming a Helper.* Pacific Grove, Calif.: Brooks/Cole, 1989.

Schroeder, S. R.; Schroeder, C. S.; and Landesman, S. "Psychological Services in Educational Settings to Persons with Mental Retardation." *American Psychologist* 42 (1987).

Schulman, E. *Intervention in Human Services.* St. Louis: C. V. Mosby, 1974.

Schur, E. M. *Narcotic Addiction in Britain and America: The Impact of Public Policy.* Bloomington: Indiana University Press, 1962.

Secretary of Health and Human Services. *Sixth Special Report to the U.S. Congress on Alcohol and Health.* Washington, D.C.: National Institute on Alcohol Abuse and Alcoholism, 1987.

Segal, S. P., and Aviram, V. *The Mentally Ill in Community-Based Sheltered Care.* New York: John Wiley and Sons, 1978.

Seidman, E. (ed.). *Handbook of Social Intervention.* Beverly Hills, Calif.: Sage Publications, 1983.

"Self-Help for the Widowed." *Innovations: Highlights of Evolving Mental Health Services.* American Institutes for Research 2 (Summer, 1975).

Selig, A. *Making Things Happen in Communities: Alternatives to Traditional Mental Health Services.* San Francisco: Research Associates, Inc., 1977.

Shelton, J. L., and Peterson, R. M. "Treatment Outcome and Maintenance in Systematic Desensitization: Professional versus Paraprofessional Effectiveness." *Journal of Consulting Psychology* 25 (1978).

Shodell, M. "The Clouded Mind." *Science 84* 5 (1984).

Shore, J. H.; Vollmer, W. M.; and Tatum, E. L. "Community Patterns of Posttraumatic Stress Disorders." *Journal of Nervous & Mental Disease* 177 (1989).

Sigerist, H. *Civilization and Disease.* Ithaca, N.Y.: Cornell University Press, 1943.

Silverman, L. "Psychoanalytic Theory: 'The Reports of My Death Are Greatly Exaggerated.' " *American Psychologist* 31 (1976).

Silverman, P. *Mutual Help Groups: Organizations and Development.* Beverly Hills, Calif.: Sage Publications, 1980.

Simons, R., and Aigner, S. *Practice Principles: A Problem Solving Approach to Social Work.* New York: Macmillan, 1985.

Skinner, B. F. *Beyond Freedom and Dignity.* New York: Alfred A. Knopf, 1971.

Slater, P. *The Pursuit of Loneliness: American Culture at the Breaking Point.* Boston: Beacon Press, 1970.

Sloane, R. B.; Staples, F. R.; Yorkston, W.; Cristol, A.; and Whipple, K. *Behavior Therapy versus Psychotherapy.* Cambridge: Commonwealth Publication of the Harvard University Press, 1975.

Slovenko, R. *Psychiatry and the Law.* Boston: Little, Brown and Co., 1973.

Smith, L. L. "A Review of Crisis Intervention Theory." *Social Casework* 59 (1978).

Smith, M. L.; Glass, G. V.; and Miller, T. I. *The Benefits of Psychotherapy.* Baltimore: The Johns Hopkins University Press, 1980.

Smith, N. K., and Meyer, A. B. "Personal Care Attendants: Key to Living Independently." *Rehabilitation Literature* 42 (1981).

Snyderman, M., and Rothman, S. *The IQ Controversy, The Media and Public Policy.* New Brunswick, N.J.: Transaction Books, 1988.

Sobey, F. *The Nonprofessional Revolution in Mental Health.* New York: Columbia University Press, 1970.

Sommer, R. *The End of Imprisonment.* New York: Oxford University Press, 1976.

Sommer, R., and Sommer, B. A. "Mystery in Milwaukee: Early Intervention, IQ, and Psychology Textbooks." *American Psychologist* 38 (1983).

Sosin, M., and Caulum, S. "Advocacy: A Conceptualization for Social Work Practice." *Social Work* 28 (1983).

Spivack, M. "Statement on Human Behavior and the Environment, To the United States Senate Select Committee on Health and Housing." In *A Handbook of Human Service Organizations,* edited by H. Demone and D. Harshbarger. New York: Behavioral Publications, 1974.

SREB. "The Creation of a Discipline: Middle Level Mental Health Workers." Southern Regional Education Board, Atlanta: 1973.

———. "Mental Health/Human Service Worker Activities: The Process and the Products." Southern Regional Education Board, Atlanta: 1979.

———. "Roles and Functions for Different Levels of Mental Health Workers." Southern Regional Education Board, Atlanta: 1969.

———. "Staff Roles for Mental Health Personnel: A History and Rationale for Paraprofessionals." Southern Regional Education Board, Atlanta: 1978.

Srole, L.; Langer, T. S.; Michael, S. T.; Kirkpatrick, P.; Opler, M. K.; and Rennie, T. A. *Mental Health in the Metropolis: The Midtown Manhattan Study.* (Rev. Ed.) New York: New York University Press, 1978.

Steadman, H. J., and Cocozza, J. J. *Careers of the Criminally Insane.* Lexington, Mass.: D.C. Heath and Company, 1974.

Stephens, L., et al. "Social Networks as Assets and Liabilities in Recovery from Stroke by Geriatric Patients." *Psychology and Aging* 2 (1987).

Stone, A. A. "Overview: The Right to Treatment—Comments on the Law and Its Impact." *American Journal of Psychiatry* 132 (1975).

Straughan, J. H.; Polter, W. K.; and Hamilton, S. H. "The Behavioral Treatment of an Elective Mute." *Journal of Child Psychology and Psychiatry* 6 (1965).

Stravynski, A.; Grey, S.; and Elie, R. "Outline of the Therapeutic Process in Social Skills Training with Socially Dysfunctional Patients." *Journal of Consulting and Clinical Psychology* 55 (1987).

Strupp, H. H., and Hadley, S. W. "Specific versus Non-Specific Factors in Psychotherapy: A Controlled Study of Outcome." *Archives of General Psychiatry* 36 (1979).

Sundberg, N. D., and Tyler, L. E. *Clinical Psychology.* New York: Appleton-Century-Crofts, 1962.

Sundel, M., and Sundel, S. *Behavior Modification in the Human Services.* New York: John Wiley and Sons, 1975.

Sunley, R. *Advocating Today: A Human Service Practitioner's Handbook.* New York: Family Service America, 1983.

Szasz, T. *The Manufacture of Madness.* New York: Harper and Row, 1970.

——. *Psychiatric Justice.* New York: Macmillan, 1965.

Talkington, L., and Watters, L. "Programming for Special Class Misfits." *Mental Retardation* 8 (1970).

Tancredi, L.; Lieb, J.; and Slaby, A. E. *Legal Issues in Psychiatric Care.* New York: Harper and Row, 1975.

Taylor, J. B., and Randolph, J. *Community Worker.* New York: Jason Aronson, 1975.

Taylor, R. D. W., and Johnson, D. A. W. "The Role of Social Networks in the Maintenance of Schizophrenic Patients." *British Journal of Social Work* 14 (1984).

Taylor, V. "The Delivery of Mental Health Services in the Xenia Tornado." Unpublished Doctoral Dissertation. Ohio State University, 1976.

Terr, L. C. "Psychic Trauma in Children: Observations Following the Chowchilla School-Bus Kidnapping." *American Journal of Psychiatry* 138 (1981).

"Texas TRIMS Some Red Tape." *Innovations: Highlights of Evolving Mental Health Services* 4 (Spring, 1977).

"Those 26 Million 'Poor'." *Time Magazine.* Chicago: Time, Inc., October 18, 1976.

Throits, P. "Social Support as Coping Assistance." *Journal of Consulting and Clinical Psychology* 54 (1986).

Thyer, B. A. (ed.). *Progress in Behavioral Social Work.* New York: The Haworth Press, 1988.

Toreland, R. W., and Hacker, L. "Self-Help Groups and Professional Involvement." *Social Work* 27 (1982).

Torrey, E. F. "Thirty Years of Shame: The Scandalous Neglect of the Mentally Ill Homeless." *Policy Review* 48 (1989).

Trattner, W. I. *From Poor Law to Welfare State: A History of Social Welfare in America.* (2d Ed.) New York: The Free Press, 1979.

——. *From Poor Law to Welfare State: A History of Social Welfare in America.* (3d Ed.) New York: The Free Press, 1986.

Truax, C. B. *An Approach Toward Training for the Aide Therapist: Research and Implications.* Fayetteville, Ark.: Arkansas Rehabilitation Research and Training Center, 1969.

Truax, C. B., and Carkuff, R. R. *Toward Effective Counseling and Psychotherapy.* Chicago: Aldine Publishing, 1967.

Turkington, C. "Linda Tarr: Therapy Can Help the Retarded." *APA Monitor* 15 (1984).

"Two From New Mexico: 1. For Ex-Offenders." *Innovations: Highlights of Evolving Mental Health Services.* American Institutes for Research 2 (Fall, 1975).

Upper, D., and Ross, S. M. (eds.). *Handbook of Behavioral Group Therapy.* New York: Plenum Press, 1985.

U.S. Department of Justice. *Bureau of Justice Statistics*. Washington, D.C.: Superintendent of Documents, 1983, 1984.

Valenstein, E. *Brain Control*. New York: John Wiley and Sons, 1973.

———. *Great and Desperate Cures: The Rise and Decline of Psychosurgery and Other Radical Treatments for Mental Illness*. New York: Basic Books, 1986.

Van der Avort, A., and Van Harberden, P. "Helping Self-Help Groups: A Developing Theory." *Psychotherapy: Theory/Research/Practice/Training* 22 (1985).

Vidaver, R. "Developments in Human Services Education and Manpower." In *Developments in Human Services* (Vol. 1), edited by H. Schulberg, F. Baker, and S. Roen. New York: Behavioral Publications, 1973.

Walker, C. E.; Bonner, B. L.; and Kaufman, K. L. *The Physically and Sexually Abused Child: Evaluation and Treatment*. New York: Pergamon Press, 1987.

Wallack, J. J. "AIDS Anxiety Among Health Care Professionals." *Hospital and Community Psychiatry* 40 (1989).

Wallerstein, R. S. *Forty-two Lives in Treatment: A Study of Psychoanalysis and Psychotherapy. The Report of the Psychotherapy Research Project of the Menninger Foundation, 1954–1982*. New York: Guilford Press, 1986.

Watson, J., and Rayner, R. "Conditioned Emotional Reaction." *Journal of Experimental Psychology* 3 (1920).

Wechsler, D. *The Measurement and Appraisal of Adult Intelligence*. Baltimore: Williams and Wilkins Co., 1958.

Weihl, H. "On the Relationship between the Size of the Residential Institutions and the Well-Being of Residents." *The Gerontologist* 21 (1981).

Weiner, D. B. "The Apprenticeship of Philippe Pinel: A New Document, 'Observations of Citizen Pussin on the Insane.'" *American Journal of Psychiatry* 136 (1979). (a)

Weiner, R. D. "The Psychiatric Use of Electrically Induced Seizures." *American Journal of Psychiatry* 136 (1979). (b)

Westermeyer, J. "Cultural Factors in Clinical Assessment." *Journal of Consulting and Clinical Psychology* 55 (1987).

White, S. L. *Managing Health and Human Service Programs: A Guide for Managers*. New York: The Free Press, 1981.

Whitman, D. "The Rise of the Hyper-Poor." *U.S. News and World Report* 109 (1990).

Whitman, D., et al. "America's Hidden Poor." *U.S. News and World Report* 104 (1988).

Whittaker, J. K.; Garbino, J.; and Associates. *Social Support Networks: Informal Helping in the Human Services*. New York: Aldine, 1983.

Wicks, R. *Correctional Psychology*. San Francisco: Canfield Press, 1974.

Wiener, L. S. "Helping Clients with AIDS: The Role of the Worker." *Public Welfare* 44 (1986).

Williams, T. (ed.). *Post-Traumatic Stress Disorders of the Vietnam Veteran*. Cincinnati: Disabled American Veterans, Inc., 1980.

Wilson, P. A. "Towards More Effective Intervention in Natural Helping Networks." *Social Work in Health Care* 9 (1983).

Wise, H. B. "The Family Health Worker." *American Journal of Public Health* 58 (1968).

Wittman, M. "The Social Welfare System: Its Relation to Community Mental Health." In *Handbook of Community Mental Health*, edited by S. Golann and C. Eisdorfer. Englewood Cliffs, N.J.: Prentice-Hall, 1972.

Wolberg, L. R. *The Technique of Psychotherapy*. (3d Ed.) New York: Grune & Stratton, 1977.

Wolpe, J. "Behavior Therapy versus Psychoanalysis: Therapeutic and Social Implications." *American Psychologist* 36 (1981).

——. "The Systematic Desensitization Treatment of Neurosis." *Journal of Nervous and Mental Disorders* 132 (1961).

Wood, A. *Deviant Behavior and Control Strategies.* Lexington, Mass.: D.C. Heath and Company, 1974.

Woody, R. H., and Associates. *The Law and the Practice of Human Services.* San Francisco: Jossey-Bass, 1984.

Yalom, I. D. *The Theory and Practice of Group Psychotherapy.* (3d Ed.) New York: Basic Books, 1985.

Yates, A. *Behavior Therapy.* New York: John Wiley and Sons, 1970.

Youngblood, G. S., and Bensberg, G. J. *Planning and Operating Group Homes for the Handicapped.* Lubbock, Tex.: Research and Training Center in Mental Retardation, 1983.

Youngstrom, N. "Seriously Mentally Ill Need Better Tracking." *APA Monitor* 21 (1990).

Zarit, S. H. *Aging and Mental Disorders.* New York: The Free Press, 1980.

Zigler, E. "Assessing Head Start at 20: An Invited Commentary." *American Journal of Orthopsychiatry* 55 (1985).

Zimbardo, P. "The Human Choice: Individuation, Reason and Order versus Deindividuation, Impulse and Chaos." In *Nebraska Symposium on Motivation, 1969,* edited by D. Levine. Lincoln: University of Nebraska, 1970.

Zingale, D. D. "The Importance of Empathic Responding in the Psychotherapeutic Interview." *International Social Work* 28 (1985).

INDEX